AFRICAN DEVELOPM
2002

AFRICA IN THE WORLD ECONOMY

RURAL DEVELOPMENT FOR POVERTY REDUCTION IN AFRICA

ECONOMIC AND SOCIAL STATISTICS ON AFRICA

PUBLISHED FOR THE AFRICAN DEVELOPMENT BANK
OXFORD UNIVERSITY PRESS

OXFORD

Great Clarendon Street, Oxford OX2 6DP

Oxford University Press is a department of the University of Oxford.
It furthers the University's objective of excellence in research, scholarship,
and education by publishing worldwide in

Oxford New York

Auckland Bangkok Buenos Aires Cape Town Chennai
Dar es Salaam Delhi Hong Kong Istanbul Karachi Kolkata
Kuala Lumpur Madrid Melbourne Mexico City Mumbai Nairobi
São Paulo Shanghai Singapore Taipei Tokyo Toronto
with an associated company in Berlin

Oxford is a registered trade mark of Oxford University Press
in the UK and in certain other countries

Published in the United States
by Oxford University Press Inc., New York

British Library Cataloguing in Publication Data
Data available

Library of Congress Cataloging-in-Publication Data
Data available

ISBN 0–19–925384-6

Typeset by African Development Bank
Printed in Great Britain
on acid-free paper by
Butler and Tanner Ltd., Frome, Somerset

FOREWORD

The year 2001 was one of marked changes in the world economy and in Africa itself. The African economy continued to grow—even if moderately —in 2001, with real GDP growth estimated to average 3.4 percent, yielding a small gain in per capita income. Despite the modest performance of the African economy as a whole, it is encouraging to note that seventeen African countries achieved rates of growth in excess of 5 percent, with sixteen others registering growth rates of between 3 and 5 percent. The number of countries recording negative growth also declined from nine to five.

The slowdown in growth owed, in large part, to the global economic slowdown, which has been exacerbated by the fallout of the September 11 attacks. The prospects for 2002 are likely to continue to be affected by the slowdown in economic activity at the global level. This is expected to hold back the expansion of Africa's economy to some 3.5 percent. With the vast majority of our people living in absolute poverty, such low growth rates are clearly incompatible with our quest for poverty reduction. Africa remains the only region in the world where poverty is rising, with 70 percent of the poor in Africa living in rural areas. Despite increasing concern about poverty at the national, regional, and international levels, progress toward the reduction of poverty and deprivation remains inadequate. The assessment documented in this *Report* shows that, at current rates of growth, the majority of African countries are unlikely to be able to meet the Millennium Development Goals of reducing poverty by half by the year 2015. The majority of African countries are also unlikely to meet the other millennium targets related to education, health and social well being.

These problems are especially challenging in rural areas, where poverty is deeper and more severe and where rates of progress towards the de-sired social targets generally lag behind those of urban areas. Rural people are not only income-poor; they are also deprived from the substantive capabilities necessary to lead a decent and meaningful life. This deprivation is reflected in, among other things, premature mortality, undernourishment, morbidity and illiteracy. Moreover, the rural poor are more susceptible to exogenous shocks emanating from the adverse external shocks, natural disasters, civil wars and conflicts. They are also the most affected by the recent resurgence of diseases including malaria, tuberculosis, and HIV/AIDS.

One of the principal lessons of recent experience in Africa is that rural people require new kinds of empowerment if they are to harness their available resources and improve their well being. Such empowerment would be significantly assisted by the widespread sharing of knowledge and experience, by generally improved access to productive assets and by the enhancement of rural peoples' legal and financial status, particularly for women. Thus, any program to reduce the widespread poverty in rural areas must require an effective combination of strategies. These include promoting growth in both agricultural and non-agricultural activities, developing the human and social capital of the rural poor, promoting access to productive assets, and ensuring productive and sustainable use of natural resources. There is also a need to make globalization, markets and institutions work for the rural poor. Depending on country-specific conditions, policy makers would need to implement the requisite policies that make liberalization stimulate trade and growth, and make growth benefit the rural poor.

Experience shows that, while market reforms, which are designed to improve price signals and enhance the efficiency of resource allocation are necessary for growth and poverty reduction in rural Africa, they will seldom be sufficient. For market reforms to be effective, they must be complemented by the provision of a number of non-price instruments including inputs, institutions, infrastructure, information, and appropriate technology and innovation. The provision of these instruments should be seen in the context of rural conditions. That is, farmers require much greater access to knowledge, technology, fertilizers and improved crop varieties. They would also benefit from a substantial improvement in access to markets and an ability to develop their financial status. In some countries, more efficient farming practices would be stimulated by a regularization of land ownership, while in all of them there is equally a clear need to promote the independent access of women to land.

The Bank's poverty reduction strategy, which has evolved over the years, takes these important aspects into consideration and recognizes poverty reduction as the most fundamental challenge facing the continent. Indeed, the Vision statement that the Bank adopted in 1999 to guide its operations places poverty reduction and sustainable economic growth as the overarching objective of the Bank. The guidelines for operations, financed from the Bank's concessional window, give priority to economic activities that generate incomes for the rural poor. In recent years, and in line with the increasing focus on poverty reduction, the lending operations of the Bank have given priority to activities that aim at improving the macroeconomic policy framework, and focus on priority sectors including agriculture, rural infrastructure, education, health and clean water supply. Operations in these fields take into account the important role of women in development and the protection of the environment.

The Bank is fully aware that the problems of poverty in Africa are so serious that no single institution can address them alone. The Bank has thus sought to collaborate with other international institutions and the donor community in supporting initiatives aimed at intensifying international co-operation on poverty reduction in Africa. In particular, it welcomes the collaboration with international institutions in the preparation of Poverty Reduction Strategy Papers (PRSPs) by African countries. In the same vein, the Bank warmly welcomes the New Partnership for Africa's Development (NEPAD) that advocates a development paradigm consistent with the Bank's Vision of poverty reduction through growth and policies that support sustainable development and equity. Under the umbrella of NEPAD, PRSPs prepared by individual African countries should provide a framework that enables governments and civil society institutions to articulate jointly national strategies and programs for poverty reduction. They should also provide the international donor community an important new framework that would enable it co-ordinate better its contributions to poverty-reduction efforts. The Bank Group, on its part, is ready to play an active role in helping to realize the ideals of NEPAD. With the commitment and resolve of Africa's leaders and with the support of the international community, Africa can and will overcome the burden of poverty and underdevelopment.

Omar Kabbaj
President
African Development Bank

The *Africa Development Report 2002* has been prepared by a staff team in the Development Research Department under the direction of Henock Kifle.

The research team was led by Temitope W. Oshikoya and Mohamed Nureldin Hussain and comprised John C. Anyanwu, Sipho Stella Moyo, and Barfour Osei (consultant) from the Research Division.

The Economic and Social Statistics on Africa were prepared by the Statistics Division led by Charles L. Lufumpa and comprised André Portella, Beejaye Kokil and Maurice Mubila.

Rhoda R. Bangurah provided production services, Richard Synge and Anthony Hawkins editorial services and Maurice K. Kponnou Research Assistance.

Preparation of the *Report* was aided by the background papers listed in the bibliographical note. Comments, from within and outside the Bank are noted with appreciation. From the Bank, Hailu Mekonnen, Kupukile Mlambo, Negatu Makonnen, Obadiah Mailafia, Zeinab El-Bakri, and from outside, Ali Abdel Gadir Ali of the Arab Planning Institute, Kuwait, Charles Chukwuma Soludo of the University of Nigeria, Nsukka, Anthony Hawkins of the University of Zimbabwe, David Sahn and David Stifel of Cornell University, Ithaca, Michael Lipton of the University of Sussex, Bereket Kebede of the Oxford University, Francis Aka of the University of Bouake, Côte d'Ivoire, Amath Ndiaye of the University of Cheik Anta Diop, Senegal, Isaac Tamba of the University of Yaounde II, Cameroon, Francis Okurut of the Uganda Women's Finance Trust Limited, Yahaya Abdou of the University of Abdou Moumouni, Niger, Constatino Marrengula of the University of Eduardo Mondlane, Maputo, Boulel Toure of the Centre d'analyse et de formulation de Politique de Developpement (CAFPD) Mali, Christiana Okojie of the University of Benin, Nigeria and Evious Zgovu of the University of Nottingham all made comments and suggestions to improve the *Report*.

ABBREVIATIONS

AAF-SAP	African Alternative Framework to Structural Adjustment Programs
ABEDA	Arab Bank for Economic Development in Africa
ACP	African, Caribbean and Pacific
ADB	African Development Bank
ADF	African Development Fund
AGOA	United States' Africa Growth and Opportunity Act
ATLE	Africa's Ten Largest Economies
AMINA	ADF Micro-finance Initiative for Africa
APPER	African Priority Program for Economic Recovery
ASIPs	Agricultural Sector Investment Programs
BCEAO	Banque centrale des états de l'Afrique de l'ouest
BEAC	Banque des états de l'Afrique centrale
BOT	Build-Operate-Transfer
CAR	Central African Republic
CEMAC	Communauté économique et monétaire de l'Afrique centrale
CFA	Communauté financière africaine
CGAP	Consultative Group to Assist the Poor
CGIAR	Consultative Group on International Agricultural Research
COMESA	Common Market for Eastern and Southern Africa
CPIA	Country Policy and Institutional Assessment
CSOs	Civil Society Organizations
CSPs	Country Strategy Papers
DRC	Democratic Republic of Congo
EBA	Everything But Arms
ECA	Economic Commission for Africa
ECOWAS	Economic Community of West African States
ESW	Economic and Sector Work
EU	European Union
FAO	Food and Agriculture Organization
FDI	Foreign Direct Investment
GDP	Gross Domestic Product
GEF	Global Environment Facility
GNI	Gross National Income
GSM	Global System for Mobile Communications
HIPCs	Heavily Indebted Poor Countries Initiative
HIV/AIDS	Human Immunodeficiency Virus/Acquired Immuno-Deficiency Syndrome
ICRAF	International Center for Research in Agro-Forestry
ICT	Information and Communication Technology
IDA	International Development Association
IDGs	International Development Goals
IFAD	International Fund for Agricultural Development
IFC	International Finance Corporation
IFDC	International Fertilizer Development Center
IFEM	Interbank Forex Market
IIMI	International Irrigation Management Institute
IITA	International Institute for Tropical Agriculture
IMF	International Monetary Fund
IRR	Internal Rate of Return
ISPs	Internet Service Providers
LDCs	Least Developed Countries
LPA	Lagos Plan of Action

MAP	Millennium African Renaissance Partnership Program
MDGs	Millennium Development Goals
MFIs	Multilateral Financial Institutions
MPC	Monetary Policy Committee
MVA	Manufacturing Value Added
NEAPs	National Environment Action Plans
NEPAD	New Economic Partnership for Africa's Development
NGOs	Non Government Organizations
NPV	Net Present Value
OAU	Organization of African Unity
ODA	Official Development Assistance
OECD	Organization for Economic Co-operation and Development
OPEC	Organization of Petroleum Exporting Countries
PAP	Poverty Alleviation Project
PEEPA	Public Enterprise Evaluation and Privatisation Agency
PERs	Public Expenditure Reviews
PRGF	Poverty Reduction and Growth Facility
PRSPs	Poverty Reduction Strategy Papers
REPA	Regional Economic Partnership Agreement
RMCs	Regional Member Countries
SACU	Southern African Customs Unions
SALs	Structural Adjustment Loans
SFM	Supplementary Financing Mechanism
SMEs	Small and Medium Sized Enterprises
SPA	Special Program of Assistance for Africa
SPFS	Special Program for Food Security
SSA	Sub-Saharan African
STDs	Sexually Transmitted Diseases
STIs	Sexually Transmitted Infections
TAF	Technical Assistance Fund
TAI	Technology Achievement Index
TEP	Technology Economy Programme.
TICAD	Tokyo International Conference on African Development
TIN	Tax Identification Number
UA	Units of Account
UN	United Nations
UNAIDS	United Nations Programme on HIV/AIDS
UNCTAD	United Nations Conference on Trade and Development
UNDP	United Nations Development Program
UNICEF	United Nations Children's Fund
UNIDO	United Nations Industrial Development Organisation
UN-NADAF	United Nations New Agenda for the Development of Africa
UNPAAERD	United Nations Program of Action for Economic Recovery and Development
US	United States
VAT	Value-added Tax
VSAT	Very Small Aperture Terminal
WAEMU	Western African Economic Monetary Union
WARDA	West African Rice Development Association
WFP	World Food Programme
WHO	World Health Organization
WTO	World Trade Organization
WUAs	Water Users' Associations
ZCCM	Zambia Consolidated Copper Mines

CONTENTS

BOXES

TEXT FIGURES

TEXT TABLES

PART ONE

AFRICA IN THE WORLD ECONOMY

Overview

The *African Development Report 2002* reviews Africa's current socio-economic performance and prospects, and examines in-depth the issue of rural development for poverty reduction in the Continent. Part I of the Report covers two chapters. The first chapter, on "The African Economy in 2001", presents and assesses the continent's economic performance as well as prospects for the medium-term. The second chapter analyses the regional economic profiles, including their recent economic trends, policy developments, privatization, and growth outlook.

Real GDP growth in 2001 was estimated at 3.4 percent, slightly above the 3.2 percent growth rate recorded in 2000. The factors responsible for the modest growth in 2001 are, in large part, due to the global economic slowdown, which was exacerbated by the September 11 attacks in the United States. Deteriorating global demand led to the collapse of most primary commodity exports in terms of both volume and prices. Consequently, African countries with very high concentrations in non-oil primary commodity exports experienced huge losses. Furthermore, countries such as Egypt, Morocco, Tunisia, Kenya, Uganda, and Tanzania, where tourism is a significant source of foreign exchange, were seriously affected.

Africa's real GDP growth reflected performance in the ten largest economies, boosted also by net oil exporters and some smaller economies with sound economic management and reforms. Despite the modest performance of the African economy, as a whole, seventeen African countries achieved rates of growth in excess of 5 percent, with sixteen other countries registering growth rates of between 3 and 5 percent. The number of countries recording negative growth also declined from nine to five. However, Africa's real per capita GDP growth in 2001 remained basically unchanged from its 2000 level. Sectorally, growth in agriculture and the industrial sector were the main contributors to output expansion in 2001. Unlike in 2000 when the agricultural sector recorded growth rate of only 1.4 percent, in 2001 it grew by 4.5 percent while the industrial sector grew by 3.5 percent, slightly down from 4.2 percent recorded in 2000.

In 2001, Eastern Africa at 4.6 percent recorded the highest economic growth rate among the five sub-regions of Africa, up from 3.9 percent in 2000. North Africa followed this at 4.0 percent in 2001, slightly up from 3.8 percent in 2000. Southern Africa had a growth rate of 2.2 percent in 2000, down slightly from 2.8 percent recorded in 2000. Western Africa grew at 3.5 percent in 2001 from 2.9 percent the previous year while Central Africa experienced an accelerated growth in 2001 to 3.2 percent from 0.3 percent recorded in 2000.

In 2002, the African economy is forecast to grow by 3.5 percent, while real per capita income is to increase by 1.2 percent, following the gradual recovery in the US and Euro Area and moderate oil prices. Growth in the world economy and Africa is expected to accelerate towards the end of 2002 and into 2003. In particular, greater prospects await 2003 as non-oil exporters are expected to see a significant improvement in performance, as commodity markets firm and prices stabilize or even moderately increase in real terms. Expected rebound in commodity prices later in 2002 will be due mainly to currency movements. These forecasts are based on assumptions of unchanged weather and hence good agricultural performance as well as unchanged political and policy stance.

Ultimately, the medium term performance will depend on the deepening of reforms – economic and political governance, structural transformation, institutional, and sound macroeconomic policy stance. One obvious implication of this is that for medium to longer-term sustainability, effort should be devoted to strengthening domestic policies and institutions for handling external shocks, diversification of export baskets as well as partnership with the international community on ways to ameliorate the effects of the adverse external shocks. As the number of countries in conflict continues to decline, and economic reconstruction and policy reforms deepen, a better environment for sustainable growth and development would increasingly emerge.

Thus, the challenge is not so much how to overcome the present short-run cyclical trends, as it is how to chart the long run trajectory, especially dealing with Africa's structural vulnerability. The New Partnership for African Development (NEPAD) launched by African leaders in 2001, as an agenda for the renewal of the Continent could well be one of the key instruments in this direction. The next years would provide the litmus test as to whether NEPAD is the long awaited visionary plan to be actively supported by the international community for Africa's renewal or yet another of the long list of unfulfilled promises and unimplemented plans.

CHAPTER 1

The African Economy in 2001

Africa's Economic Performance in 2001

The African economy continued to grow moderately in 2001, with real GDP growth estimated to average 3.4 percent as compared to 3.2 percent in 2000, yielding a small gain in per capita income (Table 1.1 and Figure 1.1). The performance of the continent as a whole was largely influenced by modest growth in Africa's ten largest economies (ATLE) which together account for some 80 percent of Africa's GDP (Table 1.2). Despite the

lacklustre performance of the African economy, as a whole, seventeen African countries managed to achieve growth rates in excess of 5 percent, while sixteen other countries grew at between 3 and 5 percent during 2001. The number of countries recording negative growth declined from nine to five (Table 1.3).

African economic growth in 2001 was constrained by the slowdown in the global economy, which was exacerbated by the September 11 attacks in the US. Global demand weakened for most primary commodity exports, resulting in an 8

Table 1.1: Africa: Macroeconomic Indicators, 1997- 2002

Indicators	1997	1998	1999	2000	2001[a/]	2002[b/]
1. Real GDP Growth Rate	3.1	3.7	3.0	3.2	3.4	3.5
2. Real Per Capita GDP Growth Rate	0.6	1.2	0.5	0.8	1.0	1.2
3. Inflation (%)	14.2	11.0	12.4	13.7	12.2	8.8
4. Investment Ratio (% of GDP)	19.3	20.9	20.8	20.2	20.8	22.5
5. Fiscal Balance (% of GDP)	-2.5	-3.6	-2.8	-1.7	-2.5	-2.8
6. Growth of Money Supply (%)	16.7	15.0	18.1	17.2	15.0	11.2
7. Export Growth, volume (%)	4.7	0.1	2.3	6.0	2.3	0.1
8. Import Growth, volume (%)	7.7	6.3	2.5	3.9	3.5	2.1
9. Terms of Trade (%)	-0.2	-10.2	8.7	20.0	-5.4	-7.8
10. Trade Balance ($ billion)	1.9	-17.5	-8.8	19.1	10.2	-3.8
11. Current Account ($ billion)	-5.6	-24.0	-16.5	6.9	-1.1	-15.3
12. Current Account (% of GDP)	-1.0	-4.4	-3.0	1.2	-0.2	-2.7
13. Debt Service (% of Exports)	19.6	20.3	19.0	16.1	15.9	17.7
14. National Savings (% of GDP)	17.6	17.1	15.8	16.6	20.0	19.5
15. Net Capital Inflows ($ billion)	24.02	23.72	21.13	14.35	...	...
16. FDI ($ billion)	11.03	8.73	10.47	9.08	...	...
17. FDI (% to developing countries)	5.88	4.63	4.72	3.78	...	...

Notes: a/ Preliminary estimates
        b/ Forecast
        ... Not available
Source: ADB Statistics Division and IMF.

Figure 1.1: Africa's Major Performance Indicators, 1997-2001

(a) Real GDP Growth and Real Per Capita Growth (Percent)

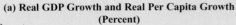
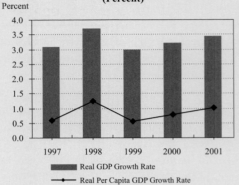

(b) Inflation (Consumer Price Index, Percent)

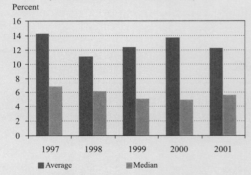

(c) Revenues-Expenditure-Fiscal Deficits (as % of GDP)

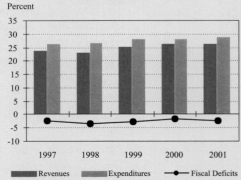

(d) Changes in Merchandise Trade (Volume) and Terms of Trade

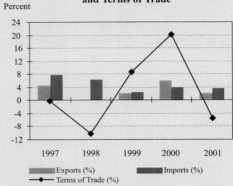

(e) Current Account Balance (In Billion of US$)

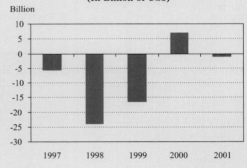

(f) Debt Service (as % of Exports) and Debt Outstanding (as % of GDP)

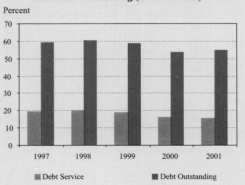

Table 1.2: Africa's Ten Largest Economies (ATLE), 2001

Country	GDP at current US$ (Billions)	Population (Millions)	GDP Growth Rate	Country Weight in total African GDP (%)
1. South Africa	112.9	43.8	2.2	20.7
2. Egypt	93.5	69.1	3.3	17.1
3. Algeria	54.6	30.8	3.5	10.0
4. Nigeria	41.5	116.9	4.0	7.6
5. Morocco	34.0	30.4	6.0	6.2
6. Libya	33.4	5.4	2.5	6.1
7. Tunisia	20.1	9.6	5.2	3.7
8. Sudan	12.6	31.8	6.0	2.3
9. Kenya	10.4	31.3	1.0	1.9
10. Angola	9.3	13.5	3.2	1.7
TOTAL ATLE	422.2	382.7	3.4	77.3

Source: ADB Statistics Division, UN and IMF.

percent decline in the prices of non-energy commodities and a fall of over 12 percent in the price of the continent's leading export, oil and gas.

Since most African countries are heavily reliant on primary commodity exports, they incurred severe terms of trade losses with adverse impacts on their balance-of-payments, exchange rates, output and employment. Furthermore, countries such as Egypt, Morocco, Tunisia, Kenya, Uganda and Tanzania, where tourism is a significant source of foreign exchange, were also seriously affected.

On the positive side, however, economic fundamentals continued to strengthen in 2001 reflecting the strong commitment of many African governments to prudent fiscal, monetary and exchange rate policies. Remarkably, in the face of deteriorating external accounts – including the terms of trade, the trade balance and the current account balance – money supply growth slowed, inflation subsided and fiscal balances improved. Furthermore, despite a hostile external environment, the investment to GDP ratio increased slightly while the ratio of debt service to exports fell marginally.

This improvement in Africa's economic fundamentals is in sharp contrast to conditions during the last two decades when the domestic policy stance was often compromised by accommodating deterioration in external accounts through increased deficit financing and excessive money supply growth.

Although economic growth in Africa marginally exceeded that for emerging markets as a whole, not only was it unevenly distributed, but it fell well short of what is needed to make a material impact on poverty. Table 1.3 demonstrates the mixed

Table 1.3: Africa: Frequency Distribution of Countries According to Real GDP and Real Per Capita GDP Growth Rates, 1997-2001

	Number of Countries				
	1997	1998	1999	2000	2001 [a/]
Real GDP Growth Rate (%)					
Negative	5	6	8	9	5
0 - 3	7	9	15	15	13
Above 3 to 5	15	18	14	13	16
Above 5	24	18	14	14	17
Not available	2	2	2	2	2
Total	53	53	53	53	53
Real Per Capita GDP Growth Rate (%)					
Negative	11	12	19	20	10
0 - 1.5	10	14	12	11	18
Above 1.5 to 5	25	20	16	15	18
Above 5	5	5	4	5	5
Not available	2	2	2	2	2
Total	53	53	53	53	53

Note: a/ Preliminary estimates
Source: ADB Statistics Division.

results. Overall, the median African country's real per capita growth rate falls within 0—1.5 percent range, with only five countries (the same as in 2000) managing real per capita income growth of more than 5 percent.

Both aggregate and real per capita growth rates are far below what is required (7 percent GDP growth and 4.5 percent per capita growth) to effect a significant reduction in poverty and attain the international development goals (IDGs) by 2015. In addition to many domestic constraints, the external environment continues to frustrate Africa's efforts to accelerate progress towards the achievements of these goals.

Economic Performance in Comparative Perspective

Is Africa insulated from the Global Economic Recession?

In 2001, the global economy experienced the worst economic conditions in over a decade, with growth in world GDP slowing to 2.4 percent from 4.7 percent in 2000. This reflected the synchronized slowdown in economic activity in leading economies with Japan plunging into recession for the fourth time in a decade, while for the first time in 20 years the Triad of regions North America, the EU and Japan stagnated as growth fell to just

1 percent. World trade tumbled from a growth rate of 13 percent in 2000 to only 0.2 percent in 2001.

Key factors contributing to the global slowdown, especially in industrial countries, included the end of the high-tech boom, the collapse of stock markets, high oil prices, volatile currency markets and the severe blow to business confidence caused by the September 11 attacks in the United States.

In marked contrast to the experience during most earlier global recessions, Africa actually outperformed all regions of the world – with the exception of Asian developing countries (Table 1.4). Indeed, while growth rates halved – or even worse – in several regions, growth in Africa actually increased marginally to 3.4 percent in 2001 and 3.2 percent the previous year although it is one of two regions said to be the least integrated into the global economy.

A similar outcome occurred in 1998 following the Asian financial crisis, when Africa again outperformed many other regions (see Figure 1.2). This has led many analysts to conclude that Africa is relatively insulated from the global economy and only outperforms other regions when the rest of the world is in crisis.

However, comparative performance in 1998 and 2001 does not imply that Africa is insulated from the world economy. The impact of the global slowdown on Africa should be measured not against the actual outcome but against what would have occurred if normal growth prevailed. Judging from the IMF's October estimates, in the absence of the September 11 attacks, the African economy would have grown at an average of 4.4 percent a year in 2001 and 2002. Current estimates suggest that the attacks will reduce Africa's GDP growth by one percentage point per annum. This translates to a cumulative reduction in Africa's GDP of about $12 billion between 2001 and 2002. This is twice as large as the average annual flows of FDI to Africa and equivalent to over two thirds of the annual average ODA flows to the continent. With the majority of Africans living below and at the brink of the poverty line, such losses exacerbate the state of poverty and impede the continent's progress toward poverty reduction.

Shocks in the global economy, especially in the OECD economies which are Africa's primary export markets and major donors, transmit to African economies through two major channels – trade and financial flows (Box 1.1).

Trade Performance

Although Africa accounts for less than 3 percent of world trade and less than 2 percent of global GDP, with a trade-to-GDP ratio of over 60 percent, it is heavily dependent on trade. The structure and direction of exports plays a decisive role in determining the extent to which the African economy is affected by global recession. Developing countries that trade most with the U.S. and Japan – especially those supplying components for high-tech manufacturers – were the hardest hit both by the collapse of the high-tech boom and the impact of the September 11 attacks.

However, African exporters of primary products are being adversely affected by weak international demand and prices for their products, with the important exceptions of oil and gas and gold. The continent's more diversified economies – South Africa and those in North Africa – have been least affected.

The impact of the slowdown was cushioned in oil exporting countries, where fuel production and exports account for 54 percent of GDP. These economies, accounting for 15 percent of Africa's GDP, and those of North Africa, which accounts

Table 1.4: Selected International Economic Indicators, 1997-2001
(Percentage changes from preceeding year, except otherwise specified)

	1997	1998	1999	2000	2001 [a]
Changes in output					
World	4.2	2.8	3.6	4.7	2.4
Advanced economies [b]	3.4	2.7	3.3	3.9	1.1
Developing Countries	5.8	3.6	3.9	5.8	4.0
-Asia	6.5	4.0	6.2	6.8	5.6
-Latin American and Caribbean countries	5.3	2.3	0.1	4.1	1.0
-Africa [c]	3.1	3.7	3.0	3.2	3.4
Countries in transition	1.6	-0.8	3.6	6.3	4.9
Changes in Consumer Price Index					
Advanced economies	2.1	1.5	1.4	2.3	2.3
Developing Countries	9.9	10.5	6.8	5.9	6.0
-Asia	4.8	7.7	2.5	1.9	2.8
-Latin American and Caribbean countries	12.9	9.8	8.8	8.1	6.3
-Africa [c]	14.2	11.0	12.4	13.7	12.1
Changes in Merchandise Trade (volume)					
World Trade	10.5	4.6	5.6	12.8	0.2
Advanced economies					
-Exports	10.8	4.3	5.1	11.8	-0.9
-Imports	9.9	5.9	8.5	11.8	-1.0
Developing Countries					
-Exports	12.6	4.8	4.7	15.4	2.3
-Imports	10.0	0.5	0.8	16.4	3.5
Africa [c]					
-Exports	4.7	0.1	2.3	6.0	2.3
-Imports	7.7	6.3	2.5	3.9	3.5
Changes in terms of trade					
Advanced economies [b]	-0.6	1.4	-0.2	-2.4	-0.3
Developing Countries	-0.8	-6.9	5.0	6.1	-0.7
-Asia	-0.4	0.2	-0.6	-5.1	1.2
-Africa [c]	-0.2	-10.2	8.7	20.0	-5.4
Countries in transition	...	...	0.7	6.0	-1.4
Changes in FDI					
World	24.2	44.9	55.2	18.2	...
Developed countries	23.5	78.0	71.7	21.1	...
Developing Countries and economies	22.9	0.5	17.9	8.2	...
-Asia	13.6	-10.8	4.3	43.9	...
-Latin American and Caribbean countries	38.8	16.9	32.6	-21.9	...
-Africa [c]	69.8	-20.8	21.1	-12.1	...
FDI (as percent of global FDI flows)					
World					
Developed countries	56.8	69.8	77.2	79.1	...
Developing Countries and economies	39.2	27.2	20.7	18.9	...
-Asia	22.4	13.8	9.3	11.3	...
-Latin American and Caribbean countries	14.9	12.0	10.3	6.8	...
-Africa [c]	2.3	1.2	1.0	0.7	...

Notes: a/ Preliminary estimates
       b/ Comprises the industrial market economies, Israel and four newly industrialized Asian economies.
       c/ ADB Regional Member Countries.
       ... Not available.
Source: IMF, World Economic Outlook, December 2001 and ADB Statistics Division.

Figure 1.2: Developing Countries' vis-à-vis Africa's Major Performance Indicators, 2000-2001

(a) Real GDP Growth and Real Per Capita Growth (Percent)

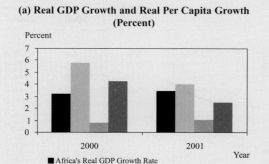

■ Africa's Real GDP Growth Rate
▨ Developing Countries' GDP Growth Rate
▨ Africa's Real Per Capita GDP Growth Rate
▨ Developing Countries' Real Per Capita GDP Growth Rate

(b) Inflation (Consumer Price Index, Percent)

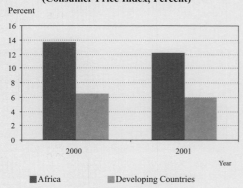

■ Africa   ▨ Developing Countries

(c) Fiscal Deficits as % of GDP

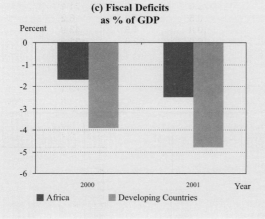

■ Africa   ▨ Developing Countries

(d) Changes in Merchandise Trade (Volume) and Terms of Trade

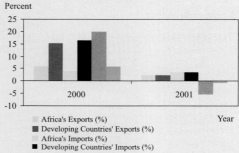

▨ Africa's Exports (%)
■ Developing Countries' Exports (%)
▨ Africa's Imports (%)
■ Developing Countries' Imports (%)
▨ Africa's Terms of Trade (%)
▨ Developing Countries' Terms of Trade (%)

(e) Current Account Balance as % of GDP

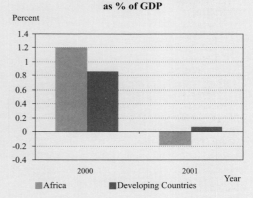

▨ Africa   ■ Developing Countries

(f) Debt Service (in % of Exports) and Debt Outstanding (in % of GDP)

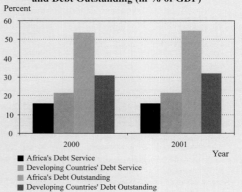

■ Africa's Debt Service
▨ Developing Countries' Debt Service
▨ Africa's Debt Outstanding
■ Developing Countries' Debt Outstanding

Box 1.1: Channels of Business Cycle Transmission from Industrial to African Countries

As African countries become more integrated into the world economy, macroeconomic fluctuations in these countries have become increasingly affected by external influences. These influences can be transmitted through three main, interrelated channels: trade, finance, and direct sectoral linkages.

The Trade Channel

- *Foreign demand shocks:* Business cycles in industrial countries have a significant effect on their demand for developing country commodities, intermediate goods, and finished products. As Africa's trade relationships with industrial countries expand, it has become increasingly affected by aggregate demand conditions in industrial countries. For some countries that rely largely on a narrow range of commodity exports and have limited trade with industrial countries, the impacts of shocks in industrial countries are much less.

- *Aggregate productivity shocks:* For many African countries, technology transfers occur mainly through imports from industrial countries. Technological spillovers and their effects on macroeconomic fluctuations therefore tend to be stronger for countries that have trade relationships with industrial countries, although this also depends on the nature of products traded. Industrial country productivity shocks have been estimated to account for 5 to 20 percent of the variation in developing country output.

- *Terms of trade fluctuations:* Some authors have estimated that terms of trade shocks could account for as much as 50 percent of output fluctuations in developing economies. These shocks include variations in commodity prices that are often influenced by cyclical conditions in advanced economies. The volatility of commodity prices tends to have large spillover effects within developing countries that rely on exports of commodities and other primary products for much of their export earnings (and in some cases for a significant fraction of their national incomes). In this context, commodity price shocks have been shown to be important determinants of investment and output fluctuations among commodity exporting African

countries (see Deaton and Miller, 1995; and Kose and Riezman, 2001).

The Financial Channel

- *Private capital flows:* Foreign direct investment and other forms of capital flows from industrial to developing countries have expanded considerably in recent decades. Many African countries now receive significant external financing for their domestic investment and current account deficits. Thus, the magnitude and volatility of capital flows from industrial countries can have a significant influence on developing country investment and output. The phenomenon of financial contagion also implies that macroeconomic disturbances in one or a few countries get transmitted rapidly via the financial channel. As African countries strengthen their linkages to international financial markets, the financial channel is likely to become an increasingly important channel.

- *Aid and other financial flows:* The volatility of aid flows can also affect macroeconomic fluctuations in some developing countries. In many African countries, which are heavily dependent on aid, aid flows are both volatile and positively related to their own cycle.

- *Global financial market conditions:* Changes in world interest rates and investors' appetite for risk, along with perceptions of riskiness of investments in developing countries, are likely to influence the quantity of capital flows to these countries. The ability of developing countries to conduct countercyclical macroeconomic policies could also be constrained by externally generated changes in interest rates and spreads. Also, the effects of interest rates might depend on the extent of the countries' indebtedness.

Sectoral Interdependence

- *Similarities in economic structure:* These similarities imply that sector-specific shocks- including productivity shocks and shocks to the composition of import demand from industrial countries—tend to have similar effects on aggregate fluctuations across national borders.

(box continues on next page)

Box 1.1: Channels of Business Cycle Transmission from Industrial to African Countries (continued)

- *Shocks to the technology sector:* This sector is relatively important to many developing countries, particularly those in East Asia, North Africa and South Africa. Shocks to this sector emanating from advanced economies have had a significant impact on aggregate output fluctuation in those countries.

African countries are becoming more closely linked to industrial countries through trade and financial linkages as well as increasing similarities in industrial structure. These forces of global integration are likely to result in increasing commonality of business cycle fluctuations across industrial and developing countries.

Source: IMF (2001), World Economic Outlook, October.

for 40 percent of regional GDP, led the resistance to the global downturn. Oil prices continued in the upper band, averaging $24.4 per barrel in 2001 and net oil exporting countries grew by an average of 3.7 percent.

In North Africa, the rebound in Morocco after the drought, together with the robust growth in the diversified economy of Algeria, helped to maintain an average growth rate of about 4 percent. This robust outcome in North Africa helped to offset decline in some Sub-Saharan economies.

In this hostile global environment, export growth slowed to 2.3 percent in 2001 from 6 percent in 2000, but import growth declined only marginally to 3.5 percent from 3.9 percent. Consequently, the continent's current account balance, as a percentage of GDP, worsened from a surplus of 1.2 percent in 2000 to a marginal deficit of 0.2 percent in 2001.

Tourism and remittances declined in the countries of North, East and Southern Africa that usually experience large inflows. Travel reservations worldwide at the end of 2001 were some 12 to 15 percent below their levels of a year earlier. The majority of Africa's tourists come from Europe, America and the Middle East. The US slowdown and the erosion of confidence after the September 11 attacks, combined with rising political tension in the Middle East had a negative impact on arrival numbers that has lasted well into 2002.

Financial Flows

Africa is becoming increasingly integrated into global capital markets, though more than half the net inflow of foreign capital takes the form of official assistance rather than private foreign direct and portfolio flows. Estimated net capital inflows to Africa decreased from $21.13 billion in 1999 to $14.3 billion in 2000. Significantly, this decline occurred before the global economic slowdown and cannot therefore be attributed to it.

Preliminary figures for 2001 point to a decline in official development assistance to Africa in line with the global reduction to $37.5 billion from $39.5 billion in 2000. (World Bank: Global Development Finance, 2002). There are concerns that official flows will decline further in 2002 reflecting tighter aid budgets in the industrialized countries and the increased diversion of aid to humanitarian assistance and to building alliances against terrorist networks.

On the other hand, project aid and foreign direct investment in the extractive sectors (which dominates Africa's FDI) are usually not significantly affected by short-term crises. In 2000, FDI inflows to Sub-Saharan Africa fell to $6.5 billion from about $8 billion in 1999. Fortunately, countries like Nigeria and Angola continued to experience significant investment in their oil and gas sectors, while the Cameroon-Chad oil pipeline project continued.

Furthermore, 20 countries have so far reached decision points under the HIPC initiative, thus relaxing the pressures on balance of payments and budgets. This was complemented by the reductions in international interest rates – led by the U.S. Federal Reserve's lowest interest rates cut in over four decades – down by more than 400 basis points in a series of 11 cuts in 2001. For African countries whose external debt is dominated by loans contracted at market interest rates, there was some relief from these reductions. This may explain the unchanged debt service to export ratio – even with falling exports – at its 2000 level of 16 percent (Table 1.1).

Sources of Diverse Economic Performance in 2001

Economic performance differed markedly across countries and regions, reflecting changes in the external environment, policy stances, production structures and diverse sectoral performances.

Oil Exporters and North Africa led the 'Resistance' to Global Trends

The marginal improvement in Africa's overall rate of economic growth, at a time when most regions were on the retreat, is largely explained by the robust performance of the North African economies and of the continent's oil exporters.

Economic growth in most African countries is influenced substantially by movements in primary commodity prices. After peaking in May 1996, non-oil commodity prices had fallen some 40 percent by the end of 2001, though in a handful of African countries continued buoyant oil prices for most of the year were the prime engine of growth.

Oil importing countries suffered greater terms of trade losses as export prices fell proportionately more than fuel import costs. Out of 44 primary commodities, only 13 experienced slight price increases in 2001, while the prices for the most of the rest weakened significantly. Compared to their 1995 peak, agricultural commodity prices in 2000 had fallen by a third, declining a further 98 percent in 2001. Prices of agricultural raw materials, on which many African economies rely, such as tropical hardwoods, cotton and natural rubber were 40 percent below their 1997 levels.

The index of nominal beverage prices comprising coffee, cocoa and tea, has declined 71 percent since 1997, while the prices of fats and oils were down 8.1 percent. Metals and mineral prices have fallen by a third from their 1995 levels with the copper price down 23 percent.

But oil prices and higher gold prices cushioned these effects somewhat. At an average of $24.4 per barrel, oil prices were lower than in 2000 but well above their decade average. Consequently, the oil exporters (Algeria, Angola, Cameroon, Congo Brazzaville, Egypt, Equatorial Guinea, Gabon, Libya, Sudan, Nigeria and Tunisia) outperformed the continent with an average growth rate of 3.7 percent. This was only marginally below the 3.9 percent achieved in 2000, but higher than the continent average of 3.4 percent.

While most sub-regions in Africa experienced a slowdown in economic activity, the more diversified North African economies as well as the oil exporters in that region posted a more robust performance, with GDP growth of 3.4 percent. The rebound in agricultural output in Morocco and other parts of the region following the end of the severe drought added further impetus to growth, more than offsetting the decline in remittances and tourism.

Despite weaker non-oil commodity prices real GDP growth in oil importing countries accelerated to 3.3 percent in 2001 from 2.7 percent the previous year.

ATLE Drove Aggregate Performance

Africa's ten largest economies (ATLE) account for nearly 80 percent of Africa's GDP and about 55 percent of the population (Table 1.2). To all intents and purposes, developments in these economies summarize the African aggregate performance (see Tables 1.2 and 1.5). Growth in 2001 maintained the lackluster trend of previous years and only Morocco, Sudan and Tunisia, featured among the continent's 15 fastest growth economies. Indeed, during the 1990s, none of the 10 large economies was a star performer and their weak performance helps account for Africa's sluggish growth over the last 10 years.

Amongst the largest economies, the most impressive performers were diversified exporters (Morocco and Tunisia) and oil exporters (Sudan and Nigeria). Meanwhile, two of Sub-Saharan Africa's more diversified economies, South Africa and – to a much lesser extent – Kenya, continued to underperform, reflecting long-term structural problems.

Small Countries Performed Well

Historically, Africa's best performers have been the small economies of Botswana and Mauritius – the only two countries that have graduated from the list of least developed countries in the past 30 years. In contrast, the ATLE countries are still largely sleeping giants though they hold the greatest potential for kickstarting the continent's economies through the diffusion of positive spillover effects, as happened in East Asia under Japan's leadership.

With ATLE growth averaging only 3 percent annually since 1997, it is the region's smaller economies that have been the most impressive performers. Equatorial Guinea leads with a five-year average growth rate of over 30 percent, followed by Mozambique, Guinea-Bissau (since 1991), Mauritius and Botswana.

There is no single explanation for this performance. The Botswana and Mauritius success stories are explained by a combination of good policy backed by good fortune. Rich diamond deposits and buoyant world markets have driven the Botswana economy, while Mauritius has successfully exploited its tourist potential and its export processing zone (clothing manufacture), while maintaining a solid base of sugar exports.

Equatorial Guinea is a classic example of the impact of the discovery of rich natural resources (oil), while the Mozambique story is one of rapid recovery from a conflict situation boosted by substantial FDI in a mega-project, the Mozal aluminum smelter.

Although the better managed economies, as shown by their Country Policy and Institutional Assessment (CPIA) scores, outperform the other group of countries on the average, it appears that the external drivers are equally important as the domestic policy stance in attaining above-average performance.

An obvious implication of this is that medium to long-term sustainability depends on export diversification and strengthening domestic policies and institutions for handling external shocks. In

Table 1.5: Macroeconomic Indicators for ATLE*, 1997- 2001

Indicators	1997	1998	1999	2000	2001
1. Real GDP Growth Rate	2.7	3.6	3.1	3.5	3.4
2. Real Per Capita GDP Growth Rate	0.4	1.4	0.9	1.4	1.3
3. Inflation (%)	14.8	8.3	6.2	5.5	5.8
4. Investment Ratio (% of GDP)	19.2	21.8	21.8	21.1	21.8
5. Fiscal Balance (% of GDP)	-2.2	-3.2	-3.4	-1.2	-2.0
6. Growth of Money Supply (%)	13.8	11.0	10.5	11.4	2.0
7. Export Growth, volume (%)	4.8	0.4	0.5	8.2	2.3
8. Import Growth, volume (%)	8.2	4.6	0.4	6.7	5.7
9. Terms of Trade (%)	0.7	-9.9	4.2	17.8	-1.7
10. Trade Balance ($ billion)	2.5	0.6	-12.6	-8.0	10.0
11. Current Account ($ billion)	1.5	1.2	-12.7	-8.2	8.1
12. Current Account (% of GDP)	0.4	0.3	-3.3	-2.0	2.1
13. Debt Service (% of Exports)	21.8	22.3	22.0	18.0	...
14. National Savings (% of GDP)	19.9	18.2	19.9	23.6	23.5
15. Net Capital Inflows ($ billion)	10.8	9.7	6.6	1.8	...
16. FDI ($ billion)	8.2	5.1	7.6	6.4	...
17. FDI (% to developing countries)	4.4	2.7	3.4	2.6	...

* ATLE: South Africa, Egypt, Algeria, Nigeria, Libya, Morocco, Tunisia, Sudan, Kenya and Angola.
... Not available.
Source: ADB Statistics Division and IMF.

addition, African governments need to strengthen co-operation with the international community on ways to ameliorate the effects of the adverse external shocks.

External Sector Had Impacts But Not Decisive for Performance

External Accounts

Reflecting adverse shifts in the terms of trade, the pre-September global slowdown and the aftermath of the September attacks, Africa's external account weakened in 2001. The terms of trade swung from a 20 percent improvement in 2000 to a 5.4 percent deterioration in 2001. Consequently, the trade balance deteriorated by an estimated $9 billion, while current account as a percentage of GDP went into deficit after a modest surplus in 2000. The current account deterioration would have been greater but for the offsetting effects of firm oil prices and the modest recovery in the gold price.

External shocks in the industrial countries are transmitted to the developing countries through a variety of channels (Box 1.1), while for Africa, the effects of the recent attacks in the United States are wide-ranging and could adversely affect economic growth for some time to come (Box 1.2).

The Debt Situation and Capital Inflows Slightly Improved

Africa's foreign debt situation in 2001 improved as 20 countries reached the decision point under the Enhanced HIPC while the continent's debt service ratio maintained its 2000 level of about 16 percent.

UNCTAD's World Investment Report (September 2001) shows that after an 18 percent surge during 2000, global FDI flows slumped by almost 50 percent in 2001, while Africa's share of global FDI fell 22 percent. In 2000, FDI to Africa fell 13 percent (from $10.5 billion to $9 billion) – the first major decline since the mid-1990s. Net capital inflows fell sharply from $21.13 billion in 1999 to $14.35 billion in 2000.

Significant declines in inflows to Angola, Gabon, Mozambique and South Africa led to the outcome in 2000. In 2001, FDI inflows to Africa increased from US$9.1 billion to US$11 billion due to a rise in investments in Morocco and South Africa, though with a downward trend in Egypt.

African FDI is driven primarily by investment in oil, gas, minerals and tourism. Exceptions, however, occur in those countries that have managed to break into global production-sharing arrangements – primarily North Africa, South Africa and Mauritius – while countries like South Africa and Egypt have become regional export platforms. In South Africa, for example, large mergers and

---

Box 1.2: Impacts of the September 11 Attacks on African Economies

Evaluating the precise impacts of the September 11 attacks on African economies is fraught with high degree of uncertainty because the full ramifications depend on the unpredictable responses of investors and consumers (especially in the US and industrial countries) as well as the extent of linkages between the industrial countries and African economies. Also, there is a more fundamental methodological problem of disentangling the effects of the attacks from what would have happened given the weak global economic fundamentals. More generally, the terrorist attacks affected economic outcomes through four major channels—the direct impact through the destruction of life and property; dampened confidence about future prospects and hence negative impacts on investment and consumption; deterioration in financial market conditions and capital flows; and fall in traded commodity volumes and prices as a result of dampened demand in industrial countries. All these channels worked to worsen an already weakened industrialized economies, with various estimates inferring that the short-run output loss in the US following the attacks is in the range of US$16 and 35 billion, and the medium to longer term impacts on the global economy much higher. These have wide-ranging consequences for the developing regions. Asian and Latin American developing countries were the worst hit because of their stronger linkages to the US and Japanese economies, as well as the high composition of their exports related to the high technology and manufactures sector. In many emerging markets (middle to high income developing countries), the aftermath of the terrorist attack reverberated with falling stock prices, widening bond spreads, and weakening currencies. Countries with substantial external financing requirements remain vulnerable to potential reassessments of global or domestic economic prospects and to further shocks to international financial markets. For countries in Latin America, especially Argentina which experienced financial turbulence, these concerns are very strong, and also for other economies with persistently high current account deficits and large external debts.

(box continues on next page)

Box 1.2: Impacts of the September 11 Attacks on African Economies (continued)

Overall, the downturn in the global economy led to the record sharpest deceleration of world trade—from 13.3 percent advance in 2000 to just 0.2 percent in 2001. U.S. investment in equipment declined by 4.5 percent, after growing by 11 percent in 2000. Given that almost 30 percent of US investment is imported, and 40 percent of total investment consisting of high-tech products, the collapse of investment demand in the US was the major force behind the slowdown of world trade and the semi-conductor market. In the first half of 2001, the US imports of capital goods had dropped at an annual rate of 32 percent, and this was worsened by the terrorist attacks. Consequently, growth in exports from developing countries dropped from 15 percent in 2000 to just 2 percent in 2001, and non-oil commodity prices fell by about 9 percent in 2001, compared to a 1.3 percent decline in 2000.

Even with Africa's relatively lower linkages with the US economy, the region was also badly hit by the spillover effects of the attacks, and the overall effect on individual countries depends on the structure of the economy and the previous stance of policies. For example, the Brent Blend oil prices temporarily jumped above $30 immediately after the attack and this benefited Nigeria and Angola, and less so to Cameroon, Chad, Congo (Brazzaville), Cote d'Ivoire, Equatorial Guinea and Gabon. Since November 2001, oil price has plummeted given the dampened global demand, and is expected to settle around $15-20 per barrel in 2002 and 2003, thereby putting immense pressures for macroeconomic adjustments on oil exporters. Already, the falling oil prices imply terms of trade losses equivalent to around 5 – 10 percent of GDP in most of the main oil exporting countries. For oil exporting countries in North Africa, the impact of the falling oil prices will be cushioned because of the conservative policies (oil stabilization funds) followed during the boom era. Nigeria will be hard hit by the falling prices as no discernible conservation policy was in place during the period of higher oil prices. During the temporary oil price boom, the oil importing countries (majority of African countries) suffered a terms of trade loss especially since the surging energy import costs coincided with declining prices for their primary commodity exports. The deteriorating oil prices since November 2001 will benefit the oil importers, and except this positive development is

offset by the falling commodity prices, these economies would sustain their growth momentum. Indeed, the net impact of the price changes on the non-fuel exporting countries is much lower than on the oil exporters— generally in the range of –1 to 1 percent of GDP.

Gold prices also experienced a temporary surge as investors substituted away from weakening currencies and into 'solid' assets (especially gold) as a store of value. With gold prices soaring to $300 per ounce, gold producing countries of South Africa, Ghana, Mali, Tanzania, and Zimbabwe reaped the gains. This is unlikely to be sustained in the medium to longer terms.

Capital flows into Africa are affected by the global slowdown and terrorist attacks. The UNCTAD had predicted a 40 percent slump in global foreign investment flows (largely the result of a slowdown in cross-border mergers and acquisitions in the industrialized countries). Aid flows also slowed down as the US and other industrialized countries stepped up security spending and allocation of aid to strategic allies (in the fight of global terrorism) rather than to countries in need. It is too early to find definite evidence of this aid 'diversion' but analysts believe that the full impact will be felt from 2002 as domestic constituencies in advanced economies insist on increased security and defense spending rather than aid.

The global downturn and the collapse of primary commodity prices have affected the major regional currencies—reinforcing the existing downward (depreciated) trend for the currencies. For the CFA franc, which is pegged to the Euro, the concern is that the appreciation of the Euro will be accompanied by weaker commodity prices, denominated in a depreciating US dollar. Such a combination may force a devaluation of the CFA franc if the zone is to maintain competitiveness.

Commodity prices fell drastically, and this had immense impacts on poverty. The falling agricultural prices impacted on the poverty status of the rural peasant farmers. The overall growth impact is muted—with the boom in oil exporting countries and the more diversified economies of North Africa offsetting the devastating effects of commodity price collapse.

Source: ADB Research Division.

acquisitions, including privatization, fuelled FDI inflows in 2001. The largest deal was Acerinox of Spain's acquisition of Columbus Stainless Steel for 232 million euros.

Although aggregate inflows increased, Africa also experienced a $1.3 billion FDI outflow, of which 43 percent represented offshore investment by South African corporates. South Africa is not only the dominant source of Africa's FDI, but also home to all four of the top 50 developing country transnational corporations (TNCs) head-quartered in Africa.

The medium term outlook is underpinned by prospects for the West African offshore oil and gas industry. Currently, oil and gas constitute Africa's hottest investment play, with a number of new oil and gas discoveries, refineries or pro-cessing projects. According to the Offshore West Africa Report, capital investment in the region led by Nigeria and Angola could exceed total flows to the Gulf of Mexico and the North Sea within 10 years. Offshore West Africa expects annual invest-ment, currently $2 billion, to increase five-fold to $10 billion by 2005. Furthermore, the develop-ment of some 176 fields will boost regional production capacity by 3 million barrels per day (mbd) over the period, of which Nigeria would account for 1.2 mbd.

Domestic Policy Developments

Economic Policy Stance Remained Mixed but Improved

Most African countries are implementing eco-nomic reforms and are committed to macroeco-nomic, structural and institutional reforms. This is not the only impetus for change. Increasingly, African countries own the reform process and the domestic constituency for reform is strengthen-ing. With the cessation of conflicts in many coun-tries and the process of reconstruction now un-derway, the overall policy environment has im-proved substantially over the last five years.

Peace and the restoration of effective politi-cal governance structure are prerequisites for sound economic governance. Policy tensions and challenges remain in some countries, especially those in, or emerging from, conflicts, as well as in those large economies with enormous pressures to deliver 'democracy dividends'.

After decades of repressive regimes in Nige-ria and South Africa, the new democratic govern-ments are under immense pressures to remedy the injustice and deprivations of the past. In South Africa, there are challenges of high unemploy-ment, growth and redistribution. Nigeria, with 70 percent of the population living under the poverty line, massive infrastructure decay, deepseated corruption and damaged institutions, is under pressure to reform so that its people can reap the dividends of the transition to liberal democracy.

Fiscal Policy Stance Remained Basically Unchanged

Fiscal performance worsened in 2001, with the overall fiscal deficit as rising from 1.7 percent of GDP in 2000 to 2.5 percent. This, however, is a remarkable achievement in the light of the im-mense pressure on public finances caused by the deterioration in trade volumes and prices. Trade taxes constitute a major source of revenue for many African governments.

Since the mid-1990s most African economies have pursued policies of fiscal consolidation re-flected in the strengthened fiscal management ca-pability. Consolidation was achieved through a combination of spending cuts, aggressive revenue-promotion strategies, the running down of reserves, including oil stabilization funds in countries with conservative fiscal attitudes to oil windfalls such as Algeria, and treating privatization proceeds as current revenue (as in Nigeria).

Consolidation was fostered also by reductions in debt service obligations arising from the Enhanced HIPC, which freed up debt-service funds for spending on poverty alleviation.

Monetary Policy Remained Moderately Tight

Monetary policy remained broadly restrictive in 2001, with broad money supply growth slowing to 15 percent from 17.2 percent in 2000. The CFA franc zone maintained its tight monetary policy, which moderated inflation and pressure on the exchange rate. From 2002, the BCEAO will introduce a more relaxed monetary policy stance. From now on government borrowing from the BCEAO will be prohibited and replaced by the use of Treasury Bills.

In other countries, particularly the ATLE, the monetary policy stance remained moderately tight. In Nigeria, monetary policy was tightened to stabilize the Naira and counteract an expansionary fiscal stance. The minimum rediscount rate was raised several times during the year to reach 18 percent while lending rates increased to between 35 and 40 percent.

In Egypt, the authorities devalued the Egyptian pound by 6.4 percent in August 2001 and doubled the trading band to 3 percent from 1.5 percent either side of the central rate. This move, designed to eliminate the parallel market, looks to have been successful. Elsewhere, except in the extreme cases of Angola, Zimbabwe and Democratic Republic of Congo, orthodox monetary polices were adopted with the aim of reining in inflation and stabilizing exchange rates.

Inflation and Exchange Rate Policies

Fiscal consolidation and relatively tight monetary policies helped to slow inflation and moderate exchange rate fluctuations in most African countries. Exceptions were the Democratic Republic of Congo and Angola, with inflation in excess of 100 percent, and Zimbabwe with 74 percent. In 39 economies, consumer level inflation remained in the single digits and the continental average fell marginally to 12.2 percent in 2001 from 13.4 percent in 2000. Median inflation however, was only 6 percent.

Inflation in Nigeria almost trebled from 6.9 percent in 2000 to 19 percent in 2001, while most other relatively high growth (RHG) countries had rates of 10 percent or less: Egypt (2.4 percent), South Africa (5.8 percent), Morocco (1.0 percent), Kenya (3 percent), Algeria (4 percent), Sudan (6 percent), and Libya (14 percent).

The weakness of the Euro relative to the US dollar meant that the CFA lost 22 percent of its value against the US dollar between January 1999, when the Euro was launched, and December 2001. However, both the Euro and the CFA franc are expected to strengthen in 2002. The Nigerian Naira had a bumpy ride in the first half of 2001 before stabilizing. In the parallel market, the Naira tumbled to a low of N140 to the dollar from N115 at the end of 2000. This reflected excess market liquidity caused by the surge in government spending, as well as arbitrage between the official and parallel markets. The Central Bank intervened strongly and tightened both foreign exchange market regulations and monetary policy to reverse the trend. Consequently, there is now a wide gap between the IFEM (interbank) rate and the parallel market rate with official IFEM rate at N112 compared to the parallel market rate of N135.

In South Africa, the Rand came under increasing pressure, falling by 10 percent in real terms in 2000 and a further 40 percent in 2001. The Rand is likely to remain vulnerable to external shocks due to South Africa's well-developed financial market that is closely integrated with the global market, its relatively low level of foreign reserves and substantial portfolio flows. High levels of unemployment in South Africa (about 30 percent) allied with the slowdown in economic activity could lend further impetus to Rand depreciation, despite analyst assertions that the currency is now substantially undervalued. Despite this, dealers expect continued Rand volatility during 2002, especially if there is no resolution of the Zimbabwe political and economic crisis, which has adversely affected Rand sentiment.

The Sudanese currency has retained its $D257 peg to the dollar since mid 1999, while the Libyan currency appreciated in the parallel market, following the easing of sanctions and economic liberalization. Morocco devalued by 5 percent, while Kenya experienced minor depreciation.

Zimbabwe maintained its two-tier exchange rate system with the official exchange rate pegged at Z$55 to the US dollar, but with the parallel market rate depreciating dramatically from Z$75 to the US unit early in 2001 to Z$330 by year-end. After falling steeply in the first few weeks of 2001, the Zambian Kwacha stabilized on the strength of a tighter monetary stance, increased aid inflows and higher copper production and exports. After depreciating 58 percent in 2000, the Kwacha appreciated 8 percent during 2001.

Major Sectoral Developments

Africa's four main economic sectors – agriculture, industry (manufacturing and mining), energy and services – continued to be prime determinants of economic performance in 2001 (Table 1.6).

Agriculture

Agriculture holds the key to Africa's short and medium term economic prospects, accounting for a third of GDP, employing about half the labor force and providing a livelihood for some 70 percent of the poor. Thus the performance of

Table 1.6: Sectoral Growth Rates, 1997-2001
(Percentage changes from preceeding year)

	1997	1998	1999	2000	2001 [a/]
Agriculture	1.0	4.5	2.3	1.4	4.5
Industry	4.2	3.2	2.5	4.2	3.5
Manufacturing	4.2	2.7	3.4	4.4	3.7
Services	3.1	3.2	3.7	3.4	3.0
GDP at constant Market prices	3.1	3.7	3.0	3.2	3.4

Note: a/ Preliminary estimates.
Source: ADB Statistics Division.

the sector is a key barometer for measuring the qualitative performance of key indices – income, employment and poverty.

In 2001, agriculture recovered strongly, growing at 4.5 percent compared with only 1.4 percent in 2000 and the best performance since 1998.

Growing Food Insecurity

Food production, which dominates the agricultural sector, increased in 2001, with improved harvests in North Africa, the Horn of Africa and bumper crops in the Sahel in West Africa. However, many countries still faced serious food shortages due to natural and/or man-made disasters and require food aid. Regionally, production increased in West Africa but adverse climatic conditions, including drought and floods in Southern Africa, led to lower output in East and Southern Africa. Overall, there was a marginal increase in estimated cereal production, from 111.5 million tonnes in 2000 to 116.7 million tonnes in 2001 (Table 1.7). Cereal imports were therefore down marginally from 47.6 million tonnes in 2000 to 44.4 million tonnes in 2001 valued at $4.1 billion. Cereal exports were slightly lower at 3.2 million tonnes (3.3 million in 2000) while food aid shipments to Africa stood at 3.1 million tonnes.

The FAO estimates that some 28 million people in Africa faced severe food shortages in 2001, of whom 18 million or 64 percent were in East Africa. Despite favorable rains over most of the **East African Region** and good secondary season harvests in parts, the effects of recent devastating droughts and earlier or ongoing civil strife and conflicts continued to undermine the food security of millions of people in the region. This was so despite a marginal increase in cereal production from 17.1 million tonnes in 2000 to 18.8 million tonnes in 2001 (FAO, 2001).

In several countries – Eritrea, Kenya, Ethiopia, Somalia, Uganda and Tanzania – the food supply situation was precarious. In Eritrea, large numbers of displaced people are dependent on emergency food assistance in spite of good main season rainfall during the second half of the year. For Kenya, apart from the negative income effects of the sharp decline in maize prices, the recent drought in the pastoral areas of the north and east of the country more than offset the impact of the favorable rains in major cereal producing areas.

In Somalia, the food situation deteriorated following a poor 2001 main season harvest, the

Table 1.7: Africa's Cereal Production, 1999-2001 (In million tonnes)

	1999	2000	2001*
North Africa	30.3	27.9	33.3
Eastern Africa	17.0	17.1	18.8
Southern Africa	21.3	24.7	20.3
Western Africa	40.0	38.7	41.3
Central Africa	3.2	3.1	3.0
Africa	111.8	111.5	116.7

*Forecast as of November 2001.
Source: FAO (2001).

smallest for seven years, due to drought. Persistent drought in Ethiopia led to renewed food shortages and the unseasonal migration of people and their livestock in the pastoral areas of the country despite abundant rains in major agricultural areas. Food difficulties remained in parts of Uganda and Tanzania due to localized drought conditions and/or insecurity.

In **Southern Africa**, close to one million people were affected by floods in February and March 2001 in Mozambique, Malawi, Zimbabwe and Zambia and governments have appealed for food aid. Also, the mid-season prolonged dry spell adversely affected crops in several countries.

In Angola, some 2.5 million people displaced by the 27-year civil war, need emergency food assistance. Coarse grain production declined in 2001 with maize output, which accounts for over 80 percent of the coarse grain output, falling 26 percent to levels 15 percent below the average for the last five years. Coarse grain output fell 23 percent in Zambia, 26 percent in Malawi, 27 percent in Zimbabwe and 28 percent in South Africa. Reduced maize production in South Africa – the region's largest producer – due to the prolonged dry spell, was the main reason for the 2.4 percent decline in agricultural production in 2001.

Although winter wheat production increased in Zimbabwe following good rains the chaotic land reform programme and a mid-season drought took its toll of maize output, which fell 30 percent. Some 700,000 people in rural Zimbabwe were estimated to be at risk from food shortages, with an additional 250,000 people in urban areas experiencing difficulties due to rapid food price inflation which exceeded 100 percent. The World Food Programme (WFP) planned the distribution of emergency food aid to an estimated 588,000 people spread across 22 districts in chronic food-deficit areas.

Total Southern African cereal production fell 18 percent to 20.3 million tonnes in 2001 from 24.7 million tonnes the previous year, largely due to the 23 percent decline to 10.3 million tonnes from 13.4 million tonnes in South Africa's output.

Apart from poor weather and floods, the HIV/AIDS pandemic continues to have a heavy toll on food security in the region where many rural farmers have died while others are no longer able to work their farms.

In **Central Africa**, the humanitarian crisis worsened in the conflict-torn Democratic Republic of Congo where some 2.5 million displaced people cannot be assisted by humanitarian agencies due to insecurity. Also in the troubled Great Lakes region, Burundi, faced a precarious food situation due to the ongoing civil conflict. In Rwanda, excessive rains in the third quarter of the year caused serious crop damage in high altitude areas mainly in the northwestern province of Gisenyi as well as in Gitarama and Gikongoro provinces.

However, reflecting favorable climatic conditions, food harvests were generally good in the Central African Republic and Cameroon. Consequently, the region witnessed only a marginal decrease cereal production from 3.1 million tonnes in 2000 to 3 million tonnes in 2001.

In **West Africa**, while favorable weather conditions ensured increased harvests in Burkina Faso, Niger, Côte d'Ivoire and Ghana, these were offset by the impact of civil disturbances and poor infrastructure in Liberia, Sierra Leone and Guinea. The region's estimated cereal production increased nearly 7 percent to 41.3 million tonnes in 2001 from 38.7 million tonnes the previous year. Despite this several West African economies were forced to import food with cereal imports of 2.6 million tonnes in Nigeria, 1.1 million tonnes in Côte d'Ivoire and 800 000 tonnes in Senegal.

The FAO estimates that in 2001 only 20 percent of Nigerians were food-secure – a situation exacerbated by increased prices for staple foods. In 2001, Nigeria's cereal production was unchanged at the 2000 level of 23 million tonnes forcing the government to introduce a special food program at a cost of $45.2 million. The government also re-introduced a 25 percent fertilizer subsidy to boost plantings and output.

In Liberia, food supply difficulties persisted as domestic production has still to fully recover from years of civil war in addition to the presence of some 70,000 Sierra Leonean refugees, mainly in Lofa county, one of Liberia's main rice producing areas. The recent eruption of fighting disrupted farming and displaced thousands of people. Although the security situation in Sierra Leone improved, the food supply situation in the country remained precarious as a result of years of civil war with over 400,000 internally displaced persons and returnees requiring food aid.

North Africa had a generally good year in

terms of food and agricultural output. Estimated cereal output for the region rose almost 20 percent to 33.3 million tonnes from 27.9 million tonnes in 2000, with wheat production up 30 percent. In Morocco, wheat production doubled from its drought-affected level in 2000 while overall cereal output increased from 2 million tonnes in 2000 to 4.8 million tonnes in 2001. Output was also higher in both Algeria and Tunisia.

Cereal production in Egypt fell marginally from 20 million tonnes in 2000 to 18.9 million tonnes, while in Sudan, extensive floods led to the displacement of thousands of people and to increased food insecurity. This was exacerbated by the closure of the normal trade routes, which prevented the movement of grain or cassava flour from surplus to deficit areas.

Although wheat production increased 40 percent in 2001 – though still remaining 22 percent below the average of the previous five years – 155,000 tonnes of food aid was required to assist 2 million displaced, drought-affected or otherwise vulnerable people. Accordingly, cereal imports into the region fell only marginally to 26.1 million tonnes from 27.9 million tonnes the previous year.

The continuing underperformance of Africa's agricultural sector has intensified dependence on food aid and food imports. Rice imports were up 3 percent in 2001 to 6.2 million tonnes from 6 million in 2000. Efforts to curtail total food imports have largely failed. Import tariffs were raised, leading to an 85 percent increase in the effective duty. Despite this, total food imports still rose 25 percent in 2001 to 1 million tonnes, with notable increases in South Africa, Cameroon, Senegal and Niger. This contrasts with the experience of other developing regions of the world where food imports either contracted or remained unchanged.

Industry, especially Manufacturing

After two decades of de-industrialization, Africa needs urgently to revive manufacturing industry as a means of diversifying economies, creating jobs, reducing dependence on imports of manufactured goods and shifting production from low technology, low-productivity sectors to those with greater growth potential. Manufacturing facilitates technology and skills transfer, while fostering knowledge, entrepreneurship and innovation. It promotes social mobility, is an important source of employment and generator of incomes and acts as a powerful magnet for attracting foreign investment.

The elasticity of industrial value-added relative to GDP was 1.10 and 1.03 during the 1960s and 1970s, respectively, but declined to 0.75 for the 1980s and to only 0.65 during the 1990s (UNCTAD, 2001). It is not surprising therefore that industrial growth fell from 4.2 percent in 2000 to 3.5 percent in 2001, with its major component – manufacturing – declining to 3.7 percent in 2001 from 4.4 percent the previous year.

In Africa's largest economy, South Africa, manufacturing growth almost halved to 2.9 percent in 2001 from over 5 percent in 2000, reflecting the global slowdown and sluggish personal consumer spending, partly offset by increased production of motor vehicles for export and related accessories, food and fabricated metal products.

Output expanded in Egypt where the manufacturing value-added (MVA) now accounts for 12 percent of GDP, while manufacturing also accounts for one fifth of formal sector employment. The private sector's share of MVA is 88 percent while the public sector contributes 12 percent (UNIDO, 2001). UNIDO estimates show that the growth rate of total MVA in Africa fell from 3.9 percent in the 1980s to 2.9 percent for the 1990s. Even so, African MVA grew faster than the world average (Table 1.8).

Over the two decades, North Africa's MVA growth rate fell from 4.5 percent to 3.4 percent while that for Central Africa was the worst hit with a fall from 2.9 percent to –0.5 percent. But in West Africa, MVA growth accelerated in the 1990s to 3.6 percent from 2.6 percent, making it the only region on the continent where the industrial growth rate increased. MVA growth in East and Southern Africa declined from 4 percent to 2.8 percent, while in South Africa's growth rates were virtually unchanged at 1.1 percent in the 1980s and 1.2 percent in the 1990s. In Egypt MVA growth slowed marginally from 6.6 percent to 6.2 percent, but was still well above the regional average.

Countries to show significant gains included Tunisia (from 3.7 to 5.4 percent), Equatorial Guinea (from 2.8 to 7.9 percent), Ethiopia (from 2.6 to 5.7 percent) and Burkina Faso (from 2 to 5 percent). The steepest decline occurred in the Democratic Republic of Congo where MVA fell 6.2 percent annually in the 1990s after growing 1.6 percent a year in the 1980s.

Growth in per capita MVA followed the same trend – slowing to 0.4 percent annually in the 1990s from 1 percent in the 1980-1990 period. While West Africa witnessed a marginal increase from – 0.4 percent to 0.8 percent during the period, the other regions experienced declines – North Africa (from 1.9 to 1.4 percent), Central Africa (from – 0.2 to –3.2 percent) and East and Southern Africa (from 0.7 to 0.1 percent).

Again, as in the case of total MVA, Tunisia (from 1.3 to 3.9 percent), Equatorial Guinea (from -2.2 to 5.1 percent), Ethiopia (from -0.5 to 2.9 percent) and Burkina Faso (from -0.6 to 2.5 percent) made gains while the DRC slumped from –

1.6 to –9.2 percent during the latter period.

In terms of the distribution of manufacturing value-added among selected branches and developing regions in 2000, wood and cork products had the largest share of 10.2 percent while the same sector in South and East Asia had a share of 55 percent. Food products and beverages with 9.8 percent, against Latin America's 44.1 percent followed Africa's branch share. This was followed by wearing apparel, leather and footwear with 8.2 percent; non-metallic mineral products (8.1 percent), textiles (7.2 percent), tobacco (6.9 percent), petroleum (including coal products, 6.6 percent), metal products (5.9 percent), and base metals (3.9 percent).

Manufacturing's lacklustre performance over the last 20 years reflects a major shift in emphasis from the much-criticized inward industrialization and "urban-bias" of earlier decades. De-industrialization, at least in some of the continent's countries, appears to have been associated with trade liberalization on the one hand and with the decline and privatization of state owned enterprises on the other, which in many countries had constituted the major component of large-scale industry.

Today, African manufacturing contributes only about 1 percent to global industrial output, with the bulk of this marginal contribution coming from just 12 of the 53 countries, where there is a relatively diversified industrial base. African manufacturing is characterized too by very low levels of capacity utilization (30-50 percent on average), as well as by extreme dependence on foreign inputs, expertise and technology. The sector has also failed to provide the boost to employment so widely predicted 30 years ago.

Other problems include the high incidence of dumping and under-invoicing of imports in a number of Africa countries such as Nigeria, which

Table 1.8: Annual Growth of MVA, 1980-2000 and Per Capita MVA, 2000[a]

Country Group or Country/Area	Total MVA							Per Capita MVA							
	Growth Rate Percentage		Index (1990 = 100)					Growth Rate Percentage		Index (1990 = 100)					Value (dollars)
	1980-1990	1990-2000	1997	1998	1999[b]	2000[c]		1980-1990	1990-2000	1997	1998	1999[b]	2000[c]		2000[c]
Africa	3.9	2.9	116	121	127	130		1	0.4	97	99	101	101		78
North Africa	4.5	3.4	119	125	132	137		1.9	1.4	103	106	111	113		198
UMA	4.2	1.6	106	107	112	115		1.5	-0.3	91	92	94	95		224
Central Africa	2.9	-0.5	83	88	91	90		-0.2	-3.2	69	70	71	68		40
Western Africa (ECOWAS)	2.6	3.6	122	131	137	137		-0.4	0.8	101	106	107	105		42
Eastern and Southern Africa	4	2.8	119	122	125	127		0.7	0.1	98	98	98	97		39
Latin America	1.4	2.9	123	124	123	130		-0.6	1.2	109	109	106	111		643
South and East Asia	9	8.9	192	195	214	231		6.9	7.3	173	173	187	199		300
West Asia and Europe	4	2.7	110	113	110	119		1.3	0.5	95	95	90	96		580
World	3.1	2.6	117	118	123	129		1.4	1.3	105	105	108	112		1037

a/ At constant 1980 prices.
b/ Provisional.
c/ Estimate.
Source: UNIDO Database

is threatening the survival of local industries. Unless effective measures to check this trend are put in place, the process of de-industrialization, will continue. Urgent policy measures are needed to raise levels of capacity utilization, encouraging the sourcing of inputs either domestically or regionally, rather than from abroad, along with a focus on competitiveness and participation in global production chains.

Mining

Although Africa is a major producer of more than 60 important minerals and a wide range of metals, its share of major metals production – copper, lead, and zinc – is less than 7 percent. Africa contains an estimated 30 percent of the world's mineral reserves, including 90 percent of platinum group metals, 60 percent of cobalt and 40 percent of gold. It is also a significant producer of uranium, manganese, ferrochrome, nickel, bauxite, cobalt and diamonds. The African mining industry is dominated by South Africa, Botswana, Namibia, Ghana, Zimbabwe, Tanzania, Zambia and the Democratic Republic of Congo.

Six trends dominated industry performance during 2001:

1. The downtrend in global demand for metals and minerals, leading to a general softening in metal prices.
2. The development of new, and expansion of existing operations in Ghana, Mali, Zambia, Tanzania, Mozambique and South Africa.
3. A partial pause in countries with high levels of political and property rights risk, most notably Zimbabwe, though development of two platinum mines is going ahead there.
4. Increased exploration in some countries,

though over the continent as a whole the major players have cut their exploration budgets;
5. The intensification of international efforts to end the trade in so-called "conflict diamonds".
6. The restructuring, consolidating and diversifying of Africa's major mining groups especially, but not only, those headquartered in South Africa.

With output running well ahead of demand, which weakened progressively through 2001, stocks rose and prices fell. Aluminum stocks at the London Metal Exchange more than doubled from 332 000 tonnes to 821 000 tonnes in December 2001, while copper stocks rose 123 percent to 800 000 tonnes from 357 000 tonnes at the end of 2000.

Consequently, the World Bank's index of metals and mineral prices (1990= 100) declined to 78.3 – its lowest since 1998.

This is not a new phenomenon. Through the 1990s, copper production grew at an average annual rate of 3.5 percent but world consumption increased only 3.3 percent a year. As a result copper inventories rose from 179 000 tonnes in 1990 to 800 000 tonnes at the end of 2001. Over the same period, the copper price plunged 40 percent from $2 770 a tonne in 1990 to $1 645 in 2001.

Global gold demand amounted to 3,235.1 tonnes in 2001, down 2 percent from 2000's 3,287.9 tonnes. The price averaged $282.5 an ounce in 2001, slightly below the $286.7 an ounce average for 2000.

Along with oil, gold was the one commodity price to benefit from the September 11 attacks and although the upsurge was shortlived, speculative demand, especially from the Far East, most notably Japan, underpinned the price during the first quarter of 2002.

Gold remains the focus for most Africa's exploration activities with the development of significant new properties in West and East Africa, especially in Mali and Tanzania where world class facilities were put in place. Tanzania and Mali have now become major gold producers in Africa, ranking third and fourth after South Africa and Ghana.

The consolidation of South Africa's gold industry that started in 2000 continued in 2001 as AngloGold disposed of its marginal gold mines, particularly in the Free State. Although output continued its longterm decline, the steep fall in the rand boosted gold producer profits. Rand depreciation is, however, a short-term panacea and not a solution to the industry's long term problems that include high levels of HIV-AIDS infection in the workforce, rising labor costs, the increasing depth of operations and a general decrease in ore grades at existing operations in the Witwatersrand Basin.

Although gold has been overtaken by platinum as the country's largest single export earner, the industry's ongoing decline largely accounts for the 2.4 percent fall in mining's contribution to GDP during 2001. In the longer-term, the industry's restructuring and consolidation programs include targeting new projects elsewhere in Africa, especially in East and West Africa, as well as looking further afield to Latin America and Australia.

In Zimbabwe, gold mining continued to decline in 2001 and production has fallen more than 30 percent since 1999. Several mines have closed largely because they are no longer viable in a hyperinflationary environment and a pegged exchange rate for their production. The authorities have sought to mitigate this with the introduction of a gold-price subsidy scheme, but there is a still a large gap between the effective price paid for exports and the exchange rate at which producers are required to source imported inputs. A turnaround in the industry is unlikely unless the government revises its exchange rate and monetary polices and there is a sustained increase in the price of gold.

In 2001, the continent remained one of the largest producers of diamonds, with Botswana, the Democratic Republic of Congo, South Africa and Namibia leading the way. However, in Namibia, diamond output declined from 1.55 million carats in 2000 to 1.5 million carats in 2001, while growth in Botswana's diamond sector slowed with the completion of its expansion program.

The conflict in Angola continued to disrupt mining and exploration activities in the prospective northern and eastern parts of the country, while neighboring Namibia and Zambia experienced cross border raids. African diamond exploration and development activities appeared to have been concentrated in West Africa as well as Liberia, Botswana, Mauritania, Namibia and Zimbabwe.

Major expansion of platinum group metals is underway in South Africa, while there are two medium mines being developed in Zimbabwe – the Ngezi and Mimosa mines. In Zimbabwe, the Australian-owned Zimplats group will reach full production at its Ngezi property in mid-2002, making platinum one of the country's larger exports.

Weak base metal prices forced some developers to shelve new and expansion projects pending a price recovery. By far the most significant was the January 2002 decision by South Africa's Anglo American group to cancel its planned Konkola Deep Mine in Zambia, which would have been the country's largest single private sector investment. Anglo American said it would divest from Zambia's copper mining industry altogether – less than two years after its return when the state-owned Zambia Consolidated copper Mines parastatal was privatized.

The future of Anglo America's three other Zambian mines will be determined during the first half of 2002. In the meantime, other copper groups in Zambia have delayed some projects while insisting that they have no intention of following the South African group's example. Indeed, a Zambian cobalt plant, Chambishi Metals, owned by the Anglovaal mining company, also South African, is set to become the largest producer of cobalt in the world.

In the face of weak demand and prices, the Zambian copper industry still achieved its best performance for many years with mining output increasing 14 percent. The sector's share in GDP rose to 6.9 percent from 6.4 percent in 2000. Copper production recovered some lost ground, increasing 15 percent to 296 500 tonnes from the 2000 low of 256 000 tonnes. Exports rose 37 percent to 297 000 tonnes but prices were down 6 percent. Cobalt sales were also sharply higher – up 47 percent – but prices fell 31 percent.

Energy

Extremely volatile conditions characterized the global energy market in 2001 with strong prices for oil and natural gas. Early in the year, it was feared that energy shortages would constrain output, especially in the US, but this was overtaken by the economic slowdown. Weak demand forced OPEC to impose oil production quota cuts totaling 5 million barrels per day in 2001, as a result of which OPEC's average production was 665,000 barrels per day less than in 2000 (Energy Information Administration, 2002).

OPEC-10 oil supply in 2001 stood at 30.1 million barrels per day against 30.9 million barrels per day in the previous year. Despite this, global oil supplies in 2001 were fractionally higher at 76.9 million barrels per day compared with 76.8 million barrels per day supplied in 2000. Africa's share in 2001 was 2.81 million barrels a day, down from 2.85 million barrels a day in 2000 (OPEC, 2002).

In 2001, global oil demand at 75.8 million barrels per day was little changed from the 75.7 million barrels per day in the previous year. Africa's demand increased marginally from 2.35 million barrels per day in 2000 to 2.37 million barrels per day in 2001. However, estimated total African oil supply fell from 301.36 million metric tonnes in 2000 to 266 million metric tonnes in 2001 (Table 1.9.)

World oil prices stayed firm through most of 2001, averaging $24.4 a barrel, down 10 percent over the year (Table 1.10), due largely to the actions led by OPEC and some non-OPEC countries to restrain oil production. However, later in the year prices weakened, after a brief surge immediately after the attacks of September 11, in response to the slowing world economy. Firm oil and gas prices benefited exporters such as Nigeria, Algeria, Angola and Equatorial Guinea, who collectively achieved an economic growth rate of 3.7 percent in 2001 against net oil importers' 3.3 percent.

In Nigeria, crude oil production rose from 2.03 million barrels per day in 2000 to 2.1 million in 2001 (OPEC, 2002). The country signed a number of production-sharing contracts, which give a 70:30 profit split (in the companies' favor) in order to encourage private local participation in the oil and gas industry. It also signed preliminary sales agreements covering the entire production of Liquified Natural Gas from its planned fourth and fifth trains, though it is yet unclear how the collapse of energy trading firm, Enron, which is the lead

Table 1.9: Crude Oil Production, 1993-2001
(In millions metrics tonnes)

Country	1993	1994	1995	1996	1997	1998	1999	2000	2001*
Algeria[a/]	36.75	37.24	37.74	40.72	42.21	41.22	37.24	40.30	41.30
Angola	24.98	27.61	30.79	34.27	36.25	36.75	38.29	38.14	36.21
Benin	0.19	0.19	0.12	0.20	0.15	0.15	0.15	na	na
Cameroon	6.34	6.54	5.05	5.46	6.16	5.07	4.97	4.22	na
Congo	9.05	9.01	8.77	10.43	12.12	11.82	11.67	14.15	na
Congo, Dem. Rep.	1.17	1.24	1.52	1.04	0.99	0.99	0.99	na	na
Egypt	46.76	44.79	44.20	45.69	45.69	43.90	42.31	40.37	38.06
Equ. Guinea	0.25	0.30	0.40	1.74	2.38	4.12	4.47	6.21	na
Gabon	14.90	15.89	17.38	17.83	18.37	17.88	16.88	16.19	14.94
Libya[a/]	68.03	68.53	70.02	69.03	70.52	69.52	67.04	70.89	67.74
Nigeria[a/]	94.85	94.35	95.84	106.77	113.22	105.28	97.83	70.89	67.74
Tunisia	4.50	4.50	4.17	5.31	5.36	4.02	4.17	na	na
Total Africa	307.78	310.20	316.00	338.48	353.43	340.72	326.02	301.36	266.00
OPEC[a/]	1297.02	1246.91	1266.57	1293.14	1350.75	1383.03	1457.52	1458.86	1352.33
World[a/]	3233.60	3278.35	3342.01	3465.51	3580.48	3648.01	3587.93	3726.23	3729.00

* Estimates
a/ Crude oil and Condensates (excluding Natural Gas Liquids).
na: Not available
Sources: Petroleum Economist, February 2002, Economist Intelligence Unit, Etudes et Statistiques BEAC and ADB Statistics Division estimates

buyer, will affect the deal. Nigeria is expected to benefit from higher investment in offshore oil fields and new gas projects, which will enhance economic growth.

Algeria's daily supply of crude oil rose from 808,000 barrels in 2000 to 820,000 barrels in 2001. During the year, Nigeria and Algeria agreed to study a 4,000-kilometer pipeline project to ferry African gas to the European market. The Trans-Saharan Gas Pipeline Project that is expected to cost US$6 billion will link Abuja, via Niger, with the Mediterranean port city of Beni Saf.

Lower oil prices may force Algeria to spend only a third of its economic recovery plan allocation in 2002, thus hampering economic growth. Egypt's oil supply fell from 80,000 barrels per day in 2000 to 76,000 barrels per day in 2001. However, there were two new gas discoveries in the Northeast of the country in 2001 while an alliance was formed during the year for the development of gas reserves for export and the creation of gas liquefaction capacities.

Libya's daily crude oil supply fell from 1,405,000 barrels in 2000 to 1.361,000 barrels in

Table 1.10: Selected Commodity Prices in Current Dollars

Commodity	Unit	2000	2001
Oil Price (dollars weighted average)	Dollars/barrels	28.2	24.4
Agricultural Commodities			
Wheat, U. S., HRW	$/mt	114.1	126.8
Rice, Thai, 5 percent	$/mt	202.4	172.8
Soybeans	$/mt	211.8	195.8
Sugar, world	Cents/kg	18.4	19.04
Coffee, other milds	Cents/kg	192	137.3
Coffee, robusta	Cents/kg	91.3	60.7
Cocoa	Cents/kg	90.6	106.9
Tea, auctions (3) average	Cents/kg	187.6	159.8
Cotton	Cents/kg	130.2	105.8
Metals and Minerals			
Aluminium	$/mt	1,549	1,444
Copper	$/mt	1,813	1,578
Gold	$/toz	279	271
Iron ore, Carajas	cents/dmtu	28.79	30.03
Lead	cents/dmtu	45.4	47.6
Nickel	$/mt	8,638	5,945
Silver	cents/toz	499.9	438.6
Tin	cents/kg	543.6	448.4
Zinc	cents/kg	112.8	88.6

Source: World Bank, Economic Policy and Prospects Group and Pink Sheet February 2002.

2001, representing 0.2 percent of world gas production in 2001. Oil production will be boosted by the discovery of an estimated 250 million barrels of oil in the Sahara Desert's Murzuq Basin, about 800 kilometers from Tripoli. The award of a contract to develop the Elephant field in the same Murzuq Basin will further boost production.

Sudan's crude oil production continues to increase – from 185,000 barrels per day in 2000 to 230,000 barrels per day in 2001 – following the development of new oil fields that have become operational. Sudan began to play a role inside OPEC in 2001 with its acceptance that it would take up observer member status as well as sending its oil minister as a delegate to one of OPEC's recent conferences. In Angola, daily crude oil production fell to 71,000 barrels in 2001 from 74,000 barrels in 2000, though this will be reversed in 2002 as major new deepwater capacity comes on stream.

Following the agreement between OPEC and non-OPEC producers to reduce world supplies for the first six months of 2002, additional stocks accumulated in 2001 will be worked off during the latter half of 2002 and in 2003, building a platform for firmer world oil prices. Indeed, with the expected recovery of the global economy by end-2002, oil demand could well increase to 1.3 million barrels per day in 2003, again boosting prices. However, political developments, including rising tensions over Iraq, could affect the oil demand-supply balance in 2002/03 rendering price forecasts meaningless.

Coal production is limited to a handful of countries, dominated by South Africa, though there are plans for major new developments in Mozambique (Moatize) and Zimbabwe. The South African coal industry is restructuring with the unbundling of steel producer Iscor, which resulted in the establishment of a new mining company, Kumba Resources. It has since set up a strategic alliance with Eyesizwe Coal, South Africa's largest black empowerment coal company, which could lead to the formation of the Africa's third largest coal producer.

Africa's electricity generating capacity is concentrated in two regions – North and Southern Africa. Together, those two regions account for 82 percent of total power-generating capacity in the continent. The Democratic Republic of Congo (Central Africa), Kenya (East Africa), and Nigeria (West Africa) are the leaders in power generating capacity for Africa's other regions. Cameroon, along with the DRC, has the greatest potential for hydroelectric power in the continent.

Services

Growth in the services sector in 2001 slowed to 3 percent from 3.4 percent the previous year and 3.7 percent in 1999. In recent years, tourism has become an increasingly important contributor to the growth of the services sector, but in 2001 growth slowed largely due to the September 11 attacks in the United States and weaker economies in the major tourism generating markets. International tourist arrivals declined slightly to 689 million in 2001 from 697 million in 2000 (Table 1.11). After increasing 3 percent during the first eight months of 2001 tourist arrivals worldwide fell 11 percent in the final quarter, with substantial decreases in most regions. In the Middle East arrivals were down 30 percent, in South Asia (-24 percent), Americas (-24 percent), East Asia/Pacific (-10 percent), Europe (-6 percent) and Africa (-3.5 percent).

Consequently, tourist arrivals in Africa in 2001 were 28.5 million compared with 27.6 million in 2000 (World Tourism Organization, 2002). This represented a growth rate of 3 percent against 4.3 percent in the previous year, with most of the gain coming from the North African countries of Tunisia and Morocco, which showed strong growth of 10 percent and 8 percent, respectively. In spite of the sharp drops in the last quarter of the year, Morocco ended the year up nearly 3 percent while Tunisia was on track for an increase of 6 percent at the end of November.

South Africa, which suffered from its dependence on the long-haul markets of the USA, UK and Germany, showed a decline of nearly 2 percent for the first 11 months of the year. Egypt,

which had a tourist growth rate of 14 percent in 2000, had a decline of 15.6 percent in 2001, while in Mauritius tourist arrivals were only fractionally higher (+ 0.6 percent) compared with an increase of 13.5 percent the previous year.

Transport

The attacks of September 11 had a dramatic impact on the airline industry, with global losses estimated at $12 billion. As a result, a number of aviation industry restructurings and privatizations ran into trouble and were either put on hold or collapsed. One casualty was the West African regional airline, Air Afrique owned by 11 African countries. Following years of financial crisis, it was forced to file for bankruptcy despite a planned bailout by Air France.

2001 was a volatile year for the transport industry as a whole as volume growth turned into declining traffic while cargo rates weakened. In Africa's ports containerization and information technologies were the driving forces of change with the mechanization of cargo necessitating heavy investment in infrastructure, equipment and new skills. One result has been increased productivity which, in turn, has translated into large reductions in port and harbor employment.

Africa's seafreight business continues to be highly concentrated with 8 ports in Egypt and South Africa responsible for more than half (almost 52 percent) of the continent's traffic. The top 10 ports account for nearly 67 percent of the total container traffic. During the 1997-2000 period, the average annual growth rate of container traffic in African ports was 9.4 percent, one percentage point above the global average, underscoring the degree to which Africa is synchronized with the rest of the world in the spectacular increase in containerized traffic over the last decade. This

Table 1.11: International Tourism Arrivals by Sub-region

	2000			2001			
		Growth Rate (%)		compared to same period last year			
			Average	Jan-	Sept-	Total	Estimate
	(Million)	2000/1999	1990/2000	Aug.	Dec.	(%)	(Million)
Africa (Excluding Egypt)	27.6	4.3	6.3	6.1	-3.5	3.2	28.5
Egypt	5.1	13.9	7.8	-5.8	na	-15.6	na
Mauritius	0.7	13,5	8,4	0.2	na	0.6	na
Morocco	4.1	7.8	0.2	7.6	na	2.7	na
South Africa	6.0	-0.4	19.3	-1.0	na	na	na
Tunisia	5.1	4.6	4.7	14.1	na	na	na
Americas	128.3	5.0	3.3	0.3	-24.5	-7.0	119.3
North America	91.2	4.9	2.4	-0.1	-27.0	-8.2	83.7
Caribbean	17.3	6.9	4.3	2.0	-16.4	-3.5	16.7
Central America	4.4	9.0	9.0	8.8	-10.5	3.0	4.5
South America	15.5	2.6	7.0	-2.2	-18.4	-7.1	11.4
East Asia and Pacific	110.6	14.3	7.3	9.9	-10.3	3.8	114.9
North-East Asia	64.0	15.9	8.6	7.3	-8.7	2.5	65.6
South- East Asia	37.0	13.0	5.6	15.3	-11.9	7.1	39.6
Oceania	9.6	8.9	6.5	6.5	-15.2	0.0	9.6
Europe	403.2	5.7	3.6	1.7	-6.2	-0.7	400.5
Northern Europe	44.2	1.2	4.3	-3.8	-5.8	-4.4	42.2
Western Europe	141.2	4.0	2.2	2.3	-7.8	-0.7	140.2
Central and Eastern Europe	77.2	4.0	5.8	2.8	-10.6	-1.2	76.3
Southern Europe	126.0	8.3	3.6	1.5	-0.6	0.9	127.1
Middle East (Including Egypt)	21.2	12.3	9.0	0.3	-30.2	-8.8	19.4
South Asia	6.4	11.2	7.4	1.2	-24.0	-6.4	6.0
World	697.5	7.0	4.3	28.0	-109.0	-1.3	688.5

na: Not available
Source: World Tourism Organization (2002).

expansion flows from rapid growth in imports, the increased transformation of raw materials for export, rising increased economic activity and the development of multimodal transport and port reforms.

Unfortunately, growth in containerized exports was far lower reflecting the primary product concentration of African exports. A number of factors need to be addressed, including the structure of trade, limited investment, inadequate transport facilities and procedures and tariffs that penalize container traffic.

Information Technology

Information and communication technology (ICT) has increasingly become an instrument for promoting growth and development worldwide. However, as the world prepares for the next generation of Internet services, most of Africa has only recently experienced the Net for the first time. Fifty-six countries and territories are now online, compared with 11 in 1996 (Bidoli, 2001). The number of computers permanently connected to the Internet passed the 10,000 mark two years ago, but most are in cities.

Estimates put the number of Internet subscribers in Africa at 1.3 million, with 750,000 in South Africa and 250,000 in North Africa, leaving 300,000 for the rest of the continent. Since each computer with an Internet or email connection usually supports a range of three to five users, this puts current estimates of the number of African Internet users at about 4 million, of which 1.5 million are outside South Africa. This works out at about one Internet user for every 200 people, compared to a world average of about one user for every 30 people, and a North American and European average of about one in every 3 persons.

By the end of 2000, Internet users in sub-Saharan Africa represented only 0.4 percent of the population compared with 54.3 percent in the United States and 28.2 percent in high-income OECD countries, excluding the US. There are currently 38 African countries with 1,000 or more Internet subscribers, 19 countries with more than 5,000 and 11 countries with more than 20,000 subscribers. This latter group comprises Algeria, Botswana, Egypt, Kenya, Mauritius, Morocco, Nigeria, South Africa, Tunisia, Tanzania and Zimbabwe.

In Zimbabwe, there are more than 35,000 dial-up Internet subscribers who have accounts with local Internet service providers but there are more than 100,000 Internet users in the country, most of whom access the Internet through cyber cafes and company accounts (Jensen, 2001).

Other countries with less than 20,000 subscribers have many more actual users due to the extensive use of wireless and University networks in countries like Côte d'Ivoire, Ghana, Madagascar, Mozambique, Namibia, Senegal, Uganda and Zambia. Though Internet connectivity in Africa is mainly city-based, South Africa stands out as one of the countries with points of presence (POPs) in many secondary towns, so that well over 100 cities and towns are connected to the web. The estimated average cost of using a local dialup Internet account for 20 hours a month in Africa is about $68 per month (excluding telephone line rental), making it the costliest in the world (Table 1.12).

Growth of mobile cellular and other wireless technologies in Africa in recent years has been exponential. The number of mobile phone users on the continent increased from 2 million in 1998 to 28 million in 2001, thereby exceeding the number of fixed-line users, estimated at 22 million. This spectacular expansion in cellphone usage is explained by the liberalization of the mobile phone market in a region where fixed line connections are both scarce and costly. Today, only six African countries do not have access to mobile phone services, while in 17 others mobile phones outnumber fixed-line connections.

Growth in the cellular telephony subscriber base exceeded 50 percent in 2001, while fixed lines grew more than 26 percent and Internet connections expanded 123 percent or 96 percent if South Africa is excluded.

After years of relative inactivity, the Nigerian Internet market is being opened up with the telecom regulator licensing over 40 ISPs to offer services. Many ISPs currently operate their own VSAT links directly into the US backbone, while broadband wireless links are also available. The government-owned telecoms utility, NITEL, has established a POP in Lagos with a 2MB link to Global One in the US and has put POPs in four other cities.

In a country where fixed line services have long been hugely inadequate, growth in cellphone usage has been spectacular since companies licensed to operate the Global System for Mobile Communications (GSM) launched their services in August 2001. Each of the companies – MTN Nigeria Communications Limited and ECONET Wireless Nigeria – has an initial 100,000 line capacity. By the end of the year about one million people had mobile phones. This compares with 500,000 people (out of over 120 million people) who have fixed-lines.

The main constraint on growth in the mobile phone sector is NITEL's inability to provide adequate interconnectivity. It is expected that the launch of a second national carrier will help to solve this problem of inter-exchange congestion.

There is also the increasing recognition of the role electronic commerce (e-commerce) can play in the global economy. It was against this background that UNCTAD in its E-Commerce and Development Report for 2001, assessed the broader economic impact of e-commerce and the ramifications for developing countries catching up or not. The analysis used two scenarios: one in which developing countries fall behind technologically and the other in which they catch up with developed countries.

Under the first scenario, developed countries would have welfare gains of $117 billion, while the developing world (excluding Asia) would lose welfare of $726 million, with Africa's loss being

Table 1.12: Selected African Country Internet Status Summary by August 2001

Country	Dialup Internet Subscribers	International Bandwidth Kbps Outgoing	Internet Hubs Number	Number ISPs	Population Millions 2001	GDP/Capita USD 2001	Cities with POPs	Dialup Access Cost*
South Africa	750000	300000	5	80	43.79	2578	100	40
Algeria	45000	2048	1	4	30.84	1770	4	
Botswana	25000	14000	1	6	1.55	3181	4	
Egypt	80000	112500	3	100	69.08	1353	14	60
Kenya	35000	6144	1	34	31.29	332	6	123
Mauritius	35000	4096	1	1	1.17	3852	1	
Morocco	80000	136000	1	250	30.43	1117	10	
Nigeria	50000	9216	5	15	116.93	355	5	40
Tanzania	20000	4096	3	14	35.97	252	2	
Tunisia	70000	41500	1	5	9.56	2100	7	30
Zimbabwe	20000	5120	1	8	12.85	568	4	46
Africa	1351075	723038	6	644	811.60	673	147	67.94

* Dialup internet access costs calculated for 20 hours a month of local call time plus internet subscription fee.
Source: Jensen (2001) and ADB Statistics Division.

$23 million. Under the second scenario, Africa would have welfare gain of $2.7 billion compared with Asia's $12 billion.

Trade services, air transport, maritime and other transport services and business services would benefit. Thus, by reducing costs, increasing efficiency, reducing time and distances, e-commerce could become an important tool for development.

To bridge the digital divide efforts must focus on infrastructural development, policy incentives, education and training, local relevance and entrepreneurship. A positive development during 2001 was the launch the "e-Africa Commission" in South Africa as the first initiative of Africa's economic regeneration program – the New Partnership for African Development (NEPAD).

Privatization of Africa's telecoms sector slowed in 2001 chiefly as a result of the global downturn in the high-technology and communications industries. South Africa's planned privatization and stock market listing of Telkom was postponed into 2002 while Nigeria's efforts to sell a substantial stake in NITEL were stillborn.

Medium-Term Prospects and Sustainability Issues

The Medium-Term Outlook

Forces Driving the Medium-term Outlook

With the global economy seemingly recovering more rapidly than first anticipated, Africa should see a modest upturn in the latter half of 2002 developing into a stronger rebound in 2003. Governments in the industrial economies have loosened fiscal and monetary policy in an attempt to kickstart recovery and by March 2002, their efforts appeared to be bearing fruit, especially in the US, though Japan remained mired in recession.

The completion of inventory corrections should boost demand while the strengthening of economic fundamentals (lower inflation, improved fiscal positions, and stronger external financial positions) in major economies will increase the scope for policy manoeuvre.

However, these are likely to be offset somewhat by the increased vulnerability of many developing countries whose policy options are seriously constrained by sluggish global demand and the marked fall-off in capital inflows.

In addition, three interrelated risks (Box 1.3) remain, including: reduced desire for risk taking in financial markets and lower commodity prices; limited market access by many developing countries; and imbalances in the global economy. Also, the September 11 attacks on the US, the ongoing global war against terrorism, stock market uncertainty and the wave of corporate bankruptcies have heightened the concerns that the world is still a very dangerous place.

Investors are therefore likely to wait until the front-loading of incentives more than compensates for the risks. These imply the need for improved market access to industrial country markets for developing economies and a rapid increase in official development assistance to reach the United Nation's target for the developed economies of 0.7 percent of their GNI. At the same time, developing economies, including many in Africa, need to strengthen macroeconomic and structural reforms, attract private capital and reduce aid dependence.

Outlook for Africa

African output growth is forecast to remain unchanged at 3.5 percent while real per capita incomes increase by 1.2 percent – the same as in 2001. World economic growth is expected to accelerate towards the end of 2002 and into 2003, with improved prospects for non-oil exporters. Non-energy commodity prices are forecast to improve fractionally in 2002, before increasing 20 percent between 2003 and 2005, though they will still remain below their 1990 levels. By contrast oil prices are forecast to remain roughly at their 2001 levels in 2002 and, although a modest upturn is predicted for 2003, by 2010 prices will still be 17 percent below their 1990 levels.

Manufactured export prices are expected to increase by 4 to 4.5 percent per year, in the light of an anticipated depreciation of the dollar. This would, however, worsen the terms of trade for primary commodity exporters, reducing their import purchasing power and thereby constraining consumption and investment in these countries.

The Outlook's Assumptions and Risks

These forecasts are based on assumptions of favorable weather conditions and an improved agricultural performance as well as an unchanged political and policy stance. Conditions could, however, be dramatically different, depending on the nature and size of changes in weather and agriculture and/or economic policies.

Following the end to the prolonged drought in Morocco and some other North African economies, agriculture is expected to spur growth in these countries in 2002-03. But hopes of a similar impulse in Southern Africa received a severe setback in the first quarter of 2002, when a number of countries, especially Zimbabwe, experienced their worst drought in a decade. Accordingly, growth forecasts for Zambia, Zimbabwe, Malawi and South Africa have been downgraded with the region requiring substantial maize imports in 2002-

---

Box 1.3: Medium-Term Outlook: Why the Current Global Recession Is Different

In the last two decades, the global economy has experienced several crisis and economic recessions. But the impacts of the current one and the dynamics of recovery seem different ostensibly because of heightened perceptions of risk and increased trade links among the global economies. These factors might affect the speed of adjustment and hence the medium term outlook.

In previous recessions, the financial channel was powerful in transmitting growth from industrial to developing countries. After the second oil crisis in the early 1980s, for example, the industrial countries tightened monetary policy to contain inflation. The resulting high interest rates generated severe debt service problems for oil-importing developing countries that had huge external debts, and this plunged these economies into an equally deep recession as in industrial countries. Financial impulse was also critical in the outcomes of the early 1990's recession when developing countries (as a region) largely escaped the recession. Then, the industrial countries pursued a more accommodative monetary policy, with a lowering of interest rates given that inflation was relatively under control. The U.S. interest rate fell by 450 basis points cumulatively over three years, and global capital market flows increased by 22 percent a year. Many developing countries were then aggressively reforming their economies, including the opening up of the capital markets. This encouraged investors to diversify away from the industrial country markets into developing countries and the inflows increased by 32 percent a year. The surge in inflows into the low and middle-income countries enabled them to escape the global downturn.

The outcome in 2001 was different, as the very loose monetary policy in the industrialized countries produced higher spreads instead of larger capital flows to developing countries. The fundamental difference between the 2001/02 slowdown and the previous one a decade ago is the risk perception of private investors. In the 1991-93 period, investors were generally optimistic about new investment opportunities in developing countries after many countries eased capital mar-

(box continues on next page)

Box 1.3: Medium-Term Outlook: Why the Current Global Recession Is Different (continued)

ket conditions. With the experiences of the 1997/98 East Asian financial crisis, the terrorist attacks, stock market dip, high consumer debt, heightened insecurity and battered consumer-cum-business confidence, the response to the 400 basis points U.S. reduction in interest rates is dramatically different. Investors have been much more cautious than on previous occasions. Net capital flows to developing countries fell in 2001, and gross flows from international capital markets, which increased by over 30 percent in 2000, fell by 20 percent in 2001. Direct foreign investment has continued to fall, and official flows also fell. Consequently, the already small share of developing countries in global capital flows has declined further in 2001.

Another difference is that the developing countries are much more integrated into the global trading system than in previous recessions. Consequently, they are also more adversely affected by falling import demand in the industrial countries. As already stated, there is unlikely to be a significant rerouting of capital from industrial to developing countries as happened in previous recessions. Given the likely delayed recovery in the industrial countries, these factors might work to further delay the recovery in developing countries as well.

However, many developing countries are now better equipped to absorb negative external shocks. This is as a result of domestic reforms and production diversification that have taken place in many of these countries during the last two decades. Such improvements raise the expectation that the developing countries would resume high growth once the downturn in the industrial countries is over.

But the recovery in industrial countries still faces several risks and the fundamentals are shakier than in previous times. Investors in the U.S are less responsive to interest rate cuts, or foreign investors might become more concerned about the persistently high U.S. current account deficit and impose an abrupt adjustment—and all these could delay the recovery of investment and its implied demand for high-tech imports. Also, the European downturn may become more severe once market sentiment deteriorates further, or monetary policy does not ease sufficiently or have the expected effects. Japan's structural reforms may falter or exact a higher toll on economic performance, and cause the recession in 2001 to linger much longer than analysts predict. Thus, with the global economy in precarious balance, unforeseen shocks from whatever sources are magnified and could push the global economy into deeper crisis.

Source: World Bank (2001), Global Economic Prospects, November.

---

03. Zimbabwe alone will need to import 1.5 million tonnes of maize following the failure of its 2001-02 harvest.

While the weak rand and export growth has helped insulate the South African economy from the global slowdown, the sharp increase in inflation in the first few months of 2002, necessitating two interest rate hikes, points to another year of sluggish growth in the region of 2.5 percent. Already the South African Reserve Bank has been forced to abandon its inflation target for 2002 (3 to 6 percent), while business confidence and regional investor sentiment have been adversely influenced by the ongoing political and social crisis in neighboring Zimbabwe.

In other economies – Mozambique, Uganda, Tanzania, Ghana and Cameroon – where macroeconomic and structural policies are generally sound, relatively healthy growth is expected in 2002 and beyond. Indeed, Mozambique is predicting growth of over 9 percent driven largely by strong export growth from the Mozal aluminum smelter.

But a number of countries, especially those affected by domestic or cross-border conflicts and governance problems, will continue to underperform. This list includes the Democratic Republic of Congo and Zimbabwe, where the combination of severe drought, limited sanctions by the U.S. and EU countries, and the steep decline in commercial agricultural production following the land resettlement programme, points to a double-digit decline in real GDP in 2002.

Exports will be constrained by commodity price weakness and sluggish global demand, though some countries will partially offset these affects by exploiting concessional trade arrangements, most notably the United States Africa Growth and Opportunity Act (AGOA). This scheme is already paying off with 13 African countries exporting $3 billion worth of goods under AGOA preferences in the first half of 2001. African exporters will benefit also from the European Union's 'Everything But Arms' (EBA) concession.

Negotiations are scheduled to start during 2002 on a successor arrangement to the Cotonou agreement that gives African Caribbean and Pacific nations non-reciprocal preferential entry into the EU market until December 2007. Non-reciprocal entry will continue beyond 2002 for Africa's least developed economies but the reminder will be required to negotiate reciprocal arrangements either individually or, preferably, as part of African regional economic agreements known as Regional Economic Partnership Agreements (REPA).

Although oil exporters must expect largely unchanged export prices in 2002-03, significant new capacity, especially in offshore areas, will boost output and export volumes. Estimates suggest that terms of trade losses will reduce GDP growth rates marginally to around 3.6 percent in 2002 from 3.8 percent in 2001.

In Nigeria, Equatorial Guinea and Angola recent offshore discoveries could significantly increase medium term oil production. Exploration and development activities, including the Chad-Cameroon pipeline project could offset terms of trade losses thereby ensuring higher real growth rates than would otherwise have been possible. Angola's economic growth should accelerate in 2002 due to increased oil production from large new offshore fields.

Some oil exporters, notably Nigeria, are moving rapidly to diversify their export portfolios. Nigeria plans to increase natural gas export capacity over the next few years with the construction of a second liquefied natural gas plant at Bonny Island that will increase production by 50 percent beginning in 2002.

Ultimately, the greatest stimulus to growth must come from the deepening of reforms – economic and political governance, structural transformation, rebuilding institutional capacities and sound as well as efficiently managed macroeconomic policies. As the number of countries in conflict declines further and economic reconstruction and policy reforms deepen, a more business- and investment-friendly environment will emerge. Recent experience shows that over the last two decades economic reformers have outperformed the continental average, while also diversifying their economies and expanding non-traditional exports. But the challenges and risks to the medium term performance remain – disease (especially the HIV/AIDS pandemic and malaria), civil strife, poor governance in several countries, erratic weather conditions, lack of economic diversification, adverse terms of trade shocks, low savings and investment, and excessive dependence on foreign aid. These problems are unlikely to disappear soon.

All these mean that the present economic slowdown has exacerbated an already fragile economic environment. Much of Africa is perennially in crisis—a crisis of underdevelopment, struggling to cope with the challenges of initiating and sustaining poverty-reducing growth and structural transformation. Within such an environment, growth rates of 3.5 percent remain the most optimistic forecast for Africa over the medium term.

This is insufficient. Africa needs growth of at least 6 percent annually just to prevent increased poverty in the region, and 7 percent – if not more - to achieve a significant reduction in poverty. African governments are committed to halving the incidence of poverty by 2015, but for this to happen, GDP growth rates must double. Accordingly, the challenge is not so much to overcome short-run setbacks as to chart the long run trajectory needed to reduce Africa's structural vulnerability (Boxes 1.4 and 1.5 and Figure 1.3).

NEPAD: Context and Background

An important consensus is also emerging that the challenge of sustaining reforms and growth in Africa requires a comprehensive agenda. Increasingly, there is a realization that domestic reforms are necessary, but by no means sufficient, to ensure the resumption of sustainable growth and development. Africa cannot do it alone—it requires massive external support, perhaps on a scale not known before.

But this is not a new discovery. Since 1960s, the ECA and OAU had initiated and galvanized over 30 global programs designed to reach a partnership between Africa and the international community in order to push towards a 'collective effort' in African development. Hardly any two years

have passed since the 1980s without a major regional or international initiative aimed at re-focusing attention on the deepening crisis, with a view to assessing past efforts and the road ahead.

Beside the monumental efforts embodied in the Lagos Plan of Action (LPA) (1980) and the African Alternative Framework to Structural Adjustment Programs (AAF-SAP) (1989), several other regional efforts have sought to redefine and strengthen various strategies for development. Some of these efforts include: the African Priority Program for Economic Recovery (APPER) which later turned into the United Nations Program of Action for Economic Recovery and Development (UNPAAERD) (1985); the Khartoum Declaration (1988); the African Charter for Popular Participation in Development (1990); and the Cairo Agenda (1995). These are in addition to Africa's participation in the South-South Commission as well as the pursuit of an African Economic Community under the aegis of the Abuja Treaty (1995).

At the same time, there has been growing concern and interest from the international community. The extra-ordinary session of the UN-General Assembly adopted APPER (with some modifications) as UNPAAERD. Later, its successor, the United Nations New Agenda for the Development of Africa in the 1990s (UN-NADAF) was launched. There have also been increasing efforts over the years to coordinate the activities of the UN system in Africa through the System-Wide Plan of Action for African Recovery and Development. The 'United Nations System-Wide Special Initiative on Africa' was launched in 1995, and the United Nations has convened three special conferences on the plight of the Least Developed countries. The Paris-based donors' club has launched its own initiative—the Special Program of Assistance for Africa (SPA).

Box 1.4: Structural Vulnerability as Threat to Sustainability

Short-run business cycles can be affected by cyclical swings in policies and shocks, but long run growth is determined by the growth fundamentals — factor accumulation and efficiency/productivity. In the literature, dozens of variables have been found to significantly impact on these core determinants, and in the various issues of this Report, we have drawn attention to many factors that threaten longer-term sustainability. These include adverse external shocks, failure to recapitalize Africa, policy reversals, societal conflicts, HIV/AIDS, etc. In various editions, we have also highlighted a number of initiatives to address the sustainability issues, including private sector-led development, regional integration, infrastructure, human capital development, debt relief, etc. These factors remain important.

In this Report, we draw attention to the threat posed by the structural vulnerability - the risk of being negatively affected by unforeseen events beyond the control of the country - of most African economies. Structural vulnerability could be a consequence of the state of underdevelopment. Understanding the nature of structural vulnerability can be important for a proper understanding of growth and feasible policy responses because, according to the World Development Report, 1996, "countries' characteristics—their unique advantages and disadvantages—influence what policies can be chosen and what leaders can accomplish". If structural vulnerability—which has an historical and social basis—is found to be central to the phenomenon of growth volatility in these countries, it would have far reaching implications for the design of policies. This is because, according to Weeks (2001, p.2), 'short-term macroeconomic policy may have limited impact on growth variability, though they may affect the average in the short term'. A major symptom of vulnerability in Africa is the lack of growth persistence,

that is, high growth variability/volatility and the average growth performances having very high standard deviation especially for sub-Saharan countries (see Figure 1.3).

There is a 'high mortality rate' for 'high performers'. Aside from Botswana and Mauritius, no African country has survived the 'high performers' list for a decade. Despite the huge inflows of ODA in the last four decades, more countries continue to join the club of LDCs rather than graduate from the league. Indeed, aside from Mauritius and Botswana, no country has graduated from the club of least developed countries and optimistic estimates indicate that even if the current best performers maintain the trend, they would still be LDCs in 2020. The largest economies—South Africa, Nigeria, Egypt, etc - are mired in low growth trap, despite evidence of improving economic policies. Countries emerging out of conflict and undertaking reforms such as Mozambique, Ethiopia, Uganda, etc and those with positive external shock such as boom in natural resource exports, especially oil— Equatorial Guinea, Sudan, etc are the current best performers in terms of growth. After a few years of 'rapid' recovery, growth performance in Uganda, and Ghana has decelerated into the lower band. Tables 1.2a and 1.2b dramatize the nature of the challenges. In 1997, 43 percent of African countries had growth rates exceeding 5 percent, and this steadily fell to 26 percent in 2001, while an increasing number now settle at growth rates between 0 and 5 percent (60 percent in 2001, as against 45 percent in 1997). Indeed, in 2001 only 4 countries had per capita income in excess of 5 percent. The growth deceleration and evident trap at around 3 percent per annum despite sustained policy reforms raise curiosity about the structural weaknesses of these economies.

Source: ADB Research Division.

All these are in addition to the multiplicity of other bilateral and multilateral advocacy and interest groups in Africa including the Global Coalition for Africa, the recent US Africa Growth and Opportunity Act (AGOA), Japan's TICAD process, the European Union's 'Everything But Arms', and the EU-ACP Cotonou Agreement.

These initiatives are reinforced by the agree-

Box 1.5: Structural Vulnerability: Causes and Possible Remedies

The list of the possible causes of structural vulnerability could be as long and as controversial as the causes of Africa's poor growth itself. A shortlist can be divided into two: a) the 'destiny' variables—geography, soil quality, tropical diseases, low population density and consequent high transport costs and lack of market integration, natural resource 'curse' and concentration on few primary products with volatile terms of trade, tiny, fragmented and economically unviable nation-states with heavy sunk and operating costs of running sovereign states which were arbitrarily marked out by the colonialists, ethno-linguistic diversity, dependence on volatile foreign aid, restrictive trade policies of advanced countries, slow democratic transition, HIV/AIDS pandemic, structure of the global financial and trading system that ensures marginalization and exclusion from the globalization process and its benefits—high admission fees that make it increasingly difficult for late starters to enter the market and compete, etc. b) the 'policy' variables— trade and exchange rates, macroeconomic management, statist and authoritarian policies that gave little fillip to the private sector and overbloated and unproductive public sector, poor civil service delivery, repressed financial sector, etc. Debates rage about the precise weights to be attached to each of these causes, and more so, as to whether the destiny or policy group of variables dominates. What is not debatable are the legacies of these factors—endemic poverty that is becoming dynastic, in the face of heavy external and domestic debt burden.

There is a growing consensus that the way out is not a straightforward one. Even analysts who put a major weight on domestic policies as being the ultimate handle in terms of growth still provide sufficient caveats. For example, Collier and Gunning (1999) conclude that growth in Africa "may be unsustainable unless there is a substantial increase in private investment". But private investment is constrained by poor public service delivery and perceptions of risk—two areas the authors believe are not easy to change. According to the authors (p.20), "Analysis of the global risk ratings shows that while they are largely explicable in terms of economic fundamentals, Africa as a whole is rated as significantly more risky than is warranted by these fundamentals. Similarly, private investment appears to be significantly lower in Africa than is explicable in terms of economic fundamentals...The perception of high risk for investing in Africa may partly be corrected by the passage of time...". Thus, the size of the 'unexplained' in thinking about investment and growth in Africa is big, and how much time is needed for these anomalies to self-correct is not known. In some sense also, the nature and efficacy of domestic policies are circumscribed by these 'unexplained' and structural factors. But the 50 percent of the population living in deep and pervasive poverty cannot wait.

Source: ADB Research Division.

---

ments and declarations reached and signed at various international gatherings such as: the World Conference on Education for All; the Children's Summit; the UN conference on Environment and Development; the UN conference on Population and Development; the Social Summit in Copenhagen, the women's conference in Beijing,

etc. Thus, the crisis continues despite the persistent efforts or expression of solidarity by the international community and donors. The snag is the mismatch between words and actions, commitments and implementation, at both global and national levels.

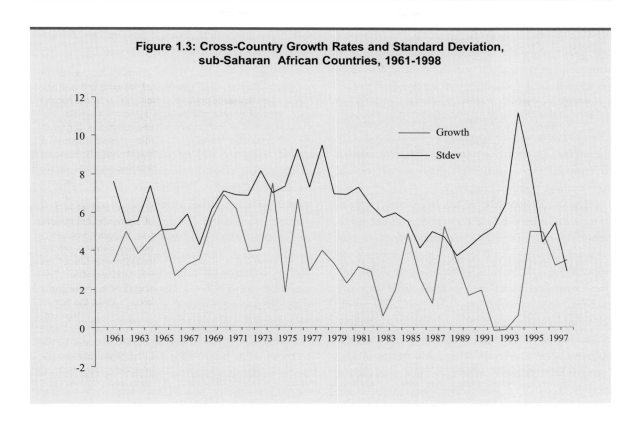

Figure 1.3: Cross-Country Growth Rates and Standard Deviation, sub-Saharan African Countries, 1961-1998

NEPAD: A New Kind of Partnership for Sustainable Development?

The year 2001 marked another milestone in the bid to develop an African development program with which to reach a partnership with the international community. The New Partnership for African Development (NEPAD) (a merger of the Millennium African Renaissance Partnership program (MAP) and the OMEGA PLAN), was launched by African leaders as an agenda for the renewal of the continent. Led by the governments of Nigeria, South Africa, Algeria and Senegal, NEPAD (Box 1.6) was launched as a plan differ-

ent from all previous plans in terms of approach and strategy and as a new framework of interaction with the rest of the world, including the industrialized countries and multilateral agencies. It centers around African ownership and management—an agenda set by African peoples through their own initiatives and of their own volition, to shape their own destiny. Through NEPAD, African leaders are making a commitment to promote peace and stability, democracy, sound economic management and people-centered development and to hold each other accountable in terms of the agreements outlined in the program.

The major distinguishing feature of the

NEPAD from previous programs is the emphasis on African ownership and a demonstrated commitment on the part of the democratic leaders to take Africa's destiny in their hands. There is a new resolve to deal with conflicts and censure deviation from the internationally accepted norms. These efforts are reinforced by voices in the civil society and by a much more resolute commitment to regional and continental goals of economic cooperation and integration.

The NEPAD initiative has been endorsed enthusiastically by the G-8 countries, and the international community. The program envisages major roles for the private sector—both African and non-African. It calls on companies in the developed world to assist in providing infrastructure and in implementing large-scale projects, while reserving some projects for African companies.

Similarly, it will approach the West for their human resources to train Africans in technical educational institutions, in universities and in the health sector. Launching the large-scale programme is expected to absorb, in the first place, all the human resources available in Africa as well as Africans working in developed countries and employ some expatriate human resources. Attracting highly skilled Africans back to work in the continent is an important element.

NEPAD is therefore a call for a new partnership between Africa and the international community, especially the highly industrialized countries, to overcome the development chasm that has widened over centuries of unequal relations.

While the NEPAD raises many hopes, key challenges remain. These include ensuring ownership of the process and programs by the ordinary citizens of Africa beyond the commitments of their Presidents. All too often, Africa's major problem has been the top-down approach to policy formulation and implementation. The NEPAD document states: "the present initiative will be successful only if it is owned by the African peoples united in their diversity". It is the hope of many that the trend would be reversed under the current initiative. Furthermore, NEPAD also recognizes that "…everything depends on the availability of funds".

If the programs of national efforts, regional cooperation, coordination and integration, as well as the expected contributions of the industrial countries materialize, they could provide a platform to tackle the continent's structural vulnerability. NEPAD would widen the economic space, ensure synergies and complementarities in production, distribution and consumption, provide regional public goods beyond the capacities of individual nation states, and ensure the infusion of required funding to escape the poverty trap.

The next decade will provide the litmus test as to whether NEPAD is the long awaited visionary plan to be actively supported by the international community for Africa's renewal or yet another of the long list of unfulfilled promises and unimplemented plans.

Box 1.6: Major Elements of the NEPAD

The NEPAD is envisaged as a long-term vision of African development based on Africans' option for a good mastery and application of the rules of the game of economics. The program of action underpinning this vision has nine top priorities structured in the same way as the strategy outlined. Some of the program areas include:

- Peace, security, democracy, human rights and political governance

- Regional and continental approach—focusing on the provision of essential regional public goods (such as transport, energy, water, ICT, disease eradication, environmental preservation, and provision of regional research capacity) as well as the promotion of intra-African trade and investments.

Sectoral priorities, including:

- Bridging the infrastructural gap, especially regional roads linking up two capital cities of two countries in the region, and continental highways crossing several regions. This would also woo private foreign finance to complement the two traditional funding methods—credit and aid.

- Bridging the education gap, especially to work with donors to ensure that the international development goals of achieving universal primary education by 2015 is realized; curriculum development, quality improvements and access to ICT; promote networks of specialized research and higher education institutions. This requires action plans in terms of regional needs assessment for educational reforms, review levels of expenditure on education by African countries, and lead the process of developing norms and standards for government expenditure on education; set up a task force to accelerate the introduction of ICT in primary schools; set up a task force to review and put forward proposals for the research capacity needed in each region of the continent.

- Appropriate and urgent attention to the health sector, water and sanitation, including the tackling of HIV/AIDS, disease prevention, vaccines against communicable diseases.
- Ensuring an agrarian revolution for sustainable de-

velopment.

- Bridging the digital gap, especially in the area of the ICT with the goal of doubling the teledensity to two lines per 100 people by 2005, with an adequate level of access for households, improve reliability, and improve the ICT competence of the productive population.

- Developing the energy sector and strive for abundant and cheap energy by exploiting all possibilities and rationalizing the territorial distribution of existing but unevenly allocated energy resources, as well as develop the solar energy resources.

- Comprehensive agenda for production diversification, export promotion, and access to industrial country markets.

- Program for promotion and protection of culture, and the environment.

- An agenda of resource mobilization through increasing domestic savings and a comprehensive plan for increasing private capital inflows, new debt and aid reform initiatives.

- Also, NEPAD articulates a comprehensive agenda for a new global partnership, which recognizes the centuries-old historical injustice and the need to correct it. Hence, the central injunction of the new partnership is for combined efforts to improve the quality of life of Africa's people as rapidly as possible with a sense of shared responsibilities and mutual benefits between Africa and her partners.

- To ensure the effective implementation of the NEPAD, the initiating Presidents propose that the following programs be fast-tracked, in collaboration with development partners.

- The programs to be tackled immediately include communicable diseases such as HIV/AIDS, malaria and tuberculosis; information and communication technology; debt reduction; market access

(box continues on next page)

Box 1.6: Major Elements of the NEPAD (continued)

- In addition, some specific projects are proposed to not only strengthen country and regional development programs, but will also go a long way in kick-starting the regeneration of the continent. Three illustrative projects include: a) agriculture: This aims to expand the ambit and operation of the integrated land and water management action plan for Africa. The project addresses the maintenance and upgrading of Africa's fragile agricultural natural resource base. Many African governments are already implementing these initiatives as part of this program. Partners include the Global Environment Facility (GEF), the World Bank, the FAO and other bilateral donor agencies. Also the project would strengthen and refocus the capacity of Africa's agricultural research and extension systems; b) promotion of the private sector through the National Business Incubators (NBI). International experience suggests that one of the best practices in promoting enterprises in highly innovative areas is through the establishment of business incubators. This project will formulate the required guidelines and policies for the establishment of such incubators at the national level, drawing on international experience and established best practice, tailored to African needs and conditions; and c) Infrastructure and regional integration. The African initiative process has identified many energy, transport, telecommunications and water projects that are crucial to Africa's integrated development. The projects are at various stages of development and require funding and in collaboration with the African Development Bank, the World Bank, and other multilateral institutions, the NEPAD hopes to accelerate their further development. It is the view of the initiating Presidents that, unless infrastructure is addressed on a planned basis—that is, linked to regional integrated development—the renewal process of the continent will not take off.

- NEPAD proposes a needs assessment action for the priority sectors, progressing from the national level, to the sub-regional, to the continental level. The point is to assess the needs in the five priority sectors in terms of structures and staff.

- NEPAD is to be managed at both the continental, sub-regional and national levels—with the Heads of State Implementation Committee at the helm, and also supported with a core technical support for the implementing mechanism in the areas of research and policy formulation.

Source: NEPAD (The New Partnership for African Development), (2001).

CHAPTER 2

Regional Economic Profiles

Introduction

This Chapter focuses on economic performance in Africa in the framework of the five sub-regional groupings into which Bank Group operations are classified namely, Central Africa, East Africa, North Africa, Southern Africa and West Africa. The analyses of the regional economic performances are intended to deepen the general analysis of the economic performance of the continent given in Chapter 1. For each of the sub-regions, in addition to an overview of the sub-regional performance, the chapter discusses in some detail the country performances highlighting the major changes that occurred during the year. The analysis focuses on the recent economic trends, policy developments and outlook for the years immediately ahead.

Table 2.1 summarizes the sub-regions' real GDP growth rates, as well as share in Africa's GDP, trade and population. It shows that real GDP increased in four of the five sub-regions between 1997-2000 and 2001—the exception being Southern Africa. Eastern Africa recorded the highest growth in 2001 at 4.6 percent, up from 3.9 percent in 2000, but in Southern Africa expansion slowed to 2.2 percent in 2001 from 2.8 percent the previous year. Growth in Central Africa accelerated to 3.2 percent from 0.3 percent in 2000. West Africa's GDP increased 3.5 percent in 2001, up from 2.9 percent the previous year, while in North Africa output increased to 4.0 percent in 2001 from 3.8 percent in 2000.

Table 2.1: A Sub-Regional Overview of African Economies' Growth, Trade and Population

| | Average Real GDP Growth 1997-2000 | 2001[a] | | | |
		Real GDP Growth	Share in Africa's GDP	Share in Africa's Trade[b]	Share in Total Population
Central Africa	0.9	3.2	5.0	6.1	12.2
Eastern Africa	3.7	4.6	8.3	6.1	23.1
Northern Africa	3.9	4.0	45.6	40.2	22.2
Southern Africa	2.6	2.2	27.1	29.6	14.5
Western Africa	3.2	3.5	14.0	18.1	28.0
Franc Zone	4.1	4.3	8.2	10.2	13.0
Net Oil Exporters	3.9	3.7	49.5	55.9	32.7
Net Oil Importers	2.8	3.3	50.5	44.1	67.3
ALL RMCs	3.2	3.4	-	-	-

Notes: a/ Preliminary estimates; b/ Exports of Goods & Nonfactor Services at Current Market Prices.
Sources: ADB Research and Statistics Divisions.

Central Africa

There are ten countries constituting Central Africa, namely Burundi, Cameroon, Central African Republic (CAR), Chad, Congo, The Democratic republic of Congo (DRC), Equatorial Guinea, Gabon, Rwanda and Sao Tome Principe. Six of the countries – Cameroon, CAR, Chad, Congo, Gabon and Equatorial Guinea belong to the Communauté économique et monétaire de l'Afrique centrale (CEMAC), which is part of the CFA franc zone. Three countries – Burundi, DRC and Rwanda – are members of the Common Market for Eastern and Southern Africa, COMESA. Of the countries in the region, Gabon and Cameroon are substantial producers of oil.

Gross output from the Central Africa is the lowest amongst the sub-regions. In the late 1990s economic performance had fallen short of potential due to the military and civil conflicts that plagued the sub-region. However, relative peace, the lack of which had undermined growth in 2000, was restored to enable economic activity to gain momentum in 2001 though per capita incomes declined from $288 in 2000 to $274.

Following the reactivation of the Lusaka ceasefire agreement, with the involvement of the United Nations, and the enhancement of the inter-Congolese dialogue, 'Africa's seven-nation war' in the DRC subsided. The political and security situation has since improved. Relative peace was also restored in the Congo and Burundi, which had been embroiled in conflicts.

In 2001, the gross domestic product originating from Central Africa represented only 5 percent of the continental total, with Cameroon, the largest country in the region (in terms of GDP), accounting for about 32 percent of regional output. In 2001, the total population of the region

was estimated at 99.07 million representing 12 percent of the continental total (Table 2.1). The population of the DRC is over half (53 percent) the regional total.

Equatorial Guinea, Gabon and Cameroon are oil exporters, while others in the region are mainly exporters of agricultural commodities. Central Region exports made up 8 percent of the continental total in 2000 with the two major oil exporters, Cameroon and Gabon, accounting for 56 percent of the total.

Recent Economic Trends

Economic activity in the Central region picked up in 2001 with real GDP growth increasing from a yearly average of 0.9 percent during 1997-2000 to 3.2 percent in 2001 (Table 2.2 and Figure 2.1).

In Burundi eight years of war and the adverse effects of the embargo imposed from 1996 to 1999 had drained the economy, weakened its administrative capacity and destroyed basic infrastructures and the economic base. Consequently, output grew by an average of only 0.8 percent annually between 1997 and 2000. In 2000, economic activity was adversely affected by drought, leading to a further decline in agricultural production but there was a rebound in 2001 when real GDP is estimated to have increased 3.2 percent.

The Cameroon economy has performed well since 1996, with growth averaging over 4.7 percent a year during the period 1997-2000. Real GDP growth is estimated at 5 percent in 2001, which would have been higher but for disruption in export crops (cocoa and coffee) and the timber sector and lower oil prices (Figure 2.2).

In Chad thirty years of civil war profoundly affected the economy but the return to democracy in the mid-1990s established a much more positive environment for economic and social

Table 2.2: Central Africa: Gross Domestic Product and Export Performances

Country	Real GDP Growth Rate (%)		GDP Per Capita (US$)		Real Export Growth (%)		Exports[b] Per Capita (US$)	
	Average 1997-2000	2001[a]	Average 1997-2000	2001[a]	Average 1997-2000	2001[a]	Average 1997-2000	2001[a]
BURUNDI	0.8	3.2	130	106	17.0	13.8	11.7	8.0
CAMEROON	4.7	5.0	624	567	8.1	2.3	166.3	178.8
CENTRAL AFRICAN REP.	4.0	1.0	282	257	-1.5	0.5	42.9	31.0
CHAD	3.1	8.9	206	197	5.0	3.8	36.1	29.7
CONGO	4.2	3.3	849	926	1.1	8.8	23.4	8.9
CONGO, DEM. REP. OF	-5.9	-4.1	104	83	10.9	-26.7	616.0	737.2
EQUATORIAL GUINEA	40.0	53.0	1784	3927	18.3	6.8	1722.9	4017.6
GABON	-0.6	-1.5	4112	3483	-12.3	-6.8	2438.9	2100.1
RWANDA	8.5	6.0	287	219	13.4	6.8	19.4	19.0
SAO TOME & PRINCIPE	2.2	3.0	332	323	-13.0	40.9	104.9	119.6
CENTRAL AFRICA	**0.94**	**3.17**	**299**	**274**	**1.6**	**-6.5**	**104.2**	**106.9**

Notes: a/ Preliminary estimates.
b/ Exports of Goods and Nonfactor Services at Market Prices.
Sources: ADB Research and Statistics Divisions.

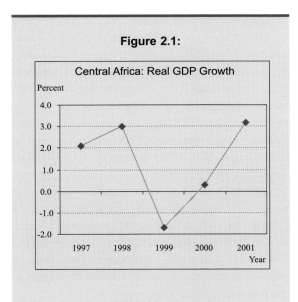

Figure 2.1:

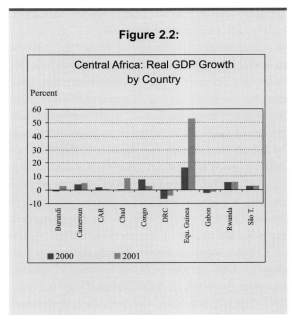

Figure 2.2:

progress. After averaging 3.1 percent a year between 1997 and 2000, GDP growth surged to 8.9
percent in 2001, largely due to increased investment linked to building the regional oil pipeline.

Recurring armed conflicts in recent years in
Congo destroyed much of the productive base of
the economy. However, there was a robust
recovery during the 1997– 2000 period, when real
GDP grew 4.2 percent annually. Following this
initial rebound, growth slowed to 3.3 percent in
2001.

The Democratic Republic of Congo has long
been characterized by economic mismanagement
and political turmoil leading to a prolonged run-
down in the economic and social infrastructure
during the 1990s. During the civil war between
1997 and 2000, real GDP declined by 5.9 percent
a year. The political and security situation has since
stabilized and in 2001 the government reached an
understandings with the IMF on a staff monitored
reform program to lay the foundation for
reconstruction and the restoration of growth.
Despite this, the decline continued in 2001 when
output fell a further 4.1 percent.

Equatorial Guinea has achieved the highest
growth path on the continent over the last five
years as a result of large oil discoveries that have
transformed the country's economic prospects,
making it one of the world's most oil-dependent
countries. GDP increased at an average annual rate
of 40 percent during the period 1997-2000. In
2001, growth was estimated at 53 percent.

Although Gabon has one of Africa's highest
per capita income levels, real income per head is
lower today than in 1980. Reflecting sluggish
growth over much of the period. Following the
economic slump in 1999, output recovered partially in 2001 on the basis of buoyant oil prices,
but over the 1997 to 2000 period, GDP declined
by 0.6 percent a year. The economy contracted

further in 2001 with output estimated to have
fallen 1.5 percent due to the decline in oil prices.

In Rwanda real GDP growth averaged 8.5
percent annually between 1997 and 2000 reflecting the improved performance of agriculture,
construction, and services. Growth would have
been even higher had it not been for the drought
that affected parts of the country until October
2000. Robust growth continued during 2001, especially in agriculture, manufacturing and construction, and GDP is estimated to have risen 6
percent.

Renewed growth in the region was achieved
with subdued inflation due mainly to stable monetary policy resulting from membership of most
of the countries in the franc zone, which has strin-
gent monetary discipline. The sub-region's inflation decreased from an annual average of 7.7
percent in the period 1997- 2000 to 6.2 percent in
2001 (Table 2.3 and Figure 2.3), which was well
below the continental average.

In Burundi consumer price inflation averaged
17.8 percent annually during the period 1997-2000
as a result of the contraction in food production
and rapid monetary expansion. However, during
the second half of 2000, the return of seasonal
rains and increased food imports helped to contain food prices. A tightening of monetary policy
at the end of 2000 also contributed to slower
inflation and inflationary pressures continued to
abate during 2001, when the rate of price increases
slowed to 12.2 percent.

After a period of relative price stability between 1997 and 2000 when inflation averaged 2.8
percent annually, inflation in Cameroon accelerated in 2001 to reach 3.4 percent, driven by higher
food prices following a drought in the northern
provinces, and increased demand from neighboring countries.

In Chad inflation accelerated sharply as a re-

Table 2.3: Central Africa: Macroeconomic Management Indicators

Country	Inflation (%)		Fiscal Balance as % of GDP		Gross Domestic			
					Investment as % of GDP		Savings as % of GDP	
	Average 1997-2000	2001[a/]	Average 1997-2000	2001[a/]	Average 1997-2000	2001[a/]	Average 1997-2000	2001[a/]
BURUNDI	17.8	12.2	-5.1	-7.1	8.5	12.2	-1.6	0.4
CAMEROON	2.8	3.4	-1.1	2.4	17.2	17.7	19.3	20.2
CENTRAL AFRICAN REP.	0.6	3.5	-1.0	-1.6	13.0	13.8	8.5	6.6
CHAD	3.7	16.8	-5.0	-10.2	14.6	44.5	1.6	5.1
CONGO	4.2	1.0	-8.5	-1.9	22.2	21.3	35.6	63.2
CONGO, DEM. REP. OF	280.6	299.0	-7.0	0.9	23.7	24.9	20.0	15.8
EQUATORIAL GUINEA	4.6	6.0	2.7	20.4	62.4	39.5	50.1	81.7
GABON	2.0	1.0	0.2	10.6	29.2	27.3	48.5	50.1
RWANDA	4.9	5.7	-2.3	-5.3	15.0	17.1	-1.8	1.2
SAO TOME & PRINCIPE	34.5	6.9	-24.9	-6.8	42.1	49.2	-9.7	-3.3
CENTRAL AFRICA	**7.7**	**6.2**	**-3.2**	**3.1**	**21.6**	**23.0**	**23.0**	**25.2**

Note: a/ Preliminary estimates.
Sources: ADB Research and Statistics Divisions.

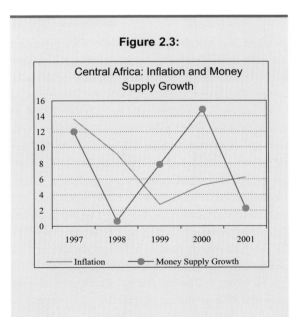

Figure 2.3:

Central Africa: Inflation and Money Supply Growth

—— Inflation   ——●—— Money Supply Growth

sult of food shortages reaching 16.8 percent in the year to December 2001, compared with a yearly average of 3.7 percent during 1997-2000. The rise in inflation reflected higher prices for staple foods as well as industrial supply problems but inflation is expected to decline to around 3.2 percent in 2002 as the harvests improve.

Civil war in the DRC gave rise to hyperinflation, so that inflation averaged 280.8 percent between 1997 and 2000. In 2001, consumer prices rose even more rapidly to 299 percent.

Rapid economic growth in Equatorial Guinea was accompanied by average inflation of 4.6 percent a year during 1997-2000, increasing to 6.0 percent in 2001. Increased inflation was driven by higher food prices and property rents in urban areas.

In Rwanda average inflation rose from an

annual average of 4.9 percent during 1997-2000
to 5.7 percent in 2001, mainly as a result of higher
food and petroleum prices, coupled with currency
depreciation. An outbreak of cattle disease leading to increased prices for meat and dairy products gave rise to higher inflation in 2001

Economic growth in the Central Region was
boosted by increased foreign-financed public sector investment. Gross domestic investment rose
above the continental average to 23 percent of
GDP in 2001 from an average of 21.6 percent
during the period 1997-2000 (Table 2.3).

Policy Developments

Fiscal developments

Improved revenue collection largely accounts for
the sub-region's stronger fiscal balance with a budget surplus of 3.1 percent of GDP in 2001 compared with an average deficit of 3.2 percent during 1997-2000 (Table 2.3 and Figure 2.4)

In Burundi the fiscal deficit averaged 5.1 percent of GDP during 1997-2000. Despite revenue-
raising and expenditure-reduction measures being
implemented in the second half of 2000, the fiscal
deficit widened to 7.1 percent of GDP in 2001.

With the advent of a new government in
Cameroon in 1996-97 policies to enhance tax revenue and tax transparency in the non-oil sector
were adopted leading to a notable improvements
in state finances. Annual audits of the national oil
company SNH *(Société Nationale des Hydrocarbures)*,
contributed to improved transparency in the oil
sector which is crucial to state revenues. Consequently, the fiscal balance in 2001 bucked the deteriorating trend of 1997-2000 to register a surplus of 2.4 percent of GDP.

The Central African Republic has a very low
government revenue-to-GDP ratio of only 9

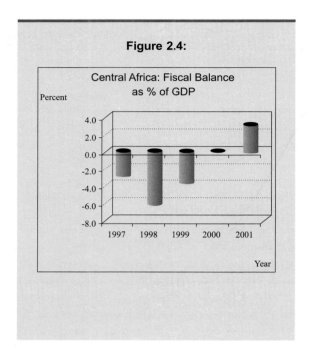

Figure 2.4:

Central Africa: Fiscal Balance as % of GDP

percent and efforts to strengthen administrative
capacity and improve the domestic tax effort have
been frustrated by recurrent political and social
crises. However, early in 2001 the government
undertook a number of measures aimed at
strengthening fiscal performance and economic
management. On January 1, a value-added tax
(VAT) was introduced and tax exemptions for non-
governmental organizations were abolished. A new
organizational structure for customs and tax
administration has been set up. The fiscal deficit
remained widened slightly to 1.6 percent of GDP
in 2001 from an annual average deficit of 1.0
percent between 1997 and 2000.

In Chad, following the broadening of the tax
base the budget deficit declined to 2.5 percent of
GDP in 1998. Growth in tax revenue was boosted

in 2000 with the introduction of VAT, which has become the main revenue source comprising about a third of all tax receipts. However, the domestic tax effort remains very low at 7 percent of GDP, well under CEMAC's 15 percent target. Consequently, the fiscal deficit doubled reaching 10.2 percent of GDP in 2001 from an average of 5.0 percent over the 1997-2000 period.

In Congo, high oil revenues in 2000 gave rise to increase in the primary budget surplus from 6 percent of GDP in 1999 to 23 percent in 2000. During 2001, oil revenues fell slightly in line with lower oil prices but non-oil revenues rose increased due to the economic upturn and strong measures to upgrade tax and customs administration. The government has strengthened mechanisms for controlling and monitoring expenditure including the organic budget law and the government accounting decree, signed on August 10, 2000. Consequently, the fiscal deficit fell sharply to 1.9 percent of GDP in 2001 from an annual average of 8.5 percent during 1997-2000.

Unsurprisingly, given the war and civil disruption, the DRC has operated with large and persistent fiscal deficits for many years reflecting the collapse of expenditure controls and a sharp decline in revenues. The proliferation of extra-budgetary spending, tax exemptions, quasi-fiscal operations, ad hoc interventions, taxpayer harassment and corruption in a number of government services, contributed significantly to the erosion of government finances. Furthermore, the war security expenses increased significantly. Since the return of relative peace to the country, the fiscal balance has improved with an estimated surplus of 0.9 percent of GDP in 2001 compared with an annual deficit of 7.0 percent during 1997-2000.

In Equatorial Guinea, fiscal policy has been influenced by the development of the oil sector and in 2000 revenues increased by 155 percent. A further rise is estimated for 2001, resulting in a sharp increase in the budget surplus to 20.4 percent of GDP in 2001 from an average of 2.7 percent over the 1997-2000 period.

Gabon's fiscal performance also depends on oil prices and revenues. The fall in oil prices in 1998, combined with fiscal indiscipline, resulted in a primary deficit of 6.3 percent of GDP and the collapse of negotiations with the IMF. Since then, the government efforts to restore fiscal discipline have begun to pay dividends leading to an estimated surplus of 10.6 percent of GDP in 2001 compared with an average of 0.2 percent in the period 1997-2000.

In Rwanda the fiscal deficit averaged of 2.3 percent of GDP during 1997-2000. In 2001, in an attempt to improve fiscal performance, the government introduced a comprehensive set of measures in the areas of customs, income taxation and excise duties. VAT, introduced in January 2001, has enhanced revenue collection while a cash-budgeting system is now in place and stricter commitment procedures are being followed. Notwithstanding these measures, and due mostly to additional social expenditure, the fiscal deficit in 2001 increased to an estimated 5.3 percent of GDP.

Monetary Developments

The regional monetary policy goal of the Bank of Central African States (BEAC) continues to be the achievement of a stable currency by targeting low inflation and a high foreign reserve coverage of the currency. Monetary policy objectives in the other countries has focused on price stability.

Monetary developments in Burundi in the first half of 2000 were characterized by rapid expansion of the monetary aggregates, which fuelled inflation. Credit expansion was driven by the central bank's (Bank of the Republic of Burundi – BRB) policy of automatically granting unsecured loans to effectively illiquid commercial banks, while failing to enforce statutory reserve requirements. In late 2000, in an attempt to slow credit growth, the BRB introduced an overall ceiling and individual quotas on bank refinancing while increasing the refinancing rate from 12 percent to 14 percent. As a result, there was a marked slowdown in credit expansion and money supply growth. This tighter monetary stance was maintained during 2001 and the BRB is committed to ending the policy of unlimited refinancing of financial institutions. It has also developed a monetary programming framework and set up a money market to ensure that central bank resources are ultimately allocated by market forces. The refinancing rate will be tied to interest rates on treasury notes resulting in positive real interest rates.

In Cameroon, private sector credit growth accelerated and broad money had increased 17 percent by end-September 2001, mainly reflecting higher bank saving deposits. The authorities were able to make net repayments to the banking system equivalent to 1.3 percent of GDP and Cameroon's contribution to the improvement in the net foreign assets position of the regional central bank (BEAC) also increased. In common with the other CEMAC countries, Cameroon's exchange rate is pegged to the Euro through the French franc and monetary policy is controlled by the BEAC.

In the DRC, monetary policy continues to be dictated by the fiscal situation, as a result of which the Central Bank (BCC) has been unable to control the monetary aggregates. In its attempt to cover the growing fiscal deficit and those of money-losing public enterprises, the BCC had to print money. However, the shortage of banknotes,

whose printing costs had risen sharply owing to hyperinflation, has contributed to the disruption of the payments system and financial disintermediation. Money supply growth accelerated from 160 percent in 1998 to 382 percent in 1999 and 493 percent in 2000. During 2001 policy was tightened and money supply slowed dramatically to an estimated 53 percent. Interest rates were deregulated allowing the BCC to set its key interest rate.

In Rwanda, broad money grew 14.2 percent during 2000 – more than double the target rate of 6.3 percent. Most of this occurred in the final quarter of 2000 due largely to an increase in the growth of credit to the private sector. At the end of 2000, the National Bank of Rwanda (NBR) strengthened its control of monetary developments by eliminating foreign exchange from commercial bank reserve requirements. The NBR introduced weekly foreign exchange auctions from February 7, 2001. Broad money growth increased to 18.4 percent in the 12 months to end-June 2001, reflecting large increases in net foreign assets and significant excess reserves held by commercial banks. Since then, the NBR has redoubled its efforts to slow monetary expansion by increasing the rediscount rate and reducing the maturity of lending.

Privatization

In common with other regions on the continent, privatization is progressing, albeit slowly. Low bidding prices, legal disputes and insolvency of firms put up for sale have contributed to the slow progress.

Privatization started late in Cameroon where the state-owned sector was extensive. The target was to privatize all its major public bodies by the end of 2001. Privatization has been completed for sugar *(Camsuco)*, rubber *(Hevecam)* and part of the palm oil sector *(Socapalm)*. The railway *(Camrail)* and, recently, the electricity company *(Sonel)* have also been privatized. Two mobile phone licences have been granted to private firms (SCM and MTN). The third wave of privatization, which began in 1999, involved major public services, but there have been delays, mainly because of the size and complexity of the enterprises concerned. The takeover of *Sonel* (electricity) by AES Sirocco was approved in July 2001. A final series of privatizations, including the national airline *Camair* and the commercial side of the port of Douala, is due to start in 2002/03.

In the Central African Republic, the government is restructuring the utilities sector, selling its stake in the petroleum distribution network that had not previously been allocated to the Trans-Oil Company and liquidating the state-owned Petroleum Company (PETROCA). Privatization will accelerate with the selection of private operators for the energy and telecoms groups, ENERCA, SOCATEL, and the water utility (SNE).

Privatization in Chad, which began in the early 1990s with the restructuring of non-strategic sectors, has since been extended to the larger public enterprises. *Sonasut* (sugar) was taken over in April 2000 by the *Compagnie Sucrière du Tchad*. The Société Tchadienne d'Eau et d'Electricité) *(STEE)* was taken over in September 2000 by the French group *Vivendi* through a management contract. In July 2001, the state-owned oil and soap factory was unbundled in preparation for privatization by the end of the year. At the same time, privatization options for the cotton company, *CotonTchad*, are under review.

In Congo, the conflict that started in late 1998 interrupted the envisaged restructuring and privatization of banks, but in 2000 the govern-ment announced a new timetable for bank restructuring and privatization. Major activities earmarked for 2001 included the outsourcing of the management of the Société Nationale de Distribution de l'Eau (SNDE, water utility), a management contract for the Société Nationale d'Electricité (SNE, electricity company), and the privatization of SOTELCO (Congo Telecommunications Company). The CORAF oil refinery is due to be privatized in 2002. The Agence Transcongolaise de Communications (ATC, port and railroad authority) has been spun off into three separate bodies: the PAPN (Pointe Noire Independent Port Authority), the CFCO (Congolese Ocean Railway Authority), and the VNPTF (Navigable Waterways, Ports and River Transport Authority). The PAPN is already under independent management while a concession contract for the CFCO is to be awarded after completion of repair works.

Privatization in Equatorial Guinea started recently and although the government is committed to the process neither a clear regulatory framework nor a public authority to supervise the process is yet in place.

Gabon begun its privatization program in 1997 with the sale of 51 percent of the water and electricity company *SEEG* to France's *Vivendi* group. Other privatizations have followed including that of the sugar enterprise and the Trans-Gabon Railway. The post and telecommunications authority was split into *Gabon Poste* and *Gabon Telecom* before the latter was privatized and the former restructured. Other state-owned firms including the agro-industrial firms *Agrogabon* (palm oil) and *Hevegab* (rubber), have, as yet, failed to attract buyers. Firms earmarked for future privatization include the Ports and Harbors Authority and *Air Gabon*.

Rwanda has established a timetable for the

divestiture of all remaining public enterprises including utility company, Electrogaz, two tea factories and the Telecommunications Company, Rwandatel. However, the privatization could be delayed because the disbursement of World Bank credit to finance the program hinges on full resolution of outstanding procedural issues.

External Accounts

Central Africa's external accounts deteriorated in 2001 due largely to a declining trade surplus, as a result of which the current account deficit widened to 7.4 percent of GDP in 2001 from 6.1 percent annually during 1997-2000 (Table 2.4 and Figure 2.5).

Burundi's external position remains weak due to the significant deterioration in its terms of trade, which have declined a cumulative 44 percent over the last three years. This coincided with increased import demand following the lifting of the trade embargo and the need to settle the external payments arrears owed to multilateral creditors. The current account deficit widened substantially to 11.0 percent of GDP in 2001 from an average of 3.1 percent a year between 1997 and 2000.

Although Cameroon has a relatively diversified export portfolio, non-oil exports have stagnated since 1995 at a time when imports have risen. While oil contributes less than 10 percent of GDP, it is the lead export accounting for a third of the total. Export crops – comprising coffee, cocoa, cotton, bananas, palm oil and rubber – contribute another third by value, while timber accounts for a further 15 percent.

Cameroon has an overall trade surplus but this masks a decline of trade in non-oil items, reflecting a gradual revival of demand following devaluation along with major adjustment problems in the country's productive capacity. In 2001, the current account continued its deterioration, with the deficit widening to 2 percent of GDP from 0.5 percent during 1997-2000.

Chad depends heavily on cotton (50 percent of exports) and livestock (25 percent) for export revenues. Over the years it has incurred merchandise trade deficits because of heavy cost of oil imports and the trade deficit increased from an average of 1.9 percent of GDP during 1997-2000 to 25.5 percent of GDP in 2001, reflecting the build-up of imports for oil project-related infrastructure investment. The trade balance will remain in substantial deficit over the next few years as the project is developed. The current account balance has worsened with the trade deficit increasing from an average of 11.2 percent of GDP during 1997-2000 to 40.1 percent in 2001.

With the implementation of the CEMAC customs and tax reforms, Equatorial Guinea has liberalized and streamlined its trade policy substantially reducing the level and dispersion of tariffs while abolishing quantitative restrictions. Exports are dominated by oil and timber, which account for 98 percent of the total, and the country has accumulated substantial trade surpluses in recent years due to buoyant oil prices and growing export volumes. Consequently, the trade surplus rose from 37.7 percent of GDP in 1999 to 50.4 percent in 2000, while the current account deficit fell from a yearly average of 47.3 percent of GDP during 1997-2000 to 18 percent in 2001.

Also a result of buoyant oil exports, Gabon's trade surplus averaged 35.2 percent of GDP during 1997-2000, falling slightly to 33.6 percent of GDP in 2001 due to weaker oil demand and prices. Despite this, the current account balance improved from a small deficit averaging 0.5 percent of GDP during 1997-2000 to a surplus of 0.5 percent of GDP in 2001.

Table 2.4: Central Africa: The External Sector

Country	Trade Balance as % of GDP		Current Account as % of GDP		Terms of Trade (%)		Total External Debt as % of GDP		Debt Service as % of Exports	
	Average 1997-2000	2001[a]	Average 1997-2000	2001[a]	Average 1997-2000	2001[a]	Average 1997-2000	2001[a]	Average 1996-1999	2000
BURUNDI	-4.3	-8.3	-3.1	-11.0	-1.7	5.9	149.2	192.1	68.7	72.4
CAMEROON	7.8	5.8	-0.5	-2.0	25.9	2.8	90.9	80.5	23.3	8.5
CENTRAL AFRICAN REP.	1.8	0.9	-3.4	-5.9	-2.5	0.8	83.2	74.5	4.6	4.5
CHAD	-1.9	-25.5	-11.2	-40.1	-3.2	18.6	65.6	63.7	0.0	13.7
CONGO	40.8	54.3	-23.7	-10.4	9.5	-12.5	219.9	157.9	19.4	5.7
CONGO, DEM. REP. OF	-0.6	-1.2	-8.7	-8.2	5.4	-11.2	203.1	186.7	0.6	0.0
EQUATORIAL GUINEA	35.1	68.3	-47.3	-18.0	6.4	23.1	34.5	7.2	4.3	1.2
GABON	35.2	33.6	-0.5	0.5	32.5	-36.6	73.4	62.7	14.7	16.4
RWANDA	-6.3	-9.0	-3.1	-10.3	-3.8	5.3	66.4	74.0	11.8	7.8
SAO TOME & PRINCIPE	0.0	-40.6	0.0	-41.6	6.2	-17.7	675.9	659.9	...	...
CENTRAL AFRICA	**11.3**	**11.6**	**-6.1**	**-7.4**	**10.2**	**-11.1**	**114.4**	**121.5**	**15.0**	**9.1**

Note: a/ Preliminary estimates
... Not available.
Sources: ADB Research and Statistics Divisions.

Figure 2.5:

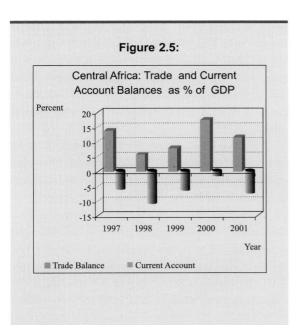

Central Africa: Trade and Current Account Balances as % of GDP

External Debt

The total debt stock of the Region increased from $33.48 billion in 2000 to $37.44 billion in 2001. The debt burden increased accordingly, with the regional debt/GDP ratio increasing from 91.9 percent to 121.5 percent over the same period (Figure 2.6).

Burundi's debt stock declined marginally from $1.14 billion in 2000 to $1.08 billion in 2001, reflecting the retirement of arrears which at end-2000 stood at $101 million, or 15 percent of GDP. These arrears were evenly divided between bilateral creditors principally the *Agence française de développement* (AFD), for $16 million and multilaterals such as the African Development Bank (AfDB) for $14.2 million and the *Arab Bank for Economic Development in Africa (ABEDA)* for $14 million. Given the country's heavy debt burden and very high debt service ratio (98 percent), do-

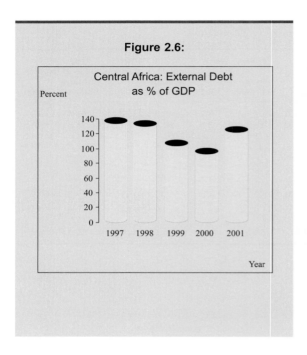

Figure 2.6:

Central Africa: External Debt
as % of GDP

Percent

nors agreed in December 2000 to set up a fund under the leadership of the World Bank to help Burundi meet current maturities while clearing its arrears with multilateral creditors.

Partly because for several years it has received less soft-loan assistance than other franc zone members, Cameroon had accumulated a substantial external debt of $7.03 billion by end-2001 (108 percent of GDP). The country, which is eligible for debt relief under the Enhanced HIPC Initiative, reached the decision point in October 2000 when it received debt cancellation worth some $2 billion in nominal terms ($1.26 billion in Net Present Value terms). This is expected to reduce the amount of government revenue spent on debt servicing from 23 percent in 2000 to 10 percent by 2008, while cutting the debt-to-export

ratio from 200 percent in 2000 to 120 percent in 2001 and 100 percent in 2007. Completion point still depends on Cameroon drafting a final version of a Poverty Reduction plan, which is expected to be finalized in 2002.

In December 2001, the total debt of the Central African Republic stood at $710 million, including arrears to multilateral creditors – the AfDB, the World Bank, the Development Bank of Central African States, the International Fund for Agricultural Development, and the OPEC Fund. The government is working with creditors on a timetable for the settlement of arrears, involving their rescheduling or deferral, while identifying resources that could be used for the payment of arrears.

Chad's debt stock was estimated at $960 million at end-2001 and, although it is eligible for relief under the enhanced HIPC Initiative, its failure to meet PRGF targets meant that it could not reach decision point on schedule in June 2000. It did so on 16 May 2001, which will entitle the country to $260 million ($170 million NPV) of debt relief in 2002. Completion point still depends on the government presenting a poverty-reduction plan for World Bank and IMF approval by first quarter 2002.

The external debt of the Democratic Republic of Congo rose to $13 billion at end-2001 representing 280 percent of GDP and with arrears accounting for some 75 percent of the total.

Owing to its remarkable growth rate, Equatorial Guinea's external debt position has changed dramatically. From 248 percent of GDP in 1995, the debt burden has fallen to 46 percent at end-2001. In absolute terms external public debt decreased from $230 million in 1995 to $100 million in 2001. The country still has some debt arrears reflecting the reluctance of the present government to take responsibility for debts contracted by previous administrations. Equatorial Guinea is not eligible for the HIPC Initiative.

Gabon's external debt was estimated at $3.10 billion at end-2001. The bulk of this accumulated during the period of major infrastructure construction in the late 1980s, notably the building of the Trans-Gabon railway. The debt burden is particularly heavy with scheduled interest payments alone accounting for over half of all tax revenue between 1995 and 2000. At the same time, due to the country's relatively high per capita income, it is not eligible under the HIPC Initiative.

Outlook

Economic growth is expected to pick up in 2002, with real GDP growth projected to increase 5.1 percent, up from 3.2 percent in 2001.

In Burundi, Central African Republic and Rwanda, real GDP growth is expected to accelerate in 2002 on the back of strengthening economic reforms but growth in oil producing countries will be constrained by weaker export prices. In Cameroon, GDP growth is expected to increase modestly from the 5 percent level attained in 2001. Chad's growth prospects for 2002 are very good reflecting the surge in oil sector investment, though this will be partially offset by weak cotton prices. In Equatorial Guinea, 2002 should be another year of exceptional growth owing to the sharp increase of oil production, while growth in Gabon will slow due to lower reduced oil production volumes and lower prices. Growth in Gabon will also be adversely influenced by the country's heavy external debt. The country is not on the list of those eligible for debt relief under the HIPC Initiative.

East Africa

The East Africa Region is made up of eleven countries: Comoros, Djibouti, Eritrea, Ethiopia, Kenya, Madagascar, Mauritius, Seychelles, Somalia, Tanzania and Uganda. In relation to the rest of Africa, the Eastern region does not possess significant mineral or energy resources. At the same time, the Eastern Region possesses some of the best natural resources on the continent for tourism. This is reflected in wealth generation in the region. The total exports of the Eastern region was the smallest in the continent in 2000 and represented only about 4 percent of the continental total. In 2001, the total gross domestic product emanating from the region constituted about 8 percent of the continental total with Kenya, the biggest economy (in terms of GDP), accounting

for about 23 percent of the sub-regional gross output. The population of the Eastern region is estimated at 188 million in 2001, representing about 23 percent of the continent's population (Table 2.1). With the relatively high regional population and low output, income per head is consequently low. In 2001, the per capita income of the region, estimated at $241 was about a third of the continental average.

Recent Economic Trends

Growth in the East Africa rebounded strongly to 4.6 percent in 2001 from an average of 3.7 percent annually during 1997-2000. The Region's growth performance in 2001 was also above the continental average of 3.4 percent (Table 2.5 and Figure 2.7).

Table 2.5: East Africa: Gross Domestic Product and Export Performances

Country	Real GDP Growth Rate (%)		GDP Per Capita (US$)		Real Export Growth (%)		Exports[b/] Per Capita (US$)	
	Average 1997-2000	2001[a/]	Average 1997-2000	2001[a/]	Average 1997-2000	2001[a/]	Average 1997-2000	2001[a/]
COMOROS	1.5	1.0	316	283	3.5	15.0	70	67
DJIBOUTI	0.7	1.5	869	889	21.8	6.0	392	398
ERITREA	1.1	5.8	187	146	.	.	34	21
ETHIOPIA	3.9	7.0	106	99	11.4	7.6	16	15
KENYA	1.2	1.0	362	332	-5.7	4.3	95	88
MADAGASCAR	4.2	6.7	243	276	10.7	5.4	60	80
MAURITIUS	5.6	6.0	3711	3852	3.5	4.1	2369	2415
SEYCHELLES	1.7	-1.0	7686	7605	26.1	5.0	5421	5975
SOMALIA	...	...	...	...	6.1	0.0	....	...
TANZANIA	4.3	4.6	251	252	-0.7	11.4	36	36
UGANDA	5.5	4.8	288	264	5.8	9.3	32	27
EAST AFRICA	**3.7**	**4.6**	**250**	**241**	**2.0**	**6.0**	**58**	**57**

Notes: a/ Preliminary estimates
            b/: Exports of Goods and Nonfactor Services at Market Prices
... Not available.
Sources: ADB Research and Statistics Divisions.

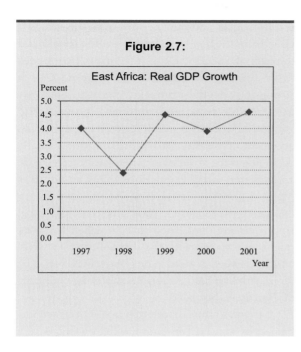

Figure 2.7:

East Africa: Real GDP Growth

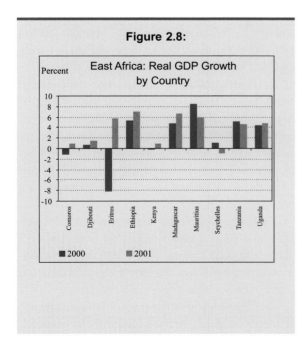

Figure 2.8:

East Africa: Real GDP Growth by Country

Although growth in Kenya – the largest economy in the sub-region – remained sluggish, improved growth performance in other economies, notably Ethiopia, Madagascar and Mauritius, spurred regional growth in 2001. The Ethiopian economy's recent performance was affected by the border war with Eritrea so that GDP growth fell to an average of 3.9 percent during 1997-2000. Growth rebounded strongly to 7 percent in 2001 following the end of hostilities in 2000, which enabled the government to shift focus from the war effort to development.

The Kenyan economy is yet to recover from its poor performance of the 1990s when output growth averaged only 2 percent, slowing further to average 1.2 percent annually between 1997 and 2000 and only one percent in 2001 (Figure 2.8). This protracted underperformance is explained by weak economic management, inefficiency in the public sector, the impact of withdrawal of donor support from 1997 and adverse weather conditions.

Tanzania maintained its above average growth performance during 2001 when GDP increased 4.6 percent compared with an annual average of 4.3 percent between 1997 and 2001, while Uganda continued to grow strongly though at a reduced rate of 4.8 percent in 2001. This compared with an annual average of 5.5 percent in 1997-2000, with the 2001 slowdown largely attributable to deteriorating terms of trade.

Growth in Mauritius accelerated to 6 percent in 2001 from the yearly average of 5.6 percent during 1997-2000. Expansion was driven by the business-friendly policies of the new administration and the rebound from drought in 1999-2000. The stimulus of faster expansion in agriculture, construction and trade gave GDP growth in Madagascar a powerful boost. Output increased 6.7 percent in 2001, compared with the trend rate of 4.2 percent in the period 1997-2000.

Although growth in Djibouti more than doubled in 2001 to 1.5 percent from the four-year average of 0.7 percent in 1997-2000 per capita incomes deteriorated further. The main drivers of this insipid growth were port activity and higher electricity production, though these were partially offset by cutbacks in public expenditures due to the reduced French military presence in the country.

Over the past ten years, the economy of Comoros has been adversely affected by the political instability arising from the activities of the separatist movement on Anjouan Island. Accordingly, economic growth in the Comoros has been sluggish with output rising only one percent in 2001, marginally down on the yearly average rate of 1.5 percent in 1997-2000. The poor performance in 2001 was partly attributable to an international embargo imposed by the Organization of African Unity (OAU). In February 2001, the OAU endorsed a political agreement among the three islands that form the Comoros, which gives greater autonomy to the smaller islands. As a result, prospects for political stability have improved and the Comoros can expect increased assistance from the international community over the next few years, which should lead to modestly faster growth.

The Seychelles economy slid into recession in 2001 when output fell one percent, largely due to the impact of the September 11 attacks in the US on tourism and especially on the number of visitors from Europe. This compared with average annual growth of 1.7 percent between 1997 and 2000. Seychelles continues to enjoy one of the highest living standards in Africa with a per capita income of $7400.

Somalia has still to recover from years of civil conflict. Agriculture, which dominates the economy, has suffered heavily over the last two years from the combination of severe drought and the lack of security. Economic growth continues to be severely constrained by the absence of a strong and effective central government. There are no effective fiscal and monetary policies and counterfeit money is periodically injected into the economy, resulting in hyperinflation. Equally damaging is the absence of a regulatory framework and proper safety regulations. This situation is blamed for the ban imposed by importing countries on livestock products from Somalia. Importers are concerned that Somalian livestock might be infected with the Rift valley fever virus, which has been evident in neighboring Kenya. The 15-month ban has severely damaged the economy of Northern Somalia.

Growth in the Eastern region has been accompanied by subdued inflation, which averaged 6.5 percent annually during 1997-2000 period, slowing to 6 percent in 2001 (Table 2.6 and Figure 2.9).

In Ethiopia, inflation slowed markedly to 0.2 percent in 2001 down from 2.7 percent during 1997-2000, primarily due to the availability of large food aid supplies which stabilized food prices.

In Kenya, inflation has followed a downward trend, falling from 6.6 percent during 1997-2000 to an estimated 2.6 percent in 2001. Inflation increased in 2000 as a result of drought-related increases in the prices of basic foodstuffs. Other factors included the increased rate of VAT, currency depreciation and higher prices for petroleum products.

In Tanzania, inflation was estimated at 5.2 percent in 2001 – a sharp reduction from the 10.7 percent average during 1997-2000. A major contributory factor was the improvement in food supply arising from the good harvests.

In Uganda, consumer price inflation is driven primarily by trends in food prices. Inflation accel-

Table 2.6: East Africa: Macroeconomic Management Indicators

Country	Inflation (%)		Fiscal Balance as % of GDP		Gross Domestic			
					Investment as % of GDP		Savings as % of GDP	
	Average		Average		Average		Average	
	1997-2000	2001[a/]	1997-2000	2001[a/]	1997-2000	2001[a/]	1997-2000	2001[a/]
COMOROS	3.7	3.5	-2.1	-3.8	12.6	11.8	-1.6	1.3
DJIBOUTI	2.6	0.4	-1.8	-1.4	12.0	13.3	-4.6	-4.3
ERITREA	9.9	18.1	...	...	...	...	...	...
ETHIOPIA	2.7	0.2	-6.9	-6.5	16.8	15.9	3.2	0.9
KENYA	6.6	2.6	-0.7	-2.1	16.9	15.3	9.2	4.3
MADAGASCAR	8.2	8.3	-3.4	-4.3	14.9	18.6	6.4	8.9
MAURITIUS	6.2	4.9	-4.6	-5.9	26.7	27.3	23.7	24.9
SEYCHELLES	3.8	7.3	-14.6	-13.8	31.1	25.7	18.8	23.2
SOMALIA	14.0	11.5	-4.5	0.0	10.0	0.0	...	...
TANZANIA	10.7	5.2	-1.1	-0.5	15.7	17.0	4.9	8.4
UGANDA	4.0	4.8	-2.7	-0.8	18.1	15.7	0.3	-8.6
EAST AFRICA	**6.5**	**6.0**	**-3.0**	**-3.0**	**17.3**	**17.5**	**6.8**	**5.8**

Note: a/ Preliminary estimates
... Not available.
Sources: ADB Research and Statistics Divisions.

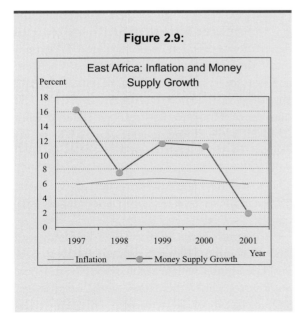

Figure 2.9:

East Africa: Inflation and Money Supply Growth

erated in the aftermath of the drought in 1997 slowing when food production recovered as in 1998. In 2001, inflation accelerated modestly from the four-year average 4 percent between 1997 and 2000 to 4.8 percent.

Inflation slowed in Mauritius during 2001 to 4.9 percent from an annual average of 6.2 percent during 1997-2000. The decline in inflation was the result of a deceleration in the rate of monetary expansion during 2001, greater stability in the exchange value of the rupee as well as subdued inflation in major trading partners.

In Djibouti, inflation remained low at 0.4 percent in 2001 down from the average of 2.6 percent during 1997-2000. This was due partly to the stabilization in transport prices that had increased during 1999/2000 in line with higher petroleum prices. Faster growth in Madagascar was accompanied by unchanged inflation of 8.3 percent in 2001, compared with an annual average of 8.2 percent during 1997-2000.

Gross domestic investment in 2001 was 17.5 percent of GDP, similar to the yearly average of 17.3 percent over the 1997-2000 period (Table 2.6). Only in Mauritius, where consumption declined, was there an increase in gross domestic investment. Elsewhere in the region investment continued to be constrained by high levels of consumption spending.

Policy Developments

Fiscal Policy

Fiscal consolidation has been the dominant theme of fiscal policy with regional deficits stabilizing at 3.0 percent of GDP over the five-year period 1997 to 2001 (Table 2.6 and Figure 2.10).

Fiscal policy in Ethiopia was dominated by the border conflict with Eritrea. Before the outbreak of hostilities, Ethiopia had made major progress towards fiscal consolidation, but these gains were lost as military spending increased and revenues declined. The fiscal deficit averaged 6.9 percent of GDP during the 1997-2000 period narrowing marginally to 6.5 percent in 2001 reflecting post-war budgetary reforms. These include a 5 percent withholding tax on imports replacing 10 percent import surcharge, an increase in the top sales tax rate to 15 percent, with effect from February 2001, and a new income tax code and legislation regarding standard assessment from 2002. Tax administration has been strengthened with legislation passed in March 2001 to introduce a Taxpayer Identification Number (TIN), while VAT will be introduced from 2003.

Kenya's fiscal position remained weak in 2001

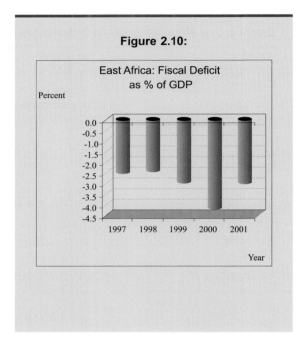

Figure 2.10:

East Africa: Fiscal Deficit as % of GDP

when the deficit rose from an annual average of 0.7 percent of GDP during 1997-2000 to 2.1 percent. Recent measures aimed at improving fiscal performance include stricter monitoring of departmental budgets, rationalization of expenditure through a review of government functions, civil service restructuring and redundancies and shedding non-core government services. The number of ministries was recently reduced from 27 to 15, while on the revenue front VAT was increased to 18 percent from 15 percent in 2000 and tax loopholes and exemptions were reduced. The Kenya Revenue Authority has stepped up its efforts in the field of tax compliance and tax education.

Tanzania's fiscal performance has improved since the country adopted cash budgeting, matching expenditures with available resources, in 1995/96. Rigorous implementation of the cash budget system, accompanied by revenue-enhancing measures, helped to restore fiscal discipline. The tax base has been broadened, the tax system streamlined and tax administration strengthened. In June 2000, a number of tax reforms were implemented including the creation of a Tax Appeals Court and the introduction of VAT and Tax Identification Numbers. These efforts successfully reduced the fiscal deficit from 1.1 percent of GDP during 1997-2000 to 0.5 percent in 2001.

Uganda too has adopted strict cash budgeting rules to curb public spending and consolidate its fiscal position, resulting in a fiscal deficit of only 0.8 percent of GDP in 2001, compared with an annual average of 2.7 percent during 1997-2000.

Comoros' fiscal balance deteriorated in 2001 as the deficit widened to 3.8 percent of GDP from an annual average of 2.1 percent during 1997-2000. This was largely caused by increased external debt service obligations. Fiscal policy in the Seychelles is driven by the extensive degree of state intervention in economic activity. During the 1997-2000 period, the budget deficit averaged 14.6 percent of GDP forcing the administration to implement remedial measures in 2000-01. These included more rigorous scrutiny of financial administration in government agencies, a tightening of eligibility requirements for public welfare programs and a reduction in transfers to state-owned enterprises. In response to these measures, the fiscal deficit contracted marginally to 13.8 percent of GDP in 2001.

The government of Djibouti's fiscal policy focuses on reducing the budget deficit while directing more resources to anti-poverty programs. The Government has taken several steps to control the growth of public spending, including reducing the size of the security forces and a retirement program for civil servants. It has also contracted out management of Djibouti port to a foreign firm. On the revenue side both direct and indirect taxes were increased in 2001 and the budget deficit contracted from an annual average of 1.8 percent of GDP during 1997-2000 to 1.4 percent.

Monetary Policy

Tight monetary policies in the Region contributed to a slowdown in inflation. Monetary policy was also designed to stabilize exchange rates while maintaining positive real interest rates.

Since the end of the war the Ethiopian government has started to sterilize excess liquidity in the economy while taking steps to streamline monetary management. In response to a tighter monetary stance by the Bank of Ethiopia, the growth of broad money slowed to 11.3 percent in 2000-01 from 14 percent the previous year. Despite this, interest rates have declined with the benchmark rate for 91-day Treasury bills falling from 4.4 percent in 1998/1999 to 3.1 percent in 1999/2000. The government is committed to a flexible exchange rate policy taking steps to narrow the exchange rate premium between the official and the parallel market rates to less than 3 percent in 2000/2001. In 2000 the *birr* dropped by 8 percent in nominal terms, following a similar depreciation in 1999.

The Kenyan government has successfully operated a tight monetary policy keeping money supply growth within the target band of less than 8 percent a year. Broad money supply, M3, expanded by 1.6 percent in 2000 compared with 2.8 percent in 1999. The deceleration in the growth of monetary aggregates was in line with the economic slowdown during 2000 and was mainly attributed to slack demand for bank credit.

A significant development in 2000 was the sharp increase in Net Foreign Assets of the banking system, reflecting a shift in asset portfolios in favor of deposits denominated in foreign currency as a hedge against the depreciation of the Kenyan shilling. Also in 2000 Parliament approved a Central Bank Amendment Bill obliging commercial banks to fix the lending and deposit rates at 4 percentage points and 8 percentage points respectively above the 91-day Treasury bill rate. However, as the economy slowed down in 2000, interest rates declined and the yield on 91-day Treasury bills eased to 9.52 percent in July 2000, before rebounding to settle at 13.47 percent in December 2000.

In Tanzania, in response to the tight monetary policy stance aimed at reducing inflation to single-digits, broad money (M3) supply growth decelerated from 18.6 percent in 1999 to 14.8 percent in 2000. This was largely attributable to the decline in government borrowing from the banking system. As inflation slowed, the benchmark rate on 91-day Treasury Bills fell from 15 percent at end-1999 to 4.5 percent at end-2000, where it has since stabilized to stand at 4.2 percent in June 2001. Commercial bank deposit and lending rates were reduced in line with the return on Treasury Bills. However, the spread between the deposit and lending rates remained considerable pointing to limited competition and structural rigidities in the banking system.

The foreign exchange market in Tanzania is market-determined with the Bank of Tanzania intervening only to smooth large seasonal fluctuations. In 2000, the shilling remained relatively stable depreciating 7.5 percent in nominal terms to follow the same rate of depreciation as in 1999.

In Uganda, the central bank also introduced Repurchase Agreements (REPOs) in August 2000 as a flexible fine-tuning instrument to help control money supply growth. Broad money grew 16.1 percent between June 1999 and June 2000 and by 13.6 percent between June 2000 and March

2001, spearheaded by the expansion of foreign currency deposits indicating a rend towards dollarization of the economy.

The Bank of Uganda has attempted to solve this problem by implementing a uniform cash reserve ratio on both domestic and foreign deposit liabilities. The rate of interest on the 91-day Treasury Bills rose from 16.8 percent in July 2000 to peak at 25.8 percent in January, 2001, reflecting the sharp rise in the volume of bills issued and held by the commercial banks. Treasury Bill rates subsequently declined to 9.96 percent in April 2001 and commercial banks followed this trend by cutting their prime lending rates.

The Ugandan shilling is market-determined with the monetary authorities intervening as necessary to maintain stability in the foreign exchange market. The Shilling has depreciated over the last five years, declining 16.4 percent against the US dollar during 1999 and a further 7 percent between June 2000 and March 2001, mirroring the deterioration in Uganda's terms of trade.

In Mauritius, monetary policy in 2000/01 was directed towards slowing inflation and stabilizing the exchange rate of the rupee. Money supply growth slowed to 9.2 percent in 2000/01 from 10.9 percent the previous year. In common with Uganda, there is some evidence of a trend towards dollarization in 2000/01, as the increase in the net foreign assets component of money supply was significantly greater than that of other components.

Exchange rate movements during 2000/01 reflected the combined effect of international trends and local market conditions. Between June 2000 and June 2001, the rupee depreciated 7.5 percent against the US dollar but appreciated 3.9 percent against the euro during 2000/01 creating some problems for exporters targeting the EU market.

Comoros' monetary policy is constrained by its participation in the French Franc Zone. The exchange rate is fixed against the French Franc (euro after 2002) and monetary policy is used to support this fixed exchange rate. As a result, Comoros has enjoyed relative price stability despite political instability. Inflation has been kept below 5 percent in recent years, partly through government price controls.

Seychelles followed a conservative monetary policy between 1995 and 1998, which resulted in low rates of inflation, but in 1999 inflation accelerated to 6.3 percent due to more rapid monetary expansion and increased fuel prices. Rupee depreciation, which led to increased import prices, including fuel, pushed inflation further ahead in 2000 to 6.7 percent. Despite this, interest rates have trended downwards with prime lending rates falling from 16.2 percent in 1996 to 11.2 percent in 2001.

Privatization

The progress of structural reform, including privatization, has been slow.

Although Ethiopia started its privatization program in 1997, a large proportion of national productive assets still remains within the public sector. The pace of the privatization picked up in 1999 when several large enterprises and state farms were brought to the point of sale and preparations began for the privatization of the Construction and Business Bank. In 2001, a foreign institution was awarded a contract to manage the Commercial Bank of Ethiopia. The government also revised its investment code in an effort to increase private participation in infrastructure provision, domestic civil aviation, power and telecommunications. But, the response to the privatization program has been poor with Ethiopia receiving no

offers for most of the enterprises on offer. Of those for which offers were received, the amounts tendered were considered inappropriate. The slow response of the domestic private sector to the privatization program reflects the small size of the sector, while the apparent lack of foreign interest underscores structural and infrastructural bottlenecks in the economy.

In 1990, the Kenyan Government owned equity in over 240 commercially oriented enterprises. Under the public enterprises reform program the government was to retain 33 of the enterprises considered "strategic", while the remaining 207 would be privatized. By end-1999, 167 enterprises had been partially or completely privatized while strategic enterprises, such as Kenya Ports Authority, Kenya Railways and Kenya Posts and Telecommunications Corporation, had also been restructured.

In Tanzania, by the end of 2000, about half of the 400 enterprises earmarked for divestiture in 1995 had been removed from government control through liquidation, share sale or asset sale. In 2001, the focus switched to the privatization of state utilities – the railways, power and remaining port services.

Uganda identified 120 enterprises for privatization in 1996. By the end of 2000 86 of them had been sold and in 2001 major new initiatives were announced including the planned privatization of Uganda Railway Corporation. The monopoly held by Entebbe Handling Services in air cargo handling has been abolished and investors invited to take up some of the equity in the business. In June 2000, 51 percent of the shares in Uganda Telecom Ltd were sold, and the generation and distribution operations of the Ugandan Electricity Board (UEB) are being offered through a long-term concession to private operators. The program has been criticized on the grounds of a lack of transparency and there have been allegations of corruption, leading Parliament to temporarily suspend the process in August 1998 to permit investigations into specific divestiture cases. In October 2001, the Bank of Uganda awarded the winning bid of Ugandan Commercial Bank (UCB) to the Standard Bank Investment Corporation of South Africa.

The Comoros government plans to privatize the capital's maritime transport company (SOCOPOTRAM) in 2002. Privatization of the postal service and the state telecommunications company are also underway.

External Accounts

The external balance of East African economies remains precarious, despite a marginal reduction in the current account balance-of-payments deficit in 2001 to 4.7 percent of GDP from 5.1 percent during 1997-2000 (Table 2.7 and Figure 2.11).

Ethiopia's weak export performance can be laid at the door of the conflict with Eritrea and, more recently, the collapse in world coffee prices over the last three years. The current account deficit, which averaged 4.4 percent of GDP during 1997-2000, widened to 5.5 percent in 2001 due to stagnant exports and a sharp increase in imports for the post-war reconstruction effort.

Kenya too continues to underperform, also partly as a consequence of adverse prices for coffee and tea in world markets. The trade deficit widened from 9.4 percent of GDP during 1997-2000 to 11.8 percent in 2001. The trade deficit spilled over into the current account deficit, which increased sharply to 5.6 percent of GDP in 2001 from 3.4 percent between 1997 and 2000. In 2000, three-quarters of Kenya's leading exports – tea, horticulture, coffee and petroleum products – experienced a decline in quantities and/or a fall in price. Horticulture export volumes fell 3.3 percent in 2000, while tea volumes were down 16.5 percent. And while coffee exports increased 21.5 percent in volume, prices were sharply lower. As exports fell, imports increased 11.6 percent in 2000.

Tanzania's trade gap narrowed slightly in 2001 to 7.6 percent of GDP from an average of 8.6 percent during the period 1997-2000, reflecting increased exports. The main boost to exports has come from the development of the gold mining sector, which has offset reductions in traditional exports of sisal, tobacco cashew nuts and cloves. The current account deficit fell from 6.2 percent of GDP a year during 1997-2000 to 2.6 percent in 2001 largely as a result of increased aid inflows.

Uganda's balance-of-payments has also been under pressure because of the coffee price slump, with coffee earnings falling 29 percent in the first quarter of 2001 compared with the same period in 2000. As a result, the trade deficit widened from an average of 13.5 percent of GDP during 1997-2000 to 18.9 percent in 2001. The current account also deteriorated from a deficit of 6.2 percent of GDP in 1997-2000 to 7.6 percent in 2001.

Three factors – higher exports, increased invisible earnings and larger net private transfers – account for the reduction in current account deficits in Comoros. The deficit declined from an average of 11.7 percent of GDP in 1997-2000 to 8.3 percent in 2001. The steady increase in price of vanilla led to significant growth in value of merchandise exports.

The current account deficit of Seychelles stood at an annual average of 13.8 percent of GDP during 1997-2000. To offset this current account imbalance, the government offered tax incentives to foreign investors, which paid off to some extent in 2001 when the deficit declined sharply to 5.6 percent of GDP.

Table 2.7: East Africa: The External Sector

Country	Trade Balance as % of GDP		Current Account as % of GDP		Terms of Trade (%)		Total External Debt as % of GDP		Debt Service as % of Exports	
	Average 1997-2000	2001[a]	Average 1997-2000	2001[a]	Average 1997-2000	2001[a]	Average 1997-2000	2001[a]	Average 1996-1999	2000
COMOROS	-16.3	-16.2	-11.7	-8.3	27.7	-10.6	97.8	103.7	12.32	3.0
DJIBOUTI	-34.1	-33.6	-2.7	-4.5	0.1	-0.1	65.4	70.4	6.3	8.0
ERITREA	...	...	-29.5	-46.4	...	...	...	...	...	...
ETHIOPIA	-14.3	-18.5	-4.4	-5.5	-2.0	-11.4	81.7	81.3	22.6	15.1
KENYA	-9.4	-11.8	-3.4	-5.6	-2.0	-4.2	52.2	54.0	25.7	17.2
MADAGASCAR	-4.5	-5.4	-6.0	-7.6	-2.9	2.4	104.8	83.0	11.6	9.1
MAURITIUS	-9.0	-10.6	-0.9	-1.2	1.5	-7.2	27.9	22.2	7.6	7.7
SEYCHELLES	-35.5	-26.2	-13.8	-5.6	-4.3	-5.3	62.9	60.3	13.9	12.3
SOMALIA	-12.8	...	-5.4	...	-0.1	-0.1	132.4	...	123.8	108.7
TANZANIA	-8.6	-7.6	-6.2	-2.6	5.3	0.0	92.9	73.2	...	12.4
UGANDA	-13.5	-18.9	-6.2	-7.6	-11.6	-11.5	55.7	62.5	18.6	14.4
EAST AFRICA	**-11.4**	**-15.5**	**-5.1**	**-4.7**	**-2.0**	**-5.3**	**78.2**	**70.0**	**19.7**	**16.4**

Note: a/ Preliminary estimates
... Not available.
Sources: ADB Research and Statistics Divisions.

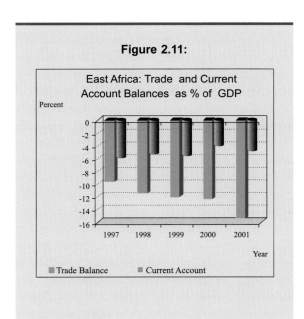

Figure 2.11:

East Africa: Trade and Current Account Balances as % of GDP

Percent

■ Trade Balance   ■ Current Account

External Debt

The region's debt burden has stabilized in recent years due largely to the positive impact of the HIPC initiative. East Africa's debt stock fell from $30.8 billion in 2000 to $28.9 billion in 2001, while the debt/GDP ratio declined to 70 percent from 75 percent (Figure 2.12).

Ethiopia's external debt was estimated at $5.06 billion at end-2000, of which multilateral debt constituted 51 percent, official bilateral debt 46 percent and commercial debt the remaining 2 percent. Significantly, the debt stock at end-2001 was nearly 50 percent of the outstanding debt at end-1998 – the result of the $4 billion debt write-off by Russia in late 1999. Despite this debt reduction, Ethiopia's external debt burden remains unsustainable and the NPV of the country's debt-to-export ratio was 243 percent in 1999 and forecast to remain above 150 percent until 2012. The debt-service ratio, before debt relief, was estimated at 55.4 percent in 1999. Ethiopia is eligible for assistance under the enhanced HIPC initiative and was expected to reach the decision point under the program at the end of 2001. The total estimated amount of HIPC assistance required to bring Ethiopia's ratio of the NPV of debt to exports to 150 percent is estimated at $1 028 million in NPV terms.

At end-2001, the total outstanding external debt of Kenya was estimated at $5.53 billion. Of the total outstanding debt 51 percent was owed to multilateral institutions. The International Development Association (IDA) accounted for 76 percent of the multilateral debt and 44 percent of total debt. Bilateral donors accounted for 35 percent of the total debt, with Japan as the main bilateral creditor accounting for 51 percent of bilateral debt and 22 percent of the total. As part of its debt management strategy, the government is limiting its external borrowing to concessionary loans only. Because the bulk of Kenya's foreign debt is concessionary, the country is regarded by the IMF and World Bank as a sustainable case, requiring no debt relief under the enhanced HIPC.

Tanzania's foreign debt stood at $6.57 billion at end-2001, of which 49 percent was owed to multilateral institutions, 47 percent to bilateral creditors and 4 percent to private creditors. Tanzania, which has remained current on its external debt obligation, obtained debt relief from Paris Club creditors in April 2000 under the enhanced HIPC initiative. Under this agreement, Tanzania reached the decision point in April 2000 making it eligible for debt relief worth more than $2 billion in NPV terms. This is equivalent to more than half of the NPV of the total debt outstanding after full use of traditional debt relief mechanisms.

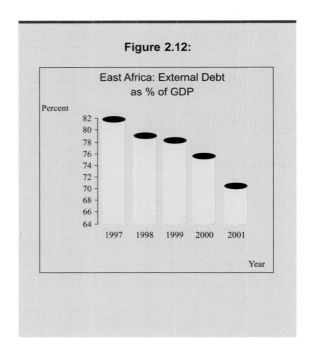

Figure 2.12:

East Africa: External Debt as % of GDP

The debt reduction operations translate into debt service relief over time of $3 billion, or about one-half of Tanzania's debt service obligations during fiscal years 2001-2003 and about one-third of Tanzania's debt service obligations thereafter. As part of its debt management strategy Tanzania uses the Debt Buyback Scheme (DBS). The first closing of the DBS took place in June 2001 when debt worth $155.7 million (principal and interest) was retired utilizing grant funds from the German government.

Uganda's external debt was estimated at $3.82 billion at end-2001, of which 72 percent was owed to multilateral creditors and 26 percent to bilaterals. Private creditors accounted for the balance of 2 percent. Uganda was the first country to benefit from the HIPC debt relief initiative in 1998 when it was granted debt relief of

$347 million in NPV terms (equivalent to $650 million in nominal terms), spread over 30 years. It was also the first country to qualify under the Enhanced HIPC Initiative in May 2000, whereby it will receive $656 million of relief in NPV terms over a period of 20 years (approximately $1.3 billion in nominal terms).

Uganda's debt/GDP ratio and its debt service payments have declined significantly as a result, with savings more than doubling over the last three years from $45 million in 1998 to $91 million in 2000. As a result, Uganda's debt service ratio is now less than half what it would have been without relief. In addition to the HIPC debt relief, Uganda also became eligible for fast-disbursing resources under the Supplementary Financing Mechanism (SFM), which helps countries service non-concessional debts owed to the African Development Bank Group. In parallel with the HIPC debt relief and SFM, Uganda has a debt management strategy whereby it contracts only concessional loans at IDA terms where it is unable to secure grants to finance development expenditure.

Outlook

East African GDP is forecast to grow 4 percent in 2002 compared with 4.6 percent in 2001.

Ethiopia is forecast to maintain its above-average growth rate in 2001/02 when GDP is expected to increase 7.1 percent (7 percent in 1999/2000) This positive outlook is contingent upon continuation of the political and social stability established following the December 2000 peace agreement. Successful implementation of Ethiopia's poverty relief programs is crucial for long term political stability, which itself is a pre-condition for sustainable economic growth.

In Kenya growth is projected to remain weak at around 1.4 percent in 2002. Much will depend on the government's ability to regain donor confidence and support, which will be difficult ahead of crucial presidential and parliamentary elections at the end of 2002. Prices for tea and coffee and the speed with which the tourist sector recovers from the September 11 attacks in the US will also have a major influence on economic performance in 2002/03.

Growth is forecast to slow marginally in Tanzania to 4.4 percent in 2002 from 4.6 percent in 2001, as Tanzania seeks to consolidate its macroeconomic stability. The major potential risk is underlying political and ethnic tension between the mainland and the island of Zanzibar. Another threat is the instability of Tanzania's neighbors, particularly Burundi and the Democratic Republic of Congo, where instability could spillover into Tanzania.

Uganda is expected to continue strong growth in 2002 with real GDP growth of 5.5 percent in the 2001/02 fiscal year. The Ugandan economy stands to benefit from any reduction in instability in the Democratic Republic of Congo, which will reduce Uganda's costly involvement in that country.

Purely economic criteria point to further strong growth in Madagascar but political instability, following the disputed presidential election early in 2002, will have a negative impact on economic performance, especially foreign investment. An average growth rate of around 6 percent was projected for 2002. However, this has been downgraded to 4 percent because of political tensions and even this could prove to be optimistic. Aside from politics, the main growth constraint is the depressed coffee price.

The 2001 political agreement between the central government of Comoros and Anjouan Island has resulted in the renewal of international support for Comoros, which should contribute to accelerated economic growth in the short run. The economy will also benefit from the economic reform programs currently underway. Positive also are strong prices for the country's main agricultural exports.

Growth in Seychelles will remain subdued at around 2 percent in 2002 given the economy's dependence on tourism. Rigidities in the foreign exchange market and structural imbalances pose a risk to Seychelles long-term growth prospects. Accordingly, it is important for the government to implement market-friendly reforms over the next few years.

While Eritrea is expected to grow at about 6 percent in the coming year, long-term economic prospects hinge on continued peace in the region, which will allow Eritrea to rebuild its economy, and the depth if the government's commitment to economic reform. The President's call for the restoration of economic ties with Ethiopia and the return of Ethiopian businessmen is a step in the right direction which is likely to encourage Ethiopia to resume its use of Port Assab, thereby boosting Eritrea's foreign currency earnings.

Because of its strategic position in the horn of Africa, Djibouti has the potential to become a transit trade route for many East African nations. The economy is expected to grow by 2.5 percent in 2002, subject to continued political stability.

The Mauritian economy is expected to grow 4 percent during 2002 but this forecast is vulnerable to several downside risks, most notably its Export Processing Zone industries may not be competitive when current export subsidies are abandoned.

North Africa

North Africa is a region of great contrasts and disparities. It comprises seven countries—Algeria, Egypt, Libya, Mauritania, Morocco, Sudan and Tunisia – whose main resource base is crude oil. It is the major source of exports as well as the largest contributor to gross output accounting for 36 percent of Africa's export revenues and 45 percent of gross output (Table 2.1).

North African economies are vulnerable to external shocks, especially weather conditions and fluctuations in oil and other commodity prices. The events of September 11 also underline the region's vulnerability to adverse influences affecting one of its most important foreign currency earners – tourism.

North Africa is home to 180 million people, about 22 percent of the continent's population but it is a region characterized by vast inequality among the seven countries. Per capita GDP in Mauritania and Sudan were $348 and $393 respectively in 2001, while the average per capita GDP for the rest of the region exceeded $1,300.

Recent Economic Trends

In 2001, GDP growth in the sub-region at 4.0 percent was marginally above the four-year average of 3.9 percent for the period 1997-2000 (Table 2.8 and Figure 2.13).

The Algerian economy expanded 3.5 percent in 2001 in response to increased investment, fiscal expansion and a rebound in agricultural output reflecting improved climatic conditions. Over the 1997 to 2000 period, growth averaged 3.0 percent a year, largely as a result of the massive drought-induced decline in agricultural output, which offset growth in the energy sector.

Egyptian economic growth slowed in 2001 to 3.3 percent (Figure 2.14) from an annual average of 5.6 percent during 1997-2000. Tourism suffered in the aftermath to the September 11 attacks in the US and escalating Middle East violence. In addition, declining oil prices dampened export growth and remittances from Egyptians working in the Gulf States.

In recent years, recurrent droughts have constrained economy growth in Morocco but there was a powerful rebound in 2001 when GDP increased 6 percent compared with an average of 1.6 percent a year during 1997-2000. Growth was driven by improved weather conditions and the strong fiscal stimulus directed at the construction, transport, and manufacturing sectors.

The Sudanese economy grew 6.0 percent in 2001 slowing slightly from the four-year average of 6.5 percent during the 1997 to 2000 period. Increased foreign investment, especially in the oil sector, has offset political uncertainty. Growth in Libya accelerated modestly to 2.5 percent in 2001 from an average of 1.8 percent a year between 1997 and 2000.

In 2001, the Tunisian economy weathered adverse domestic and external conditions to maintain a stable growth rate of 5.2 percent, similar to the annual average growth rate during 1997-2000. This strong economic performance, achieved despite dry weather conditions, was the result of efficient macroeconomic policies and a stable political environment. Tunisia's relatively well diversified economy has also helped the country to avoid the large output fluctuations characteristic of many countries on the continent.

In Mauritania, GDP growth accelerated to 5.2 percent in 2001 from the annual average of 4.0 percent during 1997-2000, reflecting the combination of progressive implementation of the reforms begun in the early 1990s and a stable

Table 2.8: North Africa: Gross Domestic Product and Export Performances

Country	Real GDP Growth Rate (%)		GDP Per Capita (US$)		Real Export Growth (%)		Exports[b/] Per Capita (US$)	
	Average 1997-2000	2001[a/]	Average 1997-2000	2001[a/]	Average 1997-2000	2001[a/]	Average 1997-2000	2001[a/]
ALGERIA	3.0	3.5	1662	1770	5.7	-0.7	518	703
EGYPT	5.6	3.3	1307	1353	10.5	0.6	218	241
LIBYA	1.8	2.5	6431	6170	-1.1	10.4	1798	2426
MAURITANIA	4.0	5.2	394	348	-4.0	4.6	156	147
MOROCCO	1.6	6.0	1186	1117	7.4	5.3	224	227
SUDAN	6.5	6.0	353	395	...	...	33	60
TUNISIA	5.2	5.2	2120	2100	7.4	7.2	918	981
NORTH AFRICA	**3.9**	**4.0**	**1363**	**1385**	**5.2**	**4.1**	**322**	**390**

Notes: a/ Preliminary estimates.

       b/: Exports of Goods and Nonfactor Services at Market Prices.
... Not available.
Sources: ADB Research and Statistics Divisions.

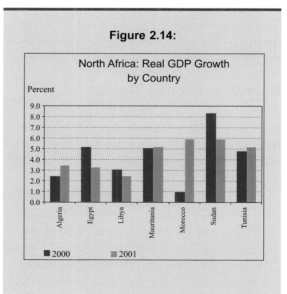

Figure 2.13:

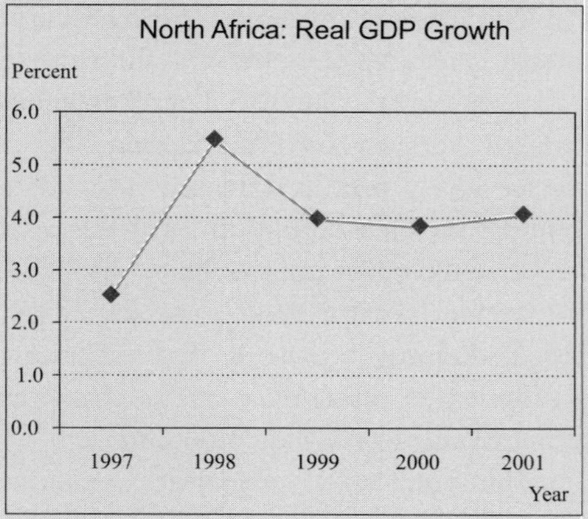

North Africa: Real GDP Growth

Figure 2.14:

North Africa: Real GDP Growth by Country

macroeconomic environment.

Average inflation in North Africa slowed markedly in 2001 to 4.5 percent compared with an average of 7.3 percent during 1997-2000 (Table 2.9 and Figure 2.15).

After averaging over 20 percent through most of the 1990s, Algerian inflation subsided to average only 2.3 percent between 1997 and 2000 following the economic reforms of the mid-1990s. Further progress was achieved in 2001 when the inflation rate declined to 1.5 percent.

Inflationary pressures in the Egyptian economy declined in the second half of the 1990s falling to an average of 3.6 percent for the period 1997-2000 and to 2.4 percent in 2001. This slowdown reflects the success of the decision to peg the currency to the US dollar supported by tight fiscal and monetary policies.

Inflation has remained under control in Morocco since the mid-1990s. In 2001 the government's decision to subsidize the domestic price of oil was a major factor cushioning domestic price increases. Inflation remained low at 1 percent for the year, compared with an annual average 1.6 percent during 1997-2000.

Price controls and strong oil revenues have helped Libya to curb inflation, which slowed from an average of 20.4 percent annually during 1997-2000 to 13.6 percent in 2001. In recent years inflation has been driven by strong import demand linked to international sanctions against the country.

In the Sudan, inflation has declined in response to improved fiscal and monetary policies, falling from 22.4 percent during 1997-2000 to 6 percent in 2001. The sharp decline of inflation in 2001

Table 2.9: North Africa: Macroeconomic Management Indicators

| Country | Inflation (%) | | Fiscal Balance as % of GDP | | Gross Domestic | | | |
| | | | | | Investment as % of GDP | | Savings as % of GDP | |
	Average 1997-2000	2001[a/]	Average 1997-2000	2001[a/]	Average 1997-2000	2001[a/]	Average 1997-2000	2001[a/]
ALGERIA	2.3	1.5	2.0	6.3	25.3	28.4	33.7	43.3
EGYPT	3.6	2.4	-3.1	-5.8	24.2	23.1	16.3	18.0
LIBYA	20.4	13.6	...	...	...	...	...	...
MAURITANIA	5.0	6.3	2.5	1.5	21.7	29.0	9.8	8.1
MOROCCO	1.6	1.0	-4.0	-7.1	23.1	24.8	18.6	18.4
SUDAN	22.4	6.0	0.0	-0.6	.	18.7	10.7	17.7
TUNISIA	3.1	1.5	-2.9	-2.5	26.7	27.9	24.3	25.0
NORTH AFRICA	**7.3**	**4.5**	**-1.9**	**-2.4**	**24.5**	**25.3**	**22.0**	**25.6**

Note: a/ Preliminary estimates.
... Not available.
Sources: ADB Research and Statistics Divisions.

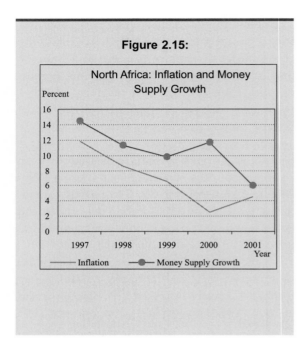

Figure 2.15:

North Africa: Inflation and Money Supply Growth

was helped by the administered domestic prices of oil that isolated the Sudanese market from the international oil price.

Tunisia has maintained single digit inflation since the mid-1990s and the rate slowed further to 1.5 percent in 2001 from a four-year average of 3.1 percent over the 1997-2000 period.

North Africa's recent growth performance is underpinned by strong domestic investment. The Region has outperformed the rest of the continent with the gross domestic investment/GDP ratio rising from an annual average of 24.5 percent during 1997-2000 to 25.3 percent in 2001 (Table 2.9).

The rich natural endowment of crude oil continues to be a major attraction to foreign investors while there has been strong international support for some privatization transactions. Algeria

continues to attract substantial foreign investment in its hydrocarbons sector. The country's enormous hydrocarbon potential, its proximity to energy markets and increased demand for gas and oil has outweighed the investment risks associated with the country's unstable political situation. Similarly, Sudan is attracting increased foreign investment in its oil sector, while public sector investment has increased in Morocco and Egypt in the construction, transport, manufacturing and infrastructural sectors.

Policy Developments

Fiscal Policy

Fiscal performance in North Africa has been poor relative to the continent as a whole, with the regional fiscal deficit continuing to widen in 2001 to 2.4 percent of GDP from a yearly average of 1.9 percent of GDP during 1997-2000 (Table 2.9 and Figure 2.16).

Algeria's recent fiscal policy focuses on reducing the country's high level of unemployment, with the result that successive administrations have adopted expansionary fiscal measures. Since 1998, these have been facilitated by buoyant energy prices giving rise to a fiscal surplus averaging 2.0 percent of GDP between 1997 and 2000, rising sharply to 6.3 percent of GDP in 2001.

Controls over public spending and the increasing efficiency of tax collection enabled Egypt to restrict the budget deficit to 3.1 percent of GDP during the 1997-2000 period. The tax administration system has been streamlined, limiting opportunities for tax evasion and increasing the efficiency of tax and custom duty collection. However, given the government's policy of not levying new taxes, further growth in tax revenues will depend increasingly on the rate of economic

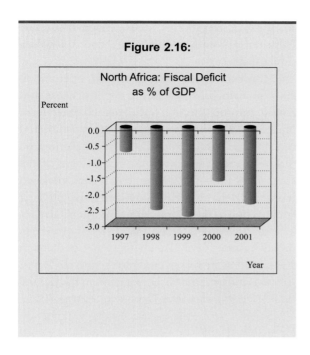

Figure 2.16:

North Africa: Fiscal Deficit as % of GDP

velopment tax, the removal of some income taxes and rationalization of custom duties. Also, the government raised oil prices by 11 percent in March 2001 to improve government revenues and compensate for the decline in tax collections as a result of significant personal income tax reductions and tax cuts in the agriculture sector. Consequently the fiscal balance showed a small deficit of 0.6 percent of GDP in 2001.

In Tunisia the fiscal deficit stabilized at 2.5 percent of GDP in 2001, compared with an average of 2.9 percent annually during 1997-2000. The government has relied on privatization to boost government revenues.

Libya's fiscal performance depends heavily on its oil revenues, and the recent strong price of oil has enabled the government to pursue an expansionary fiscal policy. A major feature of Libya's fiscal system is the size of the wage bill with the salaries of public-sector employees accounting for nearly 60 percent of government spending.

Monetary Policy

The objectives of monetary policy in North Africa have been price stability and competitive exchange rates.

Despite the surge in money supply arising from buoyant oil prices, broad money growth in Algeria was contained at 13 percent in 2000 compared with 14 percent in 1999. Increased revenues from oil exports helped reduce pressure on bank liquidity allowing the central bank to reduce its rediscount rate to 6 percent at the end of the year.

After depreciating rapidly between 1993 and 1996, the Algerian dinar stabilized in the latter half of the decade following the adoption of a comprehensive reform package in 1994, including tight monetary and fiscal policies. These, combined with favorable terms of trade in the late 1990s, con-

growth as well as the government's ability to bring the informal sector into the tax net while continuing to enhance the efficiency of tax collections. This was not achieved in 2001, which explains why the fiscal deficit widened to 5.8 percent of GDP.

In Morocco the fiscal deficit continued to widen reaching 7.1 percent of GDP in 2001 from the annual average of 4 percent of GDP during 1997-2000. Weaker export revenues, workers' remittances and an estimated 41 percent drop in privatization revenues depleted the tax base and weakened government revenues.

Until 1997, the fiscal performance in Sudan was characterized by high fiscal deficits—driven by lax controls on spending and tax collection—and loose monetary policy. The government has recently carried out fiscal reforms including tax cuts in the agriculture sector, abolition of the de-

tributed to greater exchange rate stability. The *dinar* ended 2001 at 74/dollar, compared with 71 to the dollar at the beginning of the year. The main reason for this depreciation was the weakness in the euro, as movements in the Algerian currency are closely linked with those of Algeria's main trading partners. Despite a mild recession in the United States and a relatively stronger economic performance in the EU economies, the euro failed to strengthen significantly against the dollar. However, the *dinar* recouped some of the year's losses as the U.S. dollar weakened after the September 11 terrorist attacks.

The Egyptian pound had been pegged to the dollar at a fixed rate of LE3.393: until May 2000 when the authorities appeared to abandon the peg policy by imposing controls on dollar deposits. These were reversed in October 2000 because they had triggered accelerated depreciation of the pound and a new "managed peg" policy was adopted in January 2001 at the still prevailing rate of LE3.85: US$1. The government also indicated its intention of setting the pound against a basket of currencies rather than the dollar alone.

Against this pegged rate background, the Central Bank of Egypt maintained prudent monetary policies which contained the rate of monetary (M2) expansion at 10 percent a year over the 1997 to 1999 period. But the policy came under stress in 2000 when it focused on defending the exchange rate as a result of which domestic liquidity growth halved to 5 per cent during the first nine months of the year constraining demand and economic growth.

Monetary expansion accelerated to 11 per cent per annum in the final quarter of 2000 and the first few months of 2001. Tight monetary policy and slowing inflation paved the way for lower interest rates and the CBE's discount rate declined to 11 percent in July 2001 from 12 percent in 2000

and 12.5 percent during the two preceding years. Bank deposit and lending rates have followed a similar pattern.

Morocco devalued the *dirham* by 5 percent in 2001 to help boost export competitiveness and correct the deteriorating trade balance. Previously, the *dirham* had been pegged to both the euro and the dollar. The devaluation was implemented through a readjustment of the peg in favor of the euro. At the end of 2000, the central bank loosened monetary policy to help reduce pressures on bank liquidity due to the accumulating budgetary arrears. The central bank targeted a 9.5 percent growth in broad money for 2001, up from 8.4 percent in 2000, to allow increased credit to the private sector. This was underpinned by a reduction in the Central Bank's lending rate to 4.75 percent during 2001.

Privatization

Algeria has embraced privatization as part of a package of recent reforms designed to enhance the country's investment climate. Under new legislation aimed at simplifying investment procedures and accelerating privatization, the Council of State Participation became the sole body responsible for privatization and the National Agency for the Development of Investments took charge of investment procedures. The government is also considering a new legislation to overhaul the oil, gas and energy sectors while signing two exploration agreements with Russian and UAE consortia and another contract with Malaysia's Petronas and Gaz de France for the exploration of the In Sahala gas reserves. A new mining law that provides investors with fiscal incentives and eliminates discrimination between public and private investors has been introduced. Moreover, the law on repatriation of profits has been reviewed to allow foreign investors to repatriate dividend, profits and capital. Recent privatizations include 70 percent of Alfasid and 70 percent of El Ouenza and Bukadra iron mines. The telecommunications sector was also liberalized with the award of a second GSM licence in July 2001. The Telecommunications Ministry issued a tender for a 500,000-subscriber GSM network and set up a new firm, Algerie Telecom, to upgrade and increase the efficiency of the sector.

Egypt's privatization program launched in the early 1990s involves the divestiture of 314 state-owned companies and by December 2000, 156 (49.6 per cent) had been fully or partially privatized. In 2000, there were only two sales underlining the slow pace of privatization which led to new efforts to revitalize the process. Accordingly, 49 companies, including 19 tourism and restaurant businesses, were earmarked for sale in 2001, while a further 42 state-owned hotels were listed for privatization in 2002. Many of the remaining 142 public enterprises require extensive restructuring before they can be divested and there are concerns that their sale could involve the retrenchment of some 300 000 workers, which has created serious political debate in a country where unemployment is severe.

Morocco has privatized some 60 state enterprises out of a total of over 110 since its public sector reform program was launched in 1990. The most significant recent privatization was the partial sale of *Maroc Telecom* allied with deregulation of the entire telecommunications sector. In 2002, the government plans to sell 40 percent of the national carrier, *Royal Air Maroc* to a strategic partner. Other anticipated privatizations include the automotive plant *Somaca*, and the tobacco firm *Regie des Tabacs*. The government is also committed to a gradual withdrawal from electricity and water supply sectors by offering franchises to private operators.

In its determination to restructure its economy, Sudan has announced forthcoming privatization of state companies, including the Post Office, Sudan Air, the railways, and the electricity companies.

External Accounts

The external accounts of the sub-region underline its heavy dependence on oil exports. Although export growth declined from a yearly average of 5.2 percent in 1997-2000 to 4.1 percent in 2001, the current account balance improved from an average deficit of 0.2 percent of GDP in 1997-2000 to a surplus of 2.5 percent in 2001 (Table 2.10 and Figure 2.17).

Algeria's exports are almost entirely oil-related with hydrocarbons accounting for 98 percent of total receipts. Firm energy prices account for the country's current account surplus which averaged 5.5 percent of GDP over the 1997-2000 period. In 2000, exports surged 76.4 percent due to high oil prices pushing the current account to a surplus of 12 percent of GDP in 2001.

Egypt's export portfolio is dominated by primary commodities vulnerable to severe fluctuations in global markets. Buoyant oil prices largely account for the reduction in the trade deficit from 13.3 percent of GDP during 1997-2000 to 9.7 percent in 2001. The decline in 2001 was due to a 37 per cent increase in exports, buoyed by firm oil prices, during a year in which import growth was minimal owing to the tight dollar liquidity situation and restrictive trade rules. The current account is also influenced by service income from the tourist industry, which underwent a severe setback in 2001 following the September 11 attacks in the US. The number of visitors fell to 468,000 in July 2001 from 506,000 a year earlier, and the government is projecting a 50 percent decline in

Table 2.10: North Africa: The External Sector

Country	Trade Balance as % of GDP		Current Account as % of GDP		Terms of Trade (%)		Total External Debt as % of GDP		Debt Service as % of Exports	
	Average 1997-2000	2001[a]	Average 1997-2000	2001[a]	Average 1997-2000	2001[a]	Average 1997-2000	2001[a]	Average 1996-1999	2000
ALGERIA	11.3	17.5	5.5	12.0	15.7	-0.1	58.9	41.8	45.1	20.8
EGYPT	-13.4	-9.7	-1.5	-0.2	2.4	1.2	32.9	27.9	12.6	11.4
LIBYA	...	...	...	...	...	...	...	...	...	...
MAURITANIA	2.4	-5.2	1.4	-7.2	-3.1	-0.7	225.4	182.7	22.5	17.2
MOROCCO	-7.1	-9.4	-0.7	-2.1	-0.3	-0.6	57.0	48.8	31.5	25.6
SUDAN	...	...	...	...	...	...	...	...	...	...
TUNISIA	-10.8	-11.3	-3.2	-3.1	-1.6	0.2	58.3	53.9	19.0	22.1
NORTH AFRICA	**-3.8**	**-0.2**	**-0.2**	**2.5**	**8.4**	**-10.4**	**50.4**	**42.3**	**27.3**	**19.2**

Note: a/ Preliminary estimates.
... Not available.
Sources: ADB Research and Statistics Divisions.

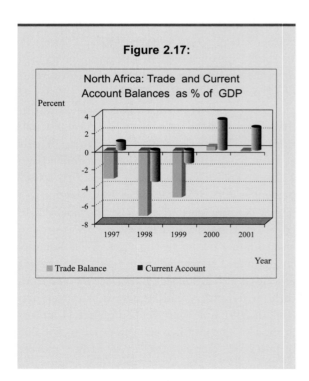

Figure 2.17:

North Africa: Trade and Current Account Balances as % of GDP

tourist arrivals over the 12 months to September 2002. Despite this, the current account deficit continued to decline reaching 0.2 percent of GDP in 2001 compared with an annual average of 1.2 percent of GDP during 1997-2000.

Morocco's terms of trade worsened considerably in 2001 as costly oil imports and weak export prices put pressure on the trade balance. Consequently, the current account deficit widened from an annual average of 0.7 percent of GDP during 1997-2000 to 2.1 percent in 2001. Surprisingly, tourism receipts surged 39 percent in 2001, despite the global slowdown in the industry following the attacks of September 11.

The recent discovery of exploitable oil deposits in Sudan has played a major role in improving the country's external balance. In 2000, oil exports increased 132 percent reflecting firm prices and increased volumes. Although the windfall in oil revenues led to a 9 percent increase in imports Sudan still achieved a modest trade surplus, which helped contain the current account deficit. The merchandise trade account was in surplus to the tune of $189 million in the first half of 2001, with exports increasing 16 percent to $1.04 billion while imports jumped 20 percent to $0.85 billion.

Libya too is heavily dependent on oil, which accounts for over 95 percent of export revenues. After running current account deficits throughout the 1980s, Libya achieved current account and trade surpluses during the 1990s. The trade surplus surged to $2.76 billion in 1999 from a $471 million the previous year thanks to export growth of 6.8 percent while imports plunged 31.8 percent. With oil prices rising in 2000, oil exports boomed and ensured a healthy trade surplus for the year. Though this is estimated to have declined in 2001 when oil demand and prices weakened. Export volumes have declined following OPEC's quota cuts.

Tunisia's current account deficit has held steady at around 3.1 percent of GDP since 1997. This is partly explained by the country's success in boosting its tourist sector with tourism receipts increasing 7.5 percent in 2000. The number of foreign visitors rose from 4.9 million in 1999 to 5.2 million in 2000.

In Mauritania, the global economic downturn has reduced world demand for the country's major export earner, iron ore, leading to reduced production and exports. Consequently, the trade gap has widened and the current account deteriorated substantially. The current account deficit increased from an annual average of 1.4 percent of GDP in 1997-2000 to 7.2 percent in 2001.

External Debt

North Africa's external debt was unchanged in 2001 at approximately $110 billion The debt/GDP ratio declined from 44.0 percent in 2000 to 42.3 percent in 2001 (Figure 2.18) and the region's debt burden, is less severe than that of Sub-Saharan countries.

Egypt is the region's largest debtor accounting for nearly 30 percent of the regional total in 2001. But its debt situation has improved with the debt stock declining from over $32 billion in the mid-1990s to $27.10 billion at end-2001. Consequently, the debt/GNI ratio has fallen from 55 per cent to 30 per cent over the period, while the debt service ratio has eased from 13.3 per cent to 9.0 per cent. In part, this reflects the impact of

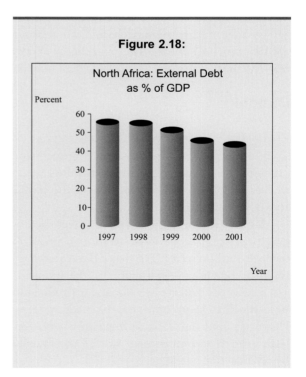

Figure 2.18:

North Africa: External Debt as % of GDP

the May 1999 debt rescheduling and reduction agreements signed with the Paris Club creditors.

Debt stocks have also declined in Algeria, Tunisia and Mauritania. In Algeria, foreign debt has fallen since 1996 to stand at $22.5 billion at end-2001 – about 41 percent of GDP. Similarly, Tunisia's external debt has fallen steadily since 1998 to $9.70 billion in December 2001. In Mauritania, the total debt at end-2001 was estimated at $1.71 billion – approximately $1 billion below the 1997 level when the debt decline began.

Morocco's external debt has also declined since 1998 following successful debt-for-equity swaps with its major creditors, including Spain, Italy and France. At end 2001 Morocco's external debt stood at $15.68 billion, nearly $5 billion below the level of debt of 1998.

Sudan continues to be a highly debt-stressed economy, with a foreign debt stock of $21 billion in 2000. The government and the IMF recently agreed a formula to reschedule Sudan's debt for the first time in 17 years. This, and the oil export boom in the country, will alleviate the debt burden.

Outlook

Economic growth in North Africa is forecast to slow to 3.6 percent in 2002 from 4 percent the previous year, with the main constraints being weaker oil prices and the impact of the global slowdown in tourism.

Algeria's economic outlook is driven by energy prices and the level of fresh investment in the hydrocarbon sector. The major BP-Amoco and state-run Sonatrach exploration of the In Sahala gas reserves is expected to boost gas production by as much as 15 percent over the medium-term. However, until the political impasse is resolved, both growth and investment will be constrained by political uncertainty.

Growth in Egypt will be constrained by lower oil prices and reduced tourist activity. The recent government decision to cancel this year's staging of the opera Aida is a clear indication of the extent to which the tourist industry is being negatively affected by the September 11 attacks. However, recent natural gas discoveries should boost investment and provide some impetus for growth although most of these projects will not come on stream before 2003 at the earliest.

The Moroccan economy will slow too in response to an anticipated reduction in tourist activity. While Morocco has achieved relative macroeconomic stability, potential political instability stemming from the continuing dispute over Western Sahara and the tense relations with Algeria represent major constraints to investment, especially in the recently discovered oil and natural gas sector. Development of these industries will boost growth while reducing the country's heavy dependence on energy imports.

Sudan will seek to use its improved international relations to attract foreign investment into the oil sector, but growth will likely be constrained by the effects of the civil war. Libya's economic prospects are clouded by weaker energy prices and ongoing structural bottlenecks in the economy emanating from the government's reluctance to embrace market-driven reforms.

With one of the most diversified economies in the region, with a large services sector, especially tourism, and manufacturing sectors, as well as a relatively young and well-educated labor force, Tunisia is well placed to become the region's star performer. These features and the country's geographic proximity and close economic ties with the European Union should boost foreign investment and growth, especially as reforms take hold and state intervention in the economy diminishes.

Southern Africa

Ten countries make up the Southern Africa sub-region – Angola, Botswana, Lesotho, Malawi, Mozambique, Namibia, South Africa, Swaziland, Zambia and Zimbabwe. The sub-region is well endowed with natural resources, notably minerals, which is reflected in production structures and exports. In 2000, exports accounted for 32 percent of the continental total, the bulk of which came from South Africa, which accounted for 64 percent of Southern Africa's exports. In 2001, Southern Africa contributed 27 percent of Africa's GDP, with South Africa accounting for 76 percent the sub-region's GDP.

Southern Africa's contribution to Africa's output and exports far exceeds its share of population. In 2001 the sub-region's population was estimated at 117 million, or 14 percent of the continent's total (Table 2.1).

Per capita incomes in Southern Africa at $1261 are more than double the African average of $673, though this masks enormous disparities between high and low income states. In Botswana and South Africa per capita incomes exceed $2500, but in the poorer countries – Mozambique, Malawi, Zambia and Angola – per capita incomes are between $200-$400.

Recent Economic Trends

GDP growth in Southern Africa slowed from an annual average of 2.6 percent during 1997-2000 to 2.2 percent in 2001 (Table 2.11 and Figure 2.19) Economic performance was diverse, ranging from growth of 7.5 percent in Botswana to an estimated decline of 7.5 percent in Zimbabwe.

Growth in Botswana accelerated in 2001 to 7.5 percent from 6.4 percent during 1997-2000, driven almost entirely by increasing diamond production. Diamond production, which accounts for 35 percent of GDP, 80 percent of exports and 50 percent of government revenue, plateaued in 2000, suggesting that growth rates will slacken in the years ahead. Other factors promoting growth include the country's efficient administration and market-friendly business environment, underpinned by sound macroeconomic policies and a well-developed and maintained infrastructure.

South Africa's economy slowed in 2001 with GDP growth of 2.2 percent compared with an annual average of 2.8 percent during 1997-2000. (Figure 2.20). South Africa was adversely affected by the economic crisis in Zimbabwe as well as the slowdown in global economic activity.

Zimbabwe has been in economic and political crisis since 1999. In 2001 GDP is estimated to have declined 7.5 percent following an average yearly decline of 0.1 percent during 1997-2000. All sectors of the economy were adversely affected by political uncertainty following the government's "fast track" land resettlement program launched in 2000. Production in the country's commercial farming sector is estimated to have fallen by at least a third since 1999, with far-reaching implications for consumption spending, exports and government revenues. Commercial agriculture accounts for over 40 percent of exports, 15 percent of GDP and 20 percent of formal sector employment.

Economic activity in Mozambique rebounded strongly in 2001, recording a growth rate of 8.7 percent compared with the average yearly growth rate of 8.2 percent during 1997-2000. In recent years Mozambique has been the continent's fastest growing economy. Private foreign direct investment has been the catalyst for economic growth, underpinned by economic reforms and Mozambique's increasing integration into the

Table 2.11: Southern Africa: Gross Domestic Product and Export Performances

Country	Real GDP Growth Rate (%)		GDP Per Capita (US$)		Real Export Growth (%)		Exports[b/] Per Capita (US$)	
	Average 1997-2000	2001[a/]	Average 1997-2000	2001[a/]	Average 1997-2000	2001[a/]	Average 1997-2000	2001[a/]
ANGOLA	4.7	3.2	579	685	3.2	-1.1	440	558
BOTSWANA	6.4	7.5	3179	3181	3.2	-0.3	1711	1793
LESOTHO	2.2	3.0	468	386	-0.2	-3.3	124	113
MALAWI	3.2	2.5	179	154	0.4	9.8	48	46
MOZAMBIQUE	8.2	8.7	212	177	12.3	54.4	28	58
NAMIBIA	3.6	2.7	2030	1727	4.0	11.6	963	1047
SOUTH AFRICA	2.2	2.2	3198	2578	4.1	1.8	833	769
SWAZILAND	3.3	2.4	1497	1186	6.6	2.2	1098	915
ZAMBIA	1.9	4.5	336	330	-2.7	12.3	94	80
ZIMBABWE	-0.1	-7.5	570	568	0.0	-3.2	222	175
SOUTHERN AFRICA	**2.6**	**2.2**	**1514**	**1261**	**3.5**	**2.2**	**455**	**440**

Notes: a/ Preliminary estimates.
          b/: Exports of Goods and Nonfactor Services at Market Prices.
Sources: ADB Research and Statistics Divisions.

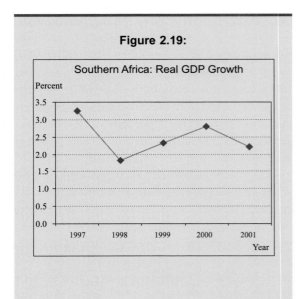

Figure 2.19:

Southern Africa: Real GDP Growth

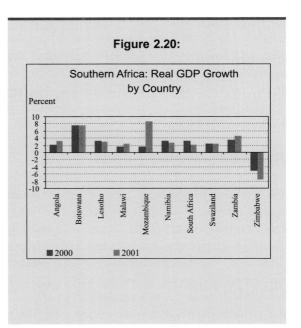

Figure 2.20:

Southern Africa: Real GDP Growth by Country

South African economy. Virtually all the country's portfolio of "mega projects" involves South Africa to some degree. Work has started on phase two of the Mozal aluminium smelter which will more than double exports between 2000 and 2004.

Namibia experienced an average growth rate of 3.6 per cent during 1997-2000, but this slowed to 2.7 percent in 2001 reflecting reduced demand and weaker prices for diamonds and the poor performance of agriculture. Growth has been driven by developments in the export-oriented primary sector, especially mining, which accounts for about 50 per cent of merchandise export earnings.

The Angolan economy achieved an estimated real GDP growth of 3.2 percent in 2001, down from the annual average rate of 4.7 percent during 1997-2000. Weaker oil prices and demand account for the 2001 slowdown in an economy where oil contributes 60 percent of GDP, 80 percent of export earnings and 90 percent of government revenue.

In Lesotho the economy has been slow to recover from the political turmoil experienced in 1998 that negatively affected investor perceptions. Growth accelerated in 2001 to reach 3 percent on increased investment in manufacturing following an average of 2.2 percent during 1997-2000.

Malawi's GDP grew a modest 2.5 percent in 2001, significantly below the four-year average of 3.1 percent between 1997 and 2000. Economic growth is heavily dependent on the performance of smallholder agriculture, which accounts for 40 percent of GDP, and on prices for tobacco and tea. In 2001, smallholder growth slowed while manufacturing production was adversely affected by kwacha depreciation, high lending rates and stiff competition from cheap imported products.

The positive effects of the privatization of Zambian Consolidated Copper Mines boosted Zambia's growth in 2001 when GDP rose 4.5 percent – a substantial improvement on the annual average of 1.9 percent during 1997-2000.

The slowdown in economic activity during 2001 was associated with heightened inflationary pressures in the sub-region with the rate of inflation increasing from a yearly average of 14.6 percent during 1997-2000 to 15.1 percent in 2001 (Table 2.12 and Figure 2.21).

Inflation in Botswana is driven by exchange rate depreciation. Although the country's economic fundamentals are strong, the exchange rate has depreciated in line with the fall in the South African rand. Because the bulk of Botswana's imports are sourced in – or though – South Africa, import prices are crucial to the inflation rate which averaged 7.8 percent during 1997-2000. However, in response to tighter monetary policies and fiscal restraint, the year-on-year rate fell to 6.8 percent in 2001.

Inflation in South Africa slowed to 5.2 percent in 1999 – the lowest figure for 30 years. During the 1997-2000 period, inflation averaged 6.5 percent declining to 5.7 percent in 2001. Inflation has since picked up, forcing the authorities to tighten monetary policy in the wake of the steep depreciation of the rand during 2001.

Inflation in Mozambique has slowed dramatically since 1995 with an average annual rate during the 1997-2000 period of only 5.2 percent compared with over 50 percent a year in the first half of the 1990s. However, following the disruption of the distribution network in the 1999/2000 floods, the annual rate in 2000 rebounded to 11.4 per cent. This was shortlived and in 2001 inflation slowed to 5.7 percent following the tightening of monetary policy.

Inflation in Namibia accelerated from 8.2 percent annually between 1997 and 2000 to 9.2 percent in 2001, mainly due to the knock-on ef-

Table 2.12: Southern Africa: Macroeconomic Management Indicators

Country	Inflation (%)		Fiscal Balance as % of GDP		Gross Domestic			
					Investment as % of GDP		Savings as % of GDP	
	Average 1997-2000	2001[a/]	Average 1997-2000	2001[a/]	Average 1997-2000	2001[a/]	Average 1997-2000	2001[a/]
ANGOLA	219.9	158.3	-12.0	5.6	27.5	29.7	26.0	41.0
BOTSWANA	7.8	6.8	2.3	-0.4	30.0	29.3	40.5	43.4
LESOTHO	7.0	6.5	-6.8	0.2	42.0	24.1	-26.8	-21.3
MALAWI	28.3	32.7	-5.3	-0.5	13.4	12.9	1.9	1.2
MOZAMBIQUE	5.2	5.7	-2.6	-9.0	29.1	31.8	8.5	12.6
NAMIBIA	8.2	9.2	-3.1	-2.8	21.3	22.1	11.3	16.3
SOUTH AFRICA	6.5	5.7	-2.5	-2.6	15.7	14.6	17.3	18.1
SWAZILAND	8.4	9.8	0.1	-2.9	35.6	36.8	18.4	20.7
ZAMBIA	25.4	21.4	-3.7	-4.4	15.0	18.7	5.0	3.6
ZIMBABWE	41.2	71.9	-10.2	-16.8	12.2	2.5	12.0	6.4
SOUTHERN AFRICA	**14.6**	**15.1**	**-3.1**	**-2.6**	**17.2**	**16.8**	**17.3**	**19.7**

Note: a/ Preliminary estimates.
Sources: ADB Research and Statistics Divisions.

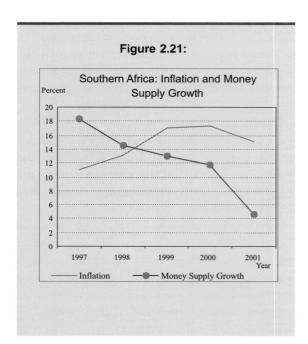

Figure 2.21:

Southern Africa: Inflation and Money Supply Growth

fect of higher import prices arising from the devaluation of the Namibian dollar which is pegged to the South African rand.

Price increases in Zimbabwe reached hyperinflation levels at the end of 2001 when inflation exceeded 100 percent. Inflation rose to 71.9 percent in 2001 from an annual average of 41 percent during 1997-2000. The main causes of triple-digit inflation were excessive monetary expansion of around 100 percent, currency devaluation in the parallel market and the steep increase in food prices.

A defining characteristic of Southern Africa's growth performance is the decline in domestic investment. Gross domestic investment fell from an average of 17.2 percent of GDP during 1997-2000 to 16.8 percent in 2001 (Table 2.12).

Although domestic investment remained strong in Botswana, Angola, Mozambique and

Zambia, this was more than offset by lower investment ratios in other countries, especially Zimbabwe.

Policy Developments

Fiscal Performance

Most Southern African countries have tightened fiscal policy in recent years with the result that the regional deficit fell from an annual average of 3.1 percent of GDP during 1997-2000 to 2.6 percent in 2001 (Table 2.12 and Figure 2.22).

Botswana's budget slipped into deficit in 1998/99 for the first time in 16 years, reflecting reduced demand for diamonds which translated into lower government revenues. There was a dramatic turnaround in the subsequent year when the budget swung from a deficit of 6 percent of GDP

to a surplus of 6 percent. Over the 1997-2000 period, the fiscal surplus averaged 2.3 percent of GDP, but this turned negative in 2001 at 0.4 percent of GDP due to larger government outlays for pensions.

The distinguishing feature of fiscal policy in South Africa since the advent of democratic rule in 1994 has been the steady reduction in the budget deficit. This reflected a combination of spending cuts, especially security spending, and the increased efficiency of revenue collection. Over the period 1997-2000, the fiscal deficit averaged of 2.5 percent of GDP, increasing fractionally to 2.6 percent in 2001.

Zimbabwe's fiscal balance began to deteriorate in 1997/98 when the government agreed to substantial, unbudgeted payments to veterans of the liberation war in the 1970s. After averaging 11.7 percent of GDP over the 1997 to 2000 period, the fiscal deficit widened to 12 percent in 2001 and is expected to double during 2002. The deficit would have been substantially greater in 2001 had it not been for the switch to a lax monetary policy and negative real interest rates, which enabled the government to reduce its debt-service expenditure.

Monetary Developments

Monetary policy in most of the countries of the sub-region has been directed towards achieving price stability through tighter control of monetary aggregates.

In Botswana following the credit boom in 1998, which saw growth in money supply of 30 percent, the Bank of Botswana raised its rediscount rate from 13.2 percent to 13.75 percent in February 2000 and then further to 14.25 percent in October. The growth rate of broad money (M2) halved from 18 percent in 1999 to 9 percent in

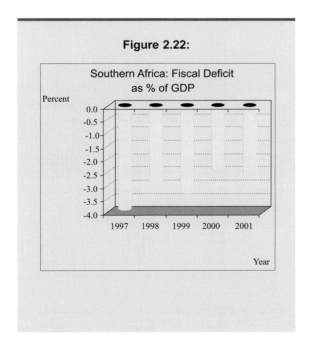

Figure 2.22:

Southern Africa: Fiscal Deficit
as % of GDP

2000, leading to lower inflation in 2001.

The South African Reserve Bank has adopted a policy of inflation targeting with a target range of between 3 and 6 percent in 2002. In 2000/01 the central bank maintained a tight monetary stance and succeeded in reducing inflation from 8.6 percent in 1997 to 5.7 percent in 2001. Following the trend set by the US Fed, the Bank of England and the European Central Bank, the South African Reserve Bank cut its repo rate by 50 basis points in September 2001, with the aim of minimizing the fall out on the South African economy and financial markets of the September 11 attacks on the US. South Africa's sluggish economic performance, political instability in the region and the September 11 attacks had a negative impact on the rand, which depreciated sharply in the final months of 2001, losing 37 percent of its value against the US dollar over the year.

Monetary policy in Zimbabwe has been driven by fiscal considerations with the government borrowing massively in the domestic market to fund the fiscal deficit. The rate of money supply growth accelerated from 30 percent in 1999 to an estimated 100 percent in 2001, during which period the inflation rate also increased dramatically. In January 2001, the authorities abandoned their policy of maintaining positive real interest rates and implemented a strategy of "interest rate targeting" designed to kickstart economic activity while reducing the cost of servicing the public sector debt.

Monetary policy in Mozambique targets control of broad money growth to curb inflation. Following the partial privatization of the state-owned banks in 1996 and 1997, money growth has been kept under control since the monetary losses of the banking system have no longer underpinned broad money expansion. Money supply growth declined from 55 per cent in 1995 to 35 per cent in 1999, contributing to a dramatic decline in inflation from 45 percent in 1996 to less than 1 percent in 1998, though it subsequently increased to 10 percent in 2000. Despite this slowdown in inflation and the impressive increase in exports, the metical - the national currency - depreciated by 18.6 per cent in 2000 and a further 32 percent in the 2001.

Monetary reform in Malawi included the establishment of a Monetary Policy Committee (MPC) under the auspices of the Reserve Bank of Malawi (RBM), leading to greater transparency and improved policy co-ordination in respect of domestic borrowing.

The Bank of Zambia has shifted the focus of its operations to the increased use of open market operations for credit control, rather than relying on statutory reserve requirements. Because most of the country's debt is in short-term instruments, the bank is trying to broaden the market by issuing medium- and long-term government bonds.

Privatization

There is little interest in privatization in Angola, despite the government's commitment in the IMF staff-monitored program to speed up the sale of state assets. The government has approved a policy document setting out a list of companies to be privatized. However, although most of the small- and medium-sized state-owned enterprises are listed, the larger, and strategic, companies are excluded.

In Botswana, parliament approved a privatization program in 2000 after which the government established a Public Enterprise Evaluation and Privatization Agency (PEEPA), tasked with drawing up a privatization master plan. Companies listed for privatization include the Botswana

Telecommunications Corporation (BTC) and the national carrier, Air Botswana. With technical assistance from the International Finance Corporation (IFC) as lead advisor, necessary reviews and consultations took place, and in December 2000 a preliminary background memorandum was issued inviting expressions of interest from potential strategic investors.

Privatization in South Africa has failed to keep pace with investor aspirations and the government has been sharply criticized for moving too slowly. In the 2001/02 Budget the South African government made provision for a R18.0 billion inflow from the proceeds of the Initial Public Offering (IPO) of Telkom, the country's telecoms provider. However, following the attacks of September 11, the IPO was postponed into 2002.

The Zimbabwe Privatization Agency has announced plans to sell controlling stakes in 12 companies listed on the Zimbabwe Stock Exchange for an estimated Z$22 billion. However the success of this program is in question given the current political and economic situation.

The Lesotho government has placed the privatization of state-owned enterprises high on its priority list. All commercially viable enterprises are to be privatized, with current efforts focused on the banking, insurance and utilities sectors. The privatization of the telecommunications company has already been completed, while a private company is expected to take over the management of the Lesotho Electricity Corporation (LEC) in an effort to restructure it and prepare it for privatization in mid-2002. A study on the future of the Muela hydroelectric power plant was commissioned in 2001, with the objective of assessing the feasibility of privatizing the plant. In addition, the Lesotho Highlands Development Authority will be restructured to enable the power plant to operate as a commercial entity with its own independent accounting records.

Details of Namibia's privatization program (which aims to reduce state-owned equity in parastatals, but falls short of full privatization) are not expected until later 2002 after consultants have completed a review of the operations of the parastatals operations. Initial candidates include Nampower and Telecom Namibia.

Zambia's otherwise successful privatization program received a sharp setback early in 2002 with the announced withdrawal of South African mining house, Anglo American. Of the 279 parastatal companies initially earmarked for privatization, 248 have been sold. The most significant was the sale of Zambia Consolidated Copper Mines (ZCCM), which was finalized in March 2000. But in January 2002, the main participant in ZCCM privatization, Anglo American abandoned plans to develop the Konkola Deep copper mines at a cost of over $1 billion and gave notice of its intention to sell its other Zambian mining interests within a year. The Zambian government has since announced that it will take over the mines temporarily until a new buyer is found.

Seventeen state enterprises are on the list for sale from 2002 including the Zambia Energy Supply Company, Zambia Railways and the Zambia Telecommunications Company. Other state-owned companies that may be privatized in the foreseeable future are the Tanzania-Zambia Railway (Tazara) and Zambia Railways.

The Mozambique government has so far privatized more than 900 parastatals. In the remaining primarily utility companies, the government is seeking private sector participation by way of concessioning, management contracts or direct equity participation.

Privatization has been slow in Malawi and under pressure from the Malawi Congress of

Trade Unions, the government has recently suspended its program altogether. Utilities earmarked for sale include electricity, banking, railway services, Air Malawi and state-owned import and export businesses, which between them employ over 500,000 people and account for 20 percent of the GDP.

The privatization of state assets is progressing slowly in Swaziland. The Royal Swazi National Airways and the commercial arm of the Swaziland Dairy Board have been privatized and the Swaziland Electricity Board and Pigs Peak Hotel will follow. The IMF has urged the government to privatize the Swaziland Development and Savings Bank.

External Accounts

The external position of the sub-region improved marginally in 2001, with the current account deficit declining from 1.9 percent of GDP during 1997-2000 to 0.4 percent in 2001 (Table 2.13 and Figure 2.23).

Botswana's strong external position over the last 20 years reflects the expansion of diamond production combined with prudent macroeconomic policy management. The country's current account surplus increased to 19.3 percent of GDP in 2001 from 12.8 percent during 1997-2000.

South Africa's external balance improved markedly during 2001 on the back of the steep depreciation of the rand and relatively sluggish import growth. In domestic currency terms, the trade surplus increased 53 percent, while the current account swung from a marginal deficit of 1 percent of GDP between 1997 and 2000 to a small surplus of 0.1 percent of GDP in 2001.

In Zimbabwe, the external position deteriorated sharply in 2000 and 2001 reflecting the combined impact of the freeze on foreign assistance,

large capital outflows and declining exports. The current account deficit of 1.6 percent of GDP per year during 1997-2000 narrowed slightly to 1.3 percent of GDP in 2001, largely as a result of a 4 percent decline in imports.

Throughout the 1990s Mozambique's external accounts were dominated by the timing and magnitude of aid disbursements. This is changing with exports growing strongly from $235 million in 1997 to almost $750 million in 2001. The main source of export growth is aluminium processed at the Mozal smelter near Maputo.

During the 1997-2000 period, the current account averaged 16.4 percent of GDP annually widening to 30 percent in 2001.

Namibia's current account situation improved in the second half of the 1990s due to strong export growth — especially diamonds and beef — coupled with sizeable transfers from the SACU revenue pool. In 2001, increased demand for fish and ostrich products after the outbreak of foot and mouth disease in Europe contributed to a current account surplus of 1.1 percent of GDP. This compares with an average surplus of 3.6 percent of GDP between 1997 and 2000.

Malawi's external accounts are closely tied to the fortunes of the tobacco industry, which accounts for 80 percent of exports and approximately 70 percent of foreign exchange earnings. Following the decline in the tobacco price, export earnings fell and the current account recorded an annual average deficit of 6.5 percent of GDP during 1997-2000. In 2001, the trade deficit narrowed marginally on the back of improved tobacco sales and the current account deficit declined to 4.4 percent of GDP.

Zambia's balance of payments deteriorated in 2001 due to depressed prices for its dominant export, copper, the delayed disbursement of donor assistance and increased imports of capital

Table 2.13: Southern Africa: The External Sector

Country	Trade Balance as % of GDP		Current Account as % of GDP		Terms of Trade (%)		Total External Debt as % of GDP		Debt Service as % of Exports	
	Average 1997-2000	2001[a]	Average 1997-2000	2001[a]	Average 1997-2000	2001[a]	Average 1997-2000	2001[a]	Average 1996-1999	2000
ANGOLA	35.2	46.5	-15.7	-2.8	9.3	-9.9	155.1	90.5	15.4	25.1
BOTSWANA	13.0	17.8	12.8	19.3	8.0	-1.1	21.7	21.1	20.6	18.1
LESOTHO	-67.7	-54.0	-24.1	-12.9	7.0	-0.7	65.7	68.4	14.7	29.7
MALAWI	-3.5	-3.3	-6.5	-4.4	-2.1	-0.5	133.4	170.6	...	...
MOZAMBIQUE	-18.3	-18.4	-16.4	-23.6	0.0	-17.8	96.1	88.1	19.8	20.5
NAMIBIA	-6.6	-4.1	3.6	1.1	-4.2	-4.6	4.3	2.2	1.4	1.4
SOUTH AFRICA	2.4	4.0	-1.0	0.1	-0.9	1.5	28.4	29.0	20.7	19.8
SWAZILAND	-9.0	-7.8	-1.8	-4.1	-0.9	0.5	22.7	31.0	...	...
ZAMBIA	-4.0	-5.6	-12.8	-14.3	-2.3	1.5	189.4	141.3	19.4	18.1
ZIMBABWE	1.1	3.8	-1.6	-1.3	7.1	1.8	74.6	72.0	19.2	5.9
SOUTHERN AFRICA	**2.8**	**5.4**	**-1.9**	**-0.4**	**1.0**	**-1.1**	**40.9**	**38.6**	**18.8**	**18.9**

Note: a/ Preliminary estimates.
... Not available.
Sources: ADB Research and Statistics Divisions.

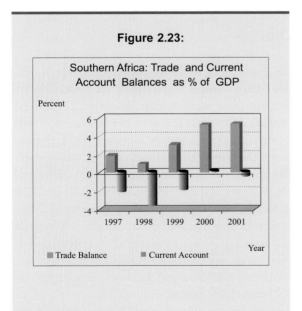

Figure 2.23:

Southern Africa: Trade and Current Account Balances as % of GDP

equipment for the copper mines following the completion of copper privatization. As a result, the current account deficit widened from an annual average of 12.8 percent of GDP during 1997-2000 to 14.3 percent of GDP in 2001.

External Debt

Southern Africa's external debt fell from $65.38 billion in 2000 to $61.60 billion in 2001 reflecting the impact of HIPC as well as reduced inflows to the region. The debt burden also declined with the Debt/GDP ratio falling from 40.4 percent in 2000 to 38.6 percent in 2001 (Figure 2.24).

Mozambique was included in the HIPC initiative in 1998, reaching completion point in June 1999. The country will receive $1.7 billion of cash flow relief in NPV terms (about $3.7 billion in debt relief over time). Mozambique is receiving additional relief under Enhanced HIPC terms for which it reached the decision point in April 2000 and completion point in September 2001. Mozambique became the third country after Bolivia and Uganda to complete this process and will receive $306 million in NPV terms (about $600 million in nominal terms) in debt relief. According to the IMF, as a result of the HIPCs assistance and bilateral debt relief already committed, Mozambique's total external debt, which stood at $3.26 billion at end-2001 has been reduced by some 73 percent.

Angola's external debt peaked at $11.68 billion in 1999, declining to $9.37 billion in 2000 and $8.52 billion in 2001. Buoyant oil prices and increased production reduced new borrowings while a rescheduling agreement was reached with Russia.

South Africa's foreign debt burden has eased since 1994 with limited fresh commitments and rapid export growth while, because of its strong external payments position, Botswana continues to avoid contracting any new debt from commercial creditors. The total external debt stock of Botswana amounted to $1.21 billion at end-2001.

Although the stock of Zimbabwe's foreign debt has remained unchanged since 1997 reflecting the cutback in aid inflows, the country's offshore obligations have risen sharply with the built-up of foreign arrears. By 2001 foreign inflows had virtually ceased and the stock of external debt, excluding arrears, had declined to the 1996 level of $4.68 billion. By the end of 2001, arrears were estimated at over $1 billion and projected to reach $1.5 billion by December 2002.

Namibia is one of Africa's least-indebted countries with a foreign debt totaling $0.08 billion at end-2001. Exposure has declined since 1997 following South Africa's write-off of its loans to Namibia.

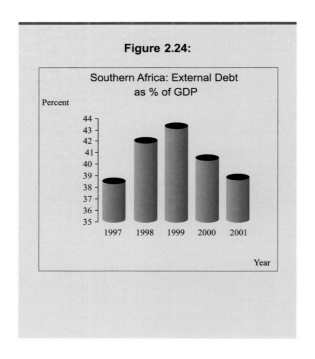

Figure 2.24:

Southern Africa: External Debt as % of GDP

Outlook

2002 is forecast to be another flat year for Southern Africa with GDP growth of no more than 2.8 percent, marginally higher than the 2.2 percent estimated for 2001. The main constraint on growth in the sub-region will be another weak performance by the South African economy, where expansion is likely to be export-led following the steep depreciation of the rand during 2001. GDP is forecast to grow at around 2 percent in 2002. Other factors that may constrain growth include low levels of fixed investment, volatility in portfolio flows, the drought, the continuing economic crisis in Zimbabwe and the worsening impact of the brain drain and of HIV/AIDS.

Growth in Botswana will continue to exceed the continental average slowing to 4.1 percent in

2002 from over 7 percent in 2000/01. Expansion of diamond production has now leveled off and weak demand and prices will constrain GDP growth during 2002, though this will be offset by increased government spending reflecting the deficit budget for 2002-03.

GDP in Zimbabwe will decline for the fourth successive year. Official projections point to a 9 percent fall in GDP, but the severe drought in the first quarter of 2002 points to an even sharper decline in the region of 12 percent. Production in Zimbabwe's leading sector – commercial agriculture – has been disrupted by "fast track" land resettlement while the maize crop, at less than 600 000 tons will be the smallest produced since the severe drought of 1992. Inflation averaged 117 percent in the first quarter of 2002 while the government faces both a serious balance-of-payments crisis, with spiraling foreign arrears and declining exports, and a fiscal crisis arising from the need to finance land reform and costly maize and other food imports.

Mozambique will remain one of Africa's fastest growing economies in 2002 with GDP rising over 9 percent for the second successive year. Growth will be underpinned by the construction of phase two of the Mozal aluminium smelter and the planned gas export pipeline to South Africa. Together these two projects will bring in an estimated $1.5 billion in FDI during 2002-03.

Growth of the Namibian economy in 2002 is expected to rebound with anticipated real GDP growth of 3.5 to 4 percent. Diamond output will rise to 1.6 million carats in 2002 from 1.45 million in 2001 while good rains will boost agricultural output. Exports of fish will increase as a result of higher fishing quotas and a Malaysian-owned clothing plant will boost manufacturing production. The new Skorpion zinc mine is now scheduled to come on stream in 2003.

Angola is well on the way to becoming Africa's second largest oil exporter after Nigeria. Output is scheduled to increase dramatically over the next few years as major new offshore oil projects, specifically the giant Girassol field, are brought into production. Production will increase 20 percent in 2002 alone. The death of the rebel leader, Jonas Savimbi, early in 2002 and the government's military successes in the civil war have raised hopes of an improved political environment that will create a platform for a recovery in the conflict-affected diamond-producing areas. A peace agreement would also open the way for the return of foreign aid and multilateral lending. GDP growth is forecast at over 10 percent in 2003, slowing to 5 percent in 2003. UK-based energy analysts Wood Mackenzie are projecting capital investment in Angola's oil sector of over $17 billion in the five years to 2006.

Lesotho's economy has been slow to recover from the political turmoil it experienced in 1998 and prospects for the medium term remain subdued. GDP growth is likely to remain restrained and growth rates of between 2 percent and 3 percent are expected in 2001 and 2002.

Malawi's growth prospects are closely tied to conditions on the tobacco market since tobacco sales account for over 70 percent of the country's foreign exchange earnings. Global tobacco prices are forecast to firm in 2002 and GDP growth will accelerate modestly to around 3 percent.

Zambia's growth prospects received a sharp setback when South African mining house, Anglo American, announced the cancellation of the planned Konkola Deep copper mine and its withdrawal from the copper in Zambia altogether by the end of 2002. This, combined with weak copper prices and demand and the probability of a slowdown in aid disbursements following the disputed presidential election in December 2001, points to a slowdown in GDP growth during 2002. Growth is expected to halve to no more than 2 percent in 2002 recovering modestly in 2003 as copper prices pick up.

West Africa

West Africa is made up of fifteen countries, divided into two distinct groups:

The CFA zone comprises eight countries – Benin, Burkina Faso, Côte d'Ivoire, Guinea Bissau, Mali, Niger, Senegal and Togo. The main distinguishing feature of the CFA zone is that the countries pegged their currencies to the French Franc (and since January 1999 to the Euro).

The other seven – Cape Verde, Ghana, Guinea, the Gambia, Nigeria, Liberia and Sierra Leone – make up the non-CFA zone. Non-CFA countries account for some 60 percent of the total regional GDP and 70 percent of the population.

The sub-region is dominated by Nigeria which accounted two thirds of total exports in 2001 – a reflection of its rich endowment of crude oil and gas. Most other countries in the sub-region depend mainly on agricultural exports. In 2001, regional GDP constituted about 14 percent of the continent's total, of which Nigeria contributed some 54 percent. Population of the region was estimated at 228 million, or 28 percent of the continent's total (Table 2.1); Nigeria accounted for 51 percent of the regional total and 14 percent of the continental total.

With GNI per capita of $337 the West Africa ranks behind the Southern and North Africa Regions in terms of living standards, but ahead of the Central and East Africa Regions.

Recent Economic Trends

In 2001, growth in West Africa increased modestly to 3.5 percent from an average of 3.2 a year during 1997-2000 (Table 2.14 and Figure 2.25). Faster growth in Nigeria was the main impetus behind the region's marginally improved performance.

In non-CFA economies growth rose to 3.9 percent in 2001, from the yearly average of 2.9 percent during 1997-2000 (Figure 2.26), again reflecting faster Nigerian expansion. Growth remained weak in Ghana at an estimated 3.9 percent, down from the yearly average of 4.3 percent during 1997-2000. The factors responsible for the marked slowdown in 2000, when output increased 3.7 percent, continued to constrain performance during 2001. The main adverse influence was a sharp deterioration in the terms of trade as cocoa and gold prices weakened while oil prices rose rapidly. This gave rise to higher inflation and rapid currency depreciation that created fiscal imbalances and excessive monetary growth.

Nigeria's economic performance began to improve in 2000 following the return to civilian rule and the surge in oil prices. GDP growth increased from one percent in 1999 to 3.8 percent in 2000 and 4 percent in 2001. The key driver was the oil price which rose from $12.8 a barrel in 1998 to $28.5 in 2000, moderating somewhat to $24.4 a barrel in 2001. Disagreement with the IMF over the use of oil windfall earnings endangered the staff-monitored program agreed in 2000, which eventually lapsed early in 2002.

Sierra Leone's three-year downturn was brought to an end by the improved security situation and output rebounded to grow at 4.5 percent in 2001 compared with the average annual contraction of 5.6 percent during 1997-2000. The economy is benefiting from the administration's successful completion of an IMF supported program in 2000.

GDP growth rates increased in Gambia and Guinea Bissau in 2001 compared with the previous four years, but in Cape Verde and Guinea output growth slowed. In 2001, Cape Verde suffered from weaker economic activity in neighbor-

Table 2.14: West Africa: Gross Domestic Product and Export Performances

Country	Real GDP Growth Rate (%)		GDP Per Capita (US$)		Real Export Growth (%)		Exports[b] Per Capita (US$)	
	Average 1997-2000	2001[a]	Average 1997-2000	2001[a]	Average 1997-2000	2001[a]	Average 1997-2000	2001[a]
BENIN	5.2	5.5	375	364	3.5	-10.8	102	104
BURKINA FASO	4.9	5.8	212	198	9.4	4.8	26	23
CAPE VERDE	7.1	3.3	1327	1297	3.5	11.5	292	317
COTE D'IVOIRE	2.8	-1.5	688	564	3.5	3.3	304	252
GAMBIA	5.1	5.7	339	304	7.1	38.6	161	156
GHANA	4.3	3.9	365	275	4.4	-0.5	130	138
GUINEA	3.7	2.9	438	346	-1.9	22.5	97	95
GUINEA-BISSAU	-1.6	4.0	197	170	40.2	9.2	45	66
LIBERIA	...	...	...	...	...	...	...	...
MALI	5.8	0.1	239	221	15.6	4.3	56	58
NIGER	3.2	5.0	189	173	1.7	4.0	31	25
NIGERIA	2.5	4.0	329	355	-1.8	-1.3	141	168
SENEGAL	5.4	5.7	501	478	3.8	5.3	160	141
SIERRA LEONE	-5.6	4.5	173	157	-3.9	9.9	24	25
TOGO	1.0	3.0	323	266	6.8	1.9	104	91
WEST AFRICA	**3.2**	**3.5**	**350**	**337**	**0.6**	**1.2**	**129**	**139**

Notes: a/ Preliminary estimates.
         b/ Exports of Goods and Nonfactor Services at Market Prices.
... Not available.
Sources: ADB Research and Statistics Divisions.

Figure 2.25:

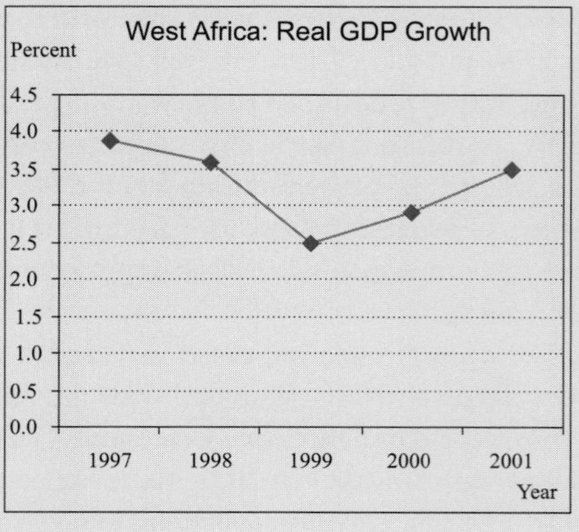

West Africa: Real GDP Growth

Figure 2.26:

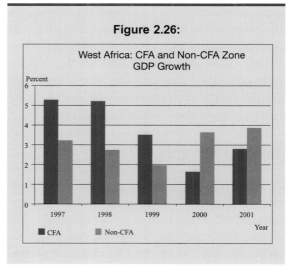

West Africa: CFA and Non-CFA Zone GDP Growth

ing countries that reduced inflows of workers' remittances - the largest source of foreign exchange. This had negative implications for domestic demand and growth. The Gambia's faster growth of 5.7 percent in 2001 was attributable to good harvests, a dynamic construction sector and increased revenues from tourism. In Guinea, the growth rate fell in 2001 due to a sharp deterioration in terms of trade and insecurity on its borders, which adversely affected the mining and agricultural sectors with knock-on effects for the economy as a whole.

In the CFA zone, economic activity slowed in 2001 with GDP growth of 2.8 percent compared with a yearly average of 3.9 percent during 1997-2000. Côte d'Ivoire, its largest economy, was plunged into recession by the combination of political instability, a freeze on foreign aid and adverse terms of trade, notably lower cocoa and coffee prices and higher fuel import costs. As a result, GDP contracted by 1.5 percent in 2001. This reversed the trend experienced following the 1994 devaluation of the CFA franc, when GDP growth averaged 5.5 percent annually.

In 2001, improved cotton output following more favorable weather conditions boosted growth in Benin, Burkina Faso and Togo. However, Mali's economy was hit by the spinoff from political instability in neighboring Côte d'Ivoire combined with the crisis in the cotton sector and the drought-induced decline in agricultural output. Cotton producers in Mali boycotted production in 2000/2001 in protest against the low farm-gate prices paid by the state-run Compagnie Malienne pour le Développement des Textiles (CMDT), the sole cotton buyer.

In Senegal, notwithstanding deteriorating terms of trade, the economy continued to grow at a rapid pace in 2001, following larger harvests and boosted by rapid expansion in the construction and telecommunication sectors, which offset the sluggish performance of services.

Economic performance improved in Guinea-Bissau and Benin in 2001, despite deteriorating terms of trade. Guinea-Bissau's economy grew 4 percent in 2001 compared with an annual average decline of 1.6 percent during 1997-2000. In Benin, higher agricultural production including cotton, pushed the growth rate to 5.5 percent in 2001, slightly above the four-year average of 5.2 percent for the period 1997 to 2000. Benin's above-average performance, achieved despite lower prices for its chief export cotton, reflects the impact of improved macroeconomic policies and structural reforms.

Increased economic activity in West Africa in 2001 was accompanied by marginal rise in inflation to 7.7 percent in 2001 from 6.3 percent during 1997-2000 (Table 2.15 and Figure 2.27).

In Ghana, inflation more than doubled in 2000 to exceed 25 percent, largely as a result of lax monetary and fiscal polices and very rapid currency depreciation. While double-digit inflation was the norm for Ghana over the last decade, the major reduction in 1998-9 to an average of 13.5 percent could not be sustained, largely due to fiscal and monetary expansion ahead of the December 2000 elections. Inflation accelerated further in 2001 to average 33 percent, but the trend was downwards with the year-end rate falling to 23.5 percent from 40.6 percent in December 2000.

In Nigeria, inflation was tamed in the first part of 2000, but fiscal expansion and rapid money supply growth stoked inflationary pressures during the latter half of 2000 and throughout 2001. The rate of inflation rose to 14 percent in December 2000 to bring the yearly average to 8 percent for the period 1997-2000 increasing further to average 15.7 percent in 2001.

After several years of double-digit inflation in

Table 2.15: West Africa: Macroeconomic Management Indicators

Country	Inflation (%)		Fiscal Balance as % of GDP		Gross Domestic			
					Investment as % of GDP		Savings as % of GDP	
	Average 1997-2000	2001[a/]	Average 1997-2000	2001[a/]	Average 1997-2000	2001[a/]	Average 1997-2000	2001[a/]
BENIN	3.4	5.2	0.6	-0.8	17.9	19.4	6.1	6.9
BURKINA FASO	1.5	5.4	-3.8	-6.1	29.4	32.5	10.9	8.9
CAPE VERDE	3.7	3.0	-11.4	-4.0	26.1	32.0	-8.7	-10.1
COTE D'IVOIRE	3.0	4.4	-2.3	-1.2	15.2	14.1	21.8	19.8
GAMBIA	2.1	3.5	-3.4	-1.0	16.7	17.7	2.9	2.7
GHANA	20.0	39.5	-8.6	-8.2	23.4	23.7	5.8	4.7
GUINEA	4.6	6.9	-2.5	-3.2	22.2	24.2	18.7	21.2
GUINEA-BISSAU	15.9	3.3	-11.9	-13.7	17.5	26.2	-3.2	-0.5
LIBERIA	10.1	10.0	...	...	...	...	...	...
MALI	0.4	4.5	-3.0	-8.9	21.1	20.7	11.6	10.5
NIGER	2.0	4.2	-3.7	-4.7	10.7	11.8	2.9	2.8
NIGERIA	8.0	19.4	-4.1	-1.0	21.8	25.0	24.7	27.5
SENEGAL	1.1	1.9	-0.4	-1.2	17.8	19.4	10.4	10.5
SIERRA LEONE	20.9	-0.9	-9.0	-13.8	2.8	20.0	-5.0	-4.0
TOGO	2.8	0.5	-3.9	-4.1	19.1	20.5	5.0	5.6
WEST AFRICA	**6.3**	**7.7**	**-4.0**	**-2.4**	**19.8**	**22.5**	**17.7**	**19.8**

Note: a/ Preliminary estimates.
... Not available.
Sources: ADB Research and Statistics Divisions.

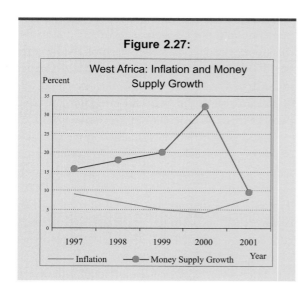

Figure 2.27:

West Africa: Inflation and Money Supply Growth

Sierra Leone, the authorities managed to stabilize prices in 2000 when consumer prices actually declined 0.9 percent despite wage awards and a surge in government spending. The decline in inflation was partly attributed to a strong appreciation of the real effective exchange rate and to a tight monetary policy. There was an inflationary rebound in 2001 when prices rose 8 percent.

In the Gambia, inflation was restrained by increased food production and the rate averaged 2.1 percent annually during the 1997-2000 period. However, in 2001, inflation resurfaced and prices increased 5.5 percent.

After experiencing two years of double-digit inflation due to the devaluation of the CFA franc, Côte d'Ivoire regained relative price stability from

1996. During the period 1997-2000, inflation averaged only 3 percent a year, partly reflecting good harvests and stable food prices. In 2001, however, inflationary pressures re-emerged as fuel and food prices increased and the rate averaged 4.4 percent.

In Senegal, following the depreciation-induced double-digit inflation in 1994, the monetary authorities succeeded in re-establishing price stability. Inflation remained at 1.1 percent annually between 1997 and 2000, accelerating modestly to 1.9 percent in 2001. This marginal increase was the result of monetary and fiscal measures including the introduction of a single-rate VAT and the liberalization in petroleum prices.

Domestic investment increased across the region in 2001 in all countries except Côte d'Ivoire, Liberia and Mali. Following the decline in the investment rate to an average of 20 percent of GDP during 1997-2000, reflecting the weaker fiscal stance in most of the countries, and socio-political instability in some others, domestic investment rose to 22.5 percent of GDP in 2001 (Table 2.15).

Policy Developments

Fiscal Policy

Fiscal balances in West Africa improved during 2001, with the budget deficit narrowing significantly to 2.4 percent of GDP from the yearly average of 4 percent during 1997-2000 (Table 2.15 and Figure 2.28).

Ghana's fiscal performance remained poor in 2001 with the deficit estimated at 8.2 percent of GDP, only marginally below the yearly average of 8.6 percent of GDP during 1997-2000. This occurred despite the government's strenuous efforts to raise domestic revenue by increasing the VAT rate by 25 percent to 12.5 percent. Tax revenues also benefited from two other taxes intro-

duced in 2000 — an ECOWAS community levy of 0.5 percent of the *cif* value of imports originating from non-ECOWAS states in April 2000; and a special tax of 20 percent on so-called non-essential imports.

In 2001, a number of new taxes were imposed including a development levy, the profit tax on mining firms and increased airport tax. In February 2001, petroleum prices were doubled in order to staunch the operating losses of the state-owned refinery, while similar increases in electricity and water tariffs took effect in May 2001 to curtail losses in these utilities.

Nigeria's budget deficit declined to 1 percent of GDP in 2001, down from the average of 4 percent during 1997-2000. This reflected strong revenue growth due to higher oil prices, but a number of questions have been raised about the calculation of the deficit, which excludes parastatal losses and understates debt-servicing obligations. Public spending increased markedly to 23.7 percent of GDP in 2001 compared with less than 20

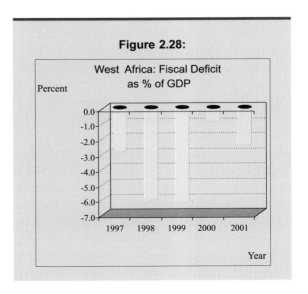

Figure 2.28:

West Africa: Fiscal Deficit as % of GDP

percent in 1999. Fiscal sustainability is under threat because of the country's fiscal federalism arrangements which require the federal government to disburse oil windfall revenues to state and local governments. Under the current revenue-sharing arrangements (guaranteed by the Constitution) the states and local governments receive full and automatic access to their share of oil revenues. In the absence of corresponding limits on spending, there is no mechanism formally to involve states and local governments in contributing to fiscal stability – for example, by saving windfall gains from oil revenues.

Sierra Leone's precarious security situation forced the government to increase security-related spending. As a result, the fiscal deficit widened to 13.8 percent of GDP in 2001 from an annual average of 9 percent during 1997-2000.

In Guinea the government's fiscal position in 2001 was affected by the economic slowdown resulting in lower customs revenues and reduced revenues from VAT. With public expenditure increasing in line with the government's social service obligations under its HIPC agreement with donors and multilateral lenders, the fiscal deficit widened to 3.2 percent of GDP in 2001, from an average of 2.5 percent between 1997 and 2000.

Faster economic growth boosted official revenues in The Gambia and the fiscal situation improved. The fiscal deficit narrowed to 1 percent of GDP in 2001 from an average of 3.4 percent of GDP in 1997-2000. Reduced inflows of foreign finance forced the government to cut capital spending, which more than offset higher current spending and lower revenues from custom receipts. Government overspent in the first quarter of 2001, as it extended financial support to three commercial banks. Conscious of the need to raise more revenues, the authorities increased gasoline, kerosene and diesel prices and reduced the number and range of customs exemptions.

The fiscal position in the CFA franc zone improved slightly in 2001, despite slower economic growth, largely due to stricter controls on public spending. In Côte d'Ivoire, two years of economic recession eroded the tax base and resulted in a weakened fiscal position. The freeze on aid disbursements and multilateral lending forced the government to cut capital expenditure and revise its initial budget. Given continued financial constraints, the government revised the 2001 budget. To compensate for lower export revenues and custom duties export taxes on cocoa were increased, while a unified 20 percent value-added tax was imposed. At the same time, VAT exemptions were reduced and a 5 percent customs duty imposed on all imports covered by the investment code. In response to donor criticism of some of these measures, seen as a retreat from earlier promises to liberalize cocoa marketing, the government lowered the cocoa export tax to 160 CFA francs per kilogram from the previously announced higher rate of 200 CFA francs.

In Senegal, the government was able to meet its fiscal targets in both 2000 and 2001, due to improved revenue collection and a cutback in capital expenditure. The fiscal deficit stood at 1.2 percent of GDP in 2001, as the revenue base increased to reach the 17 percent floor of GDP as stipulated in the West African Economic and Monetary Union convergence criteria for 2000. A pass-through mechanism for petroleum products that will adjust prices according to developments in the oil market has been re-introduced while the two VAT rates have been unified. In an attempt to cushion the impact of tax increases on the poor, the price for small bottles of butane gas has been kept unchanged while low income families have been exempted from the unified VAT rate for electricity and water. To improve tax collection efficiency the government has introduced the single taxpayer identification number in March and plans to streamline and reduce tax exemptions.

Benin's fiscal targets in 2001 were reached because revenues were stronger than expected due to improved tax administration while expenditure fell below budget.

In Burkina Faso revenues fell below the 17 percent of GDP WAEMU convergence criteria in 2001. The fall in revenue reflected reduced workers' remittances, lower agricultural production and a decline in custom revenues following the introduction of the common external tariff. Expenditures were under control, with the wages and salaries bill running higher than envisaged.

Mali's fiscal stance weakened when the government opted to maintain oil prices at March 2000 levels, to cushion the impact of surging oil prices on domestic consumers. Revenues were on track in the first three-quarters of 2000, but fell short of projections in the final quarter. Spending targets were met until the forth quarter, when government spending accelerated. In 2001, the fiscal position deteriorated significantly in light of increased election-related spending and the crisis in the cotton sector. The fiscal deficit expanded to 8.9 percent of GDP in 2001 from the average 3.6 percent between 1997 and 2000.

Monetary Policy

Price stability was the main objective of monetary policy, which was also directed at achieving foreign exchange stability in some countries.

In Ghana, the year 2000 was a particularly difficult one for the monetary authorities. The government's twin aims were to slow inflation and stabilize the *cedi*. During the year 2000, money supply growth overshot the broad money supply (M2+) growth target of 16 percent by a large

margin to reach 39.8 percent by the end of the year. The main impulse for excessive monetary expansion came from the government, which borrowed heavily from the banking system. As the money supply increased in 2000, interest rates edged upwards with the yield on 91-day Treasury Bills rising from 36.7 percent in June to a peak of 40.6 percent before declining to 38.1 percent by end-2000. Commercial banks increased their base rates accordingly.

In 2001, the new government targeted money supply growth of 32 percent, but in the first 8 months of the year public sector borrowing increased almost 80 percent. This was partially offset by an 11 percent increase in bank lending to the private sector, which was well below the inflation rate of 33 percent.

Ghana operates a fully flexible foreign exchange rate system under which the foreign exchange of the *cedi* is market-determined. At the end of 1999, the inter-bank rate and the *bureaux de change* rate were very similar, indicating a market that was relatively free of restrictions. The terms of trade shock in 2000 – falling export prices and higher oil import costs – coupled with the reduced inflows of foreign aid, caused the sharp depreciation of the *cedi,* which fell 57 percent against the US dollar in 2000 following a 49 percent depreciation in 1999. In 2001, the cedi lost a further 24 percent of its value against the US dollar.

In Nigeria, monetary policy was loosened in 2000 in an attempt to reflate the economy and the Central Bank of Nigeria lowered its benchmark interest rate by a percentage point in May 2000, following this with a similar 100 basis points cut in August. By the end of December the rediscount rate was down to 14 percent while the reserve requirement ratio had been reduced by 2 percentage points to 10 percent. Despite accelerating inflation in the second half of the year, the central bank maintained an unchanged monetary stance, allowing money supply growth to escalate to 40 percent. Monetary policy was tightened in January 2001, when interest rates were raised gradually and bank reserve and the liquid assets ratios increased. But monetary policy proved to be less effective than expected; money supply growth maintained its upward trend reaching 23 percent in September, despite the increase in the CBN's minimum rediscount rate of 20.5 percent at the end of 2001 from 14 percent a year earlier. Interest rates declined generally in 2000, reflecting the liquidity overhang in the financial system. Money market interest rates rose from 17 to 20 percent in early 2001 to 35 percent in September.

Domestic credit in Cape Verde rose 16 percent in 2000 and net credit to the government increased 21 percent reflecting the central bank's limited autonomy.

Throughout the year, a loose monetary policy was maintained to accommodate a budget deficit of 18.9 percent of GDP. In an attempt to curb credit expansion the central bank increased the rediscount rate by a percentage point to 9.5 percent in December 2000 and by another two percentage points in April 2001. Broad money was driven mainly by the central government's increased borrowing to fund the deficit and higher private credit.

Greater fiscal discipline in Sierra Leone reduced government's borrowing from the central bank and consequently broad money supply growth decelerated sharply to 10 percent in 2000 from more than 40 percent in 1999. In Gambia the monetary authority intervened heavily during 2000 to support the currency. Subsequently broad money growth accelerated to 35 percent. To reverse this trend, the authorities set a money sup-

ply growth ceiling of 8 percent, while targeting an increase in foreign exchange reserves to cover 5.3 months of imports.

West African CFA-zone countries belong to the Western African Economic Monetary Union and the monetary policy is conducted at regional level by the Central Bank of West African States (BCEAO). The main monetary policy goal is price stability and to maintain sufficient foreign exchange reserves to back the CFA franc fixed exchange rate against the euro and ensure free convertibility. The BCEAO tightened monetary policy in mid-2000 to reign in inflationary pressures stemming from higher domestic credit expansion. It raised the repurchase rate and the discount rate by 75 basis points each in mid-June 2000, to fight the monetary overhang.

The central bank also raised reserve requirement ratios and increased the numbers of assets for which reserves are required, in a bid to curb money supply expansion. In Côte d'Ivoire, in order to limit the monetization of the budget deficit, which fuels inflation, the government is required to eliminate the outstanding debt with the central bank by early 2002. In Senegal, notwithstanding the policies of the BCEAO, money supply rose 10.4 percent in 2000, almost double the rate of nominal GDP growth, on the back of a 28.6 percent surge in credit to the economy. The increase was mainly due to financial problems at SENELEC and SONACOS, which led to a rise in domestic borrowing and a run up in arrears, respectively.

Privatization

Structural reform, including privatization, is expected to pick up pace in West Africa especially in telecommunications, as many countries open up to mobile telephony.

Ghana's current privatization program started in 1995, initially attracting international attention with major sales such as Ashanti Goldfields Corporation, Ghana Telecom, Social Security Bank and the Ghana Ports and Harbors Authority. However, out of the 139 enterprises earmarked for divestiture in 1995, only 60 had been sold by end-2000. Early in 2001, the new government decided to accelerate the divestiture program, though only after first carrying out a financial and managerial audit of the Divestiture Implementation Committee (DIC) — the body responsible for the program. The government determined also to audit and review some divested companies to investigate allegations of fraud and corruption. These procedures have slowed the privatization process and only Mim Timber Company Limited out of 15 enterprises the government expected to sell in 2001 had been sold by August 2001.

Since July 1999, Nigeria has been implementing a three-phase privatization program, but progress has been uneven and slow. Phase one involved the sale of the government's shareholdings in a dozen commercially viable enterprises, including banks and petroleum marketing, cement and insurance companies. By December 2000, this had been largely completed. In the second phase, which should have been completed in 2000, the focus was on telecommunications, including the award of three GSM mobile telephone licences and the sale of the state's equity stake in the telephone company, NITEL. Two GSM licences were auctioned during 2001 but the subsequent sale of a 51 percent stake in NITEL collapsed when the buyers were unable to fund the purchase. The government secured a privatization support credit from the World Bank that will help speed up the program from 2002.

Gambia recently adopted a Privatization Act, enabling the authorities to step up the privatization process. It hopes to raise 20 million dalasi from privatization to reduce public debt. The privatization process all but stalled in Cape Verde in 2000, but the government has since promised to accelerate the divestiture process in 2001-02. Expected privatizations include the state airline (TACV) the ports authority, the municipal transport operator TRANSCOR, the ship repair facility, the inter-island shipping company ARCA Verde, two fishing service firms and the country's leading food importing and distribution business (EMPA).

In Côte d'Ivoire too privatization is making slow progress. The government has yet to privatize the SIR refinery, to restructure its postal savings services and the textile firm CIDT Nouvelle. Nor has it yet finalized the take-over of Air Ivoire by Air France, and although the audit of the Caisse Autonome d'Amortissement (CAA) has been concluded, no decisions have yet been made regarding its restructuring.

In Senegal, to eliminate structural problems at Société nationale d'électricité du Sénégal (SENELEC) (large deficits and poor generating capacity) and Société nationale de commercialisation des oléagineux du Sénégal (SONACOS) (large deficits and debts) the government agreed to privatize the two state-run enterprises. SENELEC was due to have been sold by the end of 2001 and SONACOS in late 2003. The new administration has shortlisted a further 11 enterprises for privatization.

In Benin, the government, with technical assistance from the World Bank, plans to privatize the cotton state-run enterprise SONAPRA. But little progress has been made in privatizing public utilities in telecommunications and port management and these sales are unlikely to proceed in the near future.

The Burkinabe government sold two mobile-phone licenses in 2000 to enhance competition in the telecommunications sector. It also privatized five state-owned enterprises, including Air Burkina. Progress in liberalizing the cotton industry has been slow. The government has promised to privatize the telecommunications company ONATEL, electricity company SONABEL and the divestiture of the petroleum distributor SONABHY is to be completed in 2002.

The privatization of the Malian cotton sector remains long over-due and a restructuring of the CMDT is necessary to avoid future crisis in the cotton sector. Privatization gained momentum in Niger with the sale of two mobile phone licenses in 2000 for 8.5 billion CFA franc. The government is also committed to restructure the National Post and Savings Office (ONPE). There are plans to privatize the telecommunication company SONITEL, to grant concessions to private operators for NIGELEC and to restructure the energy sector by privatizing SONIDEP.

In 2000, Togo liberalized the distribution and sale of electricity launching a program to restructure the banking, telecommunications and postal services industries.

External Accounts

West Africa's external balance improved in 2001 with the current account deficit falling to 3.4 percent of GDP from the annual average of 3.9 percent over 1997-2000 (Table 2.16 and Figure 2.29).

Ghana's balance-of-payments on current account improved marginally in 2001 when the deficit declined to 6.9 percent of GDP from over 8 percent in 2000. The trade deficit widened to $900 million from $800 million in 2000 as import growth was not matched by higher exports. But private transfers increased helping to finance the rise in imports.

Nigeria's current account swung from deficit to surplus in 2000 reflecting the massive increase in the trade surplus from $1.4 billion in 1999 to over $8 billion in 2000. The main driver behind this improvement was the sharp rise in oil prices. Due to the decline in the oil price, the current account went into a slight deficit in 2001. The current account balance fell to –0.8 percent of GDP from 5.8 percent in 2000.

In 2001, Sierra Leone's exports suffered because of abandoned cocoa and coffee plantations in rebel held areas and the suspension of rutile and bauxite mining. On the other hand, imports increased driven by a recovery in domestic demand. As a result, the trade balance deteriorated sharply, while the current account deficit more than doubled to reach 18 percent of GDP.

Although Côte d'Ivoire's trade account remained in strong surplus in 2001 at more than 1.5 billion ($1.8 billion surplus in 2000), the current account deteriorated markedly to a deficit of over $200 million from one of only $13 million the previous year. This reflected the decline in services income on the back of political uncertainty, causing the current account balance to deteriorate. The current account deficit widened to 5.5 percent of GDP from the annual average decline of 4.6 percent of GDP over the period 1997-2000.

The real effective exchange rate appreciated in WAEMU countries in 1999 and 2000, resulting in a loss in export competitiveness. This partly explains the decline in merchandise exports as a share of GDP in Benin, Burkina Faso and Mali. Weaker cotton exports, contracting workers' remittances, sustained growth in capital goods imports and higher fuel bills led to deterioration in Burkina Faso's external account last year. Continued weak economic performance in Côte d'Ivoire and the return of Burkinabe nationals from Côte

Table 2.16: West Africa: The External Sector

Country	Trade Balance as % of GDP		Current Account as % of GDP		Terms of Trade (%)		Total External Debt as % of GDP		Debt Service as % of Exports	
	Average 1997-2000	2001[a]	Average 1997-2000	2001[a]	Average 1997-2000	2001[a]	Average 1997-2000	2001[a]	Average 1996-1999	2000
BENIN	-10.4	-10.7	-7.2	-7.5	-3.9	16.6	59.7	63.9	14.4	16.4
BURKINA FASO	-12.3	-12.2	-9.4	-9.7	-2.4	12.2	59.2	66.4	20.2	21.7
CAPE VERDE	-34.4	-34.8	-11.7	-15.3	20.9	-5.1	44.4	48.0	22.2	27.9
COTE D'IVOIRE	12.2	11.1	-4.6	-5.5	-4.4	-7.0	111.7	123.3	30.5	24.5
GAMBIA	-16.0	-15.3	-4.0	-2.4	0.8	3.6	110.7	129.9	11.9	12.6
GHANA	-15.5	-16.9	-10.0	-6.9	-2.7	5.0	95.3	137.9	22.4	22.2
GUINEA	2.7	4.3	-3.5	-2.6	6.2	-7.6	95.4	...	21.9	21.3
GUINEA-BISSAU	-7.8	-14.3	-10.7	-22.8	10.0	4.3	373.9	336.0	12.8	37.8
LIBERIA	8.8	8.2	0.3	0.4	2.0	1.9	64.0	...	13.0	12.1
MALI	-0.8	0.2	-8.4	-13.1	-5.5	14.3	111.3	105.9	17.1	13.0
NIGER	-2.3	-3.4	-4.0	-5.4	-5.0	1.1	81.9	74.5	22.1	26.8
NIGERIA	10.7	9.9	-1.7	-0.8	15.0	-6.6	88.1	73.4	13.3	9.1
SENEGAL	-7.2	-8.6	-5.4	-5.1	0.2	0.9	74.8	74.0	17.4	14.1
SIERRA LEONE	-3.2	-16.3	-5.1	-11.3	-0.3	0.9	291.5	287.2	44.5	47.9
TOGO	-9.7	-10.8	-11.5	-13.2	-2.4	-5.2	87.9	81.1	9.5	26.2
WEST AFRICA	**4.3**	**4.0**	**-3.9**	**-3.4**	**6.3**	**-4.0**	**91.2**	**87.1**	**18.0**	**13.5**

Note: a/ Preliminary estimates
... Not available.
Sources: ADB Research and Statistics Divisions.

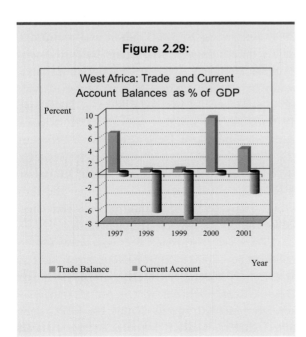

Figure 2.29:

West Africa: Trade and Current Account Balances as % of GDP

d'Ivoire undermined workers remittances for 2001.

External Debt

West Africa's total debt stock rose marginally to $71.27 billion in 2001 from $67.52 billion the year before. The debt burden, however, eased slightly as the debt/GDP ratio continued its declining trend since the beginning of the 1990s (Figure 2.30).

All except three West African countries are classified as severely indebted. The three exceptions, grouped into the moderately indebted category are: Benin, Senegal and Togo. The main debtor countries, in terms of the amount of debt, are Nigeria, Côte d'Ivoire and Ghana. Currently, the IMF and World Bank are supporting debt-relief packages for Benin, Burkina Faso, the

Gambia, Guinea, Guinea-Bissau, Mali, Niger and Senegal. Ghana and Côte d'Ivoire are yet to reach the decision point of their respective HIPC arrangements. Although Sierra Leone and Liberia are considered heavily indebted poor countries they have not yet signed up to the HIPC scheme.

Ghana's external debt stood at $6.17 billion at end-2001, of which 62 percent was owed to multilateral institutions, 25 percent to bilateral creditors and 13 percent to commercial banks. The total debt represented about 90 percent of total GNI for the year, which qualified the country for the Enhanced HIPC debt relief initiative. The NPV of external debt to fiscal revenue and the NPV of external debt to export criteria would have been 557 percent and 152 percent respectively at end-2000 after the application of traditional debt relief mechanisms, both above the enhanced HIPC thresholds of 250 percent and 150 percent respectively. In the 2001 budget, the Kufour administration announced its intention of seeking relief under the Initiative. Based on IMF calculations Ghana's debt burden will reduce significantly when it qualifies for assistance with the ratio of debt service to exports declining from 17 percent in 2001 to 11 percent by 2003 stabilizing at that level. The IMF estimates that assistance under the enhanced HIPC could translate into an average annual debt service savings of about $170 million annually over the 2002-2020 period.

Nigeria's foreign debt at the end of 2001 was estimated at $31.34 billion, or 93 percent of GNI. Bilateral creditors hold 57 per cent, followed by private creditors with 26 percent and multilateral institutions with 17 per cent. Nigeria, which does not qualify for debt relief under the Enhanced HIPC Initiative, obtained a non-concessional rescheduling of its debt in an agreement with the Paris Club of official creditors in December 2000. The agreement consolidated arrears at end-July

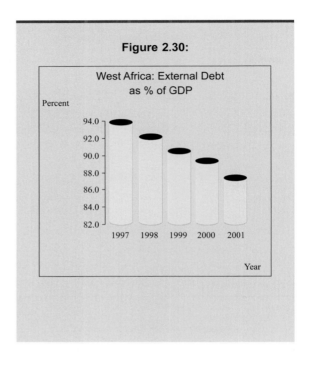

Figure 2.30:

West Africa: External Debt as % of GDP

2000 amounting to $21.3 billion and maturities falling due during the IMF stand-by Agreement (August 2000-July 2001) of $300 million. As a result of this agreement, Nigeria obtained cash savings estimated at $1.6 billion in 2000 and $970 million for the first half of 2001. Nigeria currently operates a Debt Conversion Program (DCP) as part of its debt management strategy. By the end of 2000, external debts valued at $56.7 million had been redeemed under the auction system, while $1.2 million were cancelled under the out-of-auction arrangements.

Côte d'Ivoire's foreign debt rose from $11.43 billion at end-2000 to $13.01 billion a year later as arrears accumulated. Senegal, one of the three West African countries that is not classified as severely indebted, is still eligible for HIPC debt relief, reaching decision point under the enhanced

HIPC initiative in June 2001. Interim HIPC relief is estimated to free 23.4 billion CFA francs to be channeled into poverty-reduction programs.

Benin reached decision point in July 2001 and its external public debt has declined significantly since 1999, as donors and multilateral creditors provided financial assistance of 5.6 billion CFA and 18.7 billion CFA respectively. Its debt indicators are expected to improve markedly in 2002-03 once it reaches completion point under the scheme. Burkina Faso's foreign debt exposure increased in 2000 with external public debt as a share of GDP jumping to 67.2, though it still remains well below the regional average. It has already fulfilled the conditions for reaching the completion point under both the original HIPC initiative and enhanced HIPC initiative and is benefiting from debt relief.

Guinea-Bissau is by far the most heavily indebted West African country, with external debt exceeding 340 percent of GDP. In 2000, the IMF and World Bank agreed to support a debt-relief package under the enhanced HIPC initiative with total debt service relief amounting to $790 million. In September 2000, Mali reached the completion point under the original HIPC initiative and the decision point under the enhanced HIPC initiative, with debt relief amounting to $523 million. Accordingly, its foreign debt to GDP ratio should come down significantly from the current level of 125.3 percent.

At the end of December 2000, Niger reached its decision point and the IMF and World Bank agreed to support a debt service relief package totaling $890 million, which will free an estimated $40 million per year for poverty alleviation related spending. Subsequently, external public debt is estimated to drop by 8 percent as a share of GDP to stand at 73.3 percent in 2001.

Outlook

Future growth prospects are mixed. Lower oil prices will boost growth in oil-importing nations but constrain expansion in the region's lead economy, Nigeria, and the other oil exporters. All primary product exporters will be adversely affected by the global slowdown in 2002, but thereafter the regional economy should regain its momentum, subject to the continued implementation of appropriate structural and macroeconomic reforms.

In non-CFA countries economic performance in 2002 will depend on the pace and extent of global economic recovery and its impact on commodity prices as well as on the amount of financial assistance, including debt relief. The slump in tourism and the travel industry will affect service-dependent economies such as Cape Verde and overall, economic growth in non-CFA countries is expected to increase only marginally in 2002.

Ghana's successful political transition in 2000, which has also brought about positive changes in macroeconomic policy, augurs well for the deepening of the reform process. Ghana will benefit also from access to the HIPC initiative with growth forecast to accelerate to 5 percent in 2002.

In Nigeria, weaker oil prices and the collapse of the IMF agreement point to sluggish growth of around 3 percent in 2002. Inflation is forecast to accelerate in the run-up to the presidential and national assembly elections early in 2003. Government spending will rise sharply and the Naira is likely to come under pressure in late 2002 and early 2003 reflecting political uncertainty ahead of the elections.

Sierra Leone is likely to experience another year of strong growth in 2002 with GDP forecast to increase 6 percent, provided the improved security situation is maintained. Growth will be boosted also by donor and multilateral assistance in the form of PRGF programs or debt relief under the HIPC initiative.

In 2002, growth in West African's CFA franc region is expected to rebound to about 4 percent as Côte d'Ivoire's economy recovers, with positive spinoff effects for neighboring economies, dependent on workers' remittances from Côte d'Ivoire. Resumption of financial assistance for several of these economies will further stimulate growth in the region. In Côte d'Ivoire, donor support is expected to resume in the second quarter of 2002, following implementation of the Staff Monitored Program under IMF supervision. Both investment and domestic consumption will increase while firmer cocoa prices will also boost performance. The EU has already agreed to gradually resume its aid to the country and GDP growth in 2002 is forecast at more than 3 percent.

Mali's economy is also expected to recover on the back of an increased cotton harvest, with growth projected at around 4 percent following two years of recession. Similarly, increased cotton output will help Togo, Benin and Niger to maintain moderate growth rates. In Senegal, the economy will continue its sustained growth helped by efficiency-enhancing reforms and international financial support. Improvements in external competitiveness will offset some of the negative effects of weak commodity prices.

In Guinea-Bissau, the political situation will be critical for growth prospects. Currently, the political environment remains extremely volatile, with a weak government coalition and allegations of an attempted military coup threatening its fragile peace. A return to violent conflict could reverse the strong upswing that followed political and economic disruption in 1998.

PART TWO

RURAL DEVELOPMENT FOR POVERTY REDUCTION IN AFRICA

Overview

The theme of the 2002 ADR, *Rural Development for Poverty Reduction in Africa*, is important because the international community's commitment to cutting the global incidence of absolute poverty in half by 2015 implies a massive effort in rural Africa. In addition, an understanding of the extent, nature and causes of rural poverty is a precondition for effective public action to reduce deprivation in rural areas of the Continent. The vast majority of the poor reside in rural Africa, where the incidence, depth, and severity of poverty are higher than in urban areas. The rural population is also less educated and less healthy quite apart from experiencing poorer service delivery and less employment opportunities, while relying heavily on natural resource-based production.

Thus, it is a near-universal consensus that the central development challenge that confronts African countries today is the reduction of poverty, and particularly improving the well-being of the rural poor. African leaders have in various fora – such as the Summit in Libreville in 2000 and the OAU Summit in 2001 – reaffirmed that this is indeed their primary goal. The leaders of the industrial countries have also pledged to assist developing countries in this critical endeavor. This commitment was re-affirmed last year by the adoption of the UN Millennium Development Goals (MDGs) by virtually all countries. Multilateral financial institutions and other donors have stressed the importance of refocusing on the rural poor. The important initiatives that have emerged from the consensus on the need to reduce poverty include debt relief initiatives, the New Partnership for Africa's Development (NEPAD), and the New Vision of the African Development Bank Group. Part II of this Report therefore examines the challenges and opportunities for reducing rural poverty and improving the well being of the rural poor.

Chapter 3 of the Report focuses on the question: *Why Focus on Rural Poverty?* It shows that rural poverty in Sub-Saharan Africa is widespread, deep and severe. Conventional money metric measurement reveals that most people in rural Sub-Saharan Africa live on incomes raging between 33 and 80 US cents per day. Rural people are not only income-poor but they are also deprived of basic necessities and capabilities – as reflected in low educational enrolment ratios, low literacy rates, high infant and maternal mortality and inadequate access to sanitation and clean potable water. Despite the increasing concern about poverty at the national, regional, and international levels, progress toward the reduction of poverty and deprivation remains inadequate. The assessment made in this Chapter shows that the majority of African countries will not be able to meet the international development goals of reducing poverty by half by the year 2015 and of achieving certain quantifiable improvements in education, health and social well-being. Regardless of the methodology used, the evidence for Sub-Saharan Africa is that the poverty reduction target as well as the other social goals in education, health, mortality and gender will not be met. The problems are especially challenging in rural areas, where poverty is deeper and more severe, and where rates of progress towards the desired social targets generally lag behind those of urban areas. The Chapter concludes that while rapid economic growth is necessary, it is not sufficient for reducing rural poverty and alleviating rural deprivation. Rural poverty reduction requires broad-based economic growth, which can transform the rural sector and make the rural poor the main focus of development management.

Chapter 4 examines the issue of *Empowerment and Resources for the Rural Poor*. One of the principal lessons of recent experience in Africa is that rural people require new kinds of empowerment if they are to harness their available resources so as to improve their well being. Such empowerment would be significantly assisted by the widespread sharing of knowledge and experience, by generally improved access to the most appropriate technologies and by the enhancement of rural peoples' legal and financial status. Thus, any program to reduce the widespread poverty in rural areas of Africa must require an effective combination of strategies to promote growth in both agricultural and non-agricultural activities, to develop the human and social capital of the rural poor, to promote appropriate technologies and to ensure productive and sustainable use of natural resources. In particular, there is substantial scope to improve traditional agricultural practices throughout Africa, especially with a view to improving productivity. At the same time, any intensification of cultivation of existing land has to be accompanied by measures to maintain and replenish the soil and to avoid degradation and loss. For the development of non-agricultural activities, poor rural populations would benefit greatly from increased access to credit, and a lowering of the costs of communications and transport. Empowerment of the rural population can best be achieved through the general development of their human and social capital. Investing in primary schooling is an important long-term strategy. Africa as a whole, including its rural areas, is confronted by a health crisis that has been much aggravated by the spread of HIV/AIDS and by the continuing heavy cost of malaria to human and social well being. New and effective measures, accompanied by substantial international financing, are needed to combat these threats.

Chapter 5 discusses the importance of *Making Globalization, Markets and Institutions Work for the Poor*. The globalization-induced distribution of income at the international level tends to favor countries that position themselves to benefit from increased opportunities of trade through the exportation of not only price-competitive products, but also through the promotion of products which are attractive to world income. The effect of globalization on poverty depends on its impact on trade and growth and on their distributional impact on the poor. Depending on country-specific conditions, policy makers would need to make sure that liberalization will stimulate trade and growth and that growth will benefit the rural poor. The evidence is that the often disappointing performance of internal and external liberalization in Africa is due much more to its failure to reach rural people or to induce fast agricultural growth, than to any alleged inadequacy of such growth in benefiting the poor. Many reforming countries experience poor overall and agricultural growth records even now. A policy of market liberalization must be complemented by policies to enhance market access and participation of the poor if the potentially adverse consequences of liberalization on the poor are to be minimized and potential gains realized. However, the need to complement market access reforms with changes in technology and institutions as well to enhance the supply response of agriculture must be emphasized. To benefit fully from liberalization, the abilities of the rural poor must be improved in three main areas: their ability to receive market incentives (price signals), their ability to respond to such incentives through increased production, and their ability to market their labor and excess production.

Chapter 6 discusses *The Bank Group's Rural Poverty Reduction Strategy* in line with the Bank's Vision for sustained African development in the New Millennium. The Bank's poverty reduction strategy, which has evolved over the years, recognizes poverty reduction as the most fundamental challenge facing the continent. Indeed, the Vision Statement that the Bank adopted in 1999 to guide its operations places poverty reduction and sustainable economic growth as the overarching objective of the Bank. The guidelines for operations, financed from the Bank's concessional window, give priority to economic activities that generate incomes for the rural poor. In recent years, and in line with the increasing focus on poverty reduction, the lending operations of the Bank have given priority to activities that aim at improving the macroeconomic policy framework, and focus on priority sectors including agriculture, rural infrastructure, education, health and clean water supply. In the use of its financing instruments, the Bank Group mainstreams gender, environmental sustainability, good governance, and poverty reduction into its operations as a way of facilitating sustained long-term growth and development in Africa. It also collaborates with other international institutions and the donor community in supporting initiatives aimed at intensifying international co-operation on poverty reduction in the Continent.

CHAPTER 3

Why Focus on Rural Poverty?

Introduction

At the dawn of the new century, Africa more than any other region of the world faces some of the most difficult development challenges. Close to half of the region's population still lives in absolute poverty and the continent remains the least developed region as evidenced by such indicators of well being as literacy, nutrition, health, and life expectancy. Poverty is deeply rooted in rural areas. The poor face more difficult problems with access to food, water supply, primary health care and primary education today than they did 30 years ago.

With the recent improvements in the social and political environment and in economic performance in many African countries, there is cautious optimism that Africa has indeed embarked on the right development path. Although a variety of reform programs resulted in positive per capita income growth, especially since the mid-1990s, the economic growth rate of the recent past has remained too low to make a dent in poverty reduction. The welfare of the majority of the population, as indicated by income and non-income measures of poverty, has therefore stagnated in some countries and worsened in others. It is also disquieting that the region risks losing even recent modest gains unless it succeeds in bringing under control, first, the conflicts and wars in a number of countries and, secondly, the scourge of the HIV/AIDS pandemic, two phenomena which have exacerbated the vulnerability of the rural poor. There is now near-universal consensus that the central development challenge that confronts African countries today is the reduction of poverty, and particularly improving the well-being of the rural poor.

Six major factors underline the recent focus on the rural poor:

- Poverty is growing in Africa compared to other regions;

- About 70 percent of Africans live in rural areas;

- Poverty in rural areas is not only widespread but it is also deep and severe;

- Overwhelming numbers of the rural poor are vulnerable to external shocks, natural disasters, conflicts, and the spread of diseases including HIV/AIDS;

- New initiatives bring the rural poor to the center of development dialogue;

- Few countries will be able to meet the agreed International Development Goals, particularly in the rural areas.

Part II of the African Development Report 2002 examines the challenges and opportunities for reducing rural poverty and improving the well-being of the rural poor. This Chapter discusses the factors that underline the recent focus on rural poverty and provides an overview of the conceptual framework for rural poverty reduction.

Chapter 4 examines the question of how to empower the rural poor and endow them with resources in order to combat poverty. Chapter 5 examines the question of how to make globalization, markets and institutions work for the poor. Finally, chapter 6 provides an overview of the Bank Group's rural poverty reduction strategy.

Poverty is Widespread in Africa

Compared to other regions of the world, both the incidence and depth of poverty in the continent are high whatever poverty measurement is used (see Box 3.1 on defining and measuring poverty). First, Sub-Saharan Africa is the lowest-income region in the world. Secondly, in 1998, the rate of poverty – based on the money metric approach with a poverty line of a dollar a day – was close to 50 percent. The corresponding rates for South Asia, East Asia and Latin America, were 40 percent, 15 percent, and 12 percent respectively. It is important to note, however, that the incidence of poverty in North Africa is much lower than that for Sub-Saharan Africa. In the early 1990s, it averaged about 22 percent using a poverty line of 2 dollar per day.

Non-income measures of poverty also show that Sub-Saharan Africa lags behind other regions. For instance, social indicators such as infant mortality, life expectancy and school enrolment rates are some of the lowest in the world. In Africa, 157 children out of 1,000 die before the age of five and 90 out of 1,000 before the age of one. Life expectancy of 52 years and gross primary school enrolment rates of 74 percent are the lowest in the world. In addition, in Sub-Saharan Africa, only 79 girls are enrolled in primary schools for every 100 boys, indicating a wide gender disparity in access to primary education. This gap gets wider for secondary and tertiary education.

Box 3.1: Defining and Measuring Poverty

Three broad approaches to the measurement and study of poverty can be distinguished: the quantitative money metric approach, the capability approach, and the participatory poverty assessment approach.

The Money Metric Approach

The money metric approach to poverty, which is the most dominant measure used by academics and development practitioners, has several determining parameters. Under this approach, the first step taken towards measurement is to agree on a relevant measure for the standard of living. A relevant standard for countries in the developing world is per capita consumption expenditure (including the consumption of own production). In advanced countries it is income that is taken as the relevant measure of the standard of living. Given agreement on the measure of the standard of living, there are a number of methods to determine the threshold below which a person can be identified as poor. This threshold is commonly known as the poverty line.

There is general agreement that the relevant method for determining poverty lines for developing countries is the cost of basic needs. This method involves identifying a typical diet for the poor that is necessary for leading a healthy life. Healthy life is defined in terms of nutritional requirements using WHO and FAO nutritional requirements (recommended daily allowances, e.g. 2,500 calories per adult per day). Required quantities of the goods supplying the required calories are appropriately priced to arrive at a monetary value defining a food poverty line. By adding to this amount the cost of other requirements needed by individuals to live in a social context (e.g. the cost of clothing, shelter, education and medicine) an overall poverty line can be estimated.

Third, while the international debate has been conducted in terms of a fixed poverty line (e.g. $1 per day) applied to all countries and over time, there is increasing realization that poverty lines should vary among countries depending on the level of development. Allowing the poverty line to change with the standard of living has been the practice in Europe in contrast to the practice in the US where the poverty line was held fixed for a long period of time.

Having obtained the poverty line, an immediate measure of poverty is the ratio of the poor thus identified to the total population in a given society. This is

(box continues on next page)

Box 3.1: Defining and Measuring Poverty (continued)

the well-known head-count ratio. It is the most widely used, and easily understood, measure of poverty. Thus, for example, the international development goal on poverty is to reduce the head-count ratio to half its current level by the year 2015. The head-count ratio measures the spread, or incidence, of poverty in a given society. Another useful poverty measure is the poverty-gap ratio, which takes into account the extent to which consumption of the poor falls below the poverty line. It measures the depth of poverty in a society.

To be able to identify the poor, information on the distribution of consumption expenditure, or income, in the society is needed. For Africa such information has only recently been made available for a limited number of countries. In general, any poverty measure could, thus, be expressed as depending on mean consumption expenditure in society, the poverty line and on a measure of the underlying inequality in the distribution of consumption, usually taken as the Gini coefficient (see Box 3.6). The dynamic interrelations between these three parameters are such that as per capita consumption increases, other things remaining the same, poverty declines. Similarly, as inequality in the distribution of consumption expenditure declines, other things remaining the same, poverty declines.

The Capability Approach

While the money metric approach to poverty is the dominant measure, use is often made of aggregate correlates of poverty such as life expectancy at birth (as a proxy for health status in a society) and school enrolment ratios (as a proxy for educational achievements). The use of these aggregate measures can be justified on a theoretical basis by resorting to Professor Sen's concepts of entitlements, capabilities and achievements. In contrast to the dominant approach to the measurement of poverty, which takes per capita consumption as the relevant indicator of the standard of living, the capability approach takes various kinds of freedom as the relevant indicators of the standard of living. In this perspective, poverty must be seen as the deprivation of basic capabilities rather than merely the lowness of incomes. Deprivation of elementary capabilities can be reflected in, among others, premature mortality, under-nourishment, morbidity and illiteracy. An example of applying such an approach is to be found in the Human Development Index of the UNDP.

In its relation to the dominant approach to poverty

analysis, it is perhaps important to note that the capability approach does not deny that deprivation of individual capabilities can have close links to the lowness of income. First, low income can be a major reason for illiteracy and ill health as well as hunger and malnutrition, and second, better education and health help in the earning of higher income. This type of relationship between the two approaches prompted the observation that they are complementary.

The Participatory Approach

The third approach to the study, but not necessarily the measurement, of poverty is the participatory approach to poverty assessment. This approach was popularized largely by the work of development practitioners who were involved in assessing development projects at the field level. The basic premise underlying this approach is that the poor know more than anybody else about their realities, priorities and most of all the remedies to get out of the poverty trap. As a result, the information collection process differs substantially from that of representative household surveys on which the money metric approach relies. Thus under this approach it is the poor who are involved in providing non-quantitative information about poverty in the selected community through graphic presentation, anecdotes, social mapping, case stories, life histories, and local history.

Perhaps the most extensive application of this approach was the study undertaken by the World Bank in preparation for the "World Development Report 2000/2001: Attacking Poverty". The study brought together experiences of over 60,000 poor women and men from 60 countries around the world. Despite the richness of the participatory approach to poverty assessment, however, a careful reading of the selected quotations from poor people around the world would show that material deprivation was central to the perceptions of poor people about the nature of poverty. In a technical sense, therefore, the social, physical, psychological, insecurity, and lack of freedom of choice and action dimensions of poverty can be viewed as functions of the standard of living as summarized by mean per capita consumption in a given society. Also given the close interrelations between income and other aggregate correlates of poverty, it can be argued that poverty measured by the head-count ratio screens these correlates.

Source: Ali (2001a).

In addition, among the six countries of the world (Afghanistan, Angola, Mozambique, Nepal, Sierra Leone and Somalia) with the highest maternal mortality rates between 1990-1993, four are African.

The overall trends in social indicators for Africa are also worrisome. The gross primary school enrolment rate rose from 50 percent in 1970 to only 79 percent in 1996. On the other hand, for developing countries as a whole, this rate increased from 79 percent to a high of 108 percent (gross primary school enrolment rates can exceed 100 percent in cases where children who are over the primary school age are enrolled in primary schools with those who are within the primary school age). Furthermore, among eight countries where life expectancy declined after 1990, six are African countries. In the 1990s, the decline in life expectancy is associated mainly with the HIV/AIDS pandemic.

The incidence of poverty in Africa has two distinctive features: first, it is very sensitive with respect to the poverty line used particularly in the Northern region and, secondly, it varies significantly across countries and regions. Recent evidence shows that at a poverty line of one US dollar per person per day, Sub-Saharan Africa had the highest head-count ratio (close to 50 percent) among all world regions for all the years surveyed between 1987 and 1998. Head-count ratios in excess of 40 percent of the population are recorded only for the South Asia sub-region, ranking second to SSA in terms of high incidence of poverty at the international poverty line of $1 per person per day (Ali, 2001b). At the other extreme, the North African sub-region had the lowest poverty rate among all developing regions in the world starting between 1993 and 1998. Prior to that it was only the Eastern Europe and Central Asia region that had a lower head-count ratio. How-

ever, when the poverty line is increased to $2.15 per person per day both the ranking and the magnitudes of the poverty results change with Sub-Saharan Africa ranking second to South Asia as the highest poverty incidence region. North Africa also ranks second to East Europe as the lowest poverty incidence sub-region (see Table 3.1).

Table 3.1: Head Count Ratios for African Sub-Regions and World Regions (poverty line = $2.15 per person per day in 1993 PPP)

Region	1987	1990	1993	1996	1998
North Africa	30.03	24.76	24.12	22.16	21.88
S.S. Africa	76.52	76.36	77.76	76.87	75.57
Eastern Europe*	3.59	9.55	17.17	19.19	19.92
L. America**	35.54	38.09	35.07	37.00	36.44
South Asia	86.30	86.41	85.41	85.02	83.96
East Asia***	62.90	57.33	51.61	42.78	44.96

Notes: *This region includes Central Asia.
 **This region includes the Caribbean.
 ***This region includes the Pacific.
Source: Chen and Ravallion (2000: table 3).

Most of the Poor Live in Rural Areas

Poverty in many African countries is predominantly a rural phenomenon. The rural population represents an average of 60 percent of the total population on the continent; about 90 percent of the rural labor force engages directly or indirectly in agricultural activities. Agricultural development and rural development are crucial for the structural transformation and development of Africa. Agriculture contributes 20 percent of GDP in

North Africa and 30 percent of GDP in Sub-Saharan Africa.

Rural poverty in Africa is embedded in an overall poverty context at the national level. Rural poverty in Sub-Saharan Africa contributes more than 60 percent of the incidence of total poverty as measured by the head-count ratio. The contribution of rural poverty is in excess of 90 percent of total poverty in Burkina Faso, Mali, Niger and Uganda. The contribution of rural poverty is in excess of 80 percent of total poverty in Ethiopia, Gambia, Kenya, Madagascar, and Swaziland (Ali, 2001b).

Rural people are not only income-poor, but they are also deprived from the substantive "capabilities" necessary to lead a decent and meaningful life. Deprivation of elementary capabilities can be reflected in, among other things, premature mortality, undernourishment, morbidity and illiteracy. Examining the deprivation of the rural sector in Sub-Saharan Africa from the perspective of capabilities two structural features relevant to poverty analysis need to be noted. First, the evidence shows that the average household size in the rural sector is about six persons, with a standard deviation of about two persons (which is not significantly different from that in the urban sector). The average rural household size varies from a high of 11 persons for Gambia and Senegal, to a low in Ghana with 4 persons per rural household. Secondly, and not surprisingly, the evidence shows that on average about 81 percent of rural employed labor works in the agricultural sector. Agricultural employment of 90 percent of the rural labor force or more is reported for Burkina Faso, Madagascar, Mali and Uganda. On average about 4.5 percent of the rural labor force is employed in the manufacturing sector, about 5.8 percent is employed in commerce, and about 2.1 percent in the civil service or the army.

This survey evidence confirms the aggregate evidence cited above.

Table 3.2 summarizes the most important features of capability deprivation in the rural sector of SSA, where figures between brackets are the standard deviations. To further appreciate the deprivation of the rural sector the table also provides the corresponding indicators for the urban sector as well as for the national level.

For all types of capabilities the table 3.2 paints an overall picture of very high levels of deprivation in the sample of countries considered. Looking at the sectoral figures, it can be confirmed that for all deprivation indicators there exists a statistically significant difference between the rural and urban sectors, where the level of deprivation in the rural sector is much higher than that in the urban sector.

For primary education indicators the picture is such that not only is the rural deprivation on account of this indicator higher but also the differences between countries are large. Detailed information shows relatively high net primary school enrolment ratios in the rural sector for Kenya, Ghana, Zambia and Nigeria, with an enrolment ratio of between 50 and 75 percent. The most deprived rural sectors are to be found in Ethiopia, Niger, Mali, and Senegal with a ratio of between 13 and 22 percent. For the secondary school enrolment ratio the level of deprivation of the rural sector is much deeper compared to the primary school indicator. Detailed information shows that while Nigeria, Ghana, and Central African Republic (with ratio of between 23 to 35 percent) are the best performing rural sectors in terms of secondary education, most of the countries surveyed had a ratio less than 10 percent. These countries include Côte d'Ivoire and Kenya, Gambia and Madagascar, Burkina Faso and Mauritania, Mali, Guinea and Senegal, and Ethio-

Table 3.2: Capability Deprivation in Rural SSA in the 1990s

Capability Indicator	Number of countries	Rural sector	Urban sector	National
Net Primary Enrolment Ratio	15	33.9 (19.1)	62.3 (10.1)	44.2 (17.4)
Male NPER	15	37.3 (18.2)	64.7 (9.4)	44.4 (20.0)
Female NPER	15	31.0 (21.0)	60.1 (11.5)	38.5 (18.9)
Net Secondary Enrolment Ratio	15	11.2 (11.6)	32.9 (11.4)	18.0 (12.3)
Male NSER	15	13.7 (13.3)	37.9 (11.6)	21.0 (14.1)
Female NSER	15	8.3 (10.9)	28.4 (11.9)	15.3 (11.5)
Literacy Rate	17	37.1 (26.5)	60.5 (24.3)	44.2 (24.9)
Male Literacy Rate	17	46.1 (26.0)	68.8 (23.6)	53.1 (24.7)
Female Literacy Rate	17	29.3 (27.8)	52.7 (25.8)	36.2 (26.1)
Access to Sanitation	14	41.1 (28.5)	81.3 (17.8)	51.4 (25.8)
Access to Piped Water	18	12.8 (11.9)	65.6 (21.7)	29.1 (14.5)

Source: Based on World Bank (1999). Figures between brackets are the standard deviations.

pia. Similar ratios were also recorded by the rate of literacy, which is the standard overall indicator of deprivation in terms of education. With reference to all of these educational indicators, women are especially deprived.

The deprivation of rural sectors is not only apparent in education but also in access to basic health-related services such as sanitation and piped water. Table 3.2 shows that deprivation on account of these health indicators is a national feature. The overall averages are 51.4 percent for access to sanitation and 29.1 percent for access to piped water. Within the context of this overall deprivation the rural sector is much more deprived than the urban sector. Access to sanitation in the rural sector averaged 41 percent compared to about 81 percent for the urban sector. Countries with relatively high rural access to sanitation include Tanzania, Kenya and Uganda with an access rate

of between 92 and 56 percent. At the other end, the most deprived rural populations on account of this indicator are to be found in Ethiopia, Nigeria, Burkina Faso and Niger, and Ghana with access of between 5 to 17 percent. Similar differential deprivation between the rural and urban sectors is observed for the indicator of access to piped water. Thus, compared with the urban sector, which is also poor and deprived, the rural sector is poorer and more deprived in terms of capabilities. Additional features of rural poverty in Sub-Saharan Africa come to light in answers to questions such: Who are the rural poor? Where do they live? From where do they get their income and how do they use it? What access do the rural poor have to assets? Some answers to these questions are summarized in Box 3.2.

Box 3.2: Identifying the Rural Poor: Questions and Answers

Who are the rural poor?

Wage laborers, especially landless or casually employed farmworkers, are almost everywhere among the most likely to be poor. In Africa smallholders are the largest poor group. Incidence of poverty among children is everywhere much higher than among adults. Female-headed households are not much more likely to be consumption poor than male-headed households. In North Africa a high proportion of the rural poor are women, children and the elderly, because of out-migration of prime-age males.

Where do the poor live?

The incidence and severity of rural poverty exceed those of urban poverty. Many poor people live in marginal and degraded areas. The poorest of the rural poor live in remote areas. In East and Southern Africa, the majority of the poor live in densely populated areas near capital cities. People in irrigated zones within rural areas face much lower poverty risks. In North Africa, wage-earners are located in lowlands and more densely populated areas and where work opportunities exist.

How do the poor get their income and how do they use it?

Most of the poor rural households diversify their sources of income. Smallholders in all regions often combine traditional or cash crop cultivation with raising small livestock. Own-farm income is often only a small proportion of total household income. In North, West and Central Africa, off-farm income is often the poor smallholder's main source of cash income, usually from low-return activities. Farmers dependent on rain migrate to irrigated areas for off-season work. The landless are permanently involved in daily casual work and off-farm work. Poor people typically save in good seasons but run down their reserves in lean times; overall, their consumption is seldom below their income. Of their consumption, typically 45-60 percent is on food staples – cereals, roots, and pulses – and a further 15-20 percent on other foods. In general, 55 percent of the calories come from cereals and 7 percent from roots, tubers and pulses. In Mozambique, 78 percent of the calories are derived from staples, and in Nigeria 69 percent. The importance of staples in the lives of the rural poor derives from the facts that agriculture provides 60-75 percent of rural work and that staples cover about 62 percent of arable areas. In Mozambique and Nigeria, staples cover 97 percent and 78 percent of arable areas harvested respectively. Staples provide over 67 percent of farm income from employment and self-employment. Cash crops and livestock are important for the survival of some very poor people.

What access do the rural poor have to assets?

In all regions, the rural poor lack the important asset of good quality land. Access to other productive assets is also lower among the rural poor. In North Africa water has become an important asset. In East and Southern Africa lack of draught power severely handicaps poor farmers, as lack of access to credit, agricultural inputs and technology. The rural poor also lack human capital precipitated by a strong urban bias in the provision of public services such as health, education, water and sanitation. Moreover, social support networks are important assets for the rural poor in North Africa, especially for displaced people who experience a breakdown of social connections. Lack of boats and equipment severely handicaps fishermen in East and Southern Africa.

Note: IFAD's concerns are worldwide and do not necessarily focus on Africa.
Source: IFAD (2001). Also see Ali (2001b).

Rural Poverty is Widespread, Deep and Severe

The state of rural poverty in Sub-Saharan Africa is not only widespread, but it is also deep and severe. As noted before, the spread of poverty is measured as the proportion of people who live below a given poverty line. The depth of poverty is measured by the poverty gap, which takes into account the extent to which consumption of the poor falls below the poverty line. The severity of poverty is measured by the squared poverty-gap ratio. The evidence available shows that while poverty in the majority of Sub-Saharan Africa is widespread, deep and severe, its extent varies among countries (see Table 3.3). For the three poverty measures used, Ghana emerged as a low rural poverty country where the spread of poverty is 34 percent, while its depth and severity are 8 and 2.4 percent respectively. At the other extreme, Zambia is a high rural poverty country with about 81 percent of its rural population living below a poverty line of about $25 per person per month.

In terms of depth of poverty, Central African Republic (CAR) is clearly a high rural poverty country with a poverty-gap ratio of 46.4 percent while in terms of severity Guinea Bissau is the country with the highest squared poverty-gap ratio of about 35 percent. To further appreciate the extent of the depth of rural poverty, it is to be noted that the mean expenditure of the rural poor in Guinea Bissau, Ethiopia and CAR is only about 32 US cents per person per day. For Ghana, at the other extreme, the mean expenditure of the rural poor is 81 cents per person per day. These are indeed dramatic figures reflecting the depth of poverty in rural Africa.

In the majority of Sub-Saharan countries the contribution of rural poverty to the depth of poverty at the national level is in excess of 70 percent. Rural poverty contributes more than 90 percent of the depth of poverty at the national level in Burkina Faso, Madagascar, Uganda, Mali, and Niger. Similar observations can be made about the contribution of rural poverty to the severity of poverty at the national level.

The Rural Poor are Vulnerable to Risks, Shocks and Volatility

Poor, unskilled, and uneducated people in rural areas are most vulnerable and suffer disproportionately from multiple risks, shocks and volatility, and they have few instruments for mitigating these adverse events. Poor rural Africans have become vulnerable to risks emanating from globalization and external shocks, conflicts, HIV/AIDS and natural disasters.

Globalization, Volatility and the Rural Poor

Globalization stands out as the dominant trend defining the international context for Africa's development. While globalization offers long-term opportunities, many African countries run the risk of being marginalized because their production structures are not well poised to take advantage of the unfolding opportunities. A lack of export diversification means that 39 African countries depend on only one or two primary commodities – with very low income-elasticities of demand – for over half of their export earnings. This implies that as world income grows, less and less of this income growth will be devoted to the purchase of such commodities. This process leads to increased trade marginalization of African countries and hence to lower growth prospects given the central role of export expansion in economic

Table 3.3: Poverty Measures for Rural and Urban Sectors in Sub-Saharan Africa

Country	Rural Mean Expenditure ($/person/ month)	Rural Poverty Line ($/person/ day)	Rural H (%)	Rural PG (%)	Rural SPG (%)	Urban Mean Expenditure ($/person/ month)	Urban Poverty Line ($/person/ month)	Urban H (%)	Urban PG (%)	Urban SPG (%)
B. Faso	24.4	25.4	74.05	31.14	16.11	76.9	40.9	37.20	13.95	6.90
CAR	27.2	26.7	77.84	46.37	32.57	65.3	37.2	43.68	20.82	13.16
C. d'Ivoire	45.3	31.5	36.40	9.77	3.49	71.1	39.0	30.34	7.91	2.84
Ethiopia	15.4	17.7	70.91	31.34	15.74	32.6	28.1	67.17	29.32	15.91
Gambia	22.3	25.6	69.05	30.08	17.25	64.0	36.8	37.53	12.47	5.63
Ghana	45.0	31.3	34.32	7.57	2.38	70.0	38.0	25.50	6.24	2.05
Guinea	21.9	25.5	72.15	29.81	15.33	46.4	31.7	44.11	14.52	6.52
G. Bissau	20.5	25.2	76.94	47.91	35.30	38.7	29.5	56.61	25.22	15.39
Kenya	41.5	30.3	44.12	17.48	9.78	109.3	52.8	33.91	11.93	5.63
Madagascar	25.8	26.4	68.58	29.85	16.66	61.3	35.9	42.53	16.03	7.91
Mali	22.0	25.5	76.59	36.63	21.33	71.5	39.1	35.60	11.33	5.07
Mauritania	39.1	29.7	42.99	14.31	6.84	74.4	40.1	24.54	6.48	2.56
Niger	26.3	26.5	65.47	37.40	26.28	55.4	34.2	35.26	12.84	6.50
Nigeria	48.5	32.2	48.35	19.86	10.96	55.0	34.1	32.73	10.90	5.06
Senegal	39.6	29.8	40.59	11.25	4.60	95.2	47.4	23.54	4.80	1.40
Swaziland	26.7	26.6	70.52	36.34	23.42	89.5	45.3	52.73	28.65	19.19
Tanzania	15.4	17.7	72.42	29.77	15.44	27.6	26.8	65.57	26.39	13.48
Uganda	29.5	27.3	62.01	23.69	12.06	61.5	36.0	41.29	14.12	6.61
Zambia	18.7	24.8	81.32	44.17	28.37	43.2	30.8	54.81	22.19	12.02

Notes: H = Head count Ratio; PG = Poverty-gap Ratio; SPG = Squared Poverty-gap Ratio.
Source: Calculations based on World Bank (1999).

development. The burden of such an increased marginalization is expected to fall on the rural poor whose livelihoods depends directly or indirectly on the production of primary commodities and who are often disproportionately affected by economic decline.

In the last two decades, Africa's average export growth has been only 6 percent a year, less than half that of developing countries as a whole; consequently, its share in world trade declined from about 5 percent in the early 1980s to less than 2 percent today. At the same time, the share of these commodities of world exports has fallen by over 50 percent in the last 15 years. Furthermore, as a result of weak external competitiveness, even in primary commodities Africa has lost its export

market shares: for instance, to Asian countries in cocoa, coffee, and timber; to Latin American countries in iron ore; and to Eastern European countries in cotton. Furthermore, the failure of the continent to benefit from the globalization-induced increase in private capital flows inhibits the building of its human and physical capital and constrains its ability to accelerate economic growth.

Apart from marginalization in trade and capital flows, the continent also stands the risk of the negative knock-on effects and volatility emanating from the globalization of financial markets and production structures. Such contagion effects pose clear risks that can damage developing countries' economies and can be especially harmful to the poor. A recent manifestation of contagion effects made possible by the process of globalization is the Asian crisis of 1997-1998. The crisis not only wiped out the welfare gains accumulated over the last three decades by some South East Asian countries, but its negative effects spread to other continents including the Americas, Europe and Africa. The impact of the Asian crisis on poverty, particularly in rural areas was transmitted in different ways. There was a decline in Asia's consumption of primary commodities and a decline of Africa's exports as a result of the drastic currency depreciation in Asian countries, making their exports more price competitive. The slowdown in global growth had depressing effects on commodity prices produced and exported by Africa (Hussain, Mlambo and Oshikoya, 1999).

A more recent manifestation of the contagion effects emanating from globalization followed the September 11th attack on the US, when the economic effects were felt worldwide with stark consequences for the daily lives of many Africans already resigned to poverty, disease and marginalization. The price of oil fell by $10 per barrel immediately after the attack, possibly setting the stage for lower metal and agricultural commodity prices in 2002. Also tourism was negatively affected, especially in Egypt, Morocco, Kenya, Tanzania and Zimbabwe. With so many people in Africa living at the margins of poverty, the impact of these negative effects will tend to increase the proportion of people living under the poverty line. The World Bank estimated that some 10 million more people are likely to be dragged below the poverty line of one dollar a day and that tens of thousands more children will die worldwide. In Africa falling commodity prices may impoverish another two million to three million people. Greater volatility may, thus, be one of the greatest ills of globalization as it slows growth and

exacerbates poverty.

The poor are also more vulnerable to exogenous shocks—especially those emanating from adverse weather conditions and natural disasters. The African poor are particularly exposed to adverse weather conditions given their heavy reliance on rain-fed agriculture. In the recent past, drought and floods have undermined agricultural production in countries as diverse as Morocco in North Africa, Kenya in East Africa, Zimbabwe and South Africa in Southern Africa, and those in the Sahel. In addition to causing drastic loss of life and material, adverse weather conditions and natural disasters also degrade agricultural land and destroy infrastructure on which the livelihoods of the rural poor crucially depend. Also, The fluctuations in export earnings consequent upon such adverse events create unstable macro-economic environments, making it difficult for the private sector to invest with confidence and for the government to plan its social expenditures on a volatile revenue base. Volatility affects income distribution, increases poverty, and lowers educational attainment. Box 3.3 illustrates the impact of natural disasters on the rural poor in Mozambique — one of the frequently flood-stricken African countries.

Increased Vulnerability to Diseases

Since the onset of Africa's economic crisis of the 1980s, the population of the continent, particularly the rural poor who lack access to adequate health services, became more vulnerable to illness and diseases. The main causes of illness include malaria, HIV/AIDS, and the associated tuberculosis. Malaria remains one of the leading causes of morbidity and mortality in the tropics. Pregnant women and children under five especially in rural areas continue to constitute some of the most

Box 3.3: Natural Disasters and the Rural Poor in Mozambique

Most of the rural poor in Mozambique get their liveli-hood from agriculture, isolated from regional and world markets and frequently forced to bear the burden of cyclical natural disasters. Mozambique is a disaster-prone country. In the last two decades, it has been affected eight times by droughts and cyclones, 16 times by floods and 12 times by pests (Maule, 1999). While less severe droughts occur with frequency, it has been estimated that the periodic return of a severe drought is between seven to 11 years.

These frequent natural disasters have resulted in loss of human life, flooding of cultivable land, loss of livestock and destruction of infrastructure. They have contributed substantially to the increased incidence, depth and severity of poverty. As shown in the table, natural disasters, especially drought and floods, are frequent in the central and southern part of the country, where three provinces have the worst poverty indicators, Tete, Inhambane and Sofala (IFRPI et al, 1998).

Within these areas, the rural poor are the most vulnerable. They tend to have very little land, reduced agricultural production and assets, lower levels of education and poor sanitation (WFP, 1999). They lack the necessary resources to counteract the effects of natural hazards. As result they are severely affected and their poverty status is deepened.

Natural disasters contribute to rural poverty in several ways. When floods destroy bridges and road-ways, they reinforce isolation and market fragmenta-tion. Droughts and cyclones aggravate rural poverty by reducing an already low level of agricultural output and therefore affecting food security and increasing indiscriminate use of natural resources.

Natural disasters can also affect investment expectations, the budget deficit, money supply and overall macro-economic stability.

Most of the recent agricultural expansion in Mozambique has been through better utilization of the available capacity following the 1992 peace accord. Contrary to what has been happening in other sectors, there is an extremely low level of investment in agriculture because of the persistence of natural disasters which, through increased risk and uncertainty, lead to low employment opportunities for the rural poor.

(box continues on next page)

important risk groups. The disease is often linked to the general state of poverty, movement of refu-gees, and to environmental change, including for-estry, mining and water development projects.

Since the early 1980s, the Human Immunodefi-ciency Virus (HIV) and its associated disease, AIDS, have emerged as one of the greatest causes of death in Africa. The resurgence of tuberculosis in the continent was also closely associated with the spread of AIDS as more than one-third of all new TB cases are HIV co-infected. HIV/AIDS has, thus, become one of the leading causes of deaths in Africa. Africa with only 10 percent of the world population is home to 70 percent of the world's HIV-infected people and 95 percent of the world's AIDS orphans. While the prevalence rate among adults in most of the countries has been rising, regional variations have also been observed. Southern and Eastern Africa remain the hardest hit with the HIV prevalence rate rising to 35 percent of the 15-49 adult population, followed by Central and West Africa with 13.8 percent. In some of these countries 50 percent of the 20-29 years age group of pregnant and breastfeeding mothers are infected. North Africa has the lowest rate, 0.9 percent.

Although it is difficult to project accurately the loss in terms of productivity, savings and in-vestment, studies have clearly shown the ripple effects of AIDS on badly-affected countries. The economic disaster from this epidemic stems mainly from the fact that adults and adolescents, who constitute the productive and reproductive populations in the countries, are most at risk for acquiring the disease. Furthermore, in the early years the epidemic seemed to spread fastest among people with above-average education and skills, further sharpening the economic impact. The losses in labor power and income will ultimately affect savings at all levels of the economy, which

Box 3.3: Natural Disasters and the Rural Poor in Mozambique (continued)

The table below provides information on selected natural disasters and estimated damage.

Box Table
Selected Natural Disasters (1980-2000)

When	Type	Where	Estimated Damage
1982-83	Drought	Central and Southern	5,000 dead 1,824,000 affected
1984	Cyclone	Southern	109 dead 2,500 ha destroyed Damage estimated at $73,170,731
1988	Floods	Central and Southern 11 deaths	2000 ha destroyed Roadways interrupted 1,500 displaced
1991-92	Drought	Whole Country	1,320,000 affected 1.2 million needed food aid.
1996	Floods	Central and Southern	Roadways interrupted 6 bridges destroyed 22,000 houses affected 103,000 ha destroyed 200,000 people affected
1997	Floods	Central and Northern	87 dead, 17,000 houses destroyed 356 head of cattle lost just in one district
2000	Floods	Central and Southern	568,211 affected 113 dead 79,500 ha destroyed 22, 800 tonnes of maize lost 10,900 tonnes of rice lost 2,000 cattle lost

Note: The table does not list all the damage.
Sources: Maule (1999); República de Mozambique (2001); and Marrengula (2001).

will reduce investments in social welfare and infrastructure over the long term.

The HIV/AIDS pandemic has not only aggravated the poverty situation, but it has also resulted in rising infant and adult mortality in several African countries. In some cases, these problems have prevented countries from realizing their potential for high economic growth and for reducing poverty. In others, socio-economic gains from past efforts have been reversed. The epi-

demic is also reversing Africa's progress in human capital formation. It affects individuals in their prime ages of productivity and it has an impact on the age and sex structure of the population. Africa's hard-won gains in life expectancy, an important measure of human development, are being eroded in most of the severely-affected countries. In some of these countries, life expectancy has declined from 45-60 years in 1985 to 38-50 years in 2000. As a result of the HIV/AIDS crisis, productive members of society are being lost. Children as well as adult dependants are falling into permanent poverty.

AIDS and poverty have an intimately two-way relationship. The consequences of poverty, specifically the inadequate intake of calories and nutrients, render individuals more susceptible to HIV infection and cause them to progress faster from HIV infection to AIDS and, ultimately, to death. HIV/AIDS, in turn, hinders the ability of countries, households and individuals to reduce poverty and achieve household food security through its effects on production, income and economic growth. AIDS tends to diminish the potential to increase domestic food production in order to improve household food security. Finally, by imposing heavy costs on national economies and hence reduce their ability to earn foreign exchange through increased exports, AIDS tends to make it more difficult for African countries to import the food they need to feed their people.

Civil Strife and Conflicts: a Heavy Toll

During the past ten years, more than a dozen African countries experienced significant civil or international conflict. About 100 million Africans, amounting to about 20 percent of the total population of Africa, live in these countries. Some countries, including Sudan, Somalia, Burundi, Angola, and the Democratic Republic of Congo, have been in conflict for years. Others have only recently suffered flare-ups of violence, such as Sierra Leone, Guinea-Bissau, Liberia, Zimbabwe and Côte d'Ivoire. Millions have been killed or wounded. Millions of Africans are currently refugees, displaced from their homes and deprived of their livelihoods. Conflict presents enormous challenges to rural development.

While it is difficult to provide a complete ac-count of the negative impact of civil strife and conflict on economic performance some obvious effects are generally known. The effects of a civil war include the destruction of physical and human capital, reduction of savings, diversion of portfolios from domestic investment to capital flight, and disruption of economic transactions (Collier, 1998). War also consumes resources that governments could otherwise spend on basic health care and education, infrastructure or other purposes. The combined impact of these negative trends is likely to affect the rural poor disproportionately. In combat zones, which are usually found in rural areas, conflict takes land out of production either by direct displacement of farmers, contributing to the loss of incomes, employment and livelihood, or by the placing of landmines. In some countries, such as Angola, a significant proportion of arable land is infested with landmines and cannot be farmed. Even in places not directly affected by fighting, conflict destroys incentives to invest in farms or businesses. Poverty, unemployment, low education, hunger and autocratic institutions are associated with conflict. Conflict is likely to become a bigger problem in Africa unless significant progress is made in generating widely-shared growth, reducing poverty, lowering food insecurity and creating more representative institutions.

Among the population dynamics that merit increasing attention in Africa are the movements of refugees and displaced persons. According to UN estimates, the number of refugees has more than doubled, from 8.5 to 19 million, over the past ten years. The persistent situation of war and political instability in the Great Lakes region, parts of West Africa and the Horn of Africa has brought about massive displacements of people into neighboring countries. This has had immediate and indirect impacts on macro- and household economics, environmental health (including the spread of STDs and HIV/AIDS through economic vulnerability and subsequent prostitution), additional pressure on urban social and physical infrastructures, and increased pressure on the already limited resources of the host countries. The resulting economic crisis and famine in some regions of the continent make many individuals (especially the elderly, women and children) vulnerable and in constant need of international assistance – hence the urgent need for peaceful resolution of conflicts, provision of reproductive health services, and the physical protection of refugees against exploitation, abuse and all forms of violence.

Bringing the Rural Poor to the Center of the Development Agenda

There is now near universal consensus that the central development challenge that confronts African countries today is indeed the reduction of poverty. African leaders have in various fora – such as the Summit in Libreville in 2000 and the OAU Summit in 2001 – reaffirmed that this is indeed their primary goal. The leaders of the industrial countries have also pledged to assist developing countries in this critical endeavor. This commitment was re-affirmed last year by the adoption of the UN Millennium Development Goals (MDGs) by virtually all countries. Multilateral financial institutions and other donors have stressed the importance of refocusing on the rural poor. The important initiatives that have emerged from the consensus on the need to reduce poverty include debt relief initiatives, the New Economic Partnership for Africa's Development (NEPAD), and the New Vision of the African Development Bank Group.

Debt Relief Initiatives

Most African countries suffer from unsustainable debt levels that constitute clear impediments to their development. About a quarter of total exports are applied for debt servicing annually. The large debt overhang and debt service requirements have a number of adverse impacts. Debt service requirements exert significant pressures on the budget of African countries and divert investment resources from key social and economic sectors. It also erodes the confidence of the private sector and weakens the prospects for sustainable growth and the reduction of poverty. Recognizing the important link between debt relief and poverty reduction, the international donor community took a major step to reduce the debt of Heavily Indebted Poor Countries (HIPCs) through an initiative that for the first time provided a comprehensive approach to the debt problem. The initial program involved a six-year track record of reforms by indebted countries and the provision of debt relief by creditors to bring the external indebtedness of these poor countries to a sustainable level.

Experience with the implementation of the HIPC initiative, however, demonstrated the need for additional measures. More specifically, there was a demonstrated need for: a greater emphasis on budgetary relief; strengthening the linkage of debt relief to poverty reduction; and enhancing the resources for debt relief. To meet these needs a new and an enhanced HIPC framework was agreed upon in 1999. The new framework allows for deeper and faster debt relief, retroactive coverage to allow more countries to become eligible, and closer linkage between debt relief and poverty reduction. The enhanced HIPC framework provides a mechanism for reducing, in a relatively short period of time, the stock of debt of eligible

African countries and bringing their debt servicing requirements to sustainable levels. The linkage of debt relief to economic and social reforms and to poverty reduction also offers the possibility of releasing significantly larger resources for investments in priority areas and in the social sectors. The main instrument for coordinating such donor assistance is the Poverty Reduction Strategy Papers (PRSPs) that would also provide an important framework for enhancing the collaboration between governments and their development partners.

NEPAD

In the face of the many challenges facing African countries, NEPAD represents a vision and a set of strategies for addressing them. It is a manifestation of the determination of our leaders to assume the ownership of the development process on our continent. At the same time, it represents their recognition that these challenges can only be addressed successfully in partnership with the international community. They have thus proposed to enter into a new compact based on shared principles and mutual accountability.

NEPAD advocates a development paradigm consistent with the essential ingredients of sustainable development. It calls on African leaders to take responsibility for promoting accelerated economic growth, and poverty reduction, by strengthening governance, implementing sound macroeconomic policies and boosting domestic savings mobilization. It calls on new and effective partnership between governments, civil society, and their development partners. NEPAD also stresses the cardinal importance of committing ourselves to peace, security and good governance. This is evidenced by the setting up of a Sub-Committee on Peace and Security to focus on conflict prevention and resolution on the continent.

The Bank Group Vision

In 1999, the African Development Bank Group promulgated a new Vision document: *A Re-Invigorated Bank: An Agenda for Moving Forward*. The Vision, which was prepared after a broad consultation with a wide range of stakeholders at the national and international levels, states clearly that poverty reduction is the overarching objective of the Bank. The Vision Statement, therefore, reflects the Bank's commitment to promote accelerated, sustainable and equitable economic growth that contributes a lasting impact on poverty reduction in Africa. It enumerates priority sectors for Bank operations at country and regional levels. Interventions at the country level will focus on agriculture and rural development, human resources development, and private sector development. At the regional level, interventions will target economic cooperation and regional integration. The Vision underscores the centrality of good governance, gender equity, and environmental management to all Bank Group operations.

Given that the backbone of the African economies is agriculture, the Bank regards agriculture as the starting point for supporting overall production growth and improving living standards in the continent. In addition, given that poverty in Africa is predominantly a rural phenomenon, the Bank considers infrastructure (including feeder roads, rural water supply and irrigation), agriculture and rural development as key priorities. This would be complemented with support for the development of agro-based, small and medium-scale enterprises. In addition, the Bank would facilitate rural financial intermediation by supporting bottom-up, demand-driven, micro and rural finance schemes aimed at assisting the poor and vulnerable groups of society.

Few Countries will Meet the International Development Goals

Despite the apparent commitment of African leaders, and the donor community to poverty reduction, it is clear that more would need to be done to realize this objective. It has been more than a decade since the adoption of the International Development Goals (IDGs). Yet, it is evident that, at the pace of current economic and social trends, the majority of African countries would not be able to achieve these goals. It might be recalled, in this respect, that the commitment of the international community to poverty reduction culminated in six goals set in clear quantitative terms (the seventh goal involves strategies to reverse loss of environmental resources through implementing sustainable development strategies). These included a poverty reduction target and five other social development goals. Assessing the progress made so far towards the realization of these goals, and weighing up the challenges that lie ahead, should provide the justification for continued and intensified efforts to fighting poverty. What follows is an assessment of the performance of African countries against the IDG goals related to poverty and social development.

Goal 1: "Reduce the proportion of people living in extreme poverty by half between 1990 and 2015"

Poverty in the context of the IDGs is defined and measured in terms of the head-count ratio using the money metric approach. The definition of the head-count ratio depends on mean consumption expenditure, a poverty line and a measure of the inequality in the distribution of consumption. Ac-

cording to this approach the poor are those with consumption expenditure below a certain poverty line and in the case of IDGs a global benchmark poverty line of $1 a day per person in 1985 purchasing power parity was used. For assessing the feasibility of achieving the IDG on poverty two such behavioral assumptions need to be made: the real poverty line is held constant over time; and the distribution of expenditure does not change substantially over long periods of time. With these two assumptions it can be shown that reducing poverty by half by the year 2015, starting in 2001 as a base year, would require a reduction in the head-count ratio by an annual rate of 4.83 percent. Since both the poverty line and the distribution of expenditure are assumed constant, it can also be shown that such a rate of decline of the head-count ratio would require an increase in per capita consumption given by 0.0483 divided by the elasticity of poverty with respect to consumption expenditure. This elasticity measures the percentage reduction in poverty (as defined by the head-count ratio) as a result of a one percent increase in consumption expenditure.

For a sample of 19 Sub-Saharan African countries the absolute value of the elasticity of the head-count ratio ranges from a low of 0.43 (for Ethiopia) to a high of 2.2 (for Ghana) with an average of 1.03. That is, a one percent increase in consumption expenditure reduces poverty by about 0.43 percent in Ethiopia while it reduces poverty by 2.2 percent in Ghana. For the sample as a whole, a one percent increase in consumption expenditure reduces poverty by 1.03 percent. Thus, achieving the IDG of poverty reduction by half by year 2015 for this sample of countries would require per capita consumption expenditure to grow by an annual rate of 4.71 percent. With an average population growth rate of 2.7 percent, the achievement of the IDG of poverty reduction would require a GDP growth rate of about 7.41 percent per annum. Given the historical record of growth in the continent, and given the rate of savings and the magnitude and rates of flow of foreign aid, such a growth target is clearly not feasible.

To further appreciate the unfeasibility of achieving the IDG of poverty reduction goal one should note that the incremental capital-output ratio for Sub-Saharan Africa for the period 1995-1999 averaged 5.47. This implies that to achieve the IDG goal of poverty reduction, African countries would need an annual investment rate of about 40.53 percent of GDP. This is clearly beyond the saving capacity of the African economies where the savings rate averaged 22.9 percent of GDP for the period 1975-1984, 19 percent for the period 1985-1989 and 16 percent for the 1990s (World Bank, 2001).

By contrast, for a sample of four North African countries the absolute value of the elasticity of the head-count ratio ranges from a low of 1.87 (for Algeria) to a high of 3.33 (for Egypt) with an average of 2.30. Thus, achieving the IDG of halving poverty by year 2015 would require mean per capita consumption expenditure to grow by an annual rate of 2.1 percent. With an average population growth rate of 2.0 percent, the achievement of the IDG of poverty reduction would require a GDP growth rate of about 4.1 percent per annum. Given the historical record of growth in this sub-region, and given the rate of savings achieved in the past, such a growth target is clearly feasible. To further appreciate the feasibility of achieving the IDG of poverty reduction goal note that the incremental capital-output ratio for North Africa for the period 1995-1999 averaged 5.59. This implies that to achieve the IDG goal of poverty reduction North African countries would need an annual investment

rate of about 22.9 percent of GDP. This is clearly achievable given the historical record of the saving capacity of the North African economies where the savings rate averaged 32.1 percent of GDP for the period 1975-1984, 24 percent for the period 1985-1989 and 19.8 percent for the 1990s.

An alternative way of looking at the feasibility of achieving the IDG on poverty is to ask how long would it take Sub-Saharan Africa, growing at the average rate of the second half of the 1990s, to achieve the reduction of the head-count ratio by half. During the second half of the 1990s the annual real growth rate of GDP for Sub-Saharan Africa averaged 3.28 percent (ranging from a high of 4.8 percent for 1996 to a low of 2.1 percent in 1998). With an average population growth rate of 2.7 percent. This means a real GDP per capita growth rate of 0.58 percent per annum. With such per capita growth, it is an easy matter to show that it will take Sub-Saharan Africa, growing at its currently observed rates, about 118 years to reduce poverty by half. This time horizon is about eightfold the identified time horizon in the context of the IDG for poverty reduction.

For the alternative way of looking at the feasibility of achieving the IDG on poverty for North Africa, note that the real GDP of this region was growing at an average rate of 4.02 percent per annum for the second half of the 1990s. With an average population growth rate of 2.0 percent, this implies a per capita GDP growth rate of 2.04 percent, which is almost equal to the required growth rate of per capita expenditure of 2.1 percent.

From the above, it should be clear that while the North African sub-region is poised to achieve the agreed IDG of reducing poverty by half by the year 2015, there are major difficulties facing Sub-Saharan Africa in doing so. What is true for the poverty reduction target is also true for the other social indicators given the close relationship between poverty and its other social correlates such as education and health indicators.

Sub-Saharan countries are expected to face difficulties in attaining their other social targets in education and health. A study of individual Sub-Saharan countries especially commissioned for this Report confirms this conclusion and suggests that there are large variations across countries and between rural and urban areas (Sahn, 2001). For Sub-Saharan countries where data are available, the study assesses the prospects of realizing the social goals by extrapolating past progress, and comparing these projections to the rates of change that are necessary to realize the IDG. The main findings of this study are discussed below.

Goal 2: "Enrol all children in primary school by 2015"

The possibility of achieving the social goal of enrolling all children in primary school by 2015, was examined for ten Sub-Saharan countries comprising Burkina Faso, Cameroon, Ghana, Kenya, Madagascar, Niger, Nigeria, Tanzania, Zambia, and Zimbabwe. It was found that Kenya is the only country, which is more likely to realize the goal of 100 percent enrolment in urban as well as rural areas (see Figure 3.1 for Kenya and Cameroon). In Cameroon, progress in enrolment in urban areas might also be consistent with the target-achieving path, but rural areas are unlikely to achieve the desired goal.

Goal 3: "Make progress toward gender equality and empowering women by eliminating gender disparities in primary and secondary education by 2005"

Progress toward the target of eliminating gender disparities in primary and secondary school by 2005 was examined for the same ten countries considered above. It was found that only rural Madagascar and Tanzania are on target to meet the goal of gender equality in primary and secondary education, though this only holds for Madagascar if the observed rates of change persist to the year 2015 in a linear fashion. This is also the case in urban areas of Burkina Faso, Tanzania and Zimbabwe. In rural Niger and Nigeria, there has been progress as measured by increasing ratios of girls-to-boys enrolled in primary and secondary school, but the pace of change – whether we assume linear or log-linear changes – in each of these countries is below the linear target path. In a few countries, we actually observe worsening performances in terms of gender equity in enrolments. This is most pronounced in urban areas of Madagascar (where overall enrolments are also falling), Nigeria and Zambia, as well as both urban and rural Kenya. In all of these cases the rates of decline in the ratios are sufficiently large to be a cause of serious concern.

Goal 4: "Reduce infant and child mortality rates by two-thirds between 1990 and 2015"

For health indicators, 24 Sub-Saharan countries were covered. For the two health indicators, infant mortality and chronic child malnutrition, it was found that although the evidence for both of these indicators is mixed, the common feature of urban areas being better off than rural areas generally applies here as well. In terms of targets, although 23 of the 24 countries witnessed declines in infant mortality rates in rural areas, only 11 are poised to realize the goal of reducing infant mortality by two-thirds by 2015. Also, of the 15 countries in which infant mortality rates were observed to fall in urban areas, only in Côte d'Ivoire, Ghana, Mali, and Namibia are the changes rapid enough

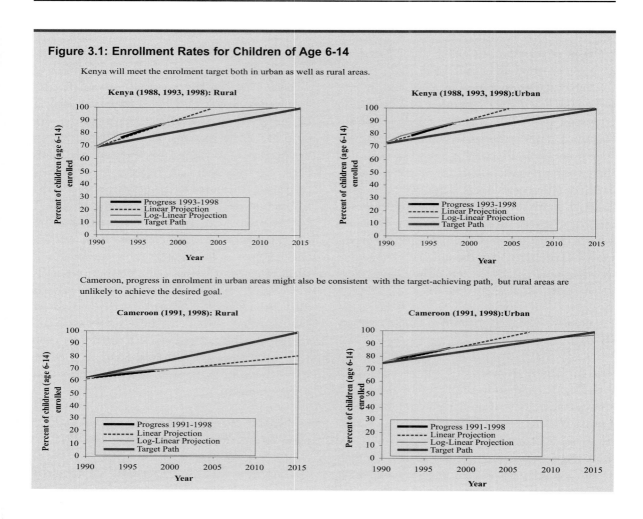

Figure 3.1: Enrollment Rates for Children of Age 6-14

Kenya will meet the enrolment target both in urban as well as rural areas.

Cameroon, progress in enrolment in urban areas might also be consistent with the target-achieving path, but rural areas are unlikely to achieve the desired goal.

to meet the target (see Figure 3.2 for Côte d'Ivoire and Namibia in rural and urban areas).

Goal 5: "Reduce maternal mortality ratios by three-quarters between 1990 and 2015"

In the case of maternal mortality, the number of births attended by skilled health personnel is used as a proxy. It is found that the only cases where there are improvements consistent with the linear

rates of progress required for realizing the targets are urban areas in Mozambique, Senegal and Togo. Furthermore, while there are other examples of urban populations within striking distance of the goal of 90 percent of births attended by skilled health personnel (a proxy for IDG of reducing maternal mortality by three-quarters), there is virtually no realistic hope for rural areas in any of the countries to meet the maternal mortality goal.

Figure 3.2: Infant Mortality Projections

Côte d'Ivoire will be able to meet the target on infant mortality in urban as well as rural areas according to the linear projection test.

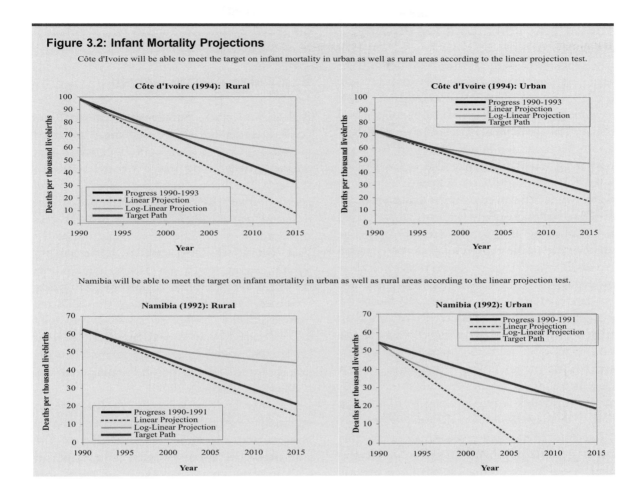

Goal 6: "Provide access for all who need reproductive health services by 2015"

More disappointing results are also found with regard to the target of providing access for all who need reproductive health services. There is no case in either urban or rural areas, where the percent of women using modern methods of contraception increases (as a proxy for access to health services) at a rate that even comes close to following the target path. With the sole exceptions of Kenya and Zimbabwe, only 10 percent of rural women are found to use modern contraceptives. The picture is not much better in urban areas. An assessment of data availability to monitor progress in the IDGs, and the summaries of the results obtained are shown in Tables 3.4, 3.5 and 3.6, respectively.

Towards A Framework for Poverty Reduction

It is clear from these results that most African countries in Sub-Saharan Africa would not be able to achieve the IDGs on poverty reduction and other social development targets. In view of these results and considering our interest in "rural development" and "rural poverty", a logical starting point for a conceptual framework is to assume that a typical African economy is a dual economy (or a two sector economy) with a rural sector and an urban sector. For the purposes of developing this framework the conventional characterization can be followed by which the rural sector is a low productivity sector and the urban sector is a high productivity sector, where productivity means the marginal, or average, productivity of labor. In addition, for the purposes of poverty analysis the rural sector is often assumed to be a low inequality sector while the urban sector is assumed to be a high inequality sector. In the context of such an economy poverty, as measured by the head-count ratio at the national level, is the weighted sum of the sectoral head-count ratios where the weights are the sectoral population shares. In this framework, it can be shown that the change in poverty over time at the national level would have two components. The first is the growth component, where poverty would be expected to decline as a result of an increase in mean consumption given the state of inequality in the distribution of consumption expenditure. The second is a distribution component, where poverty would be expected to decline as a result of a decline in the degree of inequality in the distribution of consumption, given mean consumption expenditure. The theoretical issues on the growth and distribution components are summarized in Boxes 3.4 and 3.5 respectively. In what follows, issues relating to the growth performance and income distribution in Africa are discussed.

Explaining African Growth

Reducing poverty in Sub-Saharan Africa will depend on generating, and sustaining, a long-run growth process. It is generally recognized that Africa's growth in the period after independence and up to the first oil price shock of 1973 was on par with other regions. From that time, however, economic growth faltered first and then a process of decline started. Thus, for example, during the 1980s per capita GDP declined by 1.3 percent per annum, a rate, which was 5 percentage points below the average for all low-income developing countries. During the first half of the 1990s the growth situation further deteriorated. Per capita GDP declined by an annual rate of 1.8 percent per annum, a rate 6.2 percentage points below the average for the low-income developing countries (Collier and Gunning, 1999).

A large body of literature has developed in an attempt to explain Africa's growth performance at the macro-economic level. In view of the controversy over the mainsprings of development and given the interrelated nature of the factors affecting economic growth, it is no wonder that empirical studies identify a large number of socio-economic variables that have a statistically significant impact on growth. Modern empirical growth theory has identified some 62 statistically significant explanatory variables influencing the growth performance of different economies. It needs to be noted, however that in world samples used in the specialized literature a large and significantly negative Sub-Saharan African dummy was detected implying that as far as various standard explanatory variables used SSA was somehow different. As a result a new set of stud-

Table 3.4: International Development Goals (IDGs) and Data availability from the Demographic and Health Surveys (DHS)

Goals	Goal 2	Goal 3	Goal 4	Goal 5	Goal 6	Extra
	Enrol all Children	Gender Equality in Schools	Reduce Infant Mortality Rates (IMR) by 2/3	Reduce Maternal Mortality by 3/4	Access to Reproductive Health Services	Reduce Malnutrition by 2/3
Indicator	Enrollments	Ratio of girls-to-boys enrolled	IMR	Neonatal care with skilled personnel	Contraceptive knowledge and use	Stunting
Countries						
1 Benin (1996)			X	X		
2 Burkina Faso (1992,1999)	X	X	X	X	X	X
3 Burundi (1987)			X	X		
4 Cameroon (1991, 1998)	X	X	X	X	X	X
5 Central African Republic (1994)			X	X		
6 Chad (1997)			X	X		
7 Comoros (1996)			X	X		
8 Côte d'Ivoire (1994)			X	X		
9 Ghana (1988, 1993, 1998)	X	X	X	X	X	X
10 Kenya (1988, 1993, 1998)	XX	XX	XX	XX	XX	XX
11 Madagascar (1992, 1997)	X	X	X	X	X	X
12 Malawi (1992)			X	X		
13 Mali (1987, 1995)			X	X	X	X
14 Mozambique (1997)			X	X		
15 Namibia (1992)			X	X		
16 Niger (1992, 1997)	X	X	X	X	X	X
17 Nigeria (1990, 1999)	X	X	X	X	XX	X
18 Rwanda (1992)			X	X	X	X
19 Senegal (1986, 1992, 1997)			X	X		
20 Tanzania (1991, 1996, 1999)	X	X	X	X	X	X
21 Togo (1988,1998)			X	X		X
22 Uganda (1988, 1995)			X	X	X	X
23 Zambia (1992, 1996)	X	X	X	X	X	XX
24 Zimbabwe (1988, 1994, 1999)	X	X	X	X	XX	XX

Note: X indicated that data are available to access progress on the IDGs
Source: Sahn and Stifel (2001).

Table 3.5: Progress Toward International Development Goals (IDGs) in Urban Areas (Social Development Goals)

Goals		Goal 2	Goal 3	Goal 4	Goal 5	Goal 6	Extra	
Indicator		Enrol all Children	Gender Equality in Schools	Reduce Infant Mortality Rates (IMR) by 2/3	Reduce Maternal Mortality by 3/4	Access to Reproductive Health Services	Reduce Malnutrition by 2/3	
Countries for which we can calculate progress		Enrollments	Ratio of girls-to-boys enrolled	IMR	Neonatal care with skilled personnel	Contraceptive knowledge and use	Stunting	Number of goals on target to be achieved
1	Benin (1996)			No	No			0 of 2
2	Burkina Faso (1992,1999)	No	Yes	No	Yes	No	No	2 of 6
3	Burundi (1987)			No	No			0 of 2
4	Cameroon (1991, 1998)	Yes	No	No	Yes	No	No	2 of 6
5	Central African Republic (1994)	Yes	No	No	No	No	Yes	2 of 6
6	Chad (1997)			No	No			0 of 2
7	Comoros (1996)			No	No			0 of 2
8	Côte d'Ivoire (1994)			Yes	No			1 of 2
9	Ghana (1988, 1993, 1998)	No	No	Yes	No	No	Yes	2 of 6
10	Kenya (1988, 1993, 1998)	Yes	No	No	No	No	No	1 of 6
11	Madagascar (1992, 1997)	No	No	No	No	No	Yes	1 of 6
12	Malawi (1992)			No	Yes			1 of 2
13	Mali (1987, 1995)			No	No			0 of 2
14	Mozambique (1997)			No	Yes			1 of 2
15	Namibia (1992)			Yes	Yes			2 of 2
16	Niger (1992, 1997)	No	No	No	No	No	No	0 of 6
17	Nigeria (1990, 1999)	No	No	No	No	No	No	0 of 6
18	Rwanda (1992)			No	No			0 of 2
19	Senegal (1986, 1992, 1997)			Yes	Yes	No	No	2 of 4
20	Tanzania (1991, 1996, 1999)	No	Yes	No	Yes	No	No	2 of 6
21	Togo (1988, 1998)			Yes	No		Yes	2 of 3
22	Uganda (1988, 1995)			Yes	No	No	No	1 of 4
23	Zambia (1992, 1996)	No	No	No	No	No	No	0 of 6
24	Zimbabwe (1988, 1994, 1999)	No	Yes	No	Yes	No	No	2 of 6

Do linear projections meet the target?

Source: Sahn and Stifel (2001).

Table 3.6: Progress Toward International Development Goals (IDGs) in Rural Areas (Social Development Goals)

Goals	Goal 2	Goal 3	Goal 4	Goal 5	Goal 6	Extra	
	Enrol all Children	Gender Equality in Schools	Reduce Infant Mortality Rates (IMR) by 2/3	Reduce Maternal Mortality by 3/4	Access to Reproductive Health Services	Reduce Malnutrition by 2/3	
Indicator	Enrollments	Ratio of girls-to-boys enrolled	IMR	Neonatal care with skilled personnel	Contraceptive knowledge and use	Stunting	Number of goals on target to be achieved
			Do linear projections meet the target?				
Countries for which we can calculate progress							
1 Benin (1996)			Yes	No			1 of 2
2 Burkina Faso (1992,1999)	No	No	No	No	No	No	0 of 6
3 Burundi (1987)			Yes	No			1 of 2
4 Cameroon (1991, 1998)	No	No	No	No	No	No	0 of 6
5 Central African Republic (1994)			No	No			0 of 2
6 Chad (1997)			Yes	No			1 of 2
7 Comoros (1996)			Yes	No			1 of 2
8 Cote d'Ivoire (1994)			Yes	No			1 of 2
9 Ghana (1988, 1993, 1998)	No	No	Yes	No	No	Yes	2 of 6
10 Kenya (1988, 1993, 1998)	Yes	No	No	No	No	No	1 of 6
11 Madagascar (1992, 1997)	No	Yes	No	No	No	No	1 of 6
12 Malawi (1992)			No	No			0 of 2
13 Mali (1987, 1995)			Yes	No			1 of 2
14 Mozambique (1997)			Yes	No			1 of 2
15 Namibia (1992)			Yes	No			1 of 2
16 Niger (1992, 1997)	No	No	No	No	No	No	0 of 6
17 Nigeria (1990, 1999)	No	No	No	No	No	No	0 of 6
18 Rwanda (1992)			Yes	No			1 of 2
19 Senegal (1986, 1992, 1997)	No	No	No	No	No	No	0 of 4
20 Tanzania (1991, 1996, 1999)	No	Yes	No	No	No	No	1 of 6
21 Togo (1988,1998)			Yes	No			1 of 2
22 Uganda (1988, 1995)			No	No	No	Yes	1 of 3
23 Zambia (1992, 1996)	No	No	No	No	No	No	0 of 6
24 Zimbabwe (1988, 1994, 1999)	No	No	No	No	No	No	0 of 6

Source: Sahn and Stifel (2001).

Box 3.4: Economic Growth and Poverty Reduction

While it is readily agreed that economic growth can reduce poverty, there is no universal agreement on what it takes for a country to achieve fast and accelerated growth. The mainsprings of development continue to be the fundamental question that preoccupies the minds of development theoreticians, empiricists and practitioners. During the evolutionary course of economic thought, a number of elements were singled out as central to the process of development. Earlier, and based on the works of Harrod (1939), Domar (1947), and Robert Solow (1956), the allied process of saving, capital accumulation and investment were identified as the most crucial. Lewis (1954) and others suggested that fast growth is made possible by a transfer of resources from the rural agricultural sector with low productivity to the urban industrial sector with high productivity. As in the case of Solow, the Lewis model assumed diminishing returns to capital, with the implication that in developing countries where capital is scarce, returns to capital would be higher and the income gap between the poor and rich nations would narrow overtime. The convergence of incomes predicted by these theories has not materialized and the world has witnessed an increasing income divergence between the rich and the poor.

In the mid-1980s, new growth theories such as that of Romer (1986) and Lucas (1988) came to rescue the day for the supply-side view of growth. These theories now ascribe the widening income gap as well as the process of growth itself to positive externalities associated with human capital formation and research and development, which lead to increasing returns. The dominant development paradigm still believes in the simplistic view that the key to fast growth is to increase the quantity and quality of production inputs, such as capital (investment) and labor. However, the dominant development paradigm does not recognize demand constraints on output growth and the fact that demand will affect the amount of inputs actually available and utilized.

The Balance of payments growth model (due to Thirlwall 1979 and Thirlwall and Hussain 1982) represents a complete break with this supply-side tradition. It recognizes that there is, of course, a trivial sense in which the supply-side view of growth is true and that there can be no output without input of resources. But it asserts that in order to understand the dynamics of growth, the nature and the extent of demand constraints on the utilization of resources and output growth must be understood. It postulates that the most binding constraint on growth in an open economy is likely to be the balance of payments. It argues that the balance of payments position of a country is the main constraint on economic growth, because it imposes a limit on demand to which supply can adapt.

The model provides a plain thesis for poor countries striving for faster growth and poverty reduction. While there is no disagreement that progress in poverty reduction will come through increased investment that brings about an accelerated and broad-based growth, the model implies that export expansion plays an important role not only in making such a growth possible, but also sustainable. That is, fast growth generates a large demand for manufactured capital and consumer goods. In the absence of a growing domestic production to satisfy such an increase in demand, the excess demand will spill over into imports, putting pressure on the current account balance. If export expansion is not sufficient to meet the import demand associated with faster growth (in addition to servicing foreign debt) the sustainability of fast growth will be threatened, as the heavy burden of foreign indebtedness will eventually close in, and capital inflows will eventually dry up.

In contrast to the traditional development philosophy that emphasizes investment in physical and human capital *per se*, the model implies that in the absence of strong export earnings such investments are not sustainable and would be curtailed by the lack of sufficient foreign exchange. Hence, a growth strategy that concentrates on expanding investment in human and physical capital without due regard to the "the foreign exchange productivity of investment" might be short-lived because the balance of payments constraint might eventually put an end to such an expansion, rendering domestic resources, including human capital, under-utilized.

Fast and sustainable growth thus necessitates lifting the balance of payments constraint on growth by producing the goods and services that are attractive to the domestic as well as foreign markets. The fundamental objective for countries striving for growth and poverty reduction is to adopt macro-economic and sectoral policies that reduce the income elasticity of demand for imports and/or increase the income elasticity of demand for exports. This suggests a model of socio-economic development, which is firmly anchored on the promotion of income-attractive importable and exportable goods. Regulatory, investment and trade policies, the pursuit of good governance, institutional building, infrastructure development, and human capital formation, all must be designed and implemented with this fundamental objective in mind.

Source: Extracted from Hussain (2001).

Box 3.5: Income Distribution and Poverty Reduction

There is no disagreement that fast and sustained growth is the first line of attack in the fight against poverty. What is in dispute, however, is whether the war against poverty can be won without a mechanism that ensures the distribution of growth for the benefit of the poor. In the context of a dual economy this question can be debated with reference to the famous Kuznets' hypothesis. The most celebrated result relating the effect of economic growth on inequality is that due to S. Kuznets (1955), "Economic Growth and Income Inequality", *American Economic Review*, vol. 45.

Simply put, the hypothesis asserts that as development proceeds (with increases in per capita income) inequality tends to increase at first and reaches a maximum before it decreases. The hypothesis is based on historical observations on population shifts from a low inequality, low productivity sector (e.g. a rural sector) to a high productivity, high inequality sector (e.g. an urban sector).

Measuring inequality by the Gini coefficient, the above inequality-development relationship can be looked at in terms of a curve relating the Gini coefficient to real per capita GDP. Such a curve has an inverted U-shape such that at low levels of per capita income inequality increases as per capita income increases, reaches a maximum and then declines. A number of studies have attempted to test

the existence of such a relationship. Overall the evidence is mixed with some studies confirming the existence of the relationship in the context of cross-country regressions while others show the opposite result. It seems, however, that whether the Kuznets' relationship holds or not depends on the quality of growth. If growth is broad-based and its benefits are widespread, the possibility of an inverse relationship between growth and income distribution becomes unlikely. The figure below illustrates a relationship between income per capita and the Gini coefficient where the turning point is found to be at a level of per capita income of $3,320 in 1985 PPP.

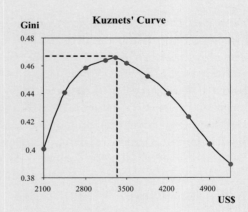

Source: Ali (2001a).

ies attempted to devise additional explanatory variables that could explain such a dummy. A representative sample of these studies was recently reviewed. Based on the review, five sets of variables are identified as explaining the observed slow growth in the sub-region. These include "lack of social capital", "lack of openness to trade", "deficient public services", "tropical location and high-risk environment", and "lack of financial depth".

In assessing such evidence, four limitations of

the growth regression methodology are noted. First, by focusing on explaining long-term average slow growth of the sub-region the methodology misses the deteriorating performance since 1973. Such a deterioration cannot be explained in terms of initial conditions such as geographical location. Secondly, African growth performance was strongly episodic in nature and as such cannot be captured by the practice of averaging variables over long periods of time. An average episode is one of six years duration during which per capita GDP would fall by about 25 percent. Thirdly, the standard growth regression methodology did not make adequate allowance for the possible neighborhood effects such as pursuing growth-oriented policies that bore fruit in a neighboring country (Collier and Gunning, 1999). Fourthly, most of these studies confine the choice of explanatory variables to those that can explain the supply of output, while paying little attention to such demand-side factors as world income as related to the demand for Africa's goods and services.

Irrespective of its methodological weaknesses, the aggregate evidence on the determinants of long-run growth is taken to describe the observed environment in Sub-Saharan Africa. That is, Africa is said to be characterized by intrinsic high risks, high transport costs and trade barriers, low levels of education, limited financial markets and high regulation. The response of economic agents and the functioning of markets in such an environment are believed to require more analysis with a view of exploring ways and means of regenerating growth. In this respect it has been argued that the African rural households responded to the highly risky and volatile environment by "self-insurance through diversification, both within agricultural activities and between agricultural activities and non-agricultural activities. They also accumulate assets for consumption smoothing. Both responses are likely to reduce growth, the former by lowering mean income and thereby savings, and the latter by the need to keep assets in liquid form" (Collier and Gunning, 1999). The response of rural households to an environment that lacked social capital is believed to have been detrimental to growth. Social capital, in this analysis, is regarded as composed of civic social capital that is generated by the community and public social capital

that is generated by the government or the state. Civic social capital embodies the economic benefits that accrue from social interaction in the form of reduced transaction costs that arise from building of trust, of knowledge externalities, of social networks and of an enhanced capacity for collective action. Public social capital is defined as the institutions of government that facilitate private activity mostly embodied in the "rule of law". While it is recognized that African traditional societies were able to devise social institutions (kin and village groups) that lowered the costs of moral hazard and adverse selection, their response to changing circumstances developed into a constraint on the growth process. In this respect it is noted that the persistence of traditional land rights and inheritance practices creates increasing divergence in factor endowments that increase the static inefficiency costs and thus reducing the growth rate directly.

The lack of evolution of rural social capital in Africa in a growth-enhancing direction is also noted with respect to the development of social networks to deepen the process of social learning through interaction and exchange of information. In this respect it is noted that social networks based on kin and village groups in Africa continue to be small, intense and closed largely to serve the fundamental insurance function that requires almost complete information. Such a structure of networks is held to be largely inappropriate for the dissemination and exchange of information on various innovations related to production methods.

In terms of the inadequacy of rural public services, the underdevelopment of rural credit markets is highlighted as particularly growth-retarding. In this respect it is noted that the lack of credit is partly due to the lack of collateral (perhaps because of prevailing land tenure systems).

The substitutes for collateral are interlinked economic transactions (e.g. with the labor market) and high observability. Because of the small sizes of African rural sectors, relevant interlinked market transactions are very limited and hence rural credit depended heavily on high observability, which is closely linked to the nature of African rural networks noted above, thus resulting in the lack of observed rural credit. Limited credit opportunities have consequences for investment strategies, choice of economic activities and rural growth. Of particular relevance is the observation that lack of rural credit could result in increased rural inequality with a two-class society in which the relatively wealthy farmers have both higher incomes and better opportunities for investment, while the poor are trapped in poverty.

The above examples of impediments to growth in the rural sector gleaned from available evidence at the household level are taken as confirmation to the results reported on the basis of aggregate cross-country growth regressions. It is noted, however, that a better understanding of the constraints to the growth of the rural sector would require more probing of rural household-level behavior.

Inequality in Africa

As measured by the standard measure of inequality – the Gini coefficient, which is explained in Box 3.6 – Africa has the second most unequal income distribution in the world next to Latin America. Africa has an expenditure Gini coefficient of 44.4 percent and an income Gini coefficient of 51 percent (Ali, 2001a). Income inequality in Africa also exhibits significant variation between countries. The highest degree of inequality in the distribution of income is reported for the CAR, with a Gini coefficient of 67.9 percent. At the other extreme, the lowest degree of inequality is recorded for Egypt with an income Gini of 35.5 percent. Income inequality in rural areas is not much different from the relatively high inequality picture painted for the whole continent.

In examining the current state of inequality in the distribution of income in Africa, a note must be made of the resurgence of interest in the study of the role of income distribution in the growth process and the possibility of reverse causation. The traditional starting point in this analysis is the hypothesis that as development proceeds (i.e. per capita income increases) inequality in the distribution of income will increase at the early stages and then declines. This is the Kuznets' hypothesis where growth in its initial stages would cause income distribution to worsen and this process will continue as income rises, up to an inflection point after which growth will improve the state of income distribution (see Box 3.5).

In a recent empirical study, which controls for relevant factors such as education, rule of law and openness to trade, it has been shown that the Kuznets' relationship exists such that inequality increases up to a per capita income level of $3,320 in 1985 PPP. Applying this to 44 African countries, it has been found that 40 of them have not yet reached the Kuznets' turning point. For these countries, this result implies that fast growth might be necessary but not sufficient for poverty reduction. It also implies that the impact of a given growth rate on poverty reduction could be enlarged by adopting the policies that correct for the socio-economic factors underpinning the Kuznets' relationship. This is where pro-poor development strategies become important.

Aside from the Kuznets' hypothesis, the relevant literature is seen as having developed along two paths. One path concentrates on the role of

Box 3.6: The Lorenz Curve and the Gini Coefficient

The most widely used way of viewing inequality in the distribution of income (wealth or consumption expenditure) is the Lorenz curve.

To draw the Lorenz curve, "the percentages of population arranged from the poorest to the richest are represented on the horizontal axis and the percentages of income enjoyed by the bottom x% of the population is shown on the vertical axis. Obviously 0% of the population enjoys 0% of the income and 100% of the population enjoys all the income. So a Lorenz curve runs from one corner of the unit square to the diametrically opposite corner. If everyone has the same income the Lorenz curve will be simply the diagonal, but in the absence of perfect equality the bottom income groups will enjoy a proportionately lower share of income. It is obvious, therefore, that any Lorenz curve must lie below the diagonal (except the one of complete equality which would be the diagonal), and its slope will increasingly rise – at any rate not fall – as we move to the richer and richer sections of the population" (Sen, 1997).

In the figure below, two Lorenz curves for Nigeria are drawn for 1985 and 1992 based on the data in the table. The figure clearly shows that the distribution of consumption expenditure in 1992 was more unequal than the distribution in 1985.

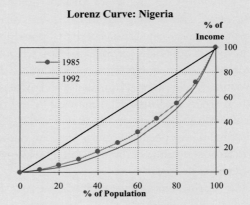

Lorenz Curve: Nigeria

Box Table: Lorenz Curves for Nigeria, 1985 and 1992

Cumulative Population Percentage	Poorest 10%	Poorest 20%	Poorest 30%	Poorest 40%	Poorest 50%	Poorest 60%	Poorest 70%	Poorest 80%	Poorest 90%	All
Cumulative Expenditure Share (%) 1985	2.43	6.24	11.05	16.88	23.87	32.36	42.71	55.46	72.01	100
Cumulative Expenditure Share (%) 1992	1.33	3.99	7.83	12.92	19.29	27.27	37.43	50.66	68.62	100

The most widely-used measure of inequality in the distribution of income (wealth or consumption expenditure) is the Gini coefficient.

The easiest way of defining the Gini coefficient is in terms of the Lorenz curve. In this respect the Gini coefficient is the ratio of the area between the line of complete equality (the diagonal of the unit square) and the Lorenz curve to the area of the triangle enclosing the Lorenz curve.

From an arithmetic point of view there "are various ways of defining the Gini coefficient, but a bit of manipulation reveals that it is exactly one-half of the relative mean difference, which is defined as the arithmetic average of the absolute values of differences between all pairs of incomes" (Sen, 1997).

For the Nigeria case, it can easily be shown that the Gini coefficient of the distribution of consumption expenditure in 1985 was 0.387 compared to a Gini of 0.45 in 1992, thus confirming that the 1992 distribution was more unequal than that of 1985.

Source: Ali (2001a).

imperfect capital markets in the growth process (Banerjee and Newman, 1998; Galor and Zeira, 1993; Aghion and Bolton, 1997). The main result of this literature is that where credit market constraints prevent the poor from making productive indivisible investments, inequalities in the wealth distribution can have significant negative impacts on growth.

The second path to reverse causation analyzes the effects on growth of the political outcome generated by a given income distribution. In this literature three political channels linking income inequality and growth are identified. The first channel envisages the existence of large incentives for the poor to engage in rent-seeking activities, which hinder investment and growth. The second channel is the fiscal one where the level of government expenditure and taxation is the result of a voting process in which income is the main determinant of a voter's preferences. The logic is that in a society with high inequality the majority of voters will vote for high taxation thus discouraging investment and growth. The third channel is that of political instability which emphasizes the effect of income inequality on social unrest. This channel has two links: the first is from inequality to social unrest, while the second is from social instability to growth, it being understood that social unrest discourages investment.

The most important hypothesis based on this work is that initial inequality is harmful to long-run growth. The bulk of the empirical work undertaken to test the hypothesis is based on running a standard growth regression by adding an inequality measure to the right hand side of the growth regression equation (Alesina and Rodrik, 1994; Persson and Tabellini, 1994; Clarke, 1995). Recent results establish a negative causal link between initial asset inequality (where the Gini coefficient of operational land holdings is used as the

inequality in the distribution of assets measure) and the growth performance of countries (Deininger and Olinto, 2001).

Despite the continuing debate on the linkages between growth and distribution, it is probably reasonable to argue that any relevant rural development strategy, with the objective of reducing rural poverty, should take into account the initial state of inequality in the distribution of income and wealth. In this respect it is relevant to note that the most recent high-quality data set on the distribution of income, or consumption expenditure, shows that Africa is characterized by a fairly high degree of initial inequality in the distribution of consumption expenditure and income.

Expenditure distribution profiles for the rural and urban sectors in Sub-Saharan Africa are not much different from the relatively high inequality picture painted for the whole continent. Available information on the state of inequality in the rural sector shows that the share of the top 20 percent in total expenditure is 3.2 times that of the lowest 40 percent of the population. This state of inequality is summarized in an expenditure Gini coefficient of about 43 percent, implying an income Gini of 49.6 percent. Comparing the distribution profiles of the urban sector with that of the rural sector, it can be shown that for all inequality measures based on the expenditure shares of population deciles there is no statistically significant difference between the two sectors at conventional test levels. This is an important conclusion in view of the standard assumption of development economics where the distribution of income in the rural sector is usually taken to be more equal than that of the urban sector.

Summary

The focus on rural poverty is justified on the grounds that (i) Africa is the only region in the world where poverty is rising, and (ii) 70 percent of the poor in Africa live in rural areas. The rural poor are more susceptible to exogenous shocks to their livelihoods emanating from the adverse effects of globalization, natural disasters, civil wars and conflicts. They are also the most affected by the recent resurgence of diseases including malaria, tuberculosis and HIV/AIDS. Rural poverty has also become the major concern of new initiative that placed poverty reduction, particularly in rural areas, in the center of the international and regional development policy agenda. This is more the case since the majority of African countries would not be able to meet the International Development Goals of reducing poverty by half by the year 2015 and of achieving certain quantifiable improvements in education, health and social well-being.

In view of the evidence presented in this Chapter, the inadequate progress in living standards in Africa seems irrefutable, regardless of the methodology and the poverty definition used. The results are particularly sobering for rural areas, where living standards are universally lower, and where rates of progress generally lag behind urban areas. With particular reference to Sub-Saharan Africa, the main conclusions and their implications are as follows:

- Rural poverty in Sub-Saharan Africa is characterized by a high level of "capability deprivation", which is reflected in educational enrolment ratios, literacy rates, access to sanitation and access to clean potable water. The average net primary school enrolment ratio is 34 percent, while the average net secondary school enrolment ratio is 11 percent and the average literacy rate is 37 percent. Average access to sanitation is 41 percent and the average access to clean water is only 13 percent.

- Rural poverty in Sub-Saharan Africa is widespread, deep and severe, as reflected by conventional money metric measures. The spread of poverty as measured by the head-count ratio ranges from a high of 81 percent to a low of 34 percent. The depth of poverty as measured by the poverty-gap ratio ranges from a high of 48 percent to a low of 8 percent. This implies an average income of the poor ranging from a high of $24 per person per month to a low of about $10 per person per month. The severity of poverty as measured by the squared poverty-gap ratio ranges from a high of 35 percent to a low of 2 percent.

- In Sub-Saharan Africa, rural poverty dominates national poverty in the sense of its share in total poverty at the national level. The share of rural poverty in the incidence of total poverty ranges from a high of 91 percent to a low of 62 percent.

- Fast growth at the macro-economic level is the first line of attack in the fight against rural poverty. While the factors determining growth are complex, the fundamentals for long-run growth in many African countries seem to be found in investments in physical capital as well as in human capital. For such investments to be sustainable, they must yield, in their totality, high rates of return in foreign exchange, which is the long-term abiding constraint on investment and growth.

■ For the rural poor to benefit from economic growth the process of growth must be broad-based. Indeed, many African countries may have not reached the inflection point beyond which economic growth will improve the distribution of income. This implies that fast growth, without paying attention to the quality of growth, might not be sufficient to reduce rural poverty and that broad-based and pro-poor growth is needed if poverty is to be reduced.

CHAPTER 4

Empowerment and Resources for the Rural Poor

Introduction

As concluded in Chapter 3, rural poverty in Sub-Saharan Africa is widespread, deep and severe. Conventional money metric measurement reveals that most people in rural Sub-Saharan Africa live on incomes raging between 33 and 80 US cents per day. Rural people are not only income-poor but they are also deprived of basic necessities and capabilities as reflected in low educational enrolment ratios, low literacy rates, high infant and maternal mortality and inadequate access to sanitation and clean potable water.

Despite the increasing concern about poverty at the national, regional, and international levels, progress toward the reduction of poverty and deprivation remains inadequate. The assessment made in Chapter 3 shows that the majority of African countries will not be able to meet the international development goals of reducing poverty by half by the year 2015 and of achieving certain quantifiable improvements in education, health and social well-being. Regardless of the methodology used, the evidence for Sub-Saharan Africa is that the poverty reduction target as well as the other social goals in education, health, mortality and gender will not be met. The problems are especially challenging in rural areas, where poverty is deeper and more severe, and where rates of progress towards the desired social targets generally lag behind those of urban areas.

Rapid economic growth is necessary but not sufficient for reducing rural poverty and alleviating rural deprivation. Rural poverty reduction requires broad-based economic growth which can transform the rural sector and make the rural poor the main focus of development management. This chapter focuses on four key elements required for achieving rural transformation and poverty reduction:

- Promoting widespread growth in agricultural and non-agricultural sectors;

- Empowering the rural poor through the development of their human and social capital;

- Promoting appropriate innovations and technologies in rural areas; and

- Ensuring that rural natural resources are productively and sustainably utilized.

The Agricultural Sector and Productivity

Agriculture is Vital...

For Africa, agricultural growth is essential to economic growth, even though, in the long run, the share of agriculture in the economy falls as an economy grows. Rapid non-agricultural growth can hardly be attained without significant agricultural growth. Most of the developing countries that grew rapidly during the last two decades experienced rapid agricultural growth in the preceding years. Agricultural growth stimulates economic growth in non-agricultural sectors and vice-versa. The overall impact is to increase employment and reduce poverty.

Agriculture thus remains important in rural Africa, and indicators of rural well-being are closely correlated with agricultural performance. According to available information for 48 countries the agricultural sector continued to dominate African economies in terms of labor force, employing about 62 percent of the total. The distribution of countries by labor force employment in the agricultural sector is given in Table 4.1.

In 36 countries, representing four-fifths of the rural population of the continent, the agricultural sector accounts for the employment of half or more of the total labor force. In nine of these – Rwanda, Burundi, Niger, Burkina Faso, Liberia, Mozambique, Uganda, Gambia, and Mali – the employment share of agriculture is in excess of 80 percent. At the other extreme, in only four countries – Algeria, Libya, Mauritius, and Tunisia – is agricultural employment fall below 30 percent of the total labor force.

Real value-added in the agricultural sector registered an average growth rate of 2.3 percent per annum in the 1990s, half the rate for the late 1980s. But this average growth rate masks the wide disparity among countries (see Table 4.2). Close to a tenth of the rural population of Africa was living in countries where real value-added in agriculture declined by an average rate of 1.8 percent per annum. Relatively high agricultural growth rate was registered in four countries accounting for about 4 percent of the rural population. In 17 countries, accounting for about two-thirds of the rural population, an average growth rate of 3.2 percent was recorded.

African countries are widely diverse in their resource and factor endowments and in their ability to commit policy actions to increasing growth and

Table 4.1: The Distribution of African Countries According to the Share of Labor Force in Agriculture in 1996

Share of Labor Force in Agriculture (%)	Number of Countries	Average Share (%)	1998 Rural Population Weight (%)
Less than 30	4	16.75	4.08
30 – 40	3	34.00	10.65
40 – 50	5	45.00	4.25
50 – 60	5	54.40	4.90
60 – 70	10	64.90	33.50
70 – 80	12	74.25	30.99
80 +	9	84.00	11.63
Total/Average	48	61.60	100.00

Source: African Development Bank (2001: 249, table 3.3).

Table 4.2: The Distribution of African Countries According to Rate of Growth of Agricultural Real Value-Added in the 1990s

Growth Rate (%)	Number of Countries	Average Growth Rate (%)	Rural Population Weight (%)
Less than zero	9	-1.67	8.07
0 – 2	9	1.13	13.80
2 – 4	17	3.17	64.89
4 – 5	8	4.41	9.30
5 +	4	6.45	3.94
Total/Average	47	2.34	100.00

Sources: Compiled from ADB data base and World Bank (2001-a: 16, table 2-2).

reducing poverty. During the 1990s 12 of the 48 countries of Sub-Saharan Africa (SSA) were able to maintain agricultural growth rates of 4 percent or better. Agricultural growth in a second group of countries has been positive, but less than 4 percent per year on average, and in many cases less than population growth. Rural poverty is gradually worsening in these countries, and about half the African nations fall into this category.

A third group of countries is still immersed in civil conflicts with sharply rising poverty, particularly of the rural people displaced by fighting. About 20 percent of the total population of the continent – over 100 million people – live in these countries. More than four million Africans are currently refugees, displaced from their homes and deprived of their livelihoods. The impact of conflict is clear from the statistics. Countries that enjoyed high rates of agricultural growth during the 1980s, including Burundi, Rwanda, Sierra Leone, Comoros and the Republic of Congo, all experienced low or negative agricultural growth when overwhelmed by conflict in the 1990s.

Sub-Saharan Africa is the only region in the world which both the number and the proportion of malnourished children have been consistently rising in recent years. In a world that has experienced tremendous advances in knowledge and growth during the past century, one-third of all children in SSA continue to go to bed hungry and have their mental and physical development compromised by the ravages of hunger. With its combination of high population growth and lagging economic performance, SSA will be caught in an increasingly perilous situation. At the current pace, the number of malnourished children in the region is forecast to increase by 6 million, or 18 percent, in 2020 compared with 1997. Food insecurity in rural Africa is closely related to agricultural production and productivity.

...But Productivity is Low

Although African farmers have increased production at even more rapid rates during the past decade, they have done so mainly by cultivating more land and not, for the most part, by using more fertilizer, better practices, or improved varieties of crops. Consequently, although crop yields in SSA were nearly equal to those in South Asia in the 1960s, they are now far lower, and the gap is even greater between SSA and other developing regions. Thus, while agricultural output is growing in Africa, productivity is not. Agricultural productivity per worker for the region as a whole has stagnated during the past ten years at an estimated $365 per worker (constant 1995 US$). This is 12 percent lower than in 1980, when value-added per worker was $424. Increasing productivity per worker helps to fuel economic growth by generating the surplus that can be used for investment in agricultural and non-agricultural activities, and is widely regarded to be the first step in the process of agricultural transformation. Agricultural yields have also been level or falling for many crops in many countries. Significantly, yields of most important food grains, tubers and legumes (maize, millet, sorghum, yams, cassava, groundnuts) in most African countries are no higher today than in 1980. Cereal yields average 1,120 kilograms per hectare, compared with 2,067 kilograms per hectare for the world as a whole.

Low agricultural productivity has seriously eroded the competitiveness of African agricultural products on world markets. Africa's share of total world agricultural trade fell from 8 percent in 1965 to about 2 percent in 2000. Reduced competitiveness derives in part from internal factors that African governments can address, such as poor development of input markets, underinvestment in agricultural research, and insufficient attention to grading and standards. It is also due to factors that are outside the control of governments, including lack of meaningful progress on the reform of global agricultural trade. The largest trading partner for most African countries is the EU, which accounts for about 50 percent of exports and about 41 percent of imports. North America is second, accounting for 15 percent of exports and 30 percent of imports. Because such a large share of African exports are destined for the protected markets of Europe and North America, opening these markets could make a big difference for Africa's rural development.

Africa's low agricultural productivity is also the result of low investment in virtually all the factors that contribute to productivity. For example, only about 4.1 percent of land under cultivation in Africa is irrigated compared with 14 percent in Latin America and the Caribbean, a region with similar population densities and resource endowments. Also, in Africa fertilizer application is 15 percent lower today than in 1980. The number of tractors per worker is 25 percent lower than in 1980, being also the lowest in the world. The most critical constraints that impede agricultural productivity in Africa are both endogenous and exogenous to the sector.

The endogenous constraints include not only poor natural resource management and heavy dependence on rain-fed agriculture (and exposure to intermittent occurrence of severe and prolonged drought), but also the weak market linkages between producers and consumers. There has been inadequate investment in appropriate infrastructure for conditioning, storage, processing, transport and marketing of agricultural commodities. The failure fully to exploit the backward and forward linkages in commodity chains has led to poor coordination between activities at different stages of sub-sectors and impeded the exploi-

tation of the potential value-added from such linkages. This has also limited the timely transmission of accurate market signals.

In many countries, the inappropriate policy environment for agricultural investment has negatively affected productivity. Foreign exchange, trade and fiscal regimes, as well as food pricing schemes directed at urban consumers discriminate against agriculture and rural enterprises and reduce incentives for rapid economic growth. Despite the policy reforms introduced and implemented by many African countries, African farmers continue to bear a substantial burden via relatively high producer taxes imposed on most of the export commodities, which are the main source of foreign exchange in relatively agrarian economies. Along with the sharp decline in real prices of these commodities on the international market, this serves as a key disincentive to generating and sustaining the requisite supply response necessary to support the fast-growing populations of Africa. Other aspects of the problem are public sector intervention, inadequate legal and regulatory systems and the weak human and institutional capacities for appropriate government support.

The complicated land tenure systems in Africa pose another endogenous problem (see Box 4.1). Traditional tenure systems for agricultural land hinder the use of land as a collateral and/or guarantee for loans from formal financial institutions. The extended family structure of most African societies tends to promote and favor communal, as opposed to private, ownership of farmland. In most rural communities, land is regarded as a resource with multiple uses, including house construction, cultivation, grazing and collection of firewood for fuel energy, among others. This makes the transferability of farmland difficult. In rural communities characterized by male dominance of inheritance rights, women are

Box 4.1: Allocation and Distribution of Land in Rural Ethiopia

The cultivation of cereals and the use of the ox-plough for very long periods of time have shaped the agricultural landscape as well as influenced institutional features of rural Ethiopia. The *gult* system (fiefdom) has played an important role in the extraction of resources from independently cultivating farmers since the 13th century. Unlike feudal estates of Medieval Europe, centralized management of production did not exist. In many northern parts of the country, local allocation of land was through the *rist* system, where members of a lineage were entitled to land. In spite of the 'communal' nature of *rist*, it was characterized by competition; the amount of *rist* right that can be activated was determined by the political and social importance of the individual. With the incorporation of the southern regions into the 'modern' Ethiopian State, the *gult* system was extended to the south. Most land that was either common property or unused became state property to be given out for individuals loyal to the State/the emperor.

As a whole, the traditional land tenure system that had evolved for centuries minimized the widespread of landlessness. The evolution of the land tenure system towards private and more individualized holdings accelerated during the second half of the twentieth century. But that evolution was abruptly stopped by the reform of 1975 that nationalized all rural land. Peasant associations were then set up to allocate and distribute land as well as function as local administrative units. In principle, peasant associations distributed and allocated land according to family size. In other words, the 'allocation rule' attempted to equalize per capita land holdings. But studies indicate that in addition to the existence of significant intra- and inter-regional differences in per capita land distribution, other socio-economic characteristics of households also seem to have influenced land distribution, including the capacity of farmers to use the land as constrained by the institutional and market conditions. The allocations also seem to reflect the absence or thinness of land and labor markets and the relatively well-developed

nature of 'market' in ox draught power. The land reform proclamation has created an institutional constraint against the implementation of a broader 'welfare' program that can take account of the amount of labor, land and other assets households have. For example, peasant associations cannot compensate a poor household for shortage of labor by allocating more land. In most of the period land distributions were implemented, land rental (or sell) and hired agricultural labor were prohibited and hence there were no 'legal' ways the poor household would have used the land. In addition, the allocation system has more or less been immune from the manipulation by richer, more educated and informed people.

The land reform of 1975 was an important landmark in the evolution of the socio-economic conditions in rural Ethiopia not only as an economic but also as a political-administrative measure. Economically, its most important immediate impact seems in terms of abolishing the obligations of tenants to landlords and giving land to landless people. The more important economic effect of the land reform appears to have been the consequence of the nationalization of all rural land. First, this stopped the evolution of land tenure towards private property; even in traditionally *rist* areas the volume of transactions in land was on the increase prior to the reform. Second, this undermined security of tenure. Third, it gave a powerful leverage for the State, allowing it to intervene in many aspects of rural life, principally, villagization, and collectivization.

With the current direction of policy, privatization of land seems the logical next step in land policy. In addition to minimizing the risks associated with the current system, privatization may even help decrease inequality in land distribution. Particularly, inter-regional inequalities in land may significantly be affected by the creation and strengthening of a rural land market (for example, as happened in Uganda).

Source: Adapted from Kebede (2001).

relatively disadvantaged and suffer from lack of title rights, which they need as real guarantees or collateral for accessing rural credit. The overall effect of these constraints is that agricultural modernization is hampered, given farmers' limited access to formal sources of rural finance for investment. This is worsened by weak financial intermediation in the rural areas.

Policy articulation and formulation have often been conducted with only limited participation by end-users. The design of activities without client participation at all levels has led to inappropriate choice of interventions, lack of end-user ownership and commitment, failure to develop effective incentives for implementation of planned activities, and gender-based exclusion of participants. In addition, the failure to mainstream gender issues in the agricultural sector has further resulted in smallholder female farmers being less productive than they could be in agricultural production and marketing activities. It is a well-established fact that women contribute significantly to household food security and poverty alleviation by spending high proportions of their incomes on investments in household welfare. Therefore, giving inadequate attention to women has had adverse impacts on agricultural productivity.

Further problems hindering African agriculture include the high level of post-harvest losses and the inadequate adoption of available technology. Poor access to markets and inappropriate storage systems are principally responsible for high post-harvest losses (15-25 percent), which in turn have the indirect effect of slowing down adoption of tested technologies for certain crops and livestock classes. Low adoption and poor application of improved technologies for management of soil fertility and soil moisture have also increased the vulnerability of crop enterprises and diminished prospects for rapid and sustainable

advances in agricultural production, even where improved seeds, plant materials, and farming practices are available. Extraction of soil nutrients without effective replacement with organic and inorganic fertilizers leads to further declines in crop yields.

The exogenous factors inhibiting agricultural productivity in Africa are varied and numerous. First, high population growth rates put tremendous pressures on low input/low output agricultural systems and contribute to accelerating the degradation of the environment. Secondly, the poor state of the basic infrastructure for delivery of social services (especially education and health) to rural areas in many countries hampers the contributions of the rural labor force to productive enterprises and limits the knowledge base of rural people in dealing with the challenges they face. Thirdly, the absence of good physical infrastructure hinders the establishment of sound market linkages between producers, processors and consumers of agricultural commodities and products. For example there are inadequate road networks in many areas and there are difficulties in the delivery of basic utilities (electricity, water and communications) to rural communities and agro-industrial facilities. Fourthly, the international prices for most primary agricultural commodity exports as well as domestic prices of non-tradeable food crops have experienced a general decline in the last two decades, making farmers generally worse off. Fifthly, persistent instability, wars and civil unrest in some countries have triggered a widespread perception among potential private sector investors (domestic and foreign) of high risks and uncertainties associated with doing business in all African countries.

Finally, in rural communities where vector-borne and viral diseases (such as malaria, schistosomiasis, onchocerciasis, HIV/AIDS and yellow fever) are endemic, they become a health hazard to rural dwellers, especially those engaged in agricultural production. The agricultural production systems of the poor are vulnerable to both stresses and shocks. Stresses take the form of environmental degradation, the availability of food at household level, and the seasonality of production calendar. Shocks take the form of weather-related events (inadequate or excessive rainfall, heat, or frost), natural calamities (such as floods or extended drought), pests and diseases (such as locusts, rinderpest), as well as civil strife and external macroeconomic changes (such as changes in global market prices or currency devaluation). All these negatively impact on the overall levels of yields.

These problems call for urgent critical actions to increase agricultural productivity. These actions should include:

- Increased mobilization of farmer capacity to serve their own needs and the improvement of the physical and organizational conditions of market access to farmers;

- Empowerment of African rural farmers in developing their capacity to respond to their own rural financial needs and interfacing with up-stream financial institutions;

- Organizational and knowledge empowerment of rural farmers with respect to rural agricultural technology;

- Changing land legislation in favor of titling rural farmers and the promotion of independent access by women to land; and

- More intensive cultivation of existing land, accompanied by measures to maintain and replenish the soil so as to avoid degradation and loss.

The Rural Non-Agricultural Economy

A Necessity for Poverty Reduction

The rural economy in developing countries is often viewed as being synonymous with agriculture, especially farming and animal husbandry activities. According to this view, rural households receive most of their income from the production of food and export crops. Consequently, rural non-agricultural employment was seen as relatively nonproductive, producing goods and services of low quality. The rural non-agricultural economy is therefore expected to wither away with development and rising incomes, and this was viewed as positive, rather than a negative, event. A corollary of this view is that the government need not be concerned about the sector or about how policies elsewhere might harm it.

In recent years, however, it has increasingly been recognized that the rural non-agricultural economy has a positive role in promoting growth and welfare (see Box 4.2). It absorbs the growing rural labor force, slows rural-urban migration, contributes to national income growth, improves household security through diversification, and promotes a more equitable distribution of income (Lanjouw, 1999). It is also particularly useful in employing women and providing off-season incomes. Furthermore, the technologies used in small-scale rural manufacturing may be more appropriate and thus generate greater income from available productive inputs (Lanjouw and Lanjouw,

Box 4.2: The Role of Rural Non-Agricultural Economy in Africa

Survey results have shown that in Africa, rural non-agricultural employment ranges from a low of 6 percent in Mali to a high of 60 percent in Nigeria. In the same vein, the percentage of rural income from non-agricultural activities ranges from 23 percent in Tanzania to 52 percent in Burkina Faso. Results from Reardon *et al* (1998) indicate that rural non-agricultural income and employment account for 36 percent of total rural income and employment in West Africa. In Africa as a whole, the study not only finds that non-agricultural income shares have been rising but also that they are greater in the continent (42 percent) than either in Latin America (40 percent) or Asia (32 percent). The reason for this high rural non-agricultural income in Africa is that, though African households are poorer, the incentive to diversify their incomes is strong (due to low agricultural incomes, risks, etc). The greater portion of rural income comes from the service sector. Also, a recent study by Barrett et al (2000) shows that there is high incidence of African households earning incomes from multiple sources – 33 percent in Cote d'Ivoire, 94 percent in Kenya, and 37 percent in Rwanda – principally to diversify their livelihoods. Adams (2001) finds that over 55 percent of the total income of rural dwellers in Egypt comes from non-agricultural sources, including non-agricultural labor, government and private sector employment plus net revenues from non-farm enterprises. In addition, in Egypt, non-agricultural income represents an inequality-decreasing source of income in the rural areas. This is particularly because inadequate land access "pushes" poorer households out of agriculture and into the non-agricultural sector.

Sources: Adapted from Reardon et al (1998), Barrett et al (2000) and Adams (2001).

1995). In addition, it provides market linkages for agriculture while being a route out of rural poverty. An increasing number of the rural poor are turning to the rural non-agricultural economy as an alternative source of income and employment. The sector is also seen as a hedge against the risk of low household income and consumption during periods of natural disaster or bad harvest (Okidegbe, 2001).

The non-agricultural economy is increasingly seen as a vehicle for rural poverty reduction, and indeed evidence suggests that non-agricultural activities are generally associated with lower absolute poverty. A recent study of Ecuador shows that poverty declines as the share of total income from non-agricultural sources rises. The study recognizes the bimodal distribution of non-agricultural occupations into low-productivity and high-productivity sub-sectors. High-productivity activities in rural areas generally accrue to the relatively wealthy. The results show that employment shares on both high-productivity and low-productivity non-agricultural activities are associated with sharply lower absolute poverty rates (Lanjouw, 1999).

While high-productivity activities tend to be positively associated with rural inequality, the sub-sector acts as an engine of growth, lifting the poor out of poverty either directly or through generally rising wage rates. The low-productivity sub-sector, on the other hand, acts as a safety net that helps to prevent more households from falling below the poverty line. These results have been confirmed by results a recent study for Ghana and Uganda. It has been shown that in Ghana the incidence of non-agricultural poverty fell from 31.7 percent in 1987/88 to 24 percent in 1991/92. In Uganda, non-agricultural poverty declined from 54.4 percent in 1992 to 39.8 percent in 1996. It has also been shown that growth in non-agricultural activities is more beneficial to women since women participate more in these activities (Newman and Canagarajah, 2000).

Linkages

A virtuous cycle exists between the agricultural and rural non-agricultural economies, whereby, due to emerging green revolution technologies, increases in rural agricultural productivity (agricultural intensification) – and thus the incomes of farmers – are magnified by multiple linkages with the rural non-agricultural economy. The production and consumption linkages are important. Production linkages could occur, for example, when the demand of agriculturalists for inputs such as plows and machinery repair would stimulate non-agricultural activity via backward linkages, or where agricultural goods required processing in spinning, milling or canning factories prior to sale and thereby stimulated non-agricultural activity through forward linkages.

On the other hand, consumption could occur as rising agricultural incomes feed primarily into increased demand for goods and services produced in nearby villages and towns. Furthermore, rising agricultural productivity could release labor or raise wages for non-agricultural activities, and agricultural surpluses could provide investment funds for the non-agricultural economy. The expanding non-agricultural economy could then act as an impetus to further agricultural intensification, through lower input costs (backward linkages), profits invested back into agriculture, and technological change. The growth in these two sectors could be mutually reinforcing with incomes and employment increasing in a dispersed pattern. In Kenya, for instance, it has been shown that farm-based non-agricultural activities have stronger linkages than town-based manufacturing. In terms of the impact on employment generating,

the service sector is found to come first followed by farm-based non-agricultural and manufacturing production. In addition, returns to education in rural areas are generally very high in non-agricultural activities, especially in high-productivity occupations (Lewis and Thorbecke, 1992).

Promoting the Rural Non-Agricultural Economy

The rural poor have special problems in exploiting non-agricultural employment opportunities. A combination of limited human and social capital, insufficient access to markets, and lack of credit results in higher barriers to entry to remunerative rural non-agricultural employment opportunities. As a result of this the rural non-agricultural economy yields unstable returns, hindering its potential to reduce poverty. While much of the rural poverty debate focuses on increasing the incomes of poor farmers, many of the rural poor, especially women, are landless and are more dependent on rural non-agricultural income strategies. There is therefore a need to formulate and implement strategies for increasing the access of the rural poor to these highly heterogeneous activities. Specifically, promoting the rural non-agricultural sector would require action on the following key areas:

- Investing in primary schooling, as a long-term strategy for stimulating the non-agricultural economy;

- An increase in rural public works – these offer an opportunity to provide non-agricultural employment opportunities directly to the extreme poor in rural areas;

- Increased investment and links to external markets, collection of market information, development of rural infrastructure, and the empowerment of rural enterprises to compete in non-local markets; and

- The establishment of specialized rural financial institutions that lend to the rural poor for use in micro-enterprise development. Micro-finance development requires a systems approach so that different types of clients are reached with different financial products adapted to their needs.

Human and Social Capital

Serious Human Capital Deprivation

A key factor that traps the poor in poverty is the low level of human capital. Such human capital is usually composed of heath, nutritional status, and education (see also ADR 1998 for detailed treatment). It involves the most basic capabilities for human development, leading to long and healthy lives, acquiring knowledge, having access to the resources needed for a decent standard of living and being able to participate in the life of the community. Although the last 30 years have witnessed impressive progress in human capital development, huge challenges remain, especially in Sub-Saharan Africa (SSA), as evidenced by the following statistics:

- In 2000, the population of Africa reached 799.3 million, growing at about 2.5 percent each year, the highest rate of growth of any continent;

- The gross primary school enrolment rate in SSA stood at 78 percent in 1996 against the developing countries' average of 107 percent;

- In 1999, the adult literacy rate in SSA was 59.6 percent against the developing countries' average of 72.9 percent;

- Access to improved water source in SSA at the end of 2000 was 55 percent compared with 79 percent in all developing countries;

- In 2000, about half of the population of SSA still lacked adequate sanitation;

- Life expectancy at birth in SSA is the lowest among all the regions of the world at only 47 years, compared with more than 60 years in other regions and 78 years in OECD countries;

- Infant mortality in SSA is the highest in the world at 92 per 1,000 live births compared with developing countries' and OECD averages of 59 and 6 per 1,000 live births respectively;

- SSA has the highest under-five mortality rate of 161 per 1,000 live births, compared with the developing countries' and OECD averages of 85 and 6 per 1,000 live births respectively;

- African countries have the highest maternal mortality rates, reaching up to 2,300 women who die for each 100,000 live births in Rwanda;

- Undernourished people in SSA constituted 34 percent of its total population in 1996-1998, compared with the developing countries' average of 18 percent.

In 1995-2000, children under-weight for age in SSA stood at 30 percent while those under-height for age stood at 37 percent, compared with 24 and 28 percent respectively for the entire world;

- Out of 40 million people living with HIV/AIDS in the world in 2001, 28.1 million or over 70 percent live in SSA while out of the 5 million newly infected with HIV, 3.4 million or 68 percent are in the region. Also, out of 3 million who died of the disease in 2001, 2.3 million or 77 percent were in SSA, which also has the highest adult prevalence rate of 8.4 percent (UNAIDS, 2001);

- Annually, there are an estimated 300-500 million clinical cases of malaria, with 90 percent of them occurring in SSA. The disease kills more than one million people each year in Africa, the vast majority of whom are young children, especially in remote rural areas with poor access to health services. Malaria is endemic in a total of 101 countries and territories 45 of which are in Africa; and

- SSA had the lowest human development index of 0.467 in 1999, compared with 0.564 in South Asia, 0.719 in East Asia and the Pacific, 0.760 in Latin America and the Caribbean, and 0.900 in OECD – far below the global average of 0.716 (UNDP, 2001).

High Population Growth

The distribution of the size of rural population among the countries of the region is such that, in 1998, 13 countries had a rural population of less than one million, with Guinea-Bissau having the largest rural sector among this group (0.925 million) and Seychelles having the lowest size (with a rural population of about 38,000 people). Another 13 countries have a rural population in excess of a million but less than 5 million. The largest size of a rural sector in this group is to be found in Guinea (4.871 million) while the smallest is to be found in the Congo (1.095 million). Rural sectors with population in excess of 5 million but less than 10 million are to be found in yet another 13 African countries with the largest in Angola (8.052 million) and the smallest in Chad (5.606 million). In 9 of the African countries the size of the rural sector is in excess of 10 million but less than 20 million. The largest rural sector in this group is to be found in Kenya (19.786 million) and the smallest in Madagascar (10.454 million). The remaining five countries had a rural sector with a population size in excess of 20 million. These include the Congo Democratic Republic (about 34 million), Ethiopia (51 million), Nigeria (about 70 million), Tanzania (22.3 million), and Egypt (33.8 million). Thus these five countries account for about 44 percent of the rural population of the continent (see Figure 4.1).

The average annual growth rate of total population in Africa is estimated at 2.5 percent over the period 1990-1998, the highest in the world. The total population of North African countries was growing at annual rate of 2 percent while that of SSA was growing at 2.7 percent. The urban population of the continent over the time period under consideration was growing at 4.4 percent: at 3 percent for North Africa and at 5 percent for SSA. Thus rural population in Africa has been growing at an average annual rate of 1.7 percent over the period 1990-1998, with a standard deviation of 0.75 percentage points.

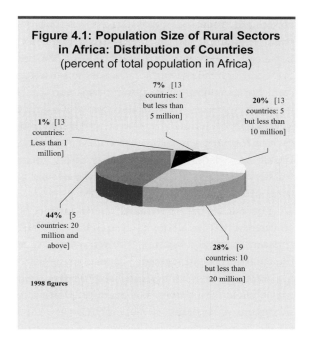

Figure 4.1: Population Size of Rural Sectors in Africa: Distribution of Countries
(percent of total population in Africa)

7% [13 countries: 1 but less than 5 million]

20% [13 countries: 5 but less than 10 million]

1% [13 countries: Less than 1 million]

44% [5 countries: 20 million and above]

28% [9 countries: 10 but less than 20 million]

1998 figures

Relatively high rates of rural population growth in excess of 2 percent per annum are to be found in 16 countries. The highest rate of population growth for this group, of 2.9 percent, is recorded for Niger and Uganda. Closely following are Congo Democratic Republic (with a growth rate of 2.89 percent), Swaziland (2.86 percent) and Zambia (2.8 percent). The lowest rates of rural population growth for this group are recorded for Mali (with a rural population growth rate of 2.02 percent) and Liberia (2.04 percent). In 15 countries the rate of rural population growth is in excess of 1.5 percent but less than 2 percent. The highest population growth for this group is recorded for Burkina Faso and Comoros (1.9 percent), followed by Côte d'Ivoire (1.89 percent), Gabon (1.88 percent), Egypt (1.84 percent), and Guinea (1.8 percent). The lowest rate of 1.5 percent is recorded for Senegal. Rural sectors with population growth rates equal to or in excess of 1 percent but less

than 1.5 percent are to be found in 8 countries. For this group the highest rate of 1.49 percent is recorded for Zimbabwe followed by Kenya and Sao Tome and Principe (1.43 percent) and Lesotho and Somalia (1.42 percent). The remaining 14 countries had rural population growth rates of less than 1 percent (see Figure 4.2). The highest rural population growth rate for this group is recorded for Sudan (0.94 percent), followed by Rwanda (0.92 percent) and South Africa (0.86 percent). The lowest rates are recorded for Tunisia (0.12 percent), Morocco (0.31 percent), Mauritania (0.34 percent) and Algeria (0.44 percent).

The population of Africa in 2015 is projected to grow to around the one billion mark. Producing food for an additional 200 million people in just 15 years will place an enormous strain on already scarce and degraded land and water resources. It will also put a strain on food processing and distribution systems needed to feed an urban population that is expected to double by 2015, from 215 million to 430 million. Food safety risks will grow with the increasing dependence of a large portion of Africa's total population on ever more complex and long distance agricultural-food supply and distribution systems. This is an important issue that will need to be addressed if rural poverty is to be reduced.

Education Indicators and Rural Poverty

Generally, education impacts on poverty through the following channels: economic growth, productivity growth, women's education and long-term development, and the quality of life (ADR 1998; IFAD, 2001). In particular, education of the rural poor is entirely inadequate because of lack of access to schooling and subsequent poor educational achievement. Available statistics indicate that school enrolment among rural children is lower

Figure 4.2: Population Growth in Rural Africa 1990-1998: Distribution of Countries

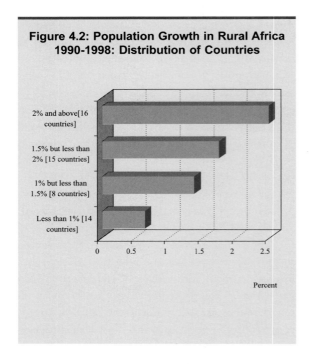

than that for urban children. For example, in 1990 in Nigeria 46.4 percent of rural children were enrolled in school against 73.1 percent in urban areas. Limited functional skills for the rural poor means that the rural laborers are impoverished when they have little control over wages or when they are out of work or unable to find work in periods of unemployment. Poor education (formal and informal) also inhibits the rural poor from taking advantage of new opportunities.

Limited education for rural households also has a gender dimension. In most African countries, poor rural girls are more unlikely to have access to education than their male counterparts, thereby denying them the skills they need to lead productive lives and escape from poverty. For example, in Algeria, in 1995 the rural literacy rates were 63 percent for males and 36 percent for females. Reversing this trend would require in-

creasing the focus of public spending on the rural poor, expanding the supply of basic education services and relaxing constraints on the demand side (through, for example, scholarships for the rural poor children). The government and international agencies should also address gender inequalities by getting girls into school by offering cash or food for schooling as practised in Mexico, Brazil, and Bangladesh, as well as hiring more teachers and offering them incentives to stay in rural areas.

Looking at the sectoral indicators, it can be confirmed that for all deprivation indicators there exists a statistically significant difference between the rural and urban sectors. The level of deprivation in the rural sector is much higher than that prevailing in urban areas. The average net primary school enrolment ratio of 34 percent for the rural sector compares with an average of about 62 percent in the urban sector. The most deprived rural sectors are to be found in Ethiopia, Niger, Mali and Senegal.

For the secondary school enrolment ratio the level of deprivation of the rural sector is much deeper, by comparison with the primary school indicators. Overall, the rural sector's secondary enrolment ratio of about 11 percent is about a third of that of the urban sector, at about 33 percent. Detailed information shows that while Nigeria (with a ratio of 38 percent), Ghana (35 percent), and Central African Republic (23 percent) have relatively high rural enrolment ratios, most of the countries of the sample had a ratio less than 10 percent. These countries include Côte d'Ivoire and Kenya (each with a ratio of 9 percent), Gambia and Madagascar (each with a ratio of 8 percent), Burkina Faso and Mauritania (each with a ratio of 6 percent), Mali (4 percent), Guinea and Senegal (each with a ratio of 3 percent), and Ethiopia with a secondary school enrolment ratio

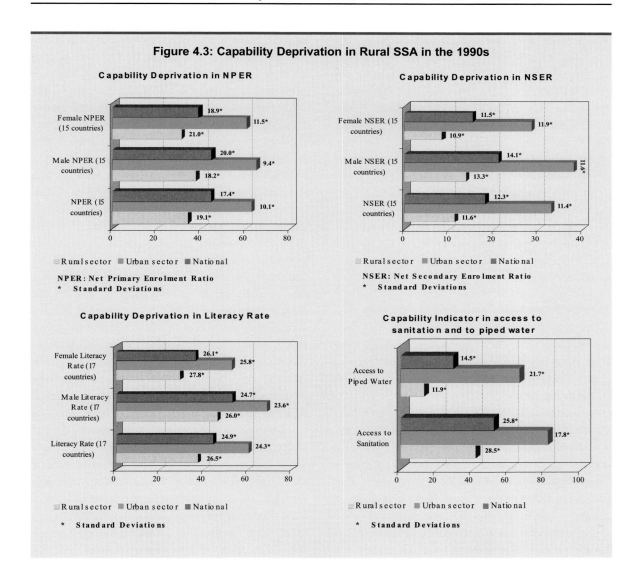

Figure 4.3: Capability Deprivation in Rural SSA in the 1990s

of only 1 percent.

A standard overall indicator of deprivation on account of education is the literacy rate. For the countries in the sample the average literacy rate is only 44 percent (with a standard deviation of 24.9 percentage points). For the rural sector the average literacy rate is 37 percent (with a standard deviation

of 26.5 percentage points) compared to an urban literacy rate of about 61 percent (with a standard deviation of 24.3 percentage points). Relatively high achievements on this indicator in the rural sector are recorded for Madagascar, Swaziland, Kenya and Tanzania and Uganda. The remaining countries had a literacy rate of 40 percent or less.

The most deprived are Mali, Guinea, Burkina Faso, Guinea-Bissau and Senegal (see Figure 4.3).

In addition to the general deprivation of the rural sector the Figure also reflects a dimension of gender discrimination. Gender inequality is usually discussed in terms of educational attainment. From the Figure, the female literacy rate for rural SSA is 29 percent compared to a male literacy rate of 46 percent, which indicates a level of social gender discrimination. The difference between the two is statistically significant at the 5 percent level. For the primary education level, however, the school enrolment ratios are 31 percent for females and 37 percent for males and the difference is not statistically significant.

Health Indicators and Rural Poverty

The linkage between ill health and poverty is two-fold: poor health keeps the poor in poverty, and poverty keeps them in poor health. Thus, ill health is both a cause and consequence of poverty. Loss of health may lead a person and his or her family to conditions of extreme poverty. This fact is exacerbated when family heads stop generating income as a consequence of their health problems. Poor families have to face costly treatment that may force them to pay excessive costs if they are to recover their health.

In the same vein, poverty is a disease that saps people's energy, dehumanizes them and creates a sense of helplessness and loss of control. The poor share an unequal burden of ill health. The poorest 20 percent of the world's population die from nearly two-thirds of the world's communicable diseases, malaria, perinatal mortality and nutritional deficiencies. Indeed, poverty has been identified as a cause, and associated factor, a catalyst and a result of ill health. One implication of this relationship is that improved health can

prevent poverty and offer a route out of poverty.

Unfortunately, the health of the rural poor is more deficient that of the urban ones because of poor nutrition and inadequate health care of the kind that is necessary to ensure bodily and mental capacity for longevity and resistance and/or quick recovery from illness. The rural poor are more malnourished because of an inadequate intake of calories (food insecurity), which in turn reduces their ability to fight off illness. This subsequently lowers their productivity and ability to earn enough income to meet their basic needs hence they find themselves trapped in a vicious cycle of perpetual poverty. Available statistics show that, for example, there is higher incidence of infant mortality in rural Africa than urban areas: 165.2 in rural Côte d'Ivoire against 120.2 in urban areas, 122 in rural Ghana against 76.8 in the urban areas, and 108.6 in rural Kenya against 88.3 in the urban areas. Access to health services is also worse in rural Africa. For example, only 11 percent rural households in Côte d'Ivoire have access to health services against an urban figure of 61 percent.

Disparities in health also have a gender dimension in rural Africa. In some societies, the lower value assigned to women and girls translate to excess infant mortality. Rural women generally have less access to health care, limited control over their reproductive health and unacceptably higher proportion die during childbirth. Among rural children lacking any vaccination in Ghana in 1993, for example, 17 percent were females while 14 percent were males. In Côte d'Ivoire, 18.2 percent were females while 16.4 percent were males. It is against this background that it has been observed that rural women have short life expectancy. For example, while women in industrial countries live, on average, almost 80 years, rural women in Ethiopia live, on average, only 41 years.

HIV/AIDS, tuberculosis and malaria have

been classified as the chief diseases of poverty, particularly in Africa – and more so in Southern Africa. These are the three diseases that alone kill more than 5 million people a year and in some countries account for half of annual deaths, especially in the rural areas. They are also classified among a group of diseases for which control efforts are being jeopardized by microbial evolution and hence they continue to spread worldwide. Urgent measures are therefore needed to stem the epidemic. Moreover, the poor tend to be affected most adversely as they usually have limited access to health services, information and protective measures, and have less power to avoid living or working within disease-infected areas.

According to the latest estimates by UNAIDS (2001), Sub-Saharan Africa accounts for 70 percent (28.1 million) of the existing HIV/AIDS cases in the world (40 million in 2001) (see Table 4.3) and about 91.6 percent of AIDS orphans. The region-wide adult prevalent rate is 8.4 percent against the global average of 1.2 percent. The epidemic appears to be increasingly concentrated in Africa where it accounted for 3.4 million of the 5 million new cases that occurred in 2001. It accounts for 77 percent (2.3 million) of the 3 million people who died of HIV/AIDS in 2001. In 16 countries in the region, at least 10 percent of those aged between 15 and 49 are infected. Moreover, in SSA the epidemic seems to be concentrated in Southern Africa and the adult prevalence rates seem to be increasing, being at least 20 percent in 2001.

The implications of HIV/AIDS for African countries are ominous. The epidemic is reversing progress in human capital formation, lowering productivity and life expectancy (47 years in 2001 instead of 62 years without HIV/AIDS), and decimating accumulated skilled labor force. Already, Botswana is being forced to import white-collar skills as a result of the impact of AIDS on the supply of trained workers. The disease is also changing the age and sex structure of the population. At the end of 2001 over 10 million children aged less than 15 years who were AIDS orphans – 90 percent of them in SSA, with its attendant social ills. The demands on the health sector for treatments of AIDS-related illnesses is overstretching already-inadequate healthcare budgets in most African countries, accounting for between 20 and 90 percent of health budgets.

The losses from absenteeism, in labor productivity and income ultimately affect savings at all levels of the economy, in turn slowing long-term investment. In South Africa, estimates show that overall economic growth rate over the next decade will be 0.3 to 0.4 percentage points a year lower than it would have been without AIDS. Cumulating the impact by 2010, real GDP will be 17 percent below what it would have been in the absence of AIDS. In 2000 values, this represents a loss of some $22 billion – more than twice the entire national production of any other country in the region except Nigeria. Estimates indicate that in the most seriously affected countries, GDP per capita will be 5 percent lower by 2010 than would have been the case without AIDS.

HIV/AIDS has now killed nearly 23 million Africans and orphaned over 10 million children. HIV/AIDS undermines agricultural systems and affects the food security of rural families. As adults fall ill and die, families lose their labor supply, as well as knowledge about indigenous farming methods. Families spend more to meet medical bills and funeral expenses, drawing down savings and disposing of assets. HIV/AIDS undermines the incentives and the ability to invest in farms, infrastructure and education, threatening future prospects for rural and national development.

While HIV/AIDS prevalence is still lower in

Table 4.3: Regional HIV/AIDS Statistics and Features, end of 2001

Region	Epidemic started	Adults and children living with HIV/AIDS	Adults and children newly infected withHIV	Adult prevalence rate (*)	% of HIV-positive adults who are women	Main mode(s) of transmission (#) for adults living with HIV/AIDS
Sub-Saharan Africa	late' 70s early '80s	28.1 million	3.4 million	8.40%	55%	Hetero
North Africa & Middle East	late' 80s	440 000	80 000	0.20%	40%	Hetero, IDU
South & South-East Asia	late' 80s	6.1 million	800 000	0.60%	35%	Hetero, IDU
East Asia	late' 80s & Pacific	1 million	270 000	0.10%	20%	IDU, hetero, MSM
Latin America	late' 70s early' 80s	1.4 million	130 000	0.50%	30%	MSM, IDU, hetero
Caribbean	late' 70s early' 80s	420 000	60 000	2.20%	50%	Hetero, MSM
Eastern Europe & Central Asia	early' 90s	1 million	250 000	0.50%	20%	IDU
Western Europe	late' 70s early' 80s	560 000	30 000	0.30%	25%	MSM, IDU
North America	late' 70s early' 80s	940 000	45 000	0.60%	20%	MSM, IDU, hetero
Australia & New Zealand	late' 70s early' 80s	15 000	500	0.10%	10%	MSM
TOTAL		**40 million**	**5 million**	**1.20%**	**48%**	

Notes: * The proportion of adults (15 to 49 years of age) living with HIV/AIDS in 2001, using 2001 population numbers.
    # Hetero (heterosexual transmission), IDU (transmission through injecting drug use), MSM (sexual transmission among men who have sex with men).
Source: UNAIDS (2001).

rural areas than in cities and towns, infections in rural areas are growing rapidly. Rural communities bear much of the burden of the disease because many urban dwellers and migrant workers return to their villages when they fall ill. As the number of productive family members declines, the number of dependents grows, putting families at great risk of poverty and food insecurity.

Women are particularly hard-hit by the HIV/AIDS pandemic. Biological and social factors make women and girls more vulnerable to HIV/AIDS than men and boys. Studies have shown that HIV infection rates in young women can be 3-5 times higher than among young men. Women and girls also face the greatest burden of caring for the sick and the children left orphaned. In many hard-hit communities, girls are being withdrawn from school to help families meet immediate needs.

In early May 2001, the World Health Organization (WHO) estimated that as much as $7 billion is needed from all sources annually to combat AIDS in low and middle income countries for effective response to the pandemic. A further $3 billion would be needed annually to drastically reduce the impact of tuberculosis and malaria. UNAIDS estimated during the same period that $3-4 billion will be needed in Africa for the same purpose annually, against current annual expenditures of $0.3-0.4 billion. The UN has therefore established a global HIV/AIDS and health fund aimed at fighting AIDS, tuberculosis and malaria.

Some countries, notably Senegal and Uganda, have demonstrated that it is possible to control the spread of the epidemic through effective prevention and AIDS awareness programs, provided this is driven by political commitment at the highest level. In contrast to the response in many African countries, Senegal did not deny the existence of the HIV/AIDS pandemic and hence faced the challenge from the start. The country enlisted all major sectors as allies in a timely and aggressive prevention campaign, as a result of which Senegal now has one of the lowest HIV infection rates in Africa of 1.8 percent of the adult population (as at June 2000).

While action at the international level to develop an AIDS vaccine is crucial for the future, experience has shown that what will really make a difference in the short term is effective leadership and societal change to prevent the spread of HIV, along with effective healthcare for those already infected. This involves confronting taboos about sexuality, while targeting information and support to high-risk groups and providing compassionate care for AIDS sufferers. This is where international assistance is urgently needed.

Mobilizing financial resources for prevention, care and support (including AIDS orphans), antiretrovirals as well as strengthening national coordinating bodies requires committing significant national funding to national HIV/AIDS plans from domestic budget resources, fund-raising campaigns, and integrating HIV/AIDS fully in national Poverty Reduction Strategy Papers and debt relief agreements under the enhanced HIPC Initiative. Industrial nations should also commit resources to the newly established Global HIV/AIDS and Health Fund.

Other effective measures include implementation of the recently adopted "African Consensus and Plan of Action", voluntary counseling and testing, prevention of mother-to-child transmission, and immediate treatment of other sexually transmitted infections (STIs). There should also be sexual education in schools and other community-based fora, provision of low cost combination drugs, and accelerated efforts at developing an effective vaccine.

Malaria, on the other hand, is by far the world's most important tropical parasitic disease, and kills more people than any other communicable disease except TB. Around the world, the malaria situation is serious and worsening. Annually, there are estimated 300-500 million clinical cases, with 90 percent of them occurring in SSA (WHO, 1998). The disease kills more than one million people each year in Africa, the vast majority of who are young children, especially in remote rural areas with poor access to health services. Malaria is endemic in a total of 101 countries and territories 45 of which are in Africa.

Malaria's cost to human and social well-being is enormous. It limits the productivity of a country's two major assets: its people and its land. The cost of prevention and treatment consumes scarce household resources. The burden on public health sector impacts on the allocation of government resources. Through its negative effect on child health as well as school attendance, performance and cognitive development, the disease reduces the accumulation of human capital. Consequently, the long-run growth potential is reduced in malarial areas.

According to estimates malaria slows economic growth in Africa by up to 1.3 percent each year (Gallup and Sachs, 1998). This is over and above the short-run costs of the disease, estimated at between $3 billion and $12 billion per year. Malaria is a principal cause of poverty, and poverty exacerbates the spread of malaria. Taken together, the effects of malaria on lives and livelihoods are devastating for economic progress in hard-hit Africa.

To achieve the Roll Back Malaria (RBM) target of halving the world's malaria burden by 2010, important new measures must be implemented. These include the adoption of multiple prevention strategies using insecticide-treated bed nets, a stratified approach to residual house spraying especially in high-risk areas, environmental management to control mosquitoes and making pregnancy safer. It is estimated that $1 billion is needed annually for malaria control, a large proportion of which should be spent in Africa. Spending this amount is economically justified as the short-term benefits of malaria control are estimated at between $3 billion and $12 billion per year. There should also be a global coalition on focussed research to develop new medicines (cheap and of high potency in view of increasing drug resistance), vaccines and insecticides and to help epidemiological and operational activities.

Social Capital is Critical in Rural Poverty Reduction

Social capital is broadly referred to as the rela-

tionships, institutions, networks and norms that enable collective action and shape the quality and quantity of a society's social interactions. Arising from families, communities, firms, civil society, the public sector, ethnicity and gender, it involves the internal social and cultural coherence of society, the norms and values that govern interactions among people and the institutions in which they are embedded (Collier, 1998).

Social capital can be bonding, bridging or linking. Bonding social capital results from the strong ties connecting family members, neighbors, close friends and business associates while bridging social capital results from weak horizontal connections between individuals from different ethnic and occupational backgrounds though with comparable economic status and political power. Linking social capital, on the other hand, is a vertical connection between poor people and people in positions of influence in formal organizations. The social interactions of social capital can be one-way (teaching, repeat trade, and authorities) or reciprocal (networks and clubs), producing externalities of knowledge, opportunism, or collective action (or free-riding). The mechanisms through which the effects occur include norms, rules, copying, pooling, repeat transactions, and/or reputation.

Social capital has important implications for poverty reduction. The poor have a lower opportunity cost of time and a lower stock of financial and physical capital than the rich. Since social interaction necessitated by social capital is time-intensive, and since social capital can often substitute for private capital, the poor may choose to rely more upon social capital than do the better-off (Collier, 1998). Social capital reduces the probability of being poor and the returns to household investment in social capital have been shown, empirically, to be higher for the poor than for the population at large. Also, social capital among the poor is critical to their short-term survival.

The poor can use social capital as an insurance mechanism which enables them to survive day-to-day when individually they cannot, for example, feed their children during the dry season, pay all their school fees, access formal credit services for their small enterprises, police their neighborhood or maintain a local well. Field survey results from Burkina Faso, for example, have shown that household social capital is positively associated with consumption, asset accumulation, and access to credit (Grootaert, 1999). Dense and overlapping social networks increase the likelihood of economic cooperation by building trust and fostering shared norms in the sense that the social capital generated within and between firms is especially important for lowering risk and uncertainty at the local level. Such social capital facilitates valuable information exchange about products and markets and reduces the costs of contracts and extensive regulations and enforcement.

At the community level, as the case of Tanzania demonstrates, social capital impacts on poverty by making government services more effective, facilitating the spread of information on agriculture, enabling groups to pool their resources and manage property as a co-operative, and giving people access to credit who have been traditionally locked out of formal financial institutions (Narayan, 1997). Social capital is also significant because it affects rural people's capacity to organize for development. It helps them to band together to raise their common concerns with the state and the private sector. Networks and norms of reciprocity facilitate common property management by providing the social relationships and trust upon which rules and monitoring can be based.

Community-based organizations have the potential to preserve the environment and local livelihoods when they band together to protect natural resources such as lakes, rivers and forests, from pollution and destruction through teaching environmentally-friendly practices locally and publicizing cases of corporate irresponsibility globally. In Côte d'Ivoire, for instance, water supply improved significantly when responsibility for maintenance was shifted from the national water distribution company to community water groups. Evidence shows that breakdown rates were reduced from 50 percent to 11 percent, while costs fell nearly 70 percent. More importantly, these results were sustained only in villages in which well-functioning community organizations existed and demand for water was high (Hino, 1993). Community level capital also helps to improve education and health facilities because schools and health institutions are more effective when parents and local citizens are actively involved.

Promoting Pro-Poor Social Capital

In spite of the benefits of social capital, a number of barriers inhibit its development in Africa. These include the segmentation of information and social exclusion, language, ethnicity, and political repression. Thus, the promotion of social capital in Africa is largely a matter of lowering costs, including those of the telephone system and transport. While information technology holds enormous potential for generating social capital, the poor are excluded from access, making the gap between the rich and poor wider. Governments, the private sector and international organizations need to focus their efforts on helping people in rural areas to set up multipurpose telecenters equipped with telephones, faxes, email and the internet, while offering requisite training and capacity building.

Governments have tended to retard the development of social capital by penalizing free association because it sees it as a threat to government control. Apart from improving institutions, public sector performance, and communications, a fairer judicial system can foster the conditions that make it possible for the poor to organize in their collective interest and to enhance their bargaining power.

Promoting Appropriate Technology

Global Technological Advance

Technology, like education, enables people to lift themselves out of poverty. It has become a tool for, not just a reward of, growth and development. Indeed, technological innovation positively impacts on human development through two channels. First, it directly enhances human capabilities. For example, many products such as drought-tolerant plant varieties for farmers in uncertain climates, vaccines for infectious diseases, clean energy sources for cooking, internet access for information and communication, can all directly improve people's health, nutrition, knowledge and living standards. They also increase people's ability to participate more actively in the social, economic and political life of a society.

The second channel through which technological innovation impacts on human development is through increased economic growth via the productivity gains it generates. Technological innovation raises the crop yields of farmers, the output of factory workers and the efficiency of service providers and small businesses. It also creates new activities and industries, including the information and communications technology sector, thus contributing to economic growth and employment creation (UNDP, 2001).

In the rural areas where majority of the poor live and where agriculture is the major occupation, one of the fastest ways to increase agricultural productivity rapidly is the adoption of new agricultural technologies. Rapid productivity growth enhances farmers' incomes and helps farmers manage risk. Agricultural innovations – such as high-yielding seeds, herbicides, fertilizers, agricultural machinery, and resource management techniques – result in increased food production. Advances in agricultural technologies not only help farmers to reduce risk, but it also helps to raise the demand for farm labor and lower food prices.

The benefits of agricultural technology can also be illustrated by the Green Revolution in South Asia during the 1960s and 1970s. During the Green Revolution small-scale farmers dramatically increased their productivity by adopting high-yielding rice and wheat varieties and using complementary inputs of irrigation and fertilizer. The adoption of new agricultural technologies has had significant positive externalities for the rural poor. Between 1965 and 2000 productivity gains in output per hectare of cereal crops averaged 71 percent globally. Improved bio-agricultural technology and water control took hundreds of millions of people out of poverty, mainly by raising production of food staples, providing employment and ensuring affordability.

Technological progress has been vitally important to the acceleration of food production and new agricultural technologies have succeeded in more than doubling global crop yields over the last 40 years. It took nearly 1,000 years for wheat yields in England to increase from 0.5 tonnes per hectare to 2, but only 40 years to go from 2 tonnes per hectare to 6. From 1960, the adoption of widespread plant breeding, fertilizer use, better seeds and water control transformed land and labor productivity around the world, eliminating much of the undernutrition and chronic famine in Asia, Latin America and the Arab states through increased food production and reduced food prices. This contributed to substantial declines in income poverty since the poorest families relied on agriculture for their livelihood and spent half of their incomes on food.

At the dawn of the 21st century, Africa is also presented with the challenge of encouraging the spread of information and communications technology and exploiting the opportunities of enhanced communications at all levels.

Appropriate Technology in Africa

Africa has not yet fared well in the adoption of the new global technologies. While the Green Revolution has led to increases in agricultural yields in Asia and Latin America, Africa still lags far behind in the use of modern seed varieties, tractors and fertilizer. Large regions and large numbers of the rural poor in Africa have gained little from the latest technological achievements and in many of these areas no technological change of any significance has yet taken place, even when new challenges arise, such as land loss and erosion, increasing salinity and urban expansion, water depletion and water diversion.

African research and extension institutions have been largely ineffective in developing technologies that respond to farmers' needs. National agricultural research and extension agencies have not only steadily deteriorated over time, governments have also have neither adequately funded the agencies nor given the local researchers the incentive to develop their skills. Even when research agencies function well, researchers often fail to develop research programs that respond to rural farmers' needs. Existing research and extension agencies are ill-adapted to diagnose

problems and offer appropriate solutions.

For most rural farmers in Africa one of the fundamental questions of technology is not just whether it exists, but also how to access it and how to adapt it to local production conditions. In Africa, technological adoption by rural farmers is among the lowest in the world. Two of the primary barriers to the adoption of new technology in these areas are lack of knowledge and over-regulation of agricultural technology transfer.

Research into agricultural technology is not enough on its own. The rural poor need more information about technological options and the capacity to evaluate advice. A social revolution in agricultural technology is required to elevate the poor from technology "objects" or recipients to technology "subjects", involved in specification of need, evaluation of responses and the choice of productive strategies. Unless the African rural poor have the power to participate in deciding which technology to use, they are unlikely to benefit from it. Improved agricultural technology will most benefit farmers who are active partners in setting priorities for both research and extension.

Evidence has shown that extension services substantially improve technology adoption rates, awareness and productivity. Information sharing on rural technology, including simple innovations for the poor and illiterate can have a large impact on productivity. Unfortunately, in most of rural Africa, public extension services are inefficient, ineffective and poorly targeted. Extension projects in these areas often suffer from inadequate client orientation, weak human resource capacity, and low levels of government commitment.

In most of Africa, a number of institutional obstacles restrict the delivery of new technology, including government's tendency to over-regulate the transfer of agricultural technologies for seeds, machinery, low-risk pesticides and feed mix (World Bank, 2001). The barriers take several forms, including the restriction of competition and the introduction of complex systems for testing, approval, and release of new varieties. The key channels of technology transfer – such as trade, technology licensing and foreign direct investment – are restricted in many countries.

The development and use of new technologies for agriculture in Africa is hindered by the lack of location-specific technologies. The inappropriateness of agricultural technologies to local conditions is compounded by the information gaps between researchers and users. In Africa, the demand for location-specific technologies is said to be too small to attract private sector investment, and there are low levels of such investment in Africa. Patterns of research expenditure indicate that most private R&D on agricultural seed focuses on development products with longer shelf life, herbicide resistance, and greater suitability for mass production techniques. By contrast, African priorities are greater nutritional content and robustness.

The widening global digital divide means that the use of new and old technologies is uneven, concentrated in industrial countries, in urban areas and among the affluent and educated communities in every country. For example, at the end of 2000, out of the world's 6.7 percent internet users, 54.3 percent were in the US, while only 0.4 percent were in Sub-Saharan Africa. In the same vein, only 0.7 percent of the population of SSA countries was using the internet at the end of 2000. But 79 percent of internet users live in OECD countries, which contain only 14 percent of the world's population. This mirrors the technology gap separating the rich countries from the poor ones, a gap that opened up during the industrial revolution and has yet to be bridged.

Constraints on the use of information technology in Africa include the absence of the requisite energy (electricity) and telecommunications (especially telephone) infrastructure as well as internet service providers in rural Africa. There is also the problem that the world wide web is beyond the reach of millions of people in Africa, partly because of the cost of computers that are the standard entry point to the web.

Ironically, however, African countries have the opportunity to push to the cutting edge by ensuring that new infrastructure is based on the latest technology. The continent could, in theory, leapfrog decades of development in telecommunications and information technology. The problem of inadequate and expensive telephone services in rural areas and the severe limitation it imposes on access to the internet can be surpassed by a combination of geo-stationary and low-earth-orbiting satellites. Indeed, the prospect of a remote school in an African village having access to the world's libraries using a one-meter dish is a change of a very large magnitude. Convenient turnkey satellite links, which can perform such services are now affordable to many African schools, and prices are expected to drop further in the future (Oshikoya and Hussain, 1998).

The high cost of computers and software represents another serious impediment to Africa's accessibility to the world of information technology. The unit price of personal computers is, for instance, higher than the per capita income of many African nations. However, the designed capacity and capability of such computers and software are not fully utilized by most users – even at top professional levels. Experts in the field suggest that bare-bone computers, perfectly serviceable for internet connections, word processing and graphics, could be built for a price six times lower than current levels. It will also be possible to produce simple stripped-down software at very low prices. Bulk purchasing could induce producers to comply with such requirements, as a commitment to purchase large quantities could convince computer suppliers to meet required specifications at sharply reduced prices. African countries need to play a collective and active role in determining the trends of the industry.

If African countries are to make their mark in determining information technology trends, rigorous visionary planning will be necessary. A government that plans for the computerization of its various sectors, say in five years, would need to draw plans detailing the quantities and the qualities of computers required and their technical specifications including compatibility and expendability. A similar approach within regional economic groupings would be more effective because of the larger purchases that could be made.

Unfortunately, most African countries do not have any explicit plans or policies on information technology. The acquisition of information technology and software is largely a result of isolated initiatives without preconceived strategies and policies. Computers and related materials are acquired by different private and public sector organizations with little coordination and planning. There is a need to devise clear national and regional long-term strategies and policies that cover the acquisition of information technology, its enabling environment and its applications. The strategies should quantify the investment requirements of the countries and identify the required changes in institutional, training, legal and regulatory frameworks to create the environment that would foster the development of the information societies in Africa. Such strategies would also serve as an explicit recognition of the challenges of the information technology and as instruments for attracting and co-ordinate donor assistance.

Promoting Inclusive Technology Policies

It has also been observed that using the technology achievement index (TAI) – developed by UNDP (2001) – including the creation of technology, diffusion of recent innovations, diffusion of old innovations and human skills, Africa is a marginalized continent. Many of the technologically-excluded nations, especially in Africa, are therefore caught in a poverty trap. Among the greatest problems are tropical disease, low agricultural productivity and environmental degradation – all requiring technological solutions beyond their means. Sometimes, the needed technologies are available in the developed world, but the countries are too poor to buy or license them on the necessary scale. Most often, the technologies do not exist in appropriate forms, and poor African markets offer scant incentives for research and development. If Africans living in the technologically-excluded countries are to join in the benefits of globalization, action must be taken on a number of fronts through an inclusive technology policy:

- The new technologically-driven character of the global economy must be properly thought through: geography, ecology, and public health must be brought into the analysis of technological change and economic growth;

- Both advanced and developing country governments need to change their approach to aid, by spending more, and more wisely;

- Participation in international assistance

needs to be broadened and recast. Multi-national firms and first-world universities and scientific establishments need to be engaged, and the official agencies charged with global development would need to be enhanced;

- Institutional reforms for improving extension services must include decentralization, privatization, and separation of funding from execution;

- Location-specific technologies for African countries will require public intervention and local research and adaptation and also addressing intellectual property rights, agricultural research institutions, and competitive grants and negotiated contracts;

- There should be increased dissemination and use of improved agricultural inputs and practices. In the area of crops, the focus should shift to the use of high-yielding inputs that increase factor productivity. Technological change will involve more efficient use of chemical, biological, and organic inputs, introduction of high-value crops, use of improved farm implements and small-scale irrigation;

- In the livestock sector, husbandry techniques will have to be updated while transhumance production is gradually abandoned due to its low productivity and its adverse ecological impact. There is need to intensify efforts to diversify beyond cattle production into the production of small ruminants and poultry, which offer opportunities for increasing rural income; and

- There must be a renewal of focus on rural-based processing of Africa's main cereals, legumes, and roots and tubers. The increased pursuit of upstream activities in the production of seeds, planting materials, farm implements, and tools as part of the strategy for rural poverty reduction will also provide the push for agro-industrialization to increase value-added in agriculture.

The Role of CGIAR

The Consultative Group on International Agricultural Research (CGIAR), working in more than 100 countries world-wide, including those in Africa, is mandated to contribute to food security and poverty eradication in developing countries through research, partnerships, capacity building, policy support, and promotion of sustainable agricultural development based on the environmentally sound management of natural resources (see Box 4.3). Sub-Saharan Africa has consistently been receiving the largest amount of the investment from the CGIAR budget. The share of Sub-Saharan averaged over 40 percent of the budget, followed by Asia with about 30 percent share. The new CGIAR vision and strategy calls for the adoption of a regional approach to research planning, priority setting and implementation.

CGIAR's research-based agriculture has contributed to growth and development, enabling millions to begin their ascent from poverty. This is supported by the evidence which shows that a 1 percent increase in agricultural growth in developing countries leads to a 1.5 percent increase in the non-agricultural economy. It is against the background of CGIAR's contribution in the fight against poverty, hunger, malnutrition, inequality, and environmental degradation in Africa that the ADB Group had been providing financial and

technical support to CGIAR since 1986. The annual support provided to CGIAR centers ranged from $800,000 in 1986/87 to $1.8 million in 1990/91, while the 1991/93 allocation from Technical

---

Box 4.3: CGIAR and Sustainable Agriculture

Over the 30 years of its existence, CGIAR scientists have consistently demonstrated that sustainable agriculture and its driving force – agricultural research – can be a powerful force for achieving sustainable development. Its research – both strategic and applied – focuses on higher-yielding food crops, more productive livestock, fish and trees; improved farming systems; better policies; and enhanced scientific capacity in developing countries. Some of the major achievements of the CGIAR system include:

- Farmers in Africa and other developing countries are now growing more than 300 varieties of wheat and rice as well as more than 200 varieties of maize developed through CGIAR-supported research. The new maize varieties, for example, have 30-50 percent higher yields even when grown in difficult drought and low-fertility soil conditions. Apart from earlier maturity than traditional maize varieties, they can be eaten green, making a vital difference in the economic and social well-being of poor farm families. This is especially important in SSA where maize accounts for almost 40 percent of all cereal production. Thus, food production has doubled, improving health and nutrition for millions. Golden rice, rich in beta carotene and other carotenoids, promises to be more effective in combating Vitamin A deficiency, a condition estimated to cause half a million cases of irreversible blindness, and up to one million deaths, worldwide annually;

- Integrated pest management, the biological control of pests, and the development of disease-resistant plant varieties have helped to reduce pesticide use in Africa and other developing countries. For example, control of cassava pests alone has increased the value of annual production in SSA by $400 million (CGIAR, 2001). In Nigeria (through its work with the International Institute for Tropical Agriculture – IITA), for instance, new intercropping practices have reduced Striga attacks (a parasitic weed) by 63

percent, greatly improving maize harvests. Also, in Kenya, farmers participating in a pilot project have increased their maize yields by 20 percent through intercropping and habitat management. A vaccine is also being developed for East Coast Fever, a cattle disease that causes losses of $200 million each year in Africa. The vaccine promises spillover benefits for cancer and malaria research;

- CGIAR's research into community-based forest management has resulted in the development of environmental indicators for tropical forests. These help scientists to monitor the environmental effects of reduced-impact logging while helping the utilization of non-timber forest products and improving the sustainable productivity of plantation forestry;

- The intensive use of CGIAR's new technologies has led to saving of land from cultivation, globally equivalent to the total arable land of the US, Canada, and Brazil. At the same time, the biodivesrity of the "saved" lands was conserved;

- Research on water management has also generated knowledge on how more sustainable farm production can be achieved in irrigated areas;

- Some 75,000 developing country scientists have been trained at CGIAR centers;

- CGIAR promotes participatory research with a bottom-up approach and collaboration with national agricultural research systems; and

- Research by CGIAR has enabled local communities to undertake their own initiatives to conserve and protect marine resources, including the protection of mangrove forests and the prevention of destructive fishing practices.

Source: Adapted from CGIAR (2001).

Assistance Fund sources was about $1.7 million. The allocation made in 1998 amounted to $3.3 million. However, the incidence, depth and severity of rural poverty call for the increased support of the donor community to technology development in Africa.

Natural Resources

Land and Water Resources for the Rural Poor

There is ample evidence that rural households in Africa depend heavily on natural resources. This is why issues related to rural poverty relate particularly to the access of the poor to natural resources, primarily to land and water resources, specifically for agricultural purposes. Apart from agricultural uses, the poor typically make use of natural resources for a wide range of purposes – as many as 100 items as shown by a recent study in Zimbabwe (IFAD, 2001). About 70 percent of Africans rely directly on natural resources for a part or all of their incomes, hence improved natural resource management can lead to higher incomes and reduce risk.

Unfortunately, the natural resource base on which most of Africa's rural poor depend is steadily deteriorating. Soils are under stress from poor cropping practices and increased exposure to wind and water. Much of the continent is subject to extreme annual variability in rainfall of plus and minus 35 percent, bringing poorly predictable droughts and floods and massive macroeconomic shocks. Despite higher than average variability in supply of water, the region has very little storage capacity. For example, in Ethiopia 43 cubic meters of water are stored per capita, compared to 746 cubic meters in South Africa, and 6,150 cubic meters in North America.

In Africa, there is increasing evidence of a "cumulative causation" link between land degradation and conversion hence agricultural cultivation is not highly productive, a problem worsened by rapid rural population growth (Barbier, 1998). The two processes of land degradation and conversion are clearly related. Overgrazing and agricultural activities are the major causes of land degradation across the continent. Many of the continent's pastoralists and farm households respond to declining productivity by abandoning existing degraded pasture and cropland, and move on to new lands. In the absence of additional investments in soil conservation, this process repeats itself. Eventually, overgrazing and over-cultivation lead to land degradation, and the search for new pasture and cropland begins again.

Available evidence shows that about 25 percent of the world's degraded land is located in Africa, and over 22 percent of the vegetated land in the continent is degraded. Overgrazing accounts for 49 percent of the human-induced soil erosion in the continent, while agricultural activities account for 24 percent. In addition, deforestation and wood harvest (for firewood) account for 14 percent of the degradation. Since soil is an essential input in farming, the impacts of land degradation and the depletion of soil resources have profound economic implications for low-income countries and poor rural regions of the continent.

Moreover, a substantial proportion of Africa's poor people is concentrated on low-potential and fragile lands that are prone to degradation. Just over half of the continent's poorest 20 percent of the rural population are found in these regions. Therefore, the economic livelihoods of many poor rural households across the continent are directly dependent on the exploitation of lands that are highly vulnerable to degradation. Unfortunately, the extreme poverty of these households influences their ability and willingness to control degradation of the lands. Thus, poverty operates as a constraining factor on poorer rural households' ability to avoid land degradation or to invest in mitigating strategies. Indeed, empirical evidence suggests that poorer households in rural areas are more constrained by access to credit, inputs and research and extension services necessary for making investments in improved land and resources management.

In many parts of Africa, land tenure is a major issue affecting farmer productivity and natural resources management. Small-scale rural farmers do not have access to sufficient land to enjoy the prospects of significant reductions in poverty through agricultural development. In parts of Southern Africa, colonial regimes encouraged the setting up of elite settler that took the best land and pushed indigenous people to marginal lands. This created a highly skewed access to land and put land reform via redistribution prominently on the political agenda, as being currently experienced in South Africa, Malawi, and Zimbabwe. In West Africa, land distribution patterns are much less skewed; it is common for farmers to have usufruct rights, with access to land largely governed by traditional village chiefs. Communal ownership rather individual ownership is the norm throughout most of West Africa. In this region, therefore, when poor people's rights to land are considered, it is generally more appropriate to focus on the level and the security of access, rather than on land ownership.

Another dimension of land tenure in most parts of Africa is that women's access to land is low, being also less secure than men's. The reasons for this include inheritance practices, bias on the part of governments in apportioning improved land (such as irrigated perimeters), and generalized marginalization of women from community decision-making. There is also the issue of high incidence of violent conflicts between farmers and herders in the semi-arid zones of Africa, in many cases resulting in ethnic conflicts and huge loss of human capital.

One of Africa's scarcest commodities – fresh water – is rapidly being depleted through inefficient use and polluted by industrial and domestic effluents, and by degradation of watersheds in major river basins. Through investments and continued reforms, Africans must manage scarce water resources effectively for agriculture, industry and human consumption, yet still leave enough to maintain healthy ecosystems.

Empirical evidence has shown that there is a close correlation between environmental degradation of water resources and poverty. The poor must often use poor quality water contaminated by sewage, industrial and agricultural pollutants or siltation from soil erosion and suffer from debilitating diseases. In poor societies, a substantial amount of time is taken to search for water and energy supply particularly by women and children. The trees cut, the crop residues and animal dung collected from the agricultural land for household energy supply result in severe soil fertility and land degradation, which eventually results in poor water quality and quantity. Unfortunately, these poor societies are incapable in terms of resources, knowledge and organizational skill, to undertake measures for mitigating environmental degradation, thus resulting in a continuous spiral of poverty and environmental deterioration.

Wetlands, forests, and rangelands are all receding or degrading at a rapid rate across much of the continent, with major adverse consequences for the poor. Negative impacts of the loss of forest ecosystems include deterioration of watersheds resulting in droughts and flooding and a deepening fuel-wood shortage.

The loss and degradation of natural resources is accompanied by loss of biodiversity, which has both short- and long-term implications for the region's poor. In the short run, people suffer from loss of access to economically important natural products such as medicinal plants, foods (including famine reserves), and building materials. Longer-run impacts include ecological instability and pest and disease outbreaks.

Many marine, coastal and freshwater fisheries that provide protein for a large part of the population are threatened by over-fishing and by reduced surface water flows and pollution. The African continent leads the world in the burden of disease arising from unclean water and poor sanitation, malaria and (together with India) indoor air pollution.

In Africa, there is heavy dependence on rainfed agriculture and exposure to intermittent occurrence of severe and prolonged drought. Vulnerability of rain-fed cropping systems to interannual variations in temporal and spatial distributions of rainfall is high, particularly in the Sahelian and Sudanian zones, in North Africa, and in semiarid Southern Africa. Incidentally, only 6.7 percent of arable land are under irrigation in Africa; a proportion which falls to 4.1 percent in subSaharan Africa. Apart from its low level of irrigation, African agriculture is also faced with severe intermittent drought, which compounds the effects of other factors on food insecurity and poverty. Prolonged droughts generate a series of negative shocks, which have the domino effect of eventually crippling agrarian societies. The immediate impact is usually reduced water supply to agricultural, industrial and domestic users. This, in turn, translates into massive crop failure and sometimes literally wipes out livestock populations in affected areas. Consequently, food prices rise, aggravating food insecurity for vulnerable groups

of society and reduced agricultural output stifles agro-industrial growth, which contracts the national income. The net effect is increased unemployment and loss of income at household and national levels. Thus, drought is not just a food security or environmental problem, but also a social, economic and political issue.

The critical role of irrigation in areas where farmers face uncertainty in water supply is well understood, since as compared with rain-fed cultivation yields and numbers of crops may be increased substantially. This is a particular issue in the region since over the last three decades agricultural production has increased on average by below 2 percent annually, which is less than the growth of population. Many of the very poor as we have seen are not self-sufficient in food and hence are highly vulnerable to shortfalls in harvests, particularly those associated with serious drought. Irrigated area remains low in Sub-Saharan Africa, roughly 6.5 million hectares compared with an estimated potential of around 40 million. For example as an extreme case in Ethiopia it is estimated that only 4 percent of the potentially irrigated area is actually developed by irrigation (World Bank, 1996b).

Irrigation projects in Africa may offer the potential for high economic returns, but there are also potential difficulties. Large and medium scale projects are generally more expensive (in investment costs per hectare of irrigated land) than in any other region of the world. This is partly due to the technical difficulties posed by the need to include storage works to regulate river flow, by the severity of the climate, requiring flood protection, and by the remoteness of many locations. However inefficiency in local construction and engineering activity and are also cited as factors (World Bank, 1996b). The current focus is now on smaller irrigation schemes that involve local farmers. Simple designs that provide primary and secondary water supply and drainage infrastructure, but allow farmers or groups of farmers to use their own resources to construct tertiary distributions systems or to install pumps to lift water to their fields, are the model recommended. What is important from the distributional standpoint however is that poor farmers are allowed to participate in such schemes or are helped to do so through either financial or technical support. The other elements of the package that need to go with irrigation water (such as new seed varieties and fertilizer) also need to be provided. Not all of the rural poor will have access to land to take advantage of such opportunities. However, in so far as irrigation projects increase agricultural production this will raise the demand for labor, so that some of the landless poor may obtain income as hired laborers on the land of farmers who can take advantage of the availability of irrigation water.

In addition to irrigation projects, a range of other less costly measures, such as improved water harvesting techniques and better water and soil conservation practices will help to achieve more efficient use of water and thus increase agricultural output in rain-fed areas.

Sustainable Natural Resources Management

Of the constraints to rural poverty reduction, the problem of identifying and implementing appropriate natural resource and environmental management systems is perhaps the most complex and difficult to address (IFAD, 2001). This is because design of appropriate measures is site-specific and depends on many factors (technical, economic, political and socio-cultural) that are interrelated in ways that are not always readily apparent. The complexity of the problem requires a learning and partnership approach to natural resource management, involving rural people, extension agents, researchers and donors.

There is also an urgent need to adapt available technologies to local circumstances, taking cognizance of the seasonality of labor availability, social organization and cultural acceptability as well as ease of replication by farmers. Greater emphasis need to be placed on participatory rural appraisal; demand-driven, multidisciplinary and participatory technology development; incorporation of social and cultural perspectives into agricultural research; and giving much more attention to the critical role women play in agriculture. Different types of agency (NGOs, government research and extension) can each bring their strengths to bear in collaborative efforts which are interdisciplinary, supportive of farmers' aspirations, and based on joint learning.

Investment in physical structures to prevent erosion is unlikely to be sustainably effective in the absence of improvements in land husbandry. A land husbandry approach focusing on higher yields and improved vegetative cover, reduced raindrop impact and runoff, and improved soil architecture can reduce erosion and improve fertility, and enhance farm livelihoods.

Where conditions are suitable, increased residues and soil cover resulting from higher yields can generate an upward spiral of improvement in soil productivity. The inclusion of leguminous green-manure/cover crops in small-farm systems have shown such effects dramatically, by contributing not only dense cover over the soil and large quantities of organic matter to the soil, but also significant quantities of microbially-fixed nitrogen as an essential plant nutrient.

Farmers can be taught to raise the natural fertility of the soil through the improvement of the texture, organic matter content, porosity and nutrient levels of the soil. This can be done by the combinations of modifications to tillage systems, incorporation of organic matter, the use of crop residues as protective mulches, mixing with other soils (sands to decrease density, clays to increase density), adding plant nutrients, drainage, and other soil-improving actions.

Rural farmers generally possess inadequate scientific knowledge to complement their own indigenous knowledge of natural resource management. Yet, access to reliable information on resource conditions and on the effects of different resource use patterns is essential for the long-term management of natural resources and the sustenance of livelihoods that depend on them. Public institutions can assist rural farmers by carrying out environmental assessments of resource use patterns and determining resources, which are being degraded or at risk, and providing training on improved management techniques.

Another particularly promising avenue for development policy and donor agency approaches to both poverty reduction and sustainable environmental management is "substituting employment for environment", or providing jobs as a central means of livelihood security for poor people. Where poor people are driven to degrade the environment, on which they depend, it is almost invariably because they lack alternative choices. The guiding principle should be to widen this range of choice, primarily to support the livelihoods of present generations of poor people. However, the imperatives of population growth add even greater urgency to this principle, so as not to compromise the ability of future generations to earn a living too.

In low-potential areas in which the thresholds of ecological sensitivity and resilience have not yet been crossed, social welfare transfers to the poor could be channeled through public works programs geared at supplementing natural resilience, such as tree-planting by means of rainwater harvesting in dry lands. However, in already degraded environments, similar kinds of public works programs could be geared to environmental rehabilitation while in high-potential areas, the emphasis should be on methods of agricultural intensification that do not displace labor to ecologically vulnerable, low-potential areas.

Some Policy Implications

The above analysis calls for urgent critical action for the reduction of rural poverty. Future increases in agricultural production will have to come increasingly from more intensive production on existing agricultural land. More intensive agricultural production will have to be accompanied by measures to maintain and replenish the soil to prevent agricultural areas from becoming degraded. Better rural infrastructure will also allow increased production to reach consumers in larger towns and cities. Achieving these will require more enlightened policies and substantial investment in agricultural inputs, such as fertilizer and irrigation, as well as in roads, clean water, and education. Indeed, reducing by one-third, the number of malnourished children in Sub-Saharan Africa from 33 to 22 million, by 2020 would require an increase in total investments on roads, irrigation, clean water, education, and agricultural research from US$76 billion to US$183 billion, between 1997 and 2020.

In addition, crop yields would have to grow at an annual rate of around 3 percent. More significantly, total gross domestic product (GDP) would have to grow at an annual rate of 8 to 10 percent. Such rates of growth, while spectacular, are not unprecedented since they occurred in Asia during the Green Revolution. Unfortunately, Sub-Saharan Africa faces more severe constraints, including more difficult agro-climatic conditions, higher cost of exploiting water resources, and more limited transportation and communications infrastructure. However, the costs of not making the necessary investments in Sub-Saharan Africa will be tremendous, not only to the region but also to the rest of the world. Sub-Saharan Africa is one of the last two bastions of hunger and malnutrition (South Asia is the other), and without progress here, the world would make only a small dent in the global burdens of malnutrition and poverty.

With respect to rural technology, as noted earlier, this will require both organizational and knowledge empowerment. In particular, sustained improvement in the rural poverty situation will require rural farmers to have access to information about technology in areas where they feel they might be able to establish profitable operations, optimizing the impact of increased access to material inputs.

Regarding land tenure systems, measures should focus on changing land legislation in favor of titling rural farmers and promoting independent access by women to land. In the area of water access, apart from promoting increased investments in the exploitation of irrigation potential, rural farmers need to be organized for effective bargaining in obtaining access to critical agricultural water resources. In all these, however, there is need for forging strategic partnerships to ensure that donor resources are focused on solving the bottlenecks facing the rural poor in developing their own social and economic strategies.

Increased investments in rural human and social capital are important in enabling rural development and empowering the rural poor. This is because the dynamic rural economies depend on active, healthy people, who are able to manage complex, diversified livelihood portfolios, are familiar with new technologies, are engaged as citizens, and have the capacity to organize and to exercise choice. Creating human and social capital that the rural poor own or can use requires action on four fronts. First, governments must increase the focus of public spending on the rural poor in particular, expanding the supply of basic social services and relaxing constraints on the demand side (through, for example, scholarships for poor rural children). Second, governments must ensure the participation of communities and households in choosing and implementing services and monitoring them to keep providers accountable. Third, governments must ensure good quality service delivery through institutional action involving sound governance and the use of markets and multiple agents. Fourth, governments and their agencies must work with and support networks of the rural poor as well as enhance their potential by linking them to intermediary organizations, broader markets, and public institutions. This will also require the improvement of legal, regulatory, and institutional environments for groups representing the rural poor.

CHAPTER 5

Making Globalization, Markets and Institutions Work for the Poor

Introduction

Poverty outcomes are closely related to the functioning of markets and institutions. The market place is where resources are allocated and incomes are generated and distributed among market participants — including profit-seekers and salary and wage earners. For the poor whose principal asset is labor, which can be hired for a wage or used for own production, both internal and external markets determine the value of their labor and output. Institutions, on the other hand, have the potential to correct market outcomes, and can empower the poor, whether through increasing their capacity to produce goods with high internal and external demand or through enhancing their ability to access markets.

What is true for an individual in a given country is true for a country in the global economy. In today's globalized world, net export earnings play a leading role in the determination of national incomes. International trade, thus, provides the link between the global market and the economic fortunes of a country. Development theory and economic history demonstrate that any open economy which has accelerated growth and raised the living standards of its people, on a sustained basis, has needed to significantly improve its trade performance. What makes the present global tide a potent force is its direct bearing on this important parameter. It is through the conduits of trade that the positive and negative forces of the global market are transmitted and the economic prospects of countries and the people that work and

live in those countries are determined. This Chapter aims to explore how globalization and markets impact the poor and what can be done to make markets (internal and external) and institutions work for the rural poor.

Globalization, Trade and Growth

In economic terms, globalization represents the integration of national markets, as impediments to cross-border transactions are reduced and international flows of ideas, capital, goods, services and people increase (see Box 5.1). The process has also been accelerated in recent years by the contraction of restrictions to international activities. International bodies like the World Trade Organization (WTO) have advanced multilateral agreements on the removal of restrictions on trade and capital flows. Many countries, particularly in the developing world, have also been undertaking these decisions unilaterally, often under the auspices of structural adjustment programs.

Trade is one of the most important and most visible aspects of globalization with the potential to make an immediate and direct impact on poverty. There is, however, intense controversy surrounding the effects of globalization on rural poverty. Some argue that the rural poor will lose out because of unfair competition from technologically advanced foreign producers, as they will be exposed to greater risk associated with price competition and fluctuations, and because they have problems accessing even liberalized domestic markets, let alone international ones. Others

---

Box 5.1: Some Definitions of Globalization

"The power to act instantaneously at a distance" – Manuel Castells.

"The tendency for the economic significance of political boundaries to diminish" – David Henderson.

"Globalization is the process whereby the world's people are becoming increasingly interconnected in all facets of their lives – cultural, economic, political, technological, and environmental" – George C. Lodge.

"Globalization…refers to a set of emerging conditions in which value and wealth are increasingly being produced and distributed within world-wide corporate networks" – The Technology/Economy Program (TEP).

"We are now beginning a reality beyond globalization – the world of globality" – Daniel Yergin.

Source: Adapted from Streeten (2001).

---

maintain that the poor can realize potential gains, providing they can be assisted to participate in markets. It is clear that complex mechanisms motivate these views. To untangle the many linkages between trade liberalization and rural poverty it is useful to examine several interrelated issues, including macroeconomic growth and productivity, micro-macro linkages, income distribution at the global level, market access, commercialization of agriculture, non-farm industries and private sector activities.

In theory, international trade and trade liberalization promote growth by causing economies to be more allocatively, productively and dynamically efficient. Allocative efficiency occurs as domestic production, less constrained by the needs

of import-substitution and encouraged by the expansion of market size, specializes in exportable goods that use the factors in which the economy is comparatively well-endowed more intensively. Improved productive efficiency results from exposure of domestic firms to international competition, as well as access to cheaper imported inputs. Dynamic efficiency is enhanced where, amongst other things, technology is embodied in imports, improved input availability makes new productive activities possible, technical assistance and product support lead to learning externalities, and where networking costs are reduced (McCulloch et al., 2001). In theory, therefore, trade liberalization will foster agricultural growth in Africa, and thus rural poverty reduction, for the reason that comparative advantage generally lies in labor-intensive activities. However, some rather unrealistic assumptions motivate this prediction.

The theory cited above assumes the existence of perfectly competitive markets and constant returns to scale. In reality, however, it will be difficult for small domestic producers to compete in imperfectly competitive world markets (as for example where they are dominated by large multinational companies). Also, the potential gains to be made from increasing exports will be precluded where goods are non-tradable and where a high degree of capital mobility (such as that brought by foreign direct investment) may reduce the degree of specialization. In these cases the effects of multilateral liberalization are less certain (McCulloch et al., 2001).

Cross-country regression analyses of the effects of trade on growth in developed and developing countries conclude that economies that trade more externally do tend to grow faster, or at least do not grow more slowly. This, however, does not mean that opening up to trade will always entail benefits that can be shared equally between poor and rich. Firstly, most measures of trade openness used in the literature (e.g. the share of trade in GDP) are outcome measures, and it is not possible to directly infer that liberalizing trade will have the same effect on growth (McKay et al., 1999). Secondly, the effect of growth on poverty (the responsiveness or elasticity of poverty with respect to growth) depends on the initial distribution of income and its subsequent dynamics.

The poor can benefit much more or much less proportionately than the average income, depending on the quality of growth. The view that income growth is not associated with systematic changes in its distributional effects, ignores the fact that the income distribution has been widening and narrowing in specific growth episodes (Ravallion, 2000; Ali and El Badawi, 2001). It is more likely that different macroeconomic policies will have different effects on the distribution of income, all other things being equal.

To sum up, in order to analyze the effects of trade liberalization on poverty more accurately it is necessary to understand the distributional consequences of liberalization, and not merely its effects on growth. As noted before, economic growth is essential for sustained poverty reduction. However, its impact on the poor will depend on how the increments are distributed. Thus, in highly unequal societies, a given rate of growth will be translated into less poverty reduction, all other things being equal. Similarly, fewer poor will gain from growth that is associated with a widening of the income distribution, although the pro-poor state transfers that growth makes possible may improve this outcome.

With regard to globalization and rural poverty reduction, policy makers would need to ascertain, given their individual country circumstances, that, first, opening up will stimulate trade and growth, and, second, that growth will benefit the rural poor. For this to be the case, rural activities ought to be directly or indirectly related to the processes of trade and growth. This requires a careful examination of the macro-micro linkages of trade liberalization and poverty.

Micro Linkages of Macroeconomic Policies

The implementation of liberalization and other macroeconomic policies affects the household level, and hence poverty, through various channels. Recalling the general formulation of any poverty measure as depending on mean consumption expenditure, the poverty line and an inequality measure, it can be surmised that these channels will include: the effect of the policies on the income-earning capacity of households, captured by the mean per capita expenditure and the underlying workings of the labor market; the prices of various commodities that affect the cost of basic needs, captured by the poverty line; and the state of distribution of household expenditure in the society and the socio-cultural factors affecting it. These are indeed the channels identified in the literature (Kanbur, 1987a, 1987b; Agenor, 1998; Ferreira, Prennushi and Ravallion, 2001). These mechanisms have been grouped into five broad channels: the relative prices channel; the labor market channel; the returns to assets channel; the public transfers channel; and the socio-economic community channel (Ferreira, Prennushi and Ravallion, 2001).

The relative prices channel is concerned with the effect of relative prices of consumer goods on real incomes and real expenditures, of households and with the extent to which the prices of the basic needs — comprising the poverty line increase relative to other goods both the spread of poverty, as captured by the head-count ratio, and the depth of poverty, as captured by the poverty-gap ratio — are likely to increase. The labor market channel is concerned with the change in demand for factors of production employed in the relevant industries and the wage level. The returns to assets channel recognizes the fact that macroeconomic policies directly affect the returns to the various assets held by households, and hence affect household income and expenditure with consequent effects on the state of poverty. More important, however, is the income distributional implication of this channel. The public transfers channel recognizes that macroeconomic policies can influence government revenue and expenditure and hence the quantity and quality of social services delivered and the rate of poverty. The socioeconomic community channel recognizes the fact that the combined effects of the various macroeconomic policies usually work themselves out in terms of the society as a whole—benefiting some and hurting others. In a societal setting, households adjust to various types of crisis by falling back on traditional ties, community networks and other forms of what has come to be known as social capital.

Given the theoretical ambiguity of the effect of policy on poverty through the working of these channels, a proper empirical investigation is needed to further explore the causal relationship between macroeconomic policies and poverty. Despite the great controversy surrounding this topic, there is very little empirical research on the possible links between macroeconomic policy, trade and poverty. This is mainly because of the difficulty of measuring certain policy variables and netting out the effect of a specific policy from the effects of other policies that are usually implemented simultaneously. For instance, removal of quantitative restrictions may have complex effects on the prices of goods. Some goods, like subsistence products,

do not have a market price, making it difficult to measure price shocks. Determining the impact of trade shocks on the prices that poor households face and on the poor through other channels, e.g. subsistence "wages", intra-household distribution is difficult. In the case of African reform programs, trade liberalization has often been implemented as part of a policy package making it difficult to separate trade shocks from other macroeconomic shocks. Furthermore, representative household surveys have been thin on the ground.

The earliest attempt of looking at the impact of macroeconomic policies on poverty, in the context of developing countries, can be credited to UNICEF (Cornia, Jolly and Stewart, 1987). On the basis of country case studies it was concluded that macroeconomic policies embodied in adjustment programs had a negative impact on the poor and vulnerable sections of society. This conclusion was the basis of the proposal by UNICEF that called for "adjustment with a human face". As it happened, some of UNICEF's suggestions were incorporated in what have come to be known as "second generation" reform packages. A recent study based on cross-country regression for a sample of 16 Sub-Saharan African countries, examined the direct relationship between the conventional measure of poverty (the head count ratio) and macroeconomic policies. The study concluded that increases in inflation increases poverty, suggesting the importance of stabilization policies for poverty reduction. Moreover, the results suggest that it is not so much the level of the fiscal variable that matters, but rather the changes in the composition of public spending. Most importantly, the results reveal that both income per capita and the share of transfers and subsidies in total government expenditure affect significantly poverty along with inflation. A study especially conducted for this Report reveals that an increase in government expenditure as a ratio of GDP seems to reduce the spread of poverty in a significant way but not the depth or the severity of poverty (Ali, 2001b). It must be concluded, however, that at this stage of the analysis, and given data limitations, the findings on the impact of macroeconomic policies should be taken as suggestive rather than conclusive. More work needs to be done in this area before firm conclusions can be established regarding the effects of macroeconomic policy on poverty.

Globalization and Income Distribution at the Global Level

The analysis above is based on an examination of whether liberalization will increase a country's trade and economic growth and whether such growth will benefit the poor. However, the effects of globalization on the rural poor through the conduit of trade are also influenced by the globalization-induced distribution of income at the international level. In the previous Chapter it was seen that rural poverty is embedded in national poverty and that the fortunes of the rural poor are inseparable from the fortunes of the nation. The globalization-induced distribution of income at the international level, which can affect national fortunes, has, thus, a direct bearing on rural poverty. An important determinant of the distribution of income at the global level is the share of international trade. Just as the share of an individual in national income is determined by the capabilities of that individual, the share of a country in global income is determined by the capabilities of that country to compete in the international market and expand its exports. It can be deduced that a country's share in global income is closely related to its share in international trade.

It must be noted that there is nothing in the doctrine of free trade that guarantees an equal or equitable distribution of the gains from trade. Indeed, Africa's average export growth during the last two decades, which witnessed increasing liberalization, was only 6 percent per year, which is less than half that of other developing countries as a whole. Consequently, Africa's share in world trade declined from about 5 percent in the early 1980s to 2 percent currently. In considering the distribution of the gains from trade, the problem for many African countries is that the nature of the goods they export have characteristics which may cause both the terms of trade to deteriorate and resources to remain unemployed. First, primary commodities have both a low price and a low income elasticity of demand, which means that when supply increases prices can drop dramatically, and demand grows only slowly with global income growth. Secondly, primary commodities are land-based activities and subject to diminishing returns, and there is a limit to employment in diminishing returns activities set by the point where the marginal product of labor falls to the minimum subsistence wage (Thirlwall, 1999; and ADR, 2000).

The above point can be illustrated by considering Ricardo's famous example of Portugal specializing in wine and England in cloth. As Portugal moves out of cloth production into wine production, there is no guarantee that viniculture will be able to employ all the labor thrown out of cloth production because at some point, as more labor is employed in the vineyards, labor's marginal product will fall below the wage. No such problem arises in manufacturing, such as cloth production, where no fixed factors of production are involved, and production may be subject to increasing returns. In practice, for countries specializing in activities prone to diminishing returns, it is possible that the real resource gains from specialization may be offset by the real income losses from unemployment. In this case, complete specialization and free trade would not be optimal (Thirlwall, 1999; ADR, 2000).

The quest for accelerating growth and reducing rural poverty is, thus, closely linked to the ability of African countries to adopt specific policies to reverse their increasing marginalization in world trade. African countries would need, first, to maintain or increase the competitive advantage they have historically enjoyed in primary commodities and, secondly, shift gradually to the production of goods that are attractive to the world market. To this end, African countries would need to maintain a competitive and market-determined exchange rate and undertake investments for the development of science-based productivity in smallholder agriculture — often the mainstay of most primary export commodities and generator of income for the rural poor. The output response of rural farmers would need to be enhanced by developing adequate physical infrastructure, rural access to finance, information and marketing services and by strengthening domestic institutional capacity. To connect the rural poor with international markets, efforts should be directed not only at removing the constraints on output supply response, but also at establishing export promotion organizations and improving export-servicing facilities. Box 5.2 provides an example of the opportunities and challenges of linking African small farmers with supermarkets in developed countries.

Besides building capacity in land-based products, African countries would need to undertake concerted efforts to enter the market for manufactures and services where world demand is high and technological progress rapid. To this end, there is a strong argument for promoting sectoral divi-

---

Box 5.2: Linking Rural Producers to International Supermarkets

During the 1990s, overseas supermarket groups became increasingly important for the diversification of agriculture in some African countries (Dolan and Humphrey, 2001). In addition to providing new external markets for a variety of agricultural produce, they also began to create new off-farm employment opportunities such as washing, wrapping and labelling, activities that are all carried out domestically.

Smallholders are less able to benefit from such supplier-driven value chains since they are unlikely to meet supermarket quality standards, at least on a consistent basis. They are also at a disadvantage in meeting demands such as the reliability of supply and the extensive range of regulatory requirements, including health, safety and ethical assurances. (Dolan and Humphrey, 2001).

However, given the evidence that small farms are more efficient in terms of resource use in land- or capital-scarce and labor-rich economies, it seems that both they and the agricultural sector would benefit from their inclusion. In Zimbabwe, around 3,000 smallholders are being contracted to produce for larger farms that are involved in packing (Oxfam-IDS, 1999; IFAD, 2001), yet only 6 percent of total export produce is being sourced from them (Dolan and Humphrey, 2001). As well as being less able to satisfy export criteria, small farmers are faced with the challenge of poor infrastructure. However, global chains involve risk for all kinds of domestic producers. Supermarkets have the power to alternate suppliers quickly, leaving even large exporters vulnerable (IFAD, 2001).

Source: Adapted from Lipton et al (2001).

---

sions of labor according to factor endowments and end-uses. The general idea of this approach is to promote three sectors: the traditional rural sector, an intermediate sector and a modern export sector. The traditional sector, employing traditional technology and labor-intensive techniques, should be developed not only to reduce poverty but also to meet, as much as possible, the basic needs of the economy including food and clothing. The modern sector, which depends on the production of knowledge-intensive goods and services, should be spearheaded by the export sector. It is envisaged that the export sector should take up the challenge of processing and manufacturing with the aim of advancing certain manufacturers into renowned market niches. This sector should encourage and host foreign investment and act as the vehicle which propels the overall economy to higher growth rates and as the window through which the country would acquire technological knowledge and managerial know-how.

Variants of this piecemeal approach have been successfully implemented by some developing countries. In Asia, for instance, the reforming economy of China moved to higher and sustained growth rates in the last decade, through the promotion of "special economic zones" and "coastal areas". In these zones the country adopted an outward-oriented strategy, with heavy reliance on manufacturing exports and foreign investment. Between 1980-2000, these special areas recorded an average real growth rate of some 15 percent while China's economy as a whole grew by an average real rate of 9 percent. In Africa, Mauritius engineered a major impetus to growth, through the promotion of its Export Processing Zone, which relied heavily on manufacturing exports and foreign investment. Tunisia is another African country that has successfully diversified its production structure towards the exportation of manufactured goods.

Policies to diversify the export baskets of African countries stand to benefit from the "special and differential treatment" offered by the WTO to developing countries. This treatment aims at providing developing countries more favorable access to the markets of the developed countries. The collaboration of developed countries is necessary in reducing their non-tariff barriers and allowing a more free access to their markets especially in the case of agricultural products. The differential treatment also allows developing countries some measure of policy discretion in their own domestic markets, including the maintenance of trade barriers at home. These and related measures supported by technical assistance to disseminate information and knowledge on markets in industrial countries could help developing countries capture the unfolding opportunities of the globalized world trade system.

Market Access for Poverty Reduction

It is widely agreed by the development community, as much as it is by the poorer countries themselves, that lack of market access presents a major constraint to rural poverty reduction (IFAD, 2001; Platteau, 1996; World Bank, 1994). It is also possible that market access barriers benefit some remote poor, some of the time. For example, in remote areas market-access barriers to competing products from "outside" may allow these products to be grown locally, whether labor-intensively or by smallholders. However, local consumers lose via higher prices, and (possibly poor) producers outside the community lose because they cannot sell the same products to the community. Market-access barriers against inputs seem clearly bad for the isolated community, but might protect its poor if those inputs were to otherwise displace local unskilled labor. Market-access barriers against selling current products might help local consumers if the products were staple foods, by keeping prices down, but at cost of farm (including smallholder) output and employment.

In the context of greater international trade and fewer market distortions in recent years, markets present a potential means for poor producers and consumers alike to benefit. In order for these gains to be realized, they must be (more easily) accessible. However, easier access is costly to taxpayers, particularly if the rural population is sparse and/or potential output gains due to better market access are small. The case for gains from trade is a case for trade subsidy via market access only if the alternative uses of the subsidizing (including state-financed road-building) resources are inferior (given that they may also be pro-growth and/or pro-poor). In addition, externalities may arise from provision of new roads between localities where third party communities that previously gained from easier access to the local markets lose out. None of this is to deny that some areas with great productive potential, as for example in southern Ethiopia, may show large net output, income, and poverty response to free roads, sufficient to justify them. But it is important to note that productive enhancements or production-side measures to raise agricultural supply elasticities compete for resources with marketing-side investments such as roads. Normally good policy needs both.

It is important for the analysis of the impact of liberalization on poverty to be clear about which markets affected by liberalization are most important to the rural poor. Effects on agricultural input and output markets will probably have the most direct effects on rural households' welfare. The channels and effects on markets for what locals consume and what they produce may differ depending on the crops and non-farm products involved. Subsistence food production is likely to involve lower technological/networking input than, for example, the production of cash crops

or more advanced forms of agriculture. Labor markets are also likely to be important, especially for landless labor and where non-negligible proportions of income are generated by (casual) labor in off-farm activities. In addition, spill-over effects on markets for assets such as land and water will be important to present and future production possibilities, particularly in areas such as dry lands.

In a study of six Ethiopian villages, it has been shown that market access is important for poverty reduction. Liberalization, devaluation and internal tax reform in Ethiopia since 1990 increased real producer prices by 26 percent on average (Dercon, 2001). Poverty, though remaining high, fell in four villages, and by a greater amount for some of the poorest households, but increased in two villages. The 50 percent of those initially poor that had good access to roads and towns, good land and high crop price increases performed better than the rest and contributed more than 80 percent of the reduction in the poverty gap. The other half that typically lived in remote regions with poor road connections and had poor (quantity or quality of) land endowments remained poor. In addition to physical and structural constraints on market access, which will be treated in more detail in the coming section, there are also social constraints. Access to markets may be severely impaired by inequities in the socio-economic environment in which people live. These systems may preclude certain groups of the poor, such as women, from access to markets and hence from sharing in the benefits of globalization (see Box 5.3).

Box 5.3: Gender and Market Access

In many African countries, where land and cultivation rights are generally ascribed to men, the possibilities for women (particularly female-headed households) to diversify into cash-crop production are limited. Women's access to labor markets (e.g. casual and seasonal work) may also be limited because of their traditional gender roles and lower educational attainment.

Concerns about adverse implications for women and household food security from agricultural liberalization are evident in Zambia. The demand for female labor in cash-crop production reduced women's input into food crops, resulting in lower nutritional standards (Oxfam-IDS, 1999; Winters, 2000a). However, in other cases some women have benefited. For example, in Mauritius, trade liberalization increased the relative wages of women and unskilled labor in the exportables sector (Milner and Wright, 1998).

Inequitable access to markets harms certain groups of the poor, and it may entail productivity losses where access to suitable inputs is also reduced. A recent study of farmers in Burkina Faso, Senegal, Uganda, Zambia and Zimbabwe, based on focus group discussions, found that women's access to land — and thus credit, education and cash from work on family holdings – is minimal (IFAD, 1998a). Where they can obtain land, through women's groups, it is usually of low quality and far from the village, and in addition may only be allocated for short periods in order to prevent them from acquiring permanent rights to it. The prevalence of migration of men to towns in these areas has aggravated these problems because women

must consequently do all the work. The study found that these constraints were manifested in poor or inappropriate production tools used by women, particularly for weeding. Many tools used were unsuitably heavy because they were designed for men. In addition, government provision of training services for more efficient farming implements, such as animal-drawn planters that significantly reduce per-acre cultivation time – from 2-4 days instead of 2-4 weeks – are biased towards men (IFAD, 1998a).

A short-term approach to the alleviation of female poverty is to promote collective off-farm activities such as micro-enterprise initiatives (IFAD, 1998b). These provide a constructive way for women to use markets to generate income. Women's enterprises in rural areas tend to be flexible because they use unskilled labor intensively and depend on local raw materials and local markets. In West Africa, women's enterprises distribute most major commodities. Such trade provides an invaluable linkage between producers and consumers in traditional markets that are not highly commercialized. However product diversification and market expansion is often low, which limits profitability. Through these off-farm activities women may also be able to afford new technologies such as fertilizer inputs which are essential for sustainable development and food security. Micro-enterprises, by empowering women, can also help to instigate and accelerate social change, which is drastically needed to reduce female poverty in the long-run.

Source: Adapted from Lipton et al (2001).

Financial Services for Poverty Reduction

Market reforms for rural poverty reduction cannot work effectively without microfinance institutions that provide not only credit but a complete set of financial services including deposits as well as insurance. This prompted a shifted from the link between micro credit and poverty reduction to the importance of providing rural financial systems that offer wide-ranging services. Micro deposit services are needed to encourage the poor to accumulate their small savings, while micro credit services are required to allow the poor to purchase the inputs of goods and services that facilitate the production process. They also help the poor to plan their consumption over the interim period from sowing to harvest. Insurance services permit them to enjoy social security and loan protection. The provision of such a complete set of services can enable the poor rural household to augment income generated by the production process as well as reduce the cost of smoothing consumption at sufficient levels.

While the provision of deposit and insurance services are deemed important for meeting the financial needs of the poor, the provision of credit and the way it is utilized remain crucial for the success of rural financial services. The poor cannot use the deposit and insurance services unless they are able to use the credit profitably so that they can repay the interest and the capital of the loan as well as earn extra profits that can be deposited in the system. It is for this reason that the provision of such services is deemed effective only when it is delivered through a specifically tailored package of other public provisions. Such public or common provision is necessary to build up the risk-taking and market-responding capacities of the poor to change their work, equipment, consumption, and above all enterprise: to swiftly learn of, and respond appropriately to, new market-based opportunities (Lipton, 1995).

In designing rural microfinance services, recent research by IFAD (2001) has shown that there is no single best type of microfinance institutions and that different types of microfinance institutions and strategies are required depending on the initial conditions of the rural location. Institutions must be tailored to the potential of the area, the cultural environment and the requirements of the clients. In the case of marginal areas with a predominance of subsistence agriculture and low-return activities, small cooperatives, which are savings-oriented and operate at nominal cost, may be most suitable. In high-potential areas with high-return on agricultural activities and profitable rural micro-enterprise activities, credit-oriented rural banks would be needed. These should include professional management, large financial cooperatives and commercial bank branches with individual or group technologies.

The choice of institutions that are suitable in a given situation is environment-specific. The degree to which financial disciplines and cost-recovery principles can be applied will depend on the extent to which the local production environment is capable of yielding reasonable returns on the activities financed through microfinance scheme. It will also depend on the effects of various exogenous shocks such as civil conflicts and natural disasters on the normal flow of economic events. In rural areas large gains can be eroded overnight, making recovery and loan repayment difficult, if not impossible. This, however, should not be taken as an excuse to halt the operation of the concerned microfinance schemes, but rather as a strong reason to provide additional concessional resources for supporting the development of such schemes. For one thing, if such costs are to be internalized most of the microfinance initiatives may cease to be feasible. The viability of microfinance institutions, on the other hand, depends on their ability to reduce transaction costs. Informal financial markets in many parts of Africa have shown their capability to efficiently mobilize savings and provide financial services. They can often show the way for cutting down on costs and ensuring fuller recovery. Efforts need to be made to integrate the informal sector with formal microfinance institutions.

A number of options, including forging links between informal and formal microfinance institutions in deposit mobilization and credit allocation can be proposed. Microfinance institutions may link up with the informal sector by offering informal deposit mobilizers preferential deposit rates higher than the rates of return on other opportunities open to them. There is also the option of developing an agency relationship in which microfinance loanable funds could be channeled through informal lenders. In countries where cooperatives are relatively developed, they could be used to realize such a potential. Another possibility is to waive all fees and charges on the demand deposits of informal deposit mobilizers. This can help forge closer relationships between the two segments of the market. A third option is to develop a three-tier approach where banks would lend, in the first instance, to credible microfinance agents who would then link up with such informal lenders as cooperatives, with rural borrowers receiving loans directly from informal agents (ADR, 1997).

Formal and informal lenders and deposit-takers would need to share risks with each other while developing improved techniques for dealing with borrowers. It is essential that techniques for lending to small borrowers minimize risk and reach small borrowers cost-effectively. Microfinance institutions will need to adjust the credit-delivery methodology to the actual patterns of demand of borrowers and to the levels of risk involved. Successful experiences indicate that, in extending and recovering credits from the rural poor, microfinance institutions need to base their lending operations on an in-depth market assessment at the design stage.

Prospects for Agricultural Commercialization

Once a food surplus is achieved, cash crop production may be the only way to achieve broad-based economic growth in agrarian economies and thus to sustain rural poverty reduction (IFAD, 2001). Regions that produce commercial crops are generally more affluent than subsistence ones and have better-off and more securely employed people (Binswanger and von Braun, 1991). However, some cash crops may be impractical for smallholder cultivation because of the long gestation and fallow periods that may be required to restore soil quality, as in the case of tree crops, including beverages, that thoroughly deplete soil nutrients (IFAD, 2001). Market bottlenecks may also arise from delays in the implementation of new processing and storage technology resulting from poor infrastructure.

Before liberalization, many farmers were dependent on parastatal organizations that bought at pre-determined prices. Thus they did not need marketing skills and lacked knowledge of how free-markets operate or indeed why prices fluctuate. This implies that it is necessary to support market intermediaries and promote competition, transparency and market access, if the transition to unregulated markets of poor farmers is to be facilitated. One way to help smallholders realize their market potential is to advocate collective organizations such as marketing cooperatives. They may enable the poor to enhance their bargaining power and gain economies of scale in transportation and storage, as well as aid the dissemination of information on market situations (PRUS, 2000a). The Cooperative for Assistance and Relief Everywhere is implementing a program in Zimbabwe that aims to facilitate the rural poor's access to agricultural inputs, marketing opportunities and technology. So far it has established over 300 community-based, independent input dealers, each of whom supply 100-200 smallholder farm households. They charge farmers lower prices than they were previously paying and some also provide on credit (IFAD, 2001).

The expansion of cash cropping in remote rural communities requires smallholders to have access to markets for assets (including land and water) and credit, as well as improved access to labor and technology. Policy must also challenge social norms and attitudes to risk, often perpetuated by inequities in access to assets such as land and water. A problem arises because the unequal distribution (and increasing scarcity) of land has ramifications for the decision logic of farmers. Land-poor farmers are often considerably risk-averse to the extent that they prefer subsistence crops to more profitable cash crops, fearing that market uncertainty and untimely payment will impair food security. For example, poor farmers in Guatemala will not diversify into cash crops unless they are two or three times more profitable than subsistence maize. Evidence from Malawi that farmers now plant fewer hybrid maize cash crops following the liberalization of maize and fertilizer markets also suggests this (Gladwin et al., 2001). Other African studies have shown that few households, even those with spare land, will increase cash crop production without first maintaining a food surplus (Killick et al., 2000; IFAD, 2001).

The performance of Uganda in liberalization, whilst relatively successful in terms of total growth and exports, has been tainted by the limited growth of agricultural exports. Uganda's poor road infrastructure and lack of formal credit markets reduce prospects for smallholder commercialization (Dijkstra and van Donge. 2001). The evidence on the effects of market and trade liberalization is both scanty and mixed. In general, however, the production impact has been less favorable on input than output markets because liberalization generally involved removal of all input subsidies on fertilizer, credit and irrigation (Gladwin et al., 2001). The decline in input use has had negative implications for sustained agricultural growth (IFAD, 2001). For example, removal of subsidies in Malawi and 100 percent devaluation of the domestic currency resulted in 200 percent to 300 percent increases in costs of fertilizers, whilst maize prices remained stable (Benson, 1997; Gladwin et al., 2001). Such increases in cost, without corresponding increases in output prices, have reduced profitability of using fertilizer on maize crops. However, there are exceptions, as in the case of Mali in 1996 where fertilizer could still be used profitably on maize, even after a 70 percent increase in its prices (Sanders, 1997).

Although the price rises that have often been caused by liberalization would tend to hurt net consumers, improvements in goods supplied may compensate for that. Some poor rural communities reported this in Tanzania (Booth et al., 1993; McKay et al., 2000). However, this was not the case in remote areas where goods availability did not improve, nor is it likely to be the case for the poorest net-consumers. Evidence suggests that the rural poor are not always affected by changes in border prices. The physical isolation of low-income households in rural Rwanda precluded them from expanding into cash-crop production and thus from being affected by price changes in the monetary economy that resulted from liberalization.

Other studies have emphasized the importance of services in enabling poor farmers to benefit from commercialization. Owens et al. (2001) find that access to extension services (one or two visits per year) raise the average value of crop production by 15 percent in resettlement areas of Zimbabwe. There is evidence that lack of facilities for storage and imperfect competition in output markets damage potential benefits. In Malawi in the 1990s, liberalization encouraged agricultural commercialization as traders sold rural produce in urban areas or export (Parris, 1999). However, lack of storage facilities means that many smallholders are forced to sell just after harvest when prices are low, and penalizes them further because traders are able to sell at high prices to smallholders during lean periods. This emphasizes the benefits of storage facilities in determining the price smallholders receive and their relative market power.

Evidence from Zambia and Zimbabwe confirms the critical role of market structure in determining the effects of liberalization on poverty). In Zimbabwe the state-controlled Cotton Marketing Board (CMB) operated a pricing policy that subsidized the textile industry by purchasing cotton at low prices (Winters, 2000a). Smallholder farmers have probably benefited a great deal from privatization. They were more likely to lack the ability to diversify crop production, and thus to mitigate losses incurred through CMB impositions, and benefited from the substantial competition that private industry has provided. The industry is now comprised of three buyers (including a farmer-owned cooperative) that compete both on prices and by offering extension and input services to smallholders. Access to inputs, including market information, has given rural smallholders the option to expand production at reduced risk.

Remote maize farmers in Zambia have not been so fortunate. This is partly because deregulation involved the removal of agricultural subsidies, which will have adversely affected them by both reducing income (raising production costs) and increasing risk, but also because the two private buyers failed to offer competitive services to remote areas, and have probably colluded to keep prices low (Winters, 2000b). If there are buyers in these regions, which is often not the case, they exploit their monopoly, or monopsony, power to trade on a barter (non-monetary) basis. The ability and willingness of many farmers to shift production to other crops has been marred by lack of knowledge of alternatives, as well as inputs, and aversion to market risk. Some farmers have shifted to production of cotton. Although less profitable, it is also less risky because traders supply inputs and credit. This reiterates a key general point that differential market access among products and inputs affects product-mix, just as production costs do. But this may be good -- it makes little sense to produce low weight/value products such as maize far from markets, or to count it as a benefit from a transport capital cost that it shifts production there.

Land redistribution will enable small farms to diversify as their land-holdings increase, but they will need market access, often for new products and with new information and systems, to do this. Old channels of market access (i.e. that formerly were for big farms) may need to change if some of the land and hence marketed surplus shifts to smaller and poorer holdings.

Water scarcity presents a major source of low supply elasticities in Sub-Saharan African agriculture. This is unlikely to be addressed adequately as long as only 3 percent of arable land is irrigated (and most of that is for the better-off farms in a few selected places). Access to water and water markets may help this allocation. Water markets are generally underdeveloped with supplies controlled by the state, often as a sanctioning device against civil disorder and at the expense of the poor, or subsidized at the expense of static allocative efficiency and conservation. When prices do not fully reflect opportunity costs then low-yield irrigation projects are more likely to be implemented and incentives to develop or implement water-conserving techniques will be minimal (IFAD, 2001). In theory, liberalization of water markets would generate prices that more accurately reflect opportunity costs and thus stimulate allocative efficiency, as well as encourage farmers both to be more efficient and implement new technologies, thus raising yields. However, free-market prices are unlikely to reflect environmental externalities such as resource depletion and pollution (and there are serious issues relating to supplier competitiveness and equitable access for all). The removal of subsidies, assuming that they are well targeted, is likely to threaten the production of smallholders that formerly received them, particularly if they were subsistence farmers or lived in remote areas, and thus aggravate rural poverty. These problems will necessitate regulation of water markets, such as a system of tradable property rights, as well as water subsidies to be eliminated gradually as new practices and social safety-nets are implemented (IFAD, 2001).

Market Liberalization and the Six *Ins*

Many African countries have embarked upon structural adjustment programs that, *inter alia*, have aimed to stimulate growth by removing artificial controls on markets. Such programs are usually intended to reduce poverty, not only by accelerating growth, but also by raising the share of the poorest (rural unskilled laborers and smallholders) in the growth benefits. This was to happen through reduced price, regulatory, and other incentive-altering biases against production of tradeables, above all trade-distorting biases against production of labor-intensive farm products -- biases which, especially in Africa, had in 1960-85 been

especially severe (Krueger, Schiff and Valdes, 1992). Yet market access constraints have impeded the success of this sequence by:

- *preventing such incentives from reaching the point of delivery*, because the difficulty or cost of accessing inputs or marketing outputs mean that improvements and de-restrictions affecting border prices, or urban prices, even if embodied in commodities that rural people buy and sell, do not adequately penetrate to rural areas (especially remote ones);

- *reducing the growth impacts of such improvements* as do reach rural people—mainly because constraints on market access reduce the capacity of farmers and farmworkers to respond to such incentives through higher output (i.e. the constraints mean low aggregate price-elasticity of agricultural supply);

- *reducing the poverty impact of agricultural growth* (even to the extent that it is induced by successful market reforms that effectively penetrate rural areas), because the poor are worst placed to overcome market-access problems, and so may lose out to the rich, relatively or even absolutely, from a reform process that does not address these problems.

Some believe that these three problems can all be adequately addressed merely by more or faster reforms, or by supporting them with a few conventional public goods to assist access (e.g. information systems). However, little evidence for this is found in Africa. Experience shows that, while market reforms (generally implying state withdrawal from providing, pricing, or over-regulating essentially private goods and services) are necessary for growth and poverty reduction in rural Africa, they will seldom be sufficient. They may occasionally be counterproductive, unless complemented by a number of non-price instruments. As illustrated by Paul Streeten (1989), there are six instruments or **Ins** that are required to stimulate the supply of output. Market liberalization and access, which lead to higher producers' price, offer the first (*In*) or **in**centives. The other five Ins comprise **in**puts, **in**stitutions, **in**frastructure, **in**formation, and **in**novation or technology. For rural poverty reduction, the provision of these **Ins** should be seen in the context of rural conditions. For instance, infrastructure might mean the construction of feeder roads, institutions might relate to implementation of land redistribution, while innovation might relate to research and delivery of most improved seeds, water-management methods, and health maintenance for humans, animals, crops, and soil-water systems.

Rural Infrastructure and Institutions

It has been concluded in the last section that macroeconomic policies that have large effects on price incentives can be ineffective or even counterproductive if they are not accompanied by appropriate measures to improve supply response and increase market access for the rural poor. In the majority of African countries which implemented macroeconomic reforms, actions on the price incentive front were not sufficient to accelerate growth and development essentially because non-price factors such as inputs; institutions; infrastructure; innovations; and information were either lacking or inadequate. For instance, the devaluation of the exchange rate and trade liberalization, which are central for increasing export supply, growth and employment, are quite

ineffective in the absence of the above noted non-price factors. Indeed, the incentive that liberalization is designed to achieve may not reach the real producer in rural areas if there are inefficient marketing boards or if there is a large body of middlemen that reap the benefits of higher prices. The supply of output might not come by if inputs necessary for production are not available; if there is inadequate transport to ensure a timely delivery of both inputs and outputs or; if appropriate technologies and products that call for more labor employment are scare or do not exist altogether. The provision of such non-price factors reduce poverty through increasing the productive capacity and the incomes of the rural poor as well as through directly affecting their social well-being. A construction of a rural road for instance, will not only increase the access of the rural poor to markets for their production and labor, but also to education and health facilities. The significance of these non-price factors to rural poverty reduction is discussed below.

Infrastructure for Poverty Reduction

There are two possible routes by which new or improved infrastructure activity can help reduce poverty. First there is the link between infrastructure and poverty reduction through economic growth. To the extent that the building of infrastructure simulates the growth of GDP, it can also reduce poverty, given income distribution. The second link between infrastructure activity and poverty reduction arises through the contribution of infrastructure to the process of pro-poor growth. To achieve this requires the identification and financing of a significant number of projects for which a high proportion of the beneficiaries are below the poverty line for the country concerned. Not all infrastructure projects will have this characteristic, but some will, and it is through this route that infrastructure activity can make its main contribution to the process of poverty reduction. Three components of infrastructure activity that are among the most likely to help in this process of pro-poor growth are irrigation, water supply and sanitation and rural transportation projects.

Rural Transport

Improvements in rural roads and paths have the potential to improve the position of the poor in several ways, although they will generally have to be provided as part of a package of measures that include credit, extension services and other investments, for example in irrigation and water. There is a strong link between poverty, transport and remoteness. Up to 90 percent of the populations of remote areas such as northern Angola, northern Zambia, northern Mozambique and southern Tanzania are estimated to be chronically poor (IFAD, 2001). Remoteness, usually defined in terms of long distances to centres of economic activity such as markets, is aggravated by poor physical infrastructure. Platteau (1996) describes the transport and communications situation in Africa as one of low density of road networks, low quality rural roads, and low rates of road utilization (ADR, 1999). The direct costs to individual households of remoteness are increased uncertainty and reduced choice, resulting in lower incentives to produce for markets and the prevalence of subsistence agriculture (see Box 5.4 on the welfare costs of inadequate infrastructure). African villages with better physical infrastructures are estimated to have crop production per acre 32 percent higher, wages per person per year 12 percent higher, and 14 percent lower fertilizer costs per kilogram of area than those with poor

---

Box 5.4: Welfare Costs of Poor Infrastructure

The following adverse consequences of poor infrastructure will be felt disproportionately by the poor:

High transport costs are reflected in high per capita costs of collecting and marketing farm products, delivering input and extension services, building decentralized storage facilities, and providing public goods such as health, education and clean water. Bottlenecks are likely to build up which impair agricultural productivity, retard output response to price changes, and discourage long-term investment in farming.

Impaired food security may occur in times of crisis where food surpluses (or food aid) cannot be easily transported to deficit regions. Poor infrastructure may also perpetuate large price differentials between regions of relative food abundance and scarcity, leading to local entitlement failures, as in the Ethiopian famine of 1983-4.

Imperfections in markets for agricultural servicing and credit result from high transport costs associated with poor roads and scattered populations.

Insulation of the domestic economy from foreign trade may result in some domestic staples being non-tradable. This tends to amplify and prolong the impact of weather shocks on both prices and wages (because production is labor-intensive), and in the process reduce competitiveness of exports. Inelastic domestic food supplies are likely to weaken the multiplier effects on macroeconomic growth from agricultural expansion because people spend a large proportion of their incomes on domestic staples in poor economies.

Slow process of social and cultural change affects overall poverty reduction by causing agricultural efficiency and growth to be lower than it might have been, because resources are not allocated according to their most profitable uses, as well as causing poverty to be concentrated among specific groups.

Marginalization of remote areas and communities may be perpetuated because the continual out-migration of young men (who may be pulled away by the attraction of modern services that less remote areas can offer them, but also pushed out by the lack of income generating opportunities in remote areas) causes per capita costs of infrastructure to rise even further.

Source: Platteau (1996).

infrastructures (IFAD, 2001).

Roads are also poorly utilized in Africa. This may partly reflect poor infrastructure, but is probably also due to the slow development of private sector transport and trading. This is linked to the restrictive environment imposed by state controls over movement of agricultural goods, as well as insufficient supply of spare parts and vehicle imports because of foreign exchange scarcity (Platteau, 1996). One study found that vehicle maintenance costs were five times more expensive in Africa than in Pakistan, whilst prices of vehicles and tires were over three times more expensive and fuel prices double (Hine and Rizet, 1991). Road transport is used much less intensively in Africa and is extremely costly in rural areas. Transport costs for food grains are estimated to account for almost one half of the 40 percent greater marketing margins in Kenya and Malawi than Bangladesh and Indonesia (IFAD, 1999, 2001). These constraints will be particularly harsh for the rural poor who tend to be producers of perishable goods with high weight/value ratios, such as roots and tubers, sorghum and millet. These cannot be traded over long distances and over long time periods given the lack of storage facilities (PRUS, 2001a).

An important trade-off in improving market access for remote communities is between building new roads and maintaining existing ones. The stock of roads in some parts of Africa has fallen because the short life span of rural (earth) roads causes them to deteriorate faster than new ones are built (Platteau, 1996). It has been estimated that each dollar put into maintaining existing roads in Africa would lower vehicle operating costs by $2 to $3 per year (Riverson et al, 1991). Construction of new roads may not only create incentives for the remote poor to trade and potentially enhance current living standards, but also may

improve access to education and health services.

However, at a wider level, there must be a balance between expenditure on roads and that on other non-price factors that could also benefit the rural poor. Failure to support productive research in agriculture and irrigation, for instance, prevents poor people from responding to improved rural infrastructure by raising production and income. Further, given credit market imperfections, the poor may not be able to afford variable inputs such as fertilizers that better physical infrastructure can make available. Policy should account for these factors. Thus, for example, if new earth roads are much cheaper than surfaced roads, they might be preferable in rural areas even if more often replaced. Additionally, they may be more conducive to poverty reduction since the labor/capital ratio in both construction and maintenance is probably far higher for earth roads, and the amount of places served per dollar more. Market financing solutions, e.g. via local petrol taxation to pay for roads, or even toll roads, would also relieve fiscal constraints.

Two further points are made here. Firstly, budget constraints will entail a trade-off between improving access to local and national markets. It is much less likely to make sense (in terms of growth and poverty reduction) to shift public-goods resources into roads to support longer-distance trade, and out of supporting production that can be consumed locally or through short-distance trade (e.g. via agricultural research). Secondly, the direction of causation between population and road density is likely to run in both directions. More roads (subsidies to transport) will also encourage scattered as against concentrated population settlement. The implications for growth, distribution or sustainability are not obvious.

It has been argued that the logical step is to

implement transport technologies that economize on scarce resources such as capital, foreign exchange, and skilled labor (Platteau, 1996). Vehicles such as bicycle trailers, hand-carts and motorized rickshaws can significantly increase load-carrying capacity over more traditional means of transport—the dominant form of transport along many rural African roads is by foot (Howe, 1994; cited in Platteau, 1996)—and will be more accessible to the rural poor than the expensive existing carriers. Unfortunately, bicycle imports have been highly taxed in many African countries, often to the order of several hundred percent above border prices (Howe, 1993; cited in Platteau, 1996), and spare parts have also been scarce, which has greatly reduced their usage. Local initiatives to develop and promote these vehicles could be a solution, especially considering that bicycle demand responded quickly in countries such as Ghana, Kenya and Tanzania that significantly reduced import taxation.

Of course, the appropriateness of bicycles depends on the type of terrain. For example in Wollaito, Ethiopia, without better roads, especially in the rainy season when much crop surplus appears and most inputs are needed, bicycles are useless. Changes in, e.g. product-mix or product timing, are needed to cut transport constraints on production and trade without the huge cost of weatherproof roads across sparsely populated arid or hilly terrain.

Evidence from the World Bank surveys in Zambia, Uganda and Burkina Faso suggest that, if they are representative, in Sub-Saharan Africa the average rural adult spends 1.25 hours per day on essential travel and transport. Of this time 75 percent is for domestic purposes (defined as including collection of water and fuelwood, and trips to a grinding mill to produce ground flour for family consumption), 18 percent for agricultural purposes (covering trips to the fields for different cultivation activities, movement of farm inputs, collection of harvested crops), no more than 1 percent for health visits to rural clinics or doctors and the remaining 6 percent for marketing of crops. The average adult also expends a carrying effort equivalent to moving a load of 20kg over 2kms a day (Barwell, 1996).

Road improvements can ease this transport burden on the rural poor; for example new or rehabilitated feeder roads can allow motor vehicles to operate down to the village level, which will allow the transport of farm inputs into villages and farm outputs from the villages to market centres. The improvement of paths or tracks can also reduce the transport burden where foot, bicycle or cart travel is involved. For example, improvements to bridges or water crossings can shorten journeys by avoiding detours, and improvements to path surfaces can allow passage by bicycle or cart as well as on foot. Involvement of the communities themselves in planning local transport interventions is likely to increase their effectiveness by allowing an accurate identification of where bottlenecks exist and ensuring regular maintenance (Weiss, 1998; ADR, 1998).

In summary, the improvements in rural transport can raise incomes of the poor through several mechanisms:

- *Reduction in time spent on water and firewood collection.* As has been noted, this will benefit women in particular since across the region they appear to be the main carriers of water and wood. The time freed can be used for leisure (resting or visiting neighbors, for example) or for productive purposes such as various agricultural activities. There is evidence that a significant portion of time saved is used productively (Malmberg-Calvo, 1994).

- *Increase in crop production.* Agricultural output can benefit, particularly where bulky low value crops are involved. For example, trucks can be hired to move bulk harvests; fertilizers can be moved to villages and stored in local storage facilities; with improved tracks and footpaths hired farm labor can move more readily to the fields.

- *Improvement in marketing opportunities.* Isolated rural communities will have great difficulty in marketing their crops. Crops can be moved in bulk by trucks, but also in smaller quantities by cart or bicycle provided adequate roads or paths are available.

- *Access to social services and non-agricultural income generating activities.* These include health clinics, for which travel time is reduced, and travel from peri-urban locations to work in services and construction in the urban informal sector.

Water Supply and Sanitation

It is widely accepted that the primary causes of disease and poor health amongst the poor in Africa are water-related. There is a lack of safe drinking water, as well as acceptable washing water and a widespread scarcity of hygienic sanitation services. As a consequence water borne diseases, such as typhoid, cholera, dysentery, bilharzia gastro-enteritis and hepatitis, as well as water based diseases, like scistosomiasis and guinea worm, are common. For example, deaths from diarrhoeal disease, a direct result of poor water quality, are higher in Sub-Saharan Africa per 1,000 of the population than in any other region. These are primarily illnesses of the poor, since one of the key characteristics of the poor in the region is a lack of access to good quality water.

Different levels of service can be provided to different water users. Whilst higher income users will demand household connections to the mains system, for the poor often the main sources of water supply provided by poverty focussed projects will be yard taps, standpipes, or handpump wells. For sanitation, whilst the better-off will require sewerage household connections, for the poor pit latrines will be the main alternative. The lower service levels for the poor are considerable cheaper than the higher levels demanded by the better-off. For the region approximate estimates of the cost of house connections as a source of water supply are $270 per capita as compared with the range of supplies to the poor that cost $80 to $120 (World Bank, 1996b).

Benefits to the poor from improved water supplies arise not just through improvements in health, which are of course desirable in their own right, but also through the impact of improved health on higher productivity and output. Estimates of the precise magnitudes of these production effects are usually uncertain. A study from West Africa on the eradication of onchocerciasis (river blindness), a water-based disease, found economic returns of 18 percent to 20 percent. Economic benefits arose in this case because with the eradication of the disease land that could not be used previously was brought back to cultivation.

Benefits from improved availability of water can also be viewed as savings in collection time, of which some portion may be used for leisure and the rest for productive activity. In rural sub-Saharan Africa it is well established that water collection is the responsibility of females and from a series of case studies the average time rural women spend on domestic transport (water and fuel wood collection) is in the range of 0.9 to 2.2 hours per day. (Barwell, 1996). Surveys conducted for the World Bank in villages suggest an average water consumption of 20 litres per capita and that this remains constant up to trip distances of 15 to 20 minutes for water collection. Once the time involved increases beyond this, the number of trips per day and hence water consumption begins to decline because of the cost of the additional time involved. Hence an improved siting of water facilities, such as stand pipes or handpump wells, closer to rural communities will act as a major stimulus to extra water consumption.

A good example of the impact of safe supply of water is provided by the river blindness program in West Africa, which has been in operation since the mid-1970s. The program aims at eradicating onchocerciasis by controlling the black fly that transmits a parasitic worm which is the source of the disease. The program benefits the rural population by removing the threat of blindness and allowing large tracts of land that were previously unusable due to the risk of contracting onchocerciasis to be brought under cultivation. A study by the World Bank has examined the economic impact of this project and estimated an economic IRR of 18 to 20 percent. Benefits from the program are defined as its productive impact and are measured by the increase in agricultural output from subsistence farming. An increase in output occurs because of the higher labor and land inputs, as additional labor and land are made available by the eradication of the disease.

The poor clearly wish to have access to improved water supplies and the existence of water vendors, often charging high prices per m3, is evidence of strong demand. A crude rule of thumb sometimes used in pricing water is that households should not spend more than 5 per-

cent of their income on water supplies. Surveys conducted in a number of countries report that many, (who would best be classified as the better-off of the poor rather than the poorest of the poor) are in fact often willing to pay considerably more than 5 percent for good quality water. Such a study conducted in Nigeria in the late 1980s found expenditures on water as a proportion of household income of nearly double this with even higher proportions in the dry season. Vendors were charging ₦12-13 per 1,000 gallons, whilst the new project was proposing to charge a tariff of ₦5 for household connections. (Whittington et al., 1991). However in the context of tariff policy the authors argue that from their survey it appears that households are willing to pay more than twice the proposed tariff.

A policy of cost recovery is frequently advocated for the water sector, both to ensure adequate funds for maintenance and also as means of allocating a scarce resource and deterring wasteful use. For individual household connections there seems little rationale in questioning this recommendation since those with such connections are highly unlikely to be amongst the very poor. Further a life-line tariff system with a low charge per cubic metre for a relatively modest amount of consumption can be implemented to protect poorer households. Higher tariffs on larger volumes of water can cross-subsidize the minimum levels of consumption. For standpipes and wells provided to communities it is not feasible to charge individual household by volume of water consumed and charging will have to be on a community basis with a view to cover the maintenance rather than the total (capital plus maintenance) costs involved.

The strongest argument for this policy is that it gives the community a stake in the water scheme and removes funding from the vagaries of local or central government budgets. The risk is that if poor communities have to find additional cash to pay for social services such as health and education the extra cash income needed may not be available. Hence charging should be reviewed in the light of the total demands on the poor from all services, not just water alone. The case for charging for water is considerably stronger than that for charging for health and education, particularly because the externality argument in terms of wider social benefits is stronger in the latter two cases (ADR, 1998; Weiss, 1998).

Private sector participation in the delivery of water is also an option to be considered. It is recognized, however, that there are limits to what can be achieved by relying on private sector entrepreneurship, particularly in the case of rural poverty reduction. Investment costs in water infrastructures tend to be large, while project economic lives are long, and the payback period is usually measured in terms of decades. On the other hand, the social – and political – nature of water means that there are enormous pressures to keep service prices low. This is exacerbated by the high incidence of poverty in the region, low and highly uncertain household incomes, and domestic consumers' low capacity to pay. All these translate into high political and commercial risks and, potentially, a low rate of return on investment.

There is strong argument that in the case of water delivery for rural households which aims at rural poverty reduction, government with the support of the donor community must take the lead. Experience has shown, however, that local communities must be consulted by the government at all stages of the project including the design and implementation. Cultural and traditional values of people in relation to water resources should be studied to provide a basis for designing an effective information, communication and education

program to deepen community understanding of sustainable utilization and management of water resources. Wherever relevant, modern civil organizations such as consumer associations, cooperatives and professional associations should be taken on board, supported and empowered to enable them to participate significantly in water resources management. In this respect, useful recommendations that emerged from a joint study by the UNDP-World Bank are discussed in Box 5.5 (See also Chapter 4).

Institutions for Rural Poverty Reduction

National Institutions

Rural poverty in Africa is entrenched in the general state of poverty at the national level. Weak national institutions, which are partly responsible for the economic malaise and the spread of poverty, will not be expected to contribute to reduction of rural poverty unless they undergo a deep restructuring process. Efforts to establish and strengthen institutions that care for the special needs of the rural poor should, therefore, start by putting national institutions in order. Too often, national agencies and institutions in Africa are synonymous with poor service, corruption and inefficiency. Lack of openness, transparency and accountability in national institutions resulted in public dissatisfaction and lack of confidence in public institutions and undermined the ability of the government to provide social services. Policies and strategies to reform national institutions were discussed in great details in the ADR 2001. Here, issues pertaining to national institutions and rural poverty reduction are outlined.

Government institutions that operate at the national level play an important role in rural pov-

Box 5.5: Recommendations for Making Rural Water Supply Sustainable

A study conducted under the UNDP-World Bank Water and Sanitation Program, provides the following useful recommendations for making rural water supply sustainable:

- *Adopting a demand-responsive approach will improve the sustainability of water systems.* The study provides evidence that better results are achieved when preferences for service levels, technology and siting are obtained directly from well-informed households, rather than from traditional leaders or water committees.

- *Training for household members and for water committees improves sustainability by building capacity and commitment.* Training should include the provision of knowledge on how to operate and maintain systems, as well as about the potential health benefits of an improved supply. It was found that the latter affects the way households value the service and thereby their willingness to sustain the system.

- *Designated and accountable community organizations are necessary components of success.* Giving clear responsibilities for management, operations, maintenance and fee collection to community organizations increases the sustainability of projects. Such organizations should be transparent, accountable, and trusted by community members.

Source: ADB (2000b).

growth and hence exacerbates the state of poverty, but also because it tends to redistribute incomes away from the poor and in favor of the rich. Strengthening the national institutions that are responsible for monetary management and inflation control is, thus, an integral part of efforts to reduce poverty. The same logic applies to all other national institutions that manage a country's economic and social affairs. Key among these is the institutions responsible for the provision of social services such as education, health and other basic needs. Despite the shift of many African countries to private sector-led growth, government institutions have still an important role to play in poverty reduction. From the point of view of poverty reduction governments ought to be active in such basic services as education and health. Likewise, from the point of view of market failure, they ought to be active in the provision of public goods including infrastructure in areas where the private sector initiatives are not forthcoming. Public sector management must also play a supportive role to allow private sector operators to assume the new role that has been assigned to them.

These functions cannot be performed effectively in the absence of strong institutions. It requires putting in place mechanisms that will enhance and guarantee the quality of public services. Greater accountability must be promoted. Systems must be put in place to strengthen mechanisms for expenditure control, exposure of and sanctions against misspending and corruption. It will also be necessary to develop and build democratic institutions and strengthen the independence of government agencies. Independent institutions to promote public and private sector accountability – such as the Auditor General's Office, the Ombudsman and the Public Accounts Committee of parliament – need to be established and

erty reduction. The functions of all national institutions including the central bank are important to poverty reduction. For instance, empirical evidence in this Report indicates that inflation is among the main causes of poverty. This is not only because it retards the process of economic

given the power to undertake their duties without fear of reprisals. Competent governing boards for public enterprises must be established and promoted. Professionalism and meritocracy must be brought to civil service to ensure effective and efficient delivery of public services and to combat bureaucratic corruption. Importantly, national institutions in Africa need to adapt to the changing international context and adopts a new approach to fight poverty in general and rural poverty in particular.

The emerging consensus is that institutions, which empower the poor are the foundation of rural poverty reduction and that rural poverty reduction requires community participation as well as the strengthening of partnerships with civil societies. Participation gives the poor a chance to make an input in the design and implementation of rural development programs, and through a transfer of responsibility it broadens their choices and gives them the power to determine ways to improve their lives. Greater emphasis is now placed on devolution and local management of common property resources and extension services. Supporting the construction of social capital and linking the poor to dynamic sectors of the economy is central to rural poverty reduction. This policy shift thus involves a new emphasis on institutions: on the organizations (for example, families, banks and trade unions) that mediate the access of the poor to assets, technologies and markets, and on the rules (laws, customs and administrative practices) that determine whether the poor benefit from such access. The poor's chance to influence rules, and to help control organizations, depends on their power and influence. These, in turn, depend on their knowledge, access and, perhaps above all, whether alternative courses of action are open to them.

Decentralization and the Paradox of Institutional Change

The relevance of local institutions for socio-economic progress stems from the need for local economic development, improved service delivery, increased popular participation in governance, and the desire to bring governments closer to the people. Good governance must be rooted in the effective participation of the people in decision-making and in the functioning of local self-governance institutions.

Effective local economic management means that development functions should be taken over by local governments. This requires that local authorities should be able to mobilize resources (financial, human and technological), initiate, plan and implement development projects, and obtain adequate support from national governments (ADR, 2001). Despite efforts by many governments to decentralize or devolve power, the local government system has not been very effective (Wohlmuth, 1999). The problems vary and are numerous. Local governments are dependent on regional and national governance systems. Political intentions notwithstanding, the creation of local governments has not necessarily led to real allocation of power and funds. Underdeveloped local civil society and turbulent economic and policy environments undercut local institutions.

Local institutions in Africa are highly inadequate with regard to development planning, financing, and administration. In many cases, there are uncertainties in the way the local authorities and national governments interact whether in project initiation and implementation or in other areas of responsibilities. Manpower and financial resources are mostly inadequate as most local governments fully depend on financially-strapped central governments. As a result, in many countries, local authorities have no political autonomy, real power and function, nor the capacity to raise revenue. Rural poverty reduction in Africa will require viable local institutions. The consolidation of local governance is necessary to create the democratic developmental state. This will require not just decentralization but also devolution of authority to local governments and building a viable local political process that can mobilize people and demand accountability from local officials.

Effective local institutions, which are capable of facilitating rural development, will require real decentralization. However, decentralization must not be used by the central governments as a way to shake off their responsibilities. They must be part of a national strategy to create more responsible and equitable local governance. Effective communication must be maintained between central and local governments. Resources should be equitably shared among the levels of government while measures to promote accountability and reduce corruption must be put in place. Local institutions will have to be strengthened and capacity of local authorities built to manage the development process.

The case for decentralization depends partially on the extent to which local institutions are not captured by the non-poor. IFAD (1989) recognizes the paradoxical nature of institutional change designed to help the poor. That is while institutional change to help the poor is desirable, institutions, including the state and NGOs, tend to be controlled by the powerful non-poor. Often, those who have good access to one institution also have good access to others. Even after land redistribution, the large farmer, for instance, may still have better access than the ex-landless laborer to production, credit, information and marketing networks. The rural rich tend to dominate the local power structure. They are often the first, and possibly the only, people consulted when a development program is undertaken in the community. Such observations warn against the assumptions that local communities are homogeneous, whether in terms of class, ethnicity, age, or gender, and point to serious accountability problems with anti-poverty programs.

The real challenge, therefore is how to design and implement institutional change that enables the poor and weak to use and benefit from those institutions, which were hitherto controlled by the rich and powerful. Paradoxically, one step in this direction is to empower the poor by decisions at the central level so as to restrain the non-poor from arranging things to their own advantage and to prevent the rural elite from wielding decentralized power over rural financial institutions or over natural resources. In cases where the democratic system functions properly, the poor may use their voting power to elect those who can deliver the institutions that serve their community and the services that empower their people. This point, of course, is not applicable in the case of token democracies where voting is based, exclusively, on tribal or religious allegiances, rather than on the expected performance or the track record of the elected.

To be sure, many non-poor, for whatever reason, often support forms of universal coverage that might benefit the poor such as the provision of free medical services and education. While the poor can potentially benefit from such free services, there are legitimate concerns related to making such services available in rural and remote areas. In many African countries, rural areas are neglected and services are concentrated in urban areas. In some cases, the cream of professionals who are providing social services (e.g. medical doctors and teachers) might be reluctant to move to rural areas. In all these cases, much depends on government incentive policies and on the ability of the rural poor to mobilize politically and put pressure on the government. For instance, for a considerable period of time after independence, the government of Sudan adopted a policy of positive discrimination with regard to the salaries of professionals in education and health. Professionals who worked in rural areas received salaries by far higher than those in urban areas. Rural locations where there were hospitals and schools were classified as hardship areas, and the higher salary was to compensate for the hardships associated with leaving urban areas and working in rural locations. As a result, professionals working in rural areas were among the highly qualified in the country, especially in education. The outcome was an outstanding success with high quality education in rural areas. Indicative of such a success is the fact that a large proportion of the intake of the University of Khartoum was from rural areas. The policy had a profound positive effect on social change and income redistribution.

Summary

The globalization-induced distribution of income at the international level tends to favor countries that position themselves to benefit from increased opportunities of trade through the exportation of not only price-competitive products, but also through the promotion of products which are attractive to world income. The effect of globalization on poverty depends on its impact on trade and growth and on their distributional impact on the poor. Depending on country-specific conditions, policy makers would need to make sure that liberalization will stimulate trade and growth and that growth will benefit the rural poor. The evidence is that the often disappointing performance of internal and external liberalization in Africa is due much more to its failure to reach rural people or to induce fast agricultural growth, than to any alleged inadequacy of such growth in benefiting the poor. Many reforming countries experience poor overall and agricultural growth records even now. A policy of market liberalization must be complemented by policies to enhance market access and participation of the poor if the potentially adverse consequences of liberalization on the poor are to be minimized and potential gains realized. However, the need to complement market access reforms with changes in technology and institutions as well to enhance the supply response of agriculture must be emphasized. To benefit fully from liberalization, the abilities of the rural poor must be improved in three main areas: their ability to receive market incentives (price signals), their ability to respond to such incentives through increased production, and their ability to market their labor and excess production.

CHAPTER 6

The Bank Group's Rural Poverty Reduction Strategy

An Overview of Past Efforts

Since it started operations in 1967, the main objective of the Bank has been the enhancement of economic and social development in its RMCs, most of which had just attained their political independence with limited economic and social infrastructure. Hence, the primacy of economic growth was widely accepted as a development goal. As a result, import substitution-based industrialization was emphasized in the 1960s and 1970s. One of the problems of industry-led growth, however, was that the urban population benefited disproportionately at the expense of the poor rural population. Development efforts of the 1970s and 1980s attempted to correct this imbalance by focusing on rural development in general and on agricultural development and the provision of social services in particular.

Projects in agriculture, infrastructure, education, health and urban development were however designed with inadequate consideration for the needs of the rural poor. Although the ADF was established to overcome these problems by addressing poverty in low-income African countries, the focus on the poor was not fully initiated until the ADF V (1988-1990). In ADF V, the aim of the Fund's operations was stipulated as "meeting the basic needs of the poorest sections of the populations in low-income countries". Other general principles such as promoting economic policies to facilitate the efficient allocation of resources, fostering employment creation, improving the environment and the inclusion of women and other members of society were not fully integrated in the development process.

Under ADF VI, (1991-1993) poverty alleviation was explicitly stated as the main aim of development activities in borrowing countries. In addition, sectoral priorities were identified, the need for appropriate policy environment recognized, and the necessity of improving the productivity of the poor, especially in agriculture and food production emphasized. Improvements in access of the poor to primary education and preventive health care were part of this strategy. The importance of providing well-targeted safety nets for the poor was also recognized during this period.

The approaches towards poverty reduction were sharpened further under ADF VII (1996-1998). As a result, poverty reduction considerations were reflected in all activities of the Fund, especially in investments in human capital, environmental management, activities aimed at creating productive opportunities for the poor and those that further strengthened the role of women in development.

Under ADF VIII (1999-2001), the Bank has further emphasized the importance of poverty reduction in all its lending and non-lending activities. The focus on poverty reduction under ADF VIII was expanded by emphasizing the importance of participatory approaches involving all stakeholders. Through this approach, the Bank aims to empower the poor at all stages of the projects and programs that it finances. In principle, therefore, all activities financed out of ADF

VIII resources are expected to adequately reflect poverty reduction considerations.

Major Elements of the Bank's Existing Poverty Reduction Strategy

The Bank's current poverty reduction strategy was articulated in the document entitled *Poverty Alleviation and Action Program* prepared in 1992. A summary of the Bank's strategy, which includes an overview of the major elements of the strategy and the mechanisms that have been put in place to implement it, is presented here.

The main components of the strategy are: an enabling policy framework, a focus on priority sectors (e.g. agriculture, rural infrastructure, education, health and clean water supply) and a recognition of the important role of women in development. Other elements encompass cross-cutting issues such as the protection of the environment, promotion of the private sector, coordination of poverty reduction efforts with development partners, provision of targeted programs for vulnerable groups and facilitation of the involvement of beneficiaries and NGOs in the development process.

Enabling Policy Framework

The Bank's poverty reduction strategy, based on the recognition of the primacy of economic growth for poverty reduction, is guided by the principle that the achievement of sustainable growth requires a prudent macro-economic environment, appropriate sectoral policies and structural as well as institutional reforms. Such reforms are necessary for the promotion of broad-based growth and the provision of opportunities for full-time employment and increased incomes for the poor.

The Bank recognizes that faster broad-based growth and increased income for the poor requires a balanced macro-economy, high adult literacy rates, well-developed infrastructure, low initial income and asset inequality, significant role of the private sector, high gender equality with respect to access to productive assets including land and credit and strong institutional structures. Therefore, economic growth is necessary but not sufficient for reducing poverty significantly. Consequently, as part of its poverty reduction strategies, the Bank continues to support macro-economic and equitable sectoral policies in a number of countries. The Bank's recent support for reform in the social and economic sectors has been accompanied by programs to mitigate possible adverse effects of the reform efforts.

Sectoral Priorities

The focus on agricultural and rural development continues to be at the center of the growth aspects of the Bank's poverty reduction strategy. This is based on the fact that in many African countries, growth within the agricultural sector is important for enhancing food security and reducing poverty. In addition, informal economic activities in rural as well as urban areas, which use the abundant labor that the poor possess, are important sources of economic growth and hence poverty reduction.

The Bank's lending program for infrastructure projects is based on the ground that investments in infrastructure such as rural roads can reduce transport costs and travel time, and can improve markets for agricultural inputs and outputs. Under these circumstances, the demand for labor, crop yields and farm incomes all show increases, thus contributing to poverty reduction. This is especially true if investments in infrastructure are made in areas that have a high potential for agricultural development.

In the past few years, Bank lending has also focused on the development of the human capital of the poor. The allocation of public resources in favor of primary education, especially girl's education, preventive health care and nutritional programs plays an important role in this respect. Even recent Bank financed structural adjustment loans have been guided by the importance of protecting the social well-being of the poor during the reduction or reallocation of public expenditures.

Cross-Cutting Issues

The existing poverty reduction strategy recognizes the importance of considering cross-cutting issues such as gender (see Box 6.1), the environment, private sector development and the involvement of non-government organizations (NGOs) as integral parts of the poverty reduction effort. The considerations for each of these cross-cutting issues are based on both economic and equity grounds.

Obviously, there are groups within society who may not benefit equally from economic growth and public expenditure policies. Targeted programs are designed for such groups. Most of these programs address pockets of poverty in neglected regions within a country. They also target disadvantaged groups, especially women. In many countries, the Bank has used micro-finance projects in general and social funds in particular to reach vulnerable groups.

The Bank's policy on poverty reduction is also based on the recognition of the strong relationship between poverty and environmental degradation. The poor are victims of environmental degradation but also contribute to environmental

---

Box 6.1: Gender, Poverty and Socio-economic Development

Gender and socio-economic development have three major dimensions that have direct implications for an equitable economic growth and poverty reduction: equity; governance and human rights; and economic development. In general, gender equity and poverty reduction go hand in hand given that women, relative to men, are discriminated against in many spheres of social and economic life. For instance, there is a bias against women in the delivery of social services, especially education and employment in the formal sector. Such biases are not only inequitable but also economically inefficient. For example, just by educating girls, African societies can reap social benefits such as reduced malnutrition for children, infant and maternal mortality and fertility. As for governance and human rights considerations, these issues are closely linked in African societies. Indeed, both the Cairo International Conference on Population and Development and the Beijing Women's Conference emphasized the fact that violence against women was an important issue to be addressed both in the context of enhancing their social and economic lives and their reproductive rights.

With regard to socio-economic development, it is recognized that in many African countries women are important inputs in the development process and Bank efforts in mainstreaming gender into poverty reduction projects are well underway. The Uganda Poverty Alleviation Project is a good illustration. Its main objective was to ensure gender balance in targeting its beneficiaries with emphasis on reaching more women specifically. The project appraisal report set as a target 60 percent of women to be beneficiaries. This target was achieved. Out of the total of about 23,900 beneficiaries by 31 December 1998, about 14,700 or 62 percent were women. The project also targeted female beneficiaries to receive more sensitization and awareness raising to break cultural barriers, which inhibited them from borrowing. As a result, they tended to respond more positively to loan repayment schedules as they scored a 95 percent repayment rate compared to 88 percent to their male counterparts. About 20 percent of these women received skill development training; credit and training in establishing

(box continues on next page)

Box 6.1: Gender, Poverty and Socio-economic Development (continued)

micro-projects. In a recent survey, 75 percent of females interviewed pointed out that PAP interventions had contributed to their empowerment in terms of overall positive impact on their lives while 80 percent indicated economic improvements, 54 percent admitted that PAP enhanced self-reliance, improved decision making, financial management, interaction with local authorities, awareness levels and social networks, all of which contributed to their ability to improve their income levels and standard of living.

The growing emphasis on private sector development in RMCs is key to reinforcing the synergy between poverty and gender. This points to, among other things, the need to enable women to transform their activities from the informal sector to more structured and formal businesses, including access to productive assets and social services. In the same vein, the combined impact of globalization, the changing patterns of trade and modern technologies calls for the enhancement of skills that most women on the continent do not possess, as they lack the requisite level of education and training.

Source: ADB (2001a).

problems because of limited planning horizons stemming from persistent poverty. As a result, the poor often engage in economic activities on marginal lands that may worsen problems of soil erosion, deforestation, desertification or air and water pollution.

Another important feature of the Bank's poverty reduction strategy is the significant role of the private sector in facilitating the creation of employment, economic growth and poverty reduction. In fact, some of the structural adjustment loans are designed to create an enabling environment for the private sector. In 1997, the Bank

transformed the Private Sector Unit (established in 1991) to a fully-fledged Department in order to encourage private sector initiatives within RMCs. In recent years, the Bank has given priority to the employment creation and income generation potential of the private sector by supporting small and medium enterprises (SMEs). The private sector activities supported by the Bank are guided by the policy papers on credit lines, agency lines and guarantees to private sector financial institutions.

In 1994, guidelines for the implementation of the poverty alleviation strategy and action program were prepared to assist staff to translate the Bank's poverty reduction policies into programs and projects. These guidelines integrate the key elements of the strategy and provide a flexible framework that enhances the Bank's operational effectiveness both at the macro- and micro-economic levels.

At the macro-economic level, the guidelines were meant to facilitate the integration of poverty reduction into the overall adjustment programs in RMCs and the preparation of Country Strategy Papers (CSPs). Accordingly, an attempt was made to enhance the capacity of Bank staff to identify, prepare, and implement projects with a high potential for contributing to poverty reduction. The importance of using poverty profiles and poverty assessments in program and project documents was emphasized.

In addition, the guidelines promoted a demand-driven approach to poverty reduction by addressing the need to support the poor and other vulnerable groups to fully participate at all stages of the project cycle. A format for beneficiary assessments was presented in the guidelines to implement the Bank's poverty reduction strategy at the project level. The need to strengthen the capacity of local institutions to internalize poverty reduction policies at the grass-roots level was equally emphasized.

Poverty Reduction in Sector Policy Papers

The Bank's poverty reduction strategy is also supported by several sector policies and guidelines. Since 1992, a number of sector policy papers have been prepared and updated. These include the Health Policy Paper (1996), the Policy Paper on Good Governance (1999), the Agricultural Policy Paper (2000), the Education Policy Paper (2000), the Integrated Water Resources Management Policy (2000), Economic Cooperation and Regional Integration Policy (2000) and Policy on Civil Society Organizations (2000). In each of these policy papers, poverty reduction considerations are incorporated in order to enhance the contribution of the sector to poverty reduction.

The main objective of the Agriculture and Rural Development Policy is to promote technological, institutional and policy changes in favor of improvements in land and labor productivity, especially within the agricultural sector. This should increase incomes of the poor, reduce their food insecurity and improve child nutrition. The policy also promotes the sustainable management of natural resources and the protection of the environment.

The Education Policy Paper addresses both equity and poverty issues within the education sector. An important aspect of this policy is the emphasis it puts on providing educational opportunity, especially for women and girls. In addition, the policy recognizes that the contribution of education to poverty reduction can be enhanced if the inter-dependence across sub-sectors and the important role that the private sector and civil society are taken into account. The issue of close

partnership among the public, private and civil society in tackling poverty as it relates to the education sector is covered in the policy paper in this respect.

Poverty reduction is also at the center of the Integrated Water Resources Management Policy Paper. In general, water is treated as a basic human need and the supply of clean water is considered as an integral part of the effort to enhance food security, promote preventive health care and ensure the sustainability of the ecosystem. The policy emphasizes the use of minimal prices for lifeline water supplies; transfer pricing between rural and urban areas to mobilize capital investments for rural water, sanitation, and hydropower services; and complementarities between water resources on one hand, and basic education (especially for girls) and community programs on the other.

The Policy Paper on Economic Cooperation and Regional Integration addresses the constraints of many African countries, especially the small ones in terms of the narrowness of their domestic markets. Thus, the policy is designed to promote the integration of African economies in the face of globalization so that both income earning and employment opportunities for the poor are expanded. Since the promotion of African agricultural exports is an important element of this policy, its implementation is expected to result in increased farm incomes and reduced poverty in RMCs.

The Bank's policy on civil society organizations (CSOs) articulates the role of civil society in the formulation of policies and the delivery of social services for the poor. In general, the policy seeks to promote the involvement of stakeholders in the development process thus ensuring that poverty reduction policies and projects are demand-driven. The implementation of the policy will facilitate the involvement of CSOs not only at all stages of the project cycle but also in the preparation of Country Strategy Papers, PRSPs, sectoral policies, public expenditure reviews and National Environment Action Plans (NEAPs).

A number of guidelines are also at an advanced stage of preparation. These include the HIV/AIDS Strategy, Malaria Control Strategy and Operational Guidelines and Guidelines on Project Design, Analysis and Management. The HIV/AIDS strategy and the guidelines on malaria are based, as indicated earlier, on the emerging consensus that both HIV/AIDS and malaria have become more of a development problem than just health issues. As a result, poverty considerations are incorporated explicitly in both guidelines.

In the past few years, the Bank has joined the international community in acknowledging the strong links between governance and development. In particular, the Bank recognizes that without good governance, the efficiency of its investments in RMCs and the success of its poverty reduction efforts will be undermined. In view of this fact, the Bank's Policy on Good Governance addresses issues related to public accountability, corruption, and participation of stakeholders at all levels to enhance the effectiveness of poverty reduction programs.

Project Lending

The Bank lends for important sectors in ADF countries with an emphasis on the agricultural and the social sectors on the grounds that the majority of Africa's poor live in rural areas. In addition, ADF supports operations that improve health and education services in order to contribute to the development of the human capital and productivity of the poor. Furthermore, ADF provides resources for stand-alone poverty projects ear-

marked mainly for the provision of basic social services and for building institutional and income-generating capacities of specific groups. ADF resources are also being allocated to support activities aimed at improving power and water supplies, sanitation facilities; transport infrastructure; debt relief through the supplementary financing mechanism (SFM) and the Heavily Indebted Poor Countries (HIPC) Initiative.

Over the last three years, the Bank earmarked substantial financial resources to assist RMCs in their development efforts. In 1998, total approvals amounted to $810.49 million: 34 specific project loans for $534.66 million; seven policy-based loans for $111.07 million; 66 grants for $85.65 million; and eight operations of $79.15 million to help reduce debt under the SFM.

On the other hand, total approvals in 1999 amounted to $681.92 million. This covered 35 project lending operations for $497.93 million; 2 policy-based loans for $20.56 million; 26 grants for $46.06 million; one HIPC operation for $97.45 million; and six operations for $19.93 million to help reduce debt under the SFM.

In 2000, total ADF approvals amounted to $1,472.42 million for 103 operations. This includes ten debt relief operations amounting to $617.84 million for approvals under the HIPC Initiative. The composition of the other operations was as follows: 38 project loans for $567.73, one line of credit for $7.52 million, five policy-based loans for $157.33 million, 45 technical assistance grants for $68.59 million, three debt alleviation operations for $55.22 million under supplementary financing mechanism.

ADF lending by sectors during 1998-2000 is represented in Figures 6.1 and 6.2. It is clear that priority was given to agricultural and rural development and the social sectors together accounting for 64, 62 and 42 percent of total ADF loan

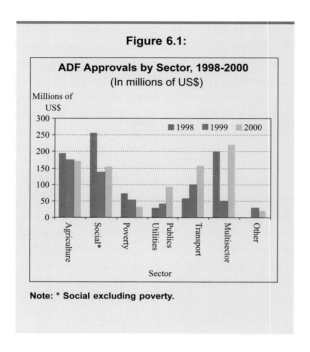

Figure 6.1:

ADF Approvals by Sector, 1998-2000
(In millions of US$)

Note: * Social excluding poverty.

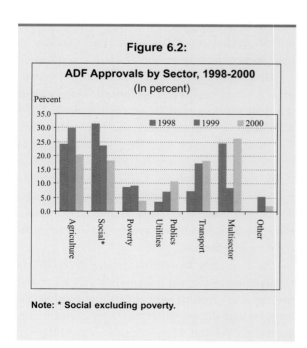

Figure 6.2:

ADF Approvals by Sector, 1998-2000
(In percent)

Note: * Social excluding poverty.

and grant approvals in 1998, 1999 and 2000 respectively. Lending to the agriculture and rural development sector amounted to $195.81 million (24.2 percent of total ADF loans and grants), $173.97 million (29.8 percent of total loans and grants) and $173.08 million (20.4 percent) in 1998, 1999, and 2000 respectively. Lending to this sector focused on improving output and household food security on a sustainable basis, and for enhancing rural incomes and reducing poverty. In addition to direct support for agriculture and rural development, approvals were given to the finance sector in the form of lines of credit to make loans available to small and medium scale farmers and other micro-entrepreneurs engaged in agriculture and related income-generating activities.

Social Sector Projects

Social sector lending for 1998, 1999, and 2000 amounted to $327.23 million, $190.67 million, and $185.77 million, respectively. Social sector activities focused on improving the access and quality of education and health services, particularly basic education and primary health care. Support to the social sector also focused on improving access to microfinance, especially for women, and building institutional and income generating capacities of target populations. In Box 6.2, examples of social sector projects with a poverty focus are provided.

Public Utilities Projects

ADF operations during the period under review also included public utilities projects, transport infrastructure and services that are important for the economic and social development of African countries. Support to public utilities were in the

Box 6.2: Examples of Social Sector Projects with a Poverty Focus, 1998-2000

- The Health Infrastructure Project in Gitega and Karuzi Provinces of Burundi is designed to improve the health status of the population in these districts. Women and children are targeted as potential beneficiaries.

- The main objective of the Rural Health Project for Kenya is to improve the health of communities in seven districts. The project focuses on improvements in public health and reduction in the incidence of preventable diseases through the promotion of participation of the communities. Improvements in access of women and children to basic health services are at the center of project activities. These two groups represent 75 percent of the potential beneficiaries of the project.

- The health sector in Malawi is characterized by poor social indicators, a high concentration of medical resources in urban areas, scarcity of well trained health personnel and a high incidence of preventable diseases, especially those related to malnutrition, environmental degradation and HIV/AIDS. The Rural Health care Support Project in Malawi is designed to address these problems in order to enhance access and quality of health care in rural areas. The project focuses on three activities. These are improvements in primary health care, development of human resources, and control of the spread of HIV/AIDS. The project is expected to contribute to the overall objective of the national Health Plan for the 1999-2004 period.

- The Education I Project for Niger is designed to facilitate the implementation of reforms within its education sector. Components of the project include construction of primary and secondary schools in order to increase enrollment rates as well as literacy, especially among girls and women.

- The main objective of Madagascar's Health Project (II) is to improve the health status of women and children, especially those within the least privileged health districts. The project is expected to benefit over 5.5 million people (39 percent of the total population in the country) living in remote and isolated districts some of, which had no health facilities before.

- The Education II Project in Uganda is designed to contribute to the Educational Sector Development Plan which was developed with extensive participation of a variety of stakeholders in the country. The highest priority of this plan is to assure universal access to primary education. The main objective of the project, therefore, is to improve access to primary education, reduce gender disparities in secondary education, and improve the quality of science education in girl's schools in rural areas. Thus, the implementation of the project will bridge the rural-urban as well as gender gap in the provision of secondary science education. Forty-five girl's secondary schools will receive a fully equipped science laboratory and school library.

- Through the Education III Project in Zambia, 188 classrooms will be built in 42 schools in rural districts. The ultimate goal is to provide 7,500 places for grades 1 and 2, the main objective being to contribute to improvements in the quality of basic education.

Source: ADB (2001a).

amount of $27.96 million, $41.90 million, and $92.77 million, in 1998, 1999 and 2000, respectively. It is important to note that lending for public utilities increased from 3.5 percent of total ADF lending in 1998 to 10.9 percent in 2000. The support was primarily to enhance public health services and reduce the prevalence of water-borne diseases, by improving sanitation and the supply of drinkable water and electricity for both urban and rural areas.

Transport Projects

In the transport sector, ADF operations focused primarily on improving the efficiency of the transport infrastructure and services to spur the economic and social development of African countries. This is achieved by rehabilitating and maintaining road networks that link agricultural areas with industrial and urban zones or ports to facilitate the transport of goods destined for export. Lending to the transport sector amounted to $59.57 million, $99.47 million and $155.85 million in 1998, 1999 and 2000, respectively. As indicated in Figure 6.1, lending for the transport sector increased from a share of 7.4 percent in 1998 to 18.3 percent of total ADF lending in 2000.

Stand-alone Poverty Projects

ADF also provided support to stand-alone poverty operations that are, by their nature, grassroots -oriented. These operations involve beneficiaries and other stakeholders increasingly in project design and implementation to meet their needs. They address some of the immediate needs of the poor, such as providing micro-credit and basic social amenities, strengthening the institutional and financial capacities of local communities in order to improve their access to basic social services,

with a particular focus on the needs of disadvantaged groups including women.

In 1998, six such stand-alone poverty projects were approved for a total of $72.15 million for activities in Burkina Faso ($22.05 million), Malawi ($12.67 million), Mozambique ($3.29 million), Niger ($9.43 million), Rwanda ($13.43 million) and Tanzania ($11.26 million).

ADF financing for stand-alone poverty projects in 1999, amounted to $53.73 million for three countries: Uganda ($20.48 million), Mali ($17.14 million), and Senegal ($16.11 million). In 2000, one stand-alone poverty project amounting to $26.06 million was approved for Nigeria and one for Cape Verde ($6.51 million). As shown in Figure 6.1, the share of lending for stand-alone projects declined between 1998 and 2000. The main reason for this decline, however, is that more and more, the Bank is mainstreaming poverty reduction in its lending programs and projects. In 2000, the classification of stand-alone projects was taken out of the multi-sector category and combined with lending for the social sector.

Technical Assistance Grants

Technical assistance grants continue to be an important component of ADF operations. They are used to enhance the capabilities of regional member countries in designing, developing, and implementing development projects and programs. They also support institutional strengthening and capacity building in the low-income countries. A total of 66 technical assistance grants, amounting to $85.65 million or 10.5 percent of total approvals, were approved in 1998. Fewer grants were approved in 1999: a total of 26 technical assistance amounting to $46.06 million, or 6.8 percent of total approvals for 1999. In 2000, 45 technical assistance grants with an amount of $68.59 million were approved. This represents 4.2 percent of total approvals. More than 50 percent of these grants are related to institutional strengthening and capacity building in RMCs.

Future Bank Objectives in Lending to the Rural Sector

Bank's lending for the sector will pursue four key developmental objectives, namely:

- accelerated economic growth with equity;
- poverty reduction and food security;
- natural resource management and environmental protection; and
- human and institutional capacity building.

Accelerated Economic Growth with Equity

The Bank aims to promote broad-based economic growth as a crucial component of its poverty-reduction strategy. This will be achieved through assistance to: promote an enabling policy, institutional and legal environment; develop and adopt an investment code that attracts private domestic and foreign capital flows into Africa; develop agri-business and agro-industries; promote exports; and assist RMCs in their regional cooperation and integration efforts (Box 6.3). Development aid to Africa has often been heavily biased towards the pre-harvest input delivery services with much less emphasis on the post-harvest aspects of the food chain. Investment in RMCs has been biased toward developing effective marketing infrastructure for export and cash crops in order to generate foreign exchange to service their debts. The relative neglect of the food crop sub-sectors has adversely affected overall economic performance of most African agrarian economies. Strong linkages with

---

Box 6.3: Reducing Poverty through Agriculture and Rural Development

Agricultural and rural development are crucial for the structural transformation and development of RMCs. Agriculture contributes 20 percent of GDP in North Africa and 30 percent of GDP in Sub-Saharan Africa. The rural population represents an average of 60 percent of the total population on the continent, and about 90 percent of the rural labor force engage directly or indirectly in agricultural activities. For the continent's rural people and economies, agricultural development could help raise efficiency, increase household income, improve standards of living, and reduce poverty.

Poverty is deeply rooted in rural areas. The poor face more difficult problems with access to food, water supply, primary health care and primary education today than they did 30 years ago. To arrest and reverse the spread of poverty requires achieving and sustaining economic growth of 7-8 percent per annum. This would require real agricultural GDP growth of at least 4 percent per annum.

Over the next decade the Bank Group assistance strategy will focus on supporting the technological, institutional, and policy changes that would trigger a lasting transformation of the rural economies of RMCs by empowering their rural populations to improve their productivity and real incomes in an equitable and environmentally sustainable manner. Bank strategy is articulated around three key development objectives:

1. More operations will directly target poverty reduction and food security. The Bank will thus support (i) the participation of stakeholders, including the poor, in investment planning and decision making; (ii) the formulation and implementation of comprehensive development policies and strategies, where investments in social services complement the agricultural activities of the poor; (iii) national food security strategies; and, (iv) labor-intensive, non-farm activities, targeting the poor more effectively.

2. The Bank's interventions aim at improving natural resource management and environmental protection by supporting: (i) activities that increase

(box continues on next page)

Box 6.3: Reducing Poverty through Agriculture and Rural Development (continued)

agricultural productivity while restoring and protecting the regenerative capacity of the natural resource base; (ii) institutional capacity to conceive and implement legal frameworks and land tenure systems, which provide incentives for long-term investments in resource-use systems; (iii) investment in cost-effective and socially acceptable irrigation technology; and, (iv) developing water-use plans which recognize the rights of all end-users.

3. The Bank will support human and institutional capacity building through assistance to: (i) building the capacity of grassroots rural institutions and associations; (ii) broad-based education, basic-skills training for youth, and adult literacy; and, (iii) primary health care and preventive health, with special attention to HIV/AIDS and water-borne diseases.

Source: ADB (2000a).

agro-industry and an efficient marketing infrastructure (for the food crop and other sub-sectors of agriculture) are necessary to improve value-added to agriculture, reduce post-harvest losses and, therefore, increase the level of adoption of improved technology. The Bank's strategy will, therefore, put more emphasis on the post-harvest end of the (input-output) continuum by improving farmers' access to markets and providing support to RMCs in identifying critical intervention points in the entire food chain.

Private Sector and Agri-business Development: Development of the private sector holds the key to future agricultural and overall economic growth in Africa. Unfortunately, however, Africa's private sector lacks capacity because it is relatively young and constrained by the weak economies in which it operates, as well as by uncertainties regarding the credibility of public policies. The investment climate is unpredictable because of a number of factors including lack of the necessary public and institutional infrastructure, weaknesses in the legal and regulatory environment, and the dominance of the public sector in the provision of private and semi-private goods and services. This has had the effect of crowding out private sector activity and discouraged the use of domestic savings for domestic investment, especially in agriculture. At the same time, Africa has been able to attract only 2.6 percent of private global capital flows, which have increased more than eightfold in the past decade.

The Bank will, therefore, play a catalytic role in helping RMCs to create the right environment for attracting both domestic and foreign investment to support agriculture and rural development in the continent. Agri-business must play a key role in generating and sustaining private sector-led economic growth. In this regard, the Bank recognizes farmers as the most dominant group to be targeted in the private sector. The strategy involves assistance to strengthen linkages between farmers and agro-industry, and to assist in the development of agribusiness and agro-industrial enterprises. The Bank will assist RMCs to build the enabling framework for financial sector development, private infrastructure development and micro-credit and savings services. It will also help RMCs to streamline their regulatory and legal environments, and to build entrepreneurial capacity of indigenous and grass-roots institutions via training and technical assistance. In order to facilitate the exposure of African entrepreneurs to the global market, the Bank will operate via its private sector window to encourage joint ventures with more experienced and interested foreign counterparts.

Technology Generation and Adoption:

To be more effective, the Bank's assistance for research will be channeled through regional research centers with clear and relevant mandates and objectives for African agriculture, and emphasize coordinated sub-regional programs to improve the production, post-harvest handling, processing, and marketing of targeted agricultural commodities. The Bank will support farming systems research to promote better understanding of applied technology development for better resource allocations at the farm level as well as specific commodity sub-sector research in a globalized market environment. In order to ensure lasting results on the ground, the Bank will allocate resources to areas of high potential that have been under-funded or neglected by other donors. These would include labor-intensive technologies; greater integration of crop, livestock, and agro-forestry enterprises within farming systems; post-harvest technologies to minimize losses; and high-value but less well-researched export commodities.

The Bank will also assist RMCs to develop strong linkages between research and extension in order to ensure effective transfer of the benefits of research to farmers. Empirical evidence shows that no single agricultural extension model has proven itself sufficiently superior to justify its uniform adoption in all farming circumstances. Thus the Bank will adopt basic efficiency principles to determine the most effective system to support. A key principle is that proposed recommendations in each system must be relevant to the actual conditions of the clientele being served. Given the dominant role of women in agriculture and household food security, the Bank will support extension systems that are gender-sensitive. The Bank will also encourage private sector efforts involving contract farming and out-grower schemes.

Rural Financial Intermediation:

The Bank considers the establishment of effective and viable rural financial institutions as one of the critical building blocks of this policy paper. It will, therefore, work with informal rural finance institutions to increase their capacity to mobilize domestic savings and to provide more effective credit services to rural households and businesses. The Bank will also work with these institutions to create and strengthen their linkages with formal private sector banking systems. These objectives will be pursued through appropriate strategies, such as the capacity-building grants of the AMINA program (see Box 6.4), which is designed to provide assistance to micro-finance institutions in the areas of organizational development, policies, procedures, management information systems, and specialized training in credit and savings account management for borrower groups and savers.

Box 6.4: The ADF Micro-finance Initiative for Africa (AMINA) Program

In recognition of the importance of the micro-enterprise sector in poverty reduction, ADF has allocated US$20 million for a two-year pilot program known as the AMINA to enhance the quality of financial services. Indeed, an important condition for poverty reduction is the availability of a range of appropriate and accessible

(box continues on next page)

Box 6.4: The ADF Micro-finance Initiative for Africa (AMINA) Program (continued)

financial services for economically active poor urban and rural households. In reaction to the failure of commercial banks to serve the poor, a variety of grass-roots organizations including: credit unions, savings and credit cooperatives, village banks and non-governmental organizations have become active in micro-finance services. Unfortunately, these institutions have typically weak institutional capacity in providing appropriate financial services to micro-entrepreneurs. The ultimate objective of the AMINA program is, therefore, to help micro-entrepreneurs, especially women, with enhanced access to financial services, including micro-credit and savings, provided by micro-finance institutions.

The AMINA program is operating in ten countries: Burkina Faso, Cameroon, Cape Verde, Chad, Ethiopia, Ghana, Malawi, Mauritania, Mozambique and Tanzania. One of the selection criteria for partners in micro-finance institutions is to demonstrate a proven track record on serving a significant number of the poor, women entrepreneurs and other disadvantaged groups. As of December 2000, more than 70 micro-finance institutions are qualified for capacity-building grants that will help them to improve their management and operational skills.

Between April 1998 and December 2000, AMINA organized 27 workshops and training activities in Mauritania, Burkina Faso, Tanzania and Cape Verde. Close to 670 participants from 48 Micro-finance Institutions (MFIs) attended these workshops. During the same period, 14 exchange visits were organized in Kenya and Mali for loan officers from Malawi and task force members from Mauritania. Regarding the activities of Bank staff training and sensitization, five workshops on rural finance, were organized during the period under review.

In terms of collaboration with RMCs, AMINA provided support for ADF Poverty Reduction Projects in Burkina Faso. Detailed analyses of all MFIs in Chad were provided to the team managing the Lake Chad Rural Development Project. Assistance was provided to a mission in Cape Verde assessing a poverty reduction project that will have a micro-finance component. Coordination was also initiated to address the training and other capacity-building needs of the NGOs participating in the Mauritania Poverty Reduction Project. AMINA also participated in a Bank mission to Uganda for an appraisal of the Poverty Alleviation Project, Phase II.

As a member of the Consultative Group to Assist the Poor (CGAP), AMINA has prepared and hosted the CGAP annual meeting in June 1999 in Abidjan. This meeting provided an opportunity for all the members to discuss issues related to savings mobilization and actions to be undertaken to reach and provide services to the poorest of the poor in Africa. In addition, AMINA is collaborating with other donors, especially with UNDP on the Micro-start Program in Ghana and Mozambique.

Source: ADB (2001a).

Poverty Reduction and Food Security

Involving the poor in the development effort will entail the establishment of mechanisms and processes that give them a voice in the investment planning and decision making process as well as the means (via fiscal decentralization) through which they can effectively participate as economic agents. Thus, participatory development, involving the poor and other stakeholders, is crucial to the sustainable alleviation of poverty in Africa, and would serve as the underlying principle the Bank would adopt to address poverty issues. To this end, the Bank will collaborate closely with multilateral development finance institutions like IFAD, FAO and the World Bank. As part of the management process at the country level, the

RMCs will need assistance to formulate comprehensive development policies and strategies, which give priority to human development needs, by increasing both the allocation and efficiency of public expenditures for social services. In this regard, the strategy to broaden the scope of agricultural development into an integrated approach of rural development, where direct agricultural activities of the poor are complemented by investments in the social services, is essentially a poverty reduction strategy.

Empirical evidence has shown that growth that hinges on labor-intensive technology (especially labor-intensive rural infrastructure) is the most direct and sustainable way to reduce poverty. The Bank will, therefore, promote labor-intensive growth in the RMCs to more effectively reach the poor. Given the dominant role of women in agriculture and the rural informal sector, the Bank will direct its assistance through programs that improve the access of women to basic social services, credit and land to enhance their capacity for direct agricultural production. It will also assist women in enterprise development and in nutrition and primary health programs to improve their capacity to cater to the needs of children. The Bank's focus on poverty will be cast within a global context, by centering it around the internationally agreed Development Goals for the 21st Century, as articulated by the Development Assistance Committee of the OECD.

The Bank will collaborate with RMCs and other donors to support preparation of RMC food security strategies and to strengthen the capacity of national institutions to update these analyses on a regular basis. Moreover, the Bank will establish systematic collaboration with specialized and experienced executing agencies throughout the cycle of its operations aimed at improving food security. In this respect, collaboration will be par-ticularly strengthened with the FAO, within the framework of its Special Program for Food Security (SPFS). The Bank will also support RMCs' efforts to ground their food security strategies on investment in agricultural research, extension, market infrastructure and services, aiming at improving both the availability of, and access to, food. The Bank will thus support long-term investment programs to:

- increase productivity and reduce temporal and spatial variability in domestic food production;
- address intermittent shortages in food supply through the promotion of private/semi privately-managed buffer stocks;
- mitigate losses in post-harvest handling, storage, processing, and marketing of domestic food supplies;
- develop and transfer technologies for diversified production, marketing and trade of higher value crops;
- reduce product transfer costs through the development of improved transport infrastructure (including the construction and maintenance of good feeder road networks), means, and policies;
- reduce transactions costs in the food systems (especially in national and sub-regional markets) through adequate market information systems, improved legal and institutional systems and effective contract enforcement mechanisms; and
- create labor-intensive, non-farm rural employment opportunities, especially off-season income-generating activities targeted at the rural poor.

Natural Resource Management

To sustain the productivity of the natural resource base, Bank lending will be directed toward interventions that increase agricultural productivity per unit of resource used and halt practices that are "mining" the resource base beyond its regenerative capacity. To this end, the Bank will collaborate with both bilateral and multilateral development partners (such as the FAO, IFDC, ICRAF and the World Bank) involved in the Soil Fertility Initiative (SFI) to assist RMCs to develop National SFI action plans and programs for effective implementation. Sustaining productivity of the natural resource base would also entail some legal changes in land tenure and in the use of common resources exploited by producers. The Bank will promote rigorous analyses at all stages of the project cycle to detect potential and actual ecological effects of investment in agriculture, and how best to avoid or minimize damages resulting therefrom.

Land Tenure: Empirical evidence shows that more and more land is falling under *de facto* private control through formal sale and lease agreements and/or informal rental arrangements. Although some progress has been made in successful privatization of a few lands and settlements, the bulk of farmland in Africa is still under communal and traditional ownership. The Bank will assist RMCs to expand their institutional capacities to assist RMCs to formulate and implement land tenure systems, which provide incentives for long-term investments in sustainable use systems and resource conservation, and prevent the fragmentation of land holdings into non-viable plots.

The Bank will promote in-depth analyses on the impacts of existing land tenure systems on program/project implementation, impact and objectives. It will work with RMC governments, via pilot programs, to find feasible solutions for agricultural enterprises on communal land, such that restrictions on unlimited access to the resource can be effectively installed where use patterns are leading to permanent degradation. In addition, the Bank will ensure that rural households participating in its programs and projects have secured resource use rights commensurate with maintenance of sustainable agricultural systems. Finally, it will provide resources for cadastral surveys and other entitlement procedures to facilitate establishment of *de jure* controls of land by rural households.

Within the framework of policy dialogue, the Bank will encourage governments to promote land tenure reforms which recognize legally the different types of socially-legitimate land ownership (both communal and private) and, where feasible and appropriate, develop financial regulations that allow formal financial intermediaries to accept other forms of collateral, especially those associated with communal ownership of farmland. Furthermore, as much as possible, the Bank will encourage reforms that promote female ownership of land in rural communities where this is a constraint to agricultural growth.

Irrigation and Conjunctive Water Use: To be viable, an irrigation system must have: water supply of suitable quality in sufficient quantity; suitable soils for irrigation; producer access to remunerative markets; and available labor and energy to operate the system. Empirical evidence from newly developed irrigation systems show that operational and management policies, which accommodate farmer preferences and safeguard small holders' sense of control over the land they irrigate, are most likely to generate higher productivity and more sustainable systems. The Bank would assist RMCs to adopt objective and monitorable criteria for selecting cost-effective, socially acceptable and appropriate irrigation technology on the basis of the foregoing guidelines.

Water resource use for irrigation will increasingly take place in the context of national water allocation planning, which in many countries will be complicated by riparian rights issues between countries which share major watersheds and river systems. The Bank will, therefore, help RMCs to: strengthen their legislative frameworks on water use and pollution control through careful analysis to set the right price for water use charges; broaden participation in management of water resources; and establish planning frameworks for preventing and resolving conflicts among competing water users. It will also support RMC efforts to formulate and implement conjunctive water use plans, which recognize the rights of all end-users for water of acceptable quality and in appropriate quantities on a sustainable basis. Special attention will also be given to lowering the relatively high costs of irrigation in Africa. In this regard, the Bank will strengthen collaboration with key development organizations (such as the FAO, WARDA and IIMI) with demonstrated expertise and field experience in irrigated agriculture.

Apart from providing assistance for irrigation, the Bank will also work with RMCs to identify alternative ways to source and manage water efficiently for agricultural uses as well as for home consumption. This would, inter alia, entail support for training of rural households in various water-harvesting and management techniques. To this end, the Bank will promote a more integrated approach to optimal water resource management which would include for instance, integration of aquaculture with irrigation and water-harvesting techniques to boost agricultural productivity at the household level.

Human and Institutional Capacity Building

Low education levels and high illiteracy rates make it difficult for rural populations, women in particular, to access training and technical assistance. Also, traditional education programs do not provide adequate response to end-user needs, particularly in rural areas. Thus, to be effective, the focus of primary education has to shift to the functional areas, such as entrepreneurial skills, business management, technical subjects of relevance to rural life, and personal analytical and organizational skills. The Bank will, therefore, collaborate with RMCs and other donor agencies to increase grassroots capacity building to enable rural populations set their own priorities and access assistance relevant to their needs. Capacity building would also focus on training in income producing activities, group mobilization, financial management and marketing. This would enable rural women to develop decision-making and management skills that can improve their income earning potential.

A concerted effort of both donors and African countries is needed to build grassroots institutions that are sustainable and equipped over time to engender and support a process of modernization and transformation of African agriculture and rural economies. On its part, the Bank will help to strengthen existing rural institutions and associations, including business groups and rural financial organizations and to create effective linkages between international NGOs with proven track records in areas such as micro-finance, development of micro-, small- and medium-scale enterprises, and functional literacy programs, and local NGOs. Finally, the Bank would focus rural education projects on more effective primary schooling, functional literacy, and adult education programs.

Complementary Investments in Social Services and Rural Infrastructure

Bank policy toward the agricultural sector recognizes that, to promote and sustain economic and social development in rural areas, RMC governments and donors must undertake other important actions that are not agricultural interventions *per se* in order to broaden development assistance to cover service areas that support the rural economy. Herein lies the rationale for broadening the scope of Bank Group agriculture sector policy to rural development. Public investments in roads, bridges, water control structures, utility services, storage and processing facilities, telecommunications systems, and market infrastructure provide basic means of linking rural households to the modern world. However, the absence of such essential infrastructure in rural areas creates disincentives to rapid rural development, drives entrepreneurs and skilled labor to look elsewhere for opportunities, accentuates the problem of rural-urban migration and growing urban unemployment, and precludes complementary private sector investment in rural enterprises.

For the education sector, the Bank will work with RMCs to identify the appropriate balance between primary, secondary, technical, and tertiary levels, in relation to demand on the ground and other supply factors (in terms of constraints faced). Also the balance between the "soft" and the "hard" aspects of investments is critical in determining the eventual benefit and outcome of the Bank's intervention in the sector. The Bank will also provide assistance for broad-based basic

educational services (including primary schooling for all), "second chance" basic-skills training for youth, and adult literary and numeracy programs.

For the health sector, special emphasis will be placed on the provision of primary health care services (including access to information on nutrition, sanitation, and reproductive health), delivery of preventive health programs to rural areas, and provision of basic medical care through local dispensaries on a cost-effective basis. Given that HIV/AIDS needs urgent attention to save the human capital of the continent, efforts will be intensified to mainstream preventive and coping measures into agriculture training programs and rural extension services to reach the rural population. In addition advocacy activities, at both the policy and grass-roots levels, will be featured in appropriate projects and programs of the sector.

To improve access of rural people to markets, the Bank will promote expansion of road networks to open up rural areas of high agricultural production potential to facilitate development of market centers and to improve linkages between collection points, terminal markets and agro-industry. The Bank will also help RMCs to develop mechanisms, institutions and participatory systems to effectively promote improved maintenance of road networks, particularly secondary and farm-to-market roads. Furthermore, intermediate means of transport, such as road tracks, with user participation will receive increased support. To this end, more assistance would be channeled through adaptive research into design standards for simple vehicles, such as bicycles, ox-carts, and wheelbarrows, to allow rural communities to fully capitalize on improved road networks. At the regional level, African governments need to collaborate with each other to build road networks that open their economies to trans-border trade.

The Bank will support such endeavors through increased assistance to multi-national projects on a demand-driven basis.

The Bank will work with RMCs to identify their overall rural energy needs and promote technological solutions that take into account renewable sources of energy (such as solar energy, biogas and windmills) that are cost-efficient and environmentally friendly. This will include support for alternative energy sources such as, solar energy and bio-gas, as well as electricity generation through hydropower and windmills; expansion of existing electricity delivery networks, particularly in areas of high agricultural potential and agro-industrial processing; and electrification of rural infrastructure that supports efficient delivery of social services to rural households, particularly health and educational services.

Empirical evidence from successful village potable water schemes has shown that active involvement of end-users in the construction and management of the schemes is key to sustainable supply of potable water in rural Africa. The Bank will work closely with RMCs to support development of Water Users' Associations (WUAs), headed by respected village or community heads, who fix user fees for their own communities, establish and maintain their own bank accounts for operations and maintenance, and train local artisans to maintain the water point. Assistance will also be given to RMCs to formulate and install conjunctive water plans that promote sustainable use of existing water resources and safeguard water quality. Finally, the Bank will promote water resource management with the active involvement of the end-users in the construction and management of the potable water supply schemes.

From Policy to Action

Project Design: Quality at Entry: The Bank will take complementary actions to facilitate successful implementation of its agricultural and rural development policy. To this end, the project cycle will be modified, as necessary, to ensure both end-user participation and better integration of projects into sector and sub-sector strategies. This will include in-depth studies in key sub-sector areas to develop medium-term (five-year) Bank/RMC rolling plans for program and project identification and design. Long-term programming of TAF funds will help to improve the quality of sub-sector analyses and development of ASIPs in collaboration with other donors. Furthermore, design missions will be planned and timed so that the Bank has effective input into the development of programs and projects in the early phases of the project cycle. This would include, *inter alia*, the application of environmental and health impact assessment of Bank Group interventions. End-user participation will be strongly encouraged in the formulation of rural development strategies and in program/project identification, design, and implementation, and monitoring and evaluation.

Monitoring and Evaluation: The capacity for monitoring and evaluation will be strengthened. To this end, monitoring and evaluation operations for programs and projects will be refocused to include the strategic aspects of the Bank's agricultural and rural development portfolio, in addition to the operational aspects of program/project implementation. To enhance the likelihood of success, projects and programs will be evaluated on a comprehensive basis to develop a synthesis of "lessons to be learned" to guide future Bank lending. Finally, the feedback system between the Evaluation and Operations Departments will be strengthened to ensure that appropriate incentives exist for timely and effective monitoring of programs/projects and quick implementation of recommendations made in evaluations.

Key Lending and Non-Lending Instruments: The Bank will adopt a balanced set of instruments for support to agriculture. Emphasis would be placed on projects and programs which build institutional capacity, along with an increased use of ASIPs and beneficiary contribution to enhance sustainability. The Bank will collaborate with the World Bank, IMF and other donor agencies to ensure a more integrated sectoral approach by RMCs and donors. Collaboration will include active participation in core sector reform programs, development of strategies for rural health, rural infrastructure, education and private sector development in rural areas. The Bank will continue its involvement in policy-based lending in close collaboration with other donors. In line with its Vision, the Bank will get more involved in the design of future adjustment programs aimed at addressing issues relevant to its areas of strategic interests, which feature agricultural and rural development. The Bank will use sector adjustment lending as a means to play an active role in policy dialogue with the RMCs in addressing sectoral policy gaps to promote an appropriate policy environment for agricultural and rural development, while ensuring that the social costs of adjustment are mitigated by appropriate interventions.

Most of the Bank's RMCs have limited institutional capacity, including in the formulation of macro-economic and sectoral policies, and in project preparation and appraisal. As a result, most of them have not been able to internalize MDB-led initiatives such as PERs and Economic and

Sector Work (ESW) and/or take the lead in formulating home grown policies to guide their development efforts. In the process, effective dialogue and ownership of development policies have been severely constrained. Systematic ESW will, therefore, be carried out in order to identify precise constraints, the needs and the potential of the agricultural sector and the overall rural economy of each RMC, and to ensure that identified projects and programs fit within the strategic framework of such sector studies. Furthermore, the Bank will collaborate with other development partners in assisting RMCs to build sustainable and viable institutions through well-tailored training and technical assistance programs. The Bank will also help ease the path to adequate private sector funding through support for deepening and regulation of the financial sector.

An Action Plan for implementing the Agricultural and Rural Development Sector Policy has been developed, taking into account the diversity in regional specificity of the agricultural and rural economies of the continent. Given that the Action Plan is an implementation tool, it would be revised and updated every two to three years to reflect the changing needs of the Bank's clients, and also to guide the lending program of the Bank. For each of the operational regions/departments of the Bank, specific actions are defined with respect to clearly identified constraints to achieving explicit development goals in a global vision. These regional Action Plans serve as the basis for the overall Bank Action Plan. In carrying out activities resulting from the Action Plan, projects and programs will emanate from the felt needs of the concerned populations in RMCs. The Bank Group interventions will therefore proceed from a "demand-driven" approach.

Conclusions

The Bank's poverty reduction strategies have evolved over time. Compared to the 1970s and the 1980s, lending and non-lending activities in recent years have focused on poverty reduction more explicitly. The renewed commitment to address poverty issues is attributed mainly to the persistence of poverty in the continent. In fact, the efforts in the last decade have culminated in the adoption of the Bank's Vision in 1999 in which it is stated clearly that poverty reduction is the Bank's overarching objective. As a result, efforts are underway to put poverty reduction at the center of Country Strategy Papers. In the past three years, the participatory approach has been used to prepare CSPs. This has enhanced the quality of the Bank's dialogue with its RMCs in terms of prioritizing sectors in order to maximize the impact of it interventions. The Bank has also developed the CPIA framework to reward ADF countries with good poverty reduction policies. In addition, projects in all sectors for ADF countries are being designed in a more participatory manner, with clearer poverty reduction objectives and specific monitorable indicators than in the past. This is expected to facilitate the assessment of the impact of Bank interventions at the project level.

In the past three years, the design of structural and sectoral adjustment loans has taken poverty reduction considerations into account. For instance, provisions are made for the protection of social expenditures and safety net programs. Some of the SALs also have components for supporting work on PRSPs in borrowing countries.

Lending for the priority sectors has remained high during this period. The agricultural and social sectors have received a significant share of ADF lending during the three years under review. In the most recent years, the Bank has approved stand-alone poverty projects that are combined with social sector projects. At the same time, lending for the public utilities and transport sectors has increased.

BIBLIOGRAPHICAL NOTE

Introduction

The background papers prepared specially for the Report are listed below, along with the selected bibliography used in the Report. These papers synthesize relevant literature. The Report has drawn on a wide range of Africa Development Bank reports, including ongoing research as well as countries' economic, sector and project work. It has also drawn on outside sources, including published and the unpublished works of institutions such as the IMF, the World Bank, IFC, the United Nations and its agencies such as the ECA, FAO, ILO, IFAD, UNAIDS, UNCTAD, UNIDO, UNDP, WHO, WTO and OECD. Other sources include publications from various national economic and statistics agencies, Africa Economic Digest, Africa Financing Review, Africa Research Bulletin; Business Africa, The Economist, Economist Intelligence Unit, Financial Times; International Capital Markets; Middle East Economic Digest; Southern Africa Monitor; and WEFA Group's economic Profiles for Africa Countries.

Background papers

(i)   Aka François (2001), "Gender, Land Access and the Rural Poor in Côte d'Ivoire".

(ii)   Ali Abdel Gadir Ali (2001a), "The Interrelations between Rural Development and Poverty: A Conceptual Framework".

(iii)   _____ (2001b), "A Profile of Rural Poverty in Africa".

(iv)   _____ (2001c), "Policies for Enhancing the Role of Rural Development in Poverty Reduction in Africa".

(v)   Kebede Bereket (2001), "Allocation and Distribution of Land in Rural Ethiopia".

(vi)   Marrengula Constantino Pedro (2001), "Natural Disasters, Market Access and the Rural Poor in Mozambique".

(vii) Lipton Micheal et al. (2001), "Globalisation and Rural Poverty: Making it Work for the Rural Poor in Africa".

(viii) Ndiaye Amath (2001), "Agriculture and Rural Poor in Senegal".

(ix)   Okojie Christiana E. E. (2001), "Rural Credit and the Rural Poor in Nigeria".

(x)   Okurut Francis Nathan (2001), "Assets and Rural Poverty in Uganda".

(xi)   Sahn David E and Stifel David C (2001), "Progress toward the International Development Goals in Rural Africa".

(xii) Tamba Isaac (2001), "Infrastructure and Rural Poverty in Cameroon".

(xiii) Toure Boulel (2001), "Livestock Assets and the Rural Poor in Mali".

(xiv) Yahaya Abdou (2001), "Développement agricole et pauvreté en milieu rural au Niger".

(xv) Zgovu Evious K. and Ng'ong'ola Davies H. (2001), "Land Policy Reforms and the Rural Poor in Malawi".

Sources for Boxes

1.1 IMF (2001), World Economic Outlook, October

1.2 ADB Research Division

1.3 World Bank (2001), Global Economic Prospects, November

1.4 ADB Research Division

1.5 ADB Research Division

1.6 NEPAD (The New Partnership for African Development) (2001)

3.1 Ali (2001a).

3.2 IFAD (2001). Also see Ali (2001b).

3.3 Maule (1999); and Marrengula (2001).

3.4 Extracted from Hussain (2001)

3.5 Ali (2001a).

3.6 Ali (2001b).

4.1 Adapted from Kebede (2001).

4.2 Adapted from Reardon et al (1998), Barrett et al (2000) and Adams (2001)

4.3 Adapted from CGIAR (2001).

5.1 Adapted from Streeten, (2001).

5.2 Adapted from Lipton et al (2001).

5.3 Adapted from Lipton et al (2001).

5.4 Platteau (1996).

5.5 ADB (2000b).
6.1 ADB (2001a).

6.2 ADB (2001a).

6.3 ADB (2000a)

6.4 ADB (2001a).

Selected Bibliography

Adams (Jr) R. H. (2001), "Nonfarm Income, Inequality and Poverty in Rural Egypt and Jordan", *Policy Research Working Paper*, WP. 2572. World Bank Washington D.C.

African Development Bank (1997-2001), *African Development Report.* Abidjan, Côte d'Ivoire.

_____ **(2000a),** *Annual Report.* Abidjan, Côte d'Ivoire.

_____ **(2000b),** "Agriculture and Rural Development Sector Bank Group Policy", OCOD, January 2000. African Development Bank/Africa Development Fund, Abidjan, Côte d'Ivoire.

_____ **(2000c),** "Policy for Integrated Water Ressources Management", OCOD, April 2000. African Development Bank/Africa Development Fund, Abidjan, Côte d'Ivoire.

_____ **(2001a),** "Progress Report on Poverty Reduction 1998 to 2000", OESU, August 2001. African Development Bank/Africa Development Fund, Abidjan, Côte d'Ivoire.

_____ **(2001b),** ADB Live Data Base. Abidjan, Côte d'Ivoire.

Agenor R-P. (1998), "Stabilization Policies, Poverty and the Labor Market", AERC, Nairobi.

Aghion P. and P. Bolton (1997), "A Theory of Trickle-down Growth and Development", Review of Economic Studies; vol. 64, pp. 151-172.

Alesina Alberto and Dani Rodrik (1994), "Distributive Politics and Economic Growth", *Quarterly Journal of Economics* 109: 465–90.

Ali Abdel Gadir Ali and I. El Badawi (2001), "Growth Could Be Good for the Poor", unpublished manuscript.

Banerjee A. and A. Newman (1998), "Information, the Dual Economy and Development", *Review of Economic Studies*, vol. 65: 631-53.

Barbier E. B. (1998), *"The Economics of Land Degradation and Rural Poverty Linkages in Africa"*, UNU/INRA Annual Lectures, 1998. The United Nations University, Tokyo.

Barrett Christopher B. et al (2000), "Heterogeneous Constraints, Incentives and Income Diversification Strategies in Rural Africa" , Project Report to USAID BASIS CRSP, University of Wisconsin-Madison Land Tenure Center.

Barwell I. (1996), *Transport and the* village. World Bank: Washington DC. Discussion Paper No. 344.

Benson Todd (1997), "The 1995/96 Fertilizer Verification Trial - Malawi", Report by Action Group I, Maize Productivity Task Force, Ministry of Agriculture and Livestock Development, Government of Malawi, Lilongwe, Malawi.

Binswanger H. P. and von Braun J. (1991), "Technological Change and Commercialization in Agriculture: The Effect on the Poor", *The World Bank Research Observer* 6(1): 57-80

Booth D., Lugngira, F., Masanja, P., Mvungi, A., Mwaipopo, R., Mwami, J., and Redmayne, A. (1993), *Social, Economic and Cultural Change in Contemporary Tanzania:- A People-Oriented Focu*s, Stockholm: Swedish International Development Authority.

Centro de Estudos da População (CEP) (1996), "A Pobreza na Província de Niassa, Cabo Delgado, Nampula, Zambézia, Tete, Manica, Sofala, Inhambane, Gaza, Maputo: Estudo de Caso", Universidade Eduardo Mondlane, Maputo.

CGIAR (Consultative Group on International Agricultural Research), (2001), *Nourishing a Peaceful Earth: the CGIAR's Contributions* , CGIAR

Chen S. and M. Ravallion (2000), "How did the World's Poorest Fare in the 1990s?", World Bank, Washington D.C.

Clarke George R. G. (1995), "More Evidence on Income Distribution and Growth." *Journal of Development Economics* 47: 403–27.

Collier Paul (1998), "Social Capital and Poverty", Social Capital Initiative. Working Paper 4. World Bank, Social Development Department, Washington, D.C.

Collier P. and J. Gunning (1999a), "Explaining African Economic Performance", *Journal of Economic Literature*, vol. 37.

_____ **(1999b),** "Why Has Africa Grown Slowly?", *Journal of Economic Perspectives*, vol. 13, No.3, pp.3-22.

Cornia G., Jolly R. and F. Stewart, (eds.), (1987), *Adjustment with a Human Face: Vol. I: Protecting the Vulnerable and Promoting Growth*; Clarendon Press, Oxford.

Coulibaly I. Traore (1991), "Etude des circuits de Commercialisation du Bétail, de la Viande et des produits d'Elevage des pays du Sahel et des pays côtiers", CILSS/ CEBV, juillet 1991.

Deaton Angus and Robert Miller (1995), "International Commodity Prices, Macroeconomic Performance, and Politics in Sub-Saharan Africa", Studies in International Finance. No.79 (Princeton: Princeton University, Department of Economics).

Deininger K. and P. Olinto (2001), "Asset Distribution, Inequality and Growth", World Bank Working Paper No. 2375, World Bank, Washington D.C..

Dercon S. (2001), "Economic Reform, Growth and the Poor: Evidence from Rural Ethiopia", Centre for Studying the African Economy WPS 2001-8.

Dijkstra A. Geske and J. K. Van Donge (2001), "What Does the 'Show Case' Show? Evidence of and Lessons from Adjustment in Uganda", *World Development,* 29 (5): 841-863.

Dolan C. and J. Humphrey (2001), "Governance and Trade in Fresh Vegetales: The Impact of UK Supermarkets on the African Horticulture Industry", *Journal of Development Studies,* 37(2): 147-176.

Domar Evsey D (1947), "Expansion and Employment", *The American Economic Review*, Vol. XXXVII, No. 2 (March 1947):34-55.

EIU (Economist Intelligence Unit) (2001), *Country Reports.*

FAO (Food and Agriculture Organization (2001a), "Food Supply Situation and Crop Prospects in Sub-Sahara Africa", Global information and early warning systems on food and agriculture, FAO, Rome. No. 3 December 2001

_____ **(2001b),** "Food Outlook", Global information and early warning systems on food and agriculture, FAO, Rome. No. 5 December 2001.

Ferreira F., Prennushi G., and M. Ravallion (2001), "Protecting the Poor from Macroeconomic Shocks: An Agenda for Action in a Crisis and Beyond", Unpublished paper, World Bank, Washington.

Gallup J. L. and Jeffrey D. Sachs (1998), "The Economic burden of Malaria", *Harvard International Review,* 1998, pp. 56-61

Galor O. and J. Zeira, (1993), "Income Distribution and Macroeconomics", *Review of Economic Studies.*
Gladwin C. , A. Thomson, J. Peterson and A. Anderson (2001), "Addressing food security in Africa via multiple livelihood strategies of women farmers", *Food Policy,* 26: 177-207.

Grootaert Christiaan (1999), "Does Social Capital Help the Poor? A Synthesis of Findings from the Local Level Institutions Studies in Bolivia, Burkina Faso and Indonesia" World Bank, Social Development Department, Washington, D.C.

Harrod Roy F. (1939), "An essay in Dynamic Theory", *The Economic Journal,* Vol XLIX, No. 193 (March 1939): 15-33.

Hine J. L. and C. Rizet (1991), " Halving Africa's freight transport costs: could it be done? ", International Symposium Transport and Communications in Africa, Brussels, 27-29 November 1991.

Hino Toshiko (1993), "Community Participation in 'Programme de restructuration de l'hydraulique villageoise' in Côte d'Ivoire" World Bank, Washington, D.C.

Hussain M. N., Kupukile Mlambo and Temitope Oshikoya (1999), "Global Financial Crisis: An African Perspective", *African Development Review, vol. 11, No. 2.* African Development Bank, Abidjan.

_____ **(2001),** "Exorcising the Ghost: An Alternative Growth Model for Measuring the Financing Gap", *Journal of Post Keynesian Economics; Fall 2001/Vol. 24, No. 1.*

IFAD (International Fund for Agricultural Development) (1989a), "Women: The Roots of Rural Development", Rome, Italy: Federgraf.

_____ **(1989b),** "Completion Evaluation Report for the Northern Pasture and Livestock Development Project, No. 0361-CH", Monitoring and Evaluation Division, Rome.

_____ **(1999a),** *Regional assessment: supporting the livelihoods of the rural poor in East and Southern Afric*a. Africa II. Division. IFAD: Rome.

_____ **(1999b),** *Rural poverty assessment: Asia and the Pacific regio*n. Asia and Pacific Division Project Management Department. IFAD: Rome. Washington DC.

_____ **(2001a),** *Rural Poverty Report 2001*: The Challenge of Ending Rural Poverty; Oxford University Press, Oxford.

_____ **(2001b),** "Assessment for Rural Poverty in Western and Central Africa", Africa I Division, Project Management Department , IFAD.

IMF (International Monetary Fund) (2001), *World Economic Outlook*. (October and December) Washington, D.C.

IFPRI et al (1998), *Pobreza e Bem-Estar em Moçambique: Primeira Avaliação* Tete, Inhambane and Sofala.

Kanbur R. (1987a), "Measurement and Alleviation of Poverty", IMF Staff Papers, vol. 36.

_____**(1987b),** "Structural Adjustment, Macroeconomic Adjustment and Poverty: A Methodology for Analysis", World Development, vol. 15.

Killick A. Kydd J. and Poulton C. (2000), *The rural poor and the wider economy: the problem of market access*. Thematic paper for IFAD's Rural Poverty Report 2001: the challenge of ending rural poverty.

Kose Ayhan and Raymond Riezman (2001), "Trade Shocks and Macroeconomic Fluctuations in Africa", *Journal of Development Economics*, vol.65 (June), pp.55-88.

Krueger A.O., Schiff, M. and Valdes A. (1992), "The Political Economy of Agricultural Protection in Developing Countries", A World Bank Comparative Study (5 volumes), Baltimore: Johns Hopkins University Press.

Kuznets S. (1955), "Economic Growth and Income Inequality", *American Economic Review*, vol. 45.

Lanjouw J. O. and Lanjouw, P. (1995), "Rural non-farm Employment: A Survey", Washington D.C.: World Bank Policy Research Working Paper No. 1463.

Lanjouw Peter (1999), "Ecuador's Rural Nonfarm Sector as a Route Out of Poverty", Policy Research Working Paper #1904, World Bank Washington D.C.

Lewis B.D. and E. Thorbecke (1992), "District-Level Economic Linkages in Kenya: Evidence Based on a Small Regional Social Accounting Matrix", *World Development*, vol. 20, No. 6, pp. 881-897.

Lewis W. Arthur (1954), "Economic Development with Unlimited Supplies of Labor", *Manchester School*, May 1954, 22, 139-92.

Lipton M. (1995), "Market, Redistributive and Proto-reform: Can Liberalization help the poor?, *Asian Development Review* 13: 1-35.

Lucas R. E. (1988), "On the Mechanics of Economic Growth", *Journal of Monetary Economics*, No. 22: 3-42.

Malmberg-Calvo Christina (1994), "Case Study on the Role of Women in Rural Transport", Washington DC : World Bank, and ECA, SSATP Working Paper No. 11.

Maule L. (1999), "Assessment of Risks of Natural Disasters in Mozambique: Review of the Existing Literature on Frequency and Impact of Such Disaster", Final report submitted to Médecins sans frontiers, consolidated Information System, Maputo.

McCulloch Neil, L. Alan Winters and Xavier Cirera (2001), *Trade Liberalisation and Poverty: A Handbook*, Centre for Economic Policy Research

McKay Andrew, Chris Milner, Abbi Kedir and Susana Franco (1999), "Trade, Technology, Poverty: the Linkages. A Review of the Linkages", Report to the International Economic Policy Department of DfID

_____ **L. Alan Winters and Abbi Kedir (2000),** "A Review of the Recent Empirical Evidence on Trade, Trade Policy and Poverty", Report to DfID
Milner C. and Wright P. (1998) , "Modelling labour market adjustment to trade liberalisation in an industrialising economy", *Economic Journal* 108, pp.509-28.

Minot Nicholas W. (1998), "Generating Disaggregated Poverty Maps: An Application to Vietnam" , MSSD Discussion Paper 25. International Food Policy Research Institute, Washington, D.C.

Narayan, D. (1997), "Bonds and Bridges: Social Capital And Poverty", The World Bank, Washington, DC:

Newman C. and Canagarajah S. (2000) "Gender, Poverty, and Nonfarm Employment in Ghana and Uganda", Policy Research Working Paper #2367., World Bank Washington D.C.

Okidegbe Nwanze (2001), "Rural Poverty: Trends and Measurement", The World Bank's Rural Development Strategy. Background Paper #3.

OPEC (Organization of Petroleum Exporting Countries) (2002) , Petroleum Economist,*The International Energy Journal*, February 2002

Oshikoya Temitope W. and M. Nureldin Hussain (1998), "Information Technology and the Challenge of Economic Development in Africa", *African Development Review*, Volume 10, No. 1. Abidjan, African Development Bank, 1998.

Oxfam-IDS (1999), *Liberalisation and Poverty.* Final Report to *DFID*, August.

Owens Trudy, John Hoddinott and Bill Kinsey (2001), "The Impact of Agricultural Extension on Farm Production in Reslttlement Areas of Zimbabwe", Centre for Monitoring the African Economy WPS/2001-6.

Parris B. (1999), "Trade for Development:- making the WTO work for the poor ", World Vision International.

Persson Torsten and Guido Tabellini (1994), "Is Inequality Harmful for Growth?", *American Economic Review* 84: 600–21.

Platteau J.-P. (1996a), "The Evolutionary Theory of Land Rights as Applied to Sub-Saharan Africa: A Critical Assessment", Development and Change, vol. 27.

_____ **(1996b),** "Physical Infrastructure as a Constraint on Agricultural Growth: the Case of Sub-Saharan Africa", *Oxford Development Studies* 24(3): 189-219.

PNUD (Programme des Nations Unies pour le Développement) **(1998)**, *Rapport sur le développement humain : la pauvreté au Cameroun.* Yaoundé-Camerron

PRUS (Poverty Research Unit at Sussex) (2001a), "Globalisation and Poverty", PRUS Notes No. 2. Mimeo. University of Sussex.

Ravallion M. (2000), "On the Urbanisation of Poverty", Mimeo. World Bank: Washington D.C..

Republica de Moçambique (2001), Programa de Reconstrução Pós-cheia da Região Centro de Moçambique, Maputo.

Riverson J. D. N. and Carapetis S. (1991), *Intermediate means of transport in Sub-Saharan Africa.* World Bank Technical Paper 161. World Bank: Washington DC.

Romer P. M. (1986), **"Increasing returns and long-run growth",** *Journal of Political Economy*, 94:-1037, **1986.**

Sanders John (1997), "Developing Technology for Agriculture in Sub-Saharan Africa: Evolution of Ideas, Some Critical Questions, and Future Research", Paper presented at the International Food Policy Research Institute, Washington, D.C., June 5.

Sen A. K. (1997), "On Economic Inequality", Expanded Edition (Oxford University Press).

Solow Robert (1956), "A Contribution to the Theory of Economic Growth", *Quarterly Journal of Economics* 70.65-94

Streeten Paul (1989), "International Cooperation", In Hollis Chenery and T. N. Srinivasan (eds.), *Handbook of Development Economics*, Vol. 2,Amsterdam: North Holland, pp. 1153-86.

_____ **(2001),** "Comment on 'On the Goals of Development'", In G. Meier and J. Stiglitz, (eds.).

Thirlwall A. P. (1979), "The Balance of Payments Constraint as an Explanation of International Growth Rate Differences", *Banca Nazionale del Lavoro Quarterly Review*, 128, 44-53.

_____ **(1999)**, "Growth and Development: with Special Reference to Developing Economies", London, Macmillan.

_____ **and Hussain M. N. (1982)**, "The Balance of Payments Constraint, Capital Flows and Growth Rate Differences Between Developing Countries", *Oxford Economic Papers,* Volume No. 3, November.

UNAIDS (Joint United Nations Programme on HIV/AIDS) (2001), *AIDS Epidemic Update - December 2001*, UNAIDS, Geneva

UNCTAD (United Nations Conference on Trade and Development)(2001), *World Investment Report*. UNCTAD, Geneva.

UNDP (United Nations Development Programme) (2000), *Human Development Report 2000*; Oxford University Press, Oxford.

_____ **(2001)**, *Human Development Report 2001*; "Making New Technologies Work for Human Development", New York: United Nations. UNDP New York.

UNIDO (United Nations Industrial Development Organization) (2001a), International Yearbook of Industrial Statistics 2001

UNIDO (2001b) Database

Union Européenne (1999), "Etude d'orientation stratégique des appuis de l'union européenne au Mali dans le sous-secteur de l'élevage: Synthèse", Mars 1999

Weeks John (2001), "Orthodox and Heterodox Policy for Growth for Africa South of the Sahara", In Terry McKinley (ed.), *Growth, Employment, and Poverty in Africa* (London: Palgrave)

Weiss J. (1998), "Infrastructure and Economic Development", Background to the ADR 1999.

Whittington D., *et al.* **(**1991), "A Study of Water Vending and Willingness to Pay for Water in Onitsha, Nige-

ria", *World Development* 19: 179-198.

WHO (World Health Organization) (1998a), *TB: A Crossroad—WHO Report on the Global Tuberculosis Epidemic 1998.* Geneva.

_____ (**1998b)**, Malaria, Fact Sheet, No. 9 WHO, Geneva.

Winters L Alan (2000a), "Trade liberalisation and poverty", PRUS Working Paper No.7, April 2000.

_____ **(2000b)**, "Trade, Trade Policy and Poverty: What are the Links? ", Mimeo, University of Sussex.

Wohlmuth Karl (1999), "Governance and Economic Development in Africa: An Introduction", In Wohlmuth, Karl, Bass, Hans H., and Messner, Frank (eds.), *Good Governance and Economic Development*. African Development Perspectives Yearbook, Hamburg, Lit Verlag Munster.

World Bank (1994a), "Adjustment in Africa: Reforms, Results, and the Road Ahead", New York: Oxford University Press. Studies and Monographs Series, no. 12. Washington.

_____ **(1994b)**, "Kingdom of Morocco: Poverty, Adjustment and Growth", report no. 11918-MOR, World Bank, Washington.

_____ **(1996a)**, "A Review of Bank Lending for Agricultural Credit and Rural Finance (1948-1992) — A Follow-Up", Report No. 15221. World Bank, Washington, D.C..

_____ **(1996b)**, *World Bank Development Report 1996:* From Plan to Market, Oxford University Press.

_____ **(1999)**, "African Development Indicators 2000", Washington D.C.

_____ **(2001a)**, "African Development Indicators", World Bank, Washington D.C.

_____**(2001b)**, *World Development Report 2000/ 2001*: Attacking Poverty; Oxford University Press, Oxford.

_____ **(2001c)**, _World Development Report 2002_: Building Institutions for Markets, Oxford University Press, Oxford.

_____ **(2001d)**, "Global Economic Prospects", Washington, D.C., The World Bank.

World Food Programme (1999), Sumário Executivo: WFP/MOZ/5938, fundo de alimentos-Projecto de Desenvolvimento Integrado Baseado Na Comunidade, Maputo

Electronic Sources

Bidoli Marina (2001), "Risk and Rewards", Telecom Africa 2001
    http://www.futurecompany.co.za/2001/11/02/featurea.htm

FAOSTAT DATABASE – Genève
    http://www.fao.org

Jensen Mike (2001), "African Country Internet Status Summary by August 2001",
    http://www3.sn.apc.org/africa/afrmain.htm#three

NEPAD (The New Partnership for African Development) (2001)
    http://www.africainitiative.org/Documents/AA0010101.pdf

Reardon Thomas (1998), "Rural Non-farm Income in Developing Countries", in Food and Agricultural Organization _The State of Food and_ Agriculture, chapter 3. Rome.
    http://www.fao.org/docrep/W9500E/w9500E00.htm

República de Moçambique (2001), Plano de Acção para a Redução da Pobreza.
Versão Final Aprovada pelo Conselho de Ministros
    http://WWW. Moçambique.mz.

UNDP (2001), "World Income Inequality Database", http:// www.undp.org/poverty/initiatives/wider.

UNIDO (United Nations Industrial Development Organization) (2001),
    http://www.unido.org/userfiles/TIMMINSK/DFID-UNIDO-2001-2005.pdf

World Bank (2001a), "Global Economic Prospects" http://www.worlbank.org/research.

_____ **(2001b)**, "Africa Rural Development Strategy: Vision to Action Update 2001: A summary", World Bank.
    http://www.worlbank.org/research.

WTO (World Tourism Organization) (2002)
    http://www.world-tourism.org/

PART THREE

ECONOMIC AND SOCIAL STATISTICS
ON AFRICA

Contents

Preface

The main purpose of this part of the Report is to present basic data that enable the monitoring of economic and social progress in regional member countries of the African Development Bank (ADB), and provide benchmark data for analysts of African development. The data cover the Bank's 53 regional member countries, with statistics on Basic Indicators, National Accounts, External Sector, Money Supply and Exchange Rates, Government Finance, External Debt and Financial Flows, Labor Force, and Social Indicators.

Throughout this part of the Report, statistical tables are arranged in sections and according to indicators. The tables contain historical data from 1980 to 2001. Period averages are provided for 1980-1990, and 1991-2001.

The data are obtained from various international sources and supplemented, to the extent possible, with data directly obtained from ADB regional member countries, and estimates by the ADB Statistics Division. Statistical practices vary from one regional member country to another with regard to data coverage, concepts, definitions, and classifications used. Although considerable efforts have been made to standardize the data, full comparability cannot be assured. Care should be exercised in their interpretation. They provide only indications on trend or structure that allow for the identification of significant differences between countries.

Technical information on these data is provided in the explanatory notes to facilitate appropriate interpretation. However, users are advised to refer to technical notes of the specialized publications of the main sources for more details.

The designations employed and the presentation of data therein do not imply any opinions whatsoever on the part of the African Development Bank concerning the legal status of any country or of its authorities. They were adopted solely for convenience of statistical presentation.

Symbols used

...	not available
0	zero or insignificant value
		break in the comparability of Data

TABLE 1.1
BASIC INDICATORS

COUNTRY	AREA ('000 Sq. Km) (US $)	POPULATION (Millions) INFLATION 2001	GNI PER CAPITA AT BIRTH (%) 2000	CONSUMER PRICE RATE (Years) 2001	LIFE EXPECTANCY RATE (per 1000) 2001	INFANT MORTALITY (%) 2001	ADULT ILLITERACY 2001
ALGERIA	2,382	30,841	1,590	1.5	70	44	31
ANGOLA	1,247	13,527	240	158.3	46	120	...
BENIN	113	6,446	380	5.2	54	82	58
BOTSWANA	600	1,554	3,300	6.8	38	68	22
BURKINA FASO	274	11,856	230	5.4	48	89	75
BURUNDI	28	6,502	110	12.2	45	113	51
CAMEROON	475	15,203	570	3.4	50	81	23
CAPE VERDE	4	437	1,330	3.0	70	51	25
CENT. AFR. REP.	623	3,782	290	3.5	44	95	52
CHAD	1,284	8,135	200	16.8	46	117	56
COMOROS	2	727	380	3.5	60	69	40
CONGO	342	3,110	630	1.0	51	67	18
CONGO DEM. REP.	2,345	52,522	...	299.0	52	80	37
COTE D'IVOIRE	322	16,349	660	4.4	48	83	52
DJIBOUTI	23	644	840	0.4	42	117	35
EGYPT	1,001	69,080	1,490	2.4	68	42	44
EQUAT. GUINEA	28	470	...	6.0	52	101	16
ERITREA	118	3,816	170	18.1	52	83	43
ETHIOPIA	1,104	64,459	100	0.2	44	108	60
GABON	268	1,262	3,180	1.0	53	82	...
GAMBIA	11	1,337	330	3.5	47	117	62
GHANA	239	19,734	350	39.5	57	63	27
GUINEA	246	8,274	450	6.9	48	116	...
GUINEA BISSAU	36	1,227	180	3.3	45	123	60
KENYA	580	31,293	360	2.6	50	60	17
LESOTHO	30	2,057	540	6.5	42	110	16
LIBERIA	111	3,108	...	10.0	54	85	45
LIBYA	1,760	5,408	...	13.6	71	26	19
MADAGASCAR	587	16,437	260	8.3	53	93	33
MALAWI	118	11,572	170	32.7	40	132	39
MALI	1,240	11,677	240	4.5	52	122	57
MAURITANIA	1,026	2,747	370	6.3	52	99	57
MAURITIUS	2	1,171	3,800	4.9	72	17	15
MOROCCO	447	30,430	1,180	1.0	68	44	50
MOZAMBIQUE	802	18,644	210	5.7	39	130	55
NAMIBIA	824	1,788	2,050	9.2	37	68	17
NIGER	1,267	11,227	180	4.2	46	128	84
NIGERIA	924	116,929	260	19.4	52	81	35
RWANDA	26	7,949	230	5.7	41	120	32
SAO T. & PRINC.	1	140	290	6.9	...	...	...
SENEGAL	197	9,662	500	1.9	54	58	62
SEYCHELLES	0.5	81	7,310	7.3	...	...	...
SIERRA LEONE	72	4,587	130	-0.9	40	150	...
SOMALIA	638	9,157	...	11.5	49	115	...
SOUTH AFRICA	1,221	43,792	3,020	5.7	49	59	14
SUDAN	2,506	31,809	320	6.0	57	80	41
SWAZILAND	17	938	1,290	9.8	41	91	20
TANZANIA	945	35,965	280	5.2	51	75	23
TOGO	57	4,657	300	0.5	52	77	42
TUNISIA	164	9,562	2,090	1.5	71	27	28
UGANDA	241	24,023	310	4.8	45	96	32
ZAMBIA	753	10,649	300	21.4	42	83	21
ZIMBABWE	391	12,852	480	71.9	43	57	11
AFRICA	**30,061**	**811,605**	**671**	**12.2**	**53**	**79**	**38**

TABLE 2.1
GROSS DOMESTIC PRODUCT, REAL
(MILLIONS US DOLLARS, CONSTANT 1995 PRICES)

COUNTRY	1980	1990	1995	2000	2001	Av. Ann. Real Growth Rate (%) 1981-1990	1991-2001
ALGERIA	31,386	41,236	41,767	48,681	50,363	2.8	1.9
ANGOLA	4,826	6,189	5,040	6,647	6,857	2.6	1.4
BENIN	1,310	1,705	2,009	2,595	2,738	2.8	4.4
BOTSWANA	1,363	3,574	4,427	5,979	6,425	10.1	5.5
BURKINA FASO	1,258	1,743	2,184	2,841	3,006	3.4	5.1
BURUNDI	728	1,126	1,000	946	977	4.5	-1.2
CAMEROON	6,319	8,765	7,965	10,044	10,546	3.6	1.8
CAPE VERDE	171	381	491	670	692	8.7	5.6
CENT. AFR. REP.	964	1,069	1,122	1,258	1,271	1.2	1.7
CHAD	788	1,311	1,438	1,664	1,812	5.6	3.2
COMOROS	167	223	232	243	245	3.0	0.9
CONGO	1,294	2,070	2,116	2,381	2,460	5.1	1.7
CONGO DEM. REP.	7,524	8,203	5,643	4,368	4,187	0.9	-5.8
COTE D'IVOIRE	8,566	9,198	9,992	11,890	11,712	0.8	2.3
DJIBOUTI	507	544	498	495	502	0.8	-0.7
EGYPT	29,899	50,921	60,177	78,454	81,003	5.5	4.3
EQUAT. GUINEA	94	117	164	775	1,186	2.3	25.2
ERITREA	...	...	574	635	672	...	3.0
ETHIOPIA	4,541	5,137	5,782	7,445	7,966	1.6	4.2
GABON	3,633	4,345	4,959	4,985	4,910	2.1	1.2
GAMBIA	243	347	382	494	522	3.7	3.8
GHANA	4,231	5,236	6,457	7,978	8,286	2.3	4.3
GUINEA	2,265	3,075	3,692	4,465	4,595	3.1	3.7
GUINEA BISSAU	134	217	254	251	262	5.1	2.3
KENYA	5,612	8,360	9,047	9,876	9,971	4.1	1.6
LESOTHO	500	768	933	1,117	1,150	4.5	3.8
LIBERIA	...	...	...	...	...	...	...
LIBYA	37,811	32,265	29,717	32,853	33,661	-1.3	0.4
MADAGASCAR	3,048	3,212	3,160	3,814	4,069	0.6	2.2
MALAWI	992	1,234	1,429	1,739	1,782	2.2	3.7
MALI	1,985	2,107	2,377	3,101	3,103	0.7	3.7
MAURITANIA	753	887	1,068	1,318	1,387	1.7	4.2
MAURITIUS	1,743	3,127	3,973	5,223	5,536	6.0	5.3
MOROCCO	21,590	31,506	32,985	39,322	41,662	4.0	2.7
MOZAMBIQUE	1,938	1,967	2,311	3,380	3,674	0.5	6.0
NAMIBIA	1,483	1,677	3,503	4,156	4,268	1.2	9.8
NIGER	1,833	1,813	1,881	2,197	2,307	0.1	2.3
NIGERIA	22,357	24,864	28,109	32,947	34,250	1.3	3.0
RWANDA	1,661	2,031	1,286	2,059	2,183	2.1	3.2
SAO T. & PRINC.	48	42	45	50	52	-1.1	2.0
SENEGAL	3,057	4,150	4,476	5,806	6,140	3.2	3.7
SEYCHELLES	315	441	508	569	563	3.6	2.3
SIERRA LEONE	1,013	1,211	962	763	797	1.9	-3.4
SOMALIA	...	...	...	...	...	...	...
SOUTH AFRICA	127,410	144,763	151,113	172,074	175,902	1.4	1.8
SUDAN	4,917	5,484	7,194	9,641	10,215	1.2	5.8
SWAZILAND	608	1,121	1,304	1,542	1,579	6.6	3.2
TANZANIA	3,474	4,808	5,255	6,513	6,812	3.3	3.2
TOGO	1,175	1,304	1,309	1,479	1,523	1.1	1.7
TUNISIA	10,509	14,915	18,030	23,693	24,914	3.6	4.8
UGANDA	2,799	4,102	5,756	7,741	8,110	4.0	6.4
ZAMBIA	3,351	3,716	3,471	3,978	4,156	1.1	1.1
ZIMBABWE	5,362	6,703	7,115	7,818	7,228	2.3	0.9
AFRICA	**382,000**	**467,303**	**498,379**	**593,541**	**612,916**	**2.4**	**2.6**

TABLE 2.2
GROSS DOMESTIC PRODUCT, NOMINAL
(MILLIONS OF US DOLLARS AT CURRENT MARKET PRICES)

COUNTRY	1980	1990	1995	2000	2001	Av. Ann. Nominal Change (%) 1981-1990	Av. Ann. Nominal Change (%) 1991-2001
ALGERIA	42,318	62,031	41,767	53,306	54,598	4.2	-0.5
ANGOLA	5,400	10,260	5,040	8,828	9,271	7.0	3.4
BENIN	1,405	1,845	2,009	2,248	2,349	3.6	3.6
BOTSWANA	1,126	3,516	4,427	4,943	4,944	13.1	3.3
BURKINA FASO	1,709	2,765	2,184	2,192	2,343	5.7	-0.4
BURUNDI	920	1,132	1,000	679	688	2.3	-4.1
CAMEROON	6,741	11,152	7,965	8,879	8,615	5.7	-1.4
CAPE VERDE	107	339	491	558	566	15.0	5.1
CENT. AFR. REP.	797	1,488	1,122	963	972	7.5	-2.7
CHAD	1,033	1,739	1,438	1,407	1,601	6.0	0.2
COMOROS	124	250	232	202	206	8.3	-0.9
CONGO	1,706	2,799	2,116	3,215	2,879	5.7	2.2
CONGO DEM. REP.	14,391	9,348	5,643	4,406	4,350	-3.2	-5.9
COTE D'IVOIRE	10,175	10,796	9,992	9,370	9,215	1.4	-0.5
DJIBOUTI	296	418	498	553	572	3.5	2.9
EGYPT	22,913	43,094	60,177	98,680	93,490	6.8	7.7
EQUAT. GUINEA	61	132	164	1,341	1,844	9.7	32.1
ERITREA	...	...	574	608	558	...	3.3
ETHIOPIA	5,024	6,842	5,782	6,331	6,377	3.5	0.1
GABON	4,279	5,952	4,959	5,024	4,394	4.3	-2.0
GAMBIA	241	317	382	434	406	3.9	2.4
GHANA	4,445	5,886	6,457	5,102	5,429	3.3	0.3
GUINEA	6,684	2,818	3,692	3,077	2,861	4.8	0.3
GUINEA BISSAU	110	244	254	215	209	9.7	-0.9
KENYA	7,265	8,531	9,047	10,356	10,383	1.9	3.8
LESOTHO	431	615	933	899	794	4.7	2.8
LIBERIA	1,117	384	...	...	...	-8.2	...
LIBYA	36,272	28,587	29,717	35,716	33,368	-1.9	1.8
MADAGASCAR	4,042	3,081	3,160	3,878	4,541	-1.9	4.3
MALAWI	1,238	1,803	1,429	1,692	1,781	4.2	3.9
MALI	1,787	2,473	2,377	2,544	2,584	4.1	1.6
MAURITANIA	709	1,020	1,068	935	955	4.0	-0.2
MAURITIUS	1,132	2,642	3,973	4,513	4,510	9.7	5.1
MOROCCO	18,805	25,821	32,985	33,346	33,999	4.2	2.8
MOZAMBIQUE	3,526	2,463	2,311	3,813	3,302	-0.3	3.6
NAMIBIA	2,166	2,350	3,503	3,427	3,088	1.6	2.8
NIGER	2,509	2,481	1,881	1,826	1,937	0.9	-1.3
NIGERIA	64,202	28,472	28,109	41,083	41,526	-6.4	5.0
RWANDA	1,163	2,585	1,286	1,794	1,739	8.4	2.0
SAO T. & PRINC.	47	58	45	46	45	2.9	-1.8
SENEGAL	2,987	5,699	4,476	4,371	4,616	8.0	-0.9
SEYCHELLES	147	368	508	623	619	9.9	4.9
SIERRA LEONE	1,166	897	962	636	722	-0.3	-1.0
SOMALIA	604	917	...	...	...	4.7	...
SOUTH AFRICA	80,423	112,014	151,113	127,927	112,874	4.5	0.3
SUDAN	7,617	13,167	7,194	11,516	12,562	7.5	1.8
SWAZILAND	581	842	1,304	1,348	1,112	5.2	3.0
TANZANIA	4,771	4,259	5,255	9,027	9,076	2.0	7.6
TOGO	1,136	1,628	1,309	1,219	1,237	4.9	-1.3
TUNISIA	8,743	12,314	18,030	19,462	20,079	3.7	4.8
UGANDA	1,245	4,304	5,756	6,170	6,335	16.9	4.9
ZAMBIA	3,878	3,288	3,471	3,205	3,518	1.4	1.0
ZIMBABWE	6,679	8,773	7,115	7,076	7,306	3.5	-0.4
AFRICA	398,391	466,998	498,379	563,560	545,984	1.7	1.5

TABLE 2.3
GROSS NATIONAL SAVINGS
(PERCENTAGE OF GDP)

COUNTRY	1980	1990	1995	2000	2001	Annual Average 1980-1990	Annual Average 1991-2001
ALGERIA	30.4	31.6	24.9	40.6	39.8	26.9	30.5
ANGOLA	20.8	3.9	-0.8	32.8	31.1	12.3	14.3
BENIN	29.3	12.0	13.0	11.1	12.0	9.9	11.6
BOTSWANA	30.7	37.3	32.7	53.5	51.0	33.5	39.9
BURKINA FASO	13.3	16.9	18.2	19.7	19.4	16.7	17.2
BURUNDI	4.8	3.5	8.8	-0.5	0.0	7.0	5.2
CAMEROON	20.4	16.2	13.6	23.9	23.7	20.0	15.4
CAPE VERDE	16.4	19.0	31.9	21.0	33.4	35.1	23.1
CENT. AFR. REP.	-2.8	2.6	7.2	7.3	7.8	2.4	8.1
CHAD	11.3	0.4	5.8	3.1	4.6	2.6	4.1
COMOROS	14.7	18.3	6.6	10.0	3.2	17.1	9.8
CONGO	59.3	6.9	20.9	7.9	7.9	53.8	6.5
CONGO DEM. REP.	6.4	4.1	3.1	2.7	2.8	6.1	2.8
COTE D'IVOIRE	22.1	-2.1	10.6	7.0	7.1	8.3	6.9
DJIBOUTI	25.3	11.8	5.0	4.5	3.2	8.1	7.0
EGYPT	16.5	19.1	22.6	22.7	23.6	16.0	22.6
EQUAT. GUINEA	...	...	...	...	...	...	...
ERITREA	...	...	...	...	...	...	...
ETHIOPIA	7.3	8.6	19.7	8.0	-3.2	9.5	10.6
GABON	41.9	24.2	27.2	32.0	29.7	34.7	27.4
GAMBIA	-1.1	17.8	11.7	12.5	23.8	16.3	15.0
GHANA	4.9	10.7	17.6	14.8	14.7	8.1	14.1
GUINEA	9.0	8.9	19.6	19.2	21.9	7.7	19.7
GUINEA BISSAU	9.5	14.2	4.7	0.8	0.1	9.3	5.8
KENYA	7.5	19.9	16.8	12.7	9.6	18.1	15.8
LESOTHO	43.1	46.4	25.4	15.4	13.7	31.9	21.0
LIBERIA	31.8	12.0	...	...	...	17.9	...
LIBYA	...	...	...	...	...	...	...
MADAGASCAR	1.2	4.1	2.4	9.5	12.4	3.2	6.0
MALAWI	8.1	12.1	4.7	-0.4	-0.5	11.2	2.0
MALI	7.0	14.9	14.9	11.0	12.4	9.7	13.9
MAURITANIA	14.2	6.4	13.9	31.1	13.7	11.4	15.6
MAURITIUS	14.9	25.9	25.4	26.3	30.2	20.5	26.9
MOROCCO	16.5	22.9	17.3	23.1	23.2	19.3	21.0
MOZAMBIQUE	-2.7	0.5	3.4	21.6	29.4	-2.3	6.3
NAMIBIA	20.6	35.0	27.4	26.8	32.9	19.8	25.5
NIGER	17.1	7.4	2.6	5.5	8.8	10.0	6.5
NIGERIA	23.3	28.0	14.9	27.6	22.2	15.2	18.3
RWANDA	8.8	3.6	19.2	...	...	8.8	...
SAO T. & PRINC.	-10.4	-9.3	27.6	23.0	12.9	-6.2	12.1
SENEGAL	-1.8	10.4	11.5	11.9	12.4	4.4	11.1
SEYCHELLES	11.5	20.0	20.0	20.0	25.9	16.6	21.0
SIERRA LEONE	3.6	-1.5	-11.7	-1.8	-0.9	3.2	-3.4
SOMALIA	10.5	6.8	...	...	...	19.4	...
SOUTH AFRICA	33.9	19.1	16.5	15.2	15.2	23.9	15.8
SUDAN	0.5	9.3	...	...	...	4.9	...
SWAZILAND	16.7	25.5	30.6	33.4	33.5	21.2	29.8
TANZANIA	20.7	20.9	1.9	0.7	0.6	16.7	7.9
TOGO	18.3	26.9	14.2	9.6	9.1	15.9	9.6
TUNISIA	24.6	21.6	20.4	23.2	23.8	22.6	22.3
UGANDA	42.4	5.9	14.7	17.8	...	16.6	13.5
ZAMBIA	11.8	14.8	8.9	4.5	4.7	8.9	7.2
ZIMBABWE	14.5	15.6	14.5	2.7	2.7	14.7	11.9
AFRICA	**21.5**	**18.6**	**16.5**	**20.0**	**19.5**	**18.3**	**17.2**

TABLE 2.4
GROSS CAPITAL FORMATION
(PERCENTAGE OF GDP)

COUNTRY	1980	1990	1995	2000	2001	Annual Average 1980-1990	Annual Average 1991-2001
ALGERIA	39.1	28.9	30.2	23.8	28.4	33.7	27.7
ANGOLA	20.4	7.3	27.9	26.1	27.5	17.2	26.2
BENIN	35.6	14.2	19.6	18.8	19.5	19.8	17.0
BOTSWANA	40.4	37.8	26.4	31.5	29.3	32.4	29.2
BURKINA FASO	14.6	20.6	23.9	33.0	32.5	19.0	25.8
BURUNDI	13.9	14.5	9.3	8.3	14.8	16.4	11.4
CAMEROON	21.0	17.8	14.5	16.4	17.7	23.3	16.2
CAPE VERDE	38.7	24.4	43.0	34.4	30.6	43.7	30.2
CENT. AFR. REP.	12.3	11.7	14.4	11.3	13.8	12.5	13.0
CHAD	11.2	11.5	8.8	17.9	44.0	10.9	15.3
COMOROS	20.5	19.7	19.5	10.4	11.8	21.9	16.3
CONGO	12.4	15.9	36.6	18.9	17.4	17.4	27.4
CONGO DEM. REP.	9.2	9.1	9.4	23.2	27.1	11.2	16.4
COTE D'IVOIRE	22.8	6.7	16.4	12.3	14.1	15.0	12.6
DJIBOUTI	13.1	17.4	8.4	14.6	12.9	16.1	12.8
EGYPT	35.7	29.4	19.9	23.9	23.1	30.5	21.7
EQUAT. GUINEA	35.7	17.4	74.9	37.5	39.6	23.9	58.9
ERITREA	...	...	...	...	...	...	...
ETHIOPIA	12.6	12.0	15.2	12.6	15.9	13.9	14.1
GABON	32.9	21.7	23.3	22.1	27.5	36.8	25.6
GAMBIA	28.9	20.4	16.0	17.1	17.7	21.4	18.2
GHANA	5.6	14.4	20.0	24.0	23.7	9.2	21.2
GUINEA	13.4	17.5	24.1	22.1	24.2	14.7	23.6
GUINEA BISSAU	53.4	27.9	22.3	21.0	27.3	36.3	25.0
KENYA	22.8	24.2	21.8	15.6	15.3	22.8	18.2
LESOTHO	35.2	50.9	59.9	33.6	31.5	37.5	48.3
LIBERIA	26.8	13.2	...	...	...	16.0	...
LIBYA	...	...	...	...	...	...	...
MADAGASCAR	15.0	14.8	12.1	17.1	18.6	11.0	13.3
MALAWI	24.7	20.6	17.0	13.1	12.9	18.8	16.3
MALI	14.8	20.7	24.1	20.4	19.8	17.1	21.0
MAURITANIA	36.1	18.8	19.3	30.3	29.1	28.6	20.7
MAURITIUS	24.8	31.2	30.8	25.8	26.8	24.4	28.0
MOROCCO	24.2	25.3	20.7	24.8	24.9	24.4	22.5
MOZAMBIQUE	8.3	16.4	23.9	38.6	40.8	10.8	24.5
NAMIBIA	20.3	33.8	21.2	23.7	22.1	18.1	21.2
NIGER	28.1	11.0	7.3	10.6	12.1	14.9	9.4
NIGERIA	18.5	21.5	16.3	22.7	25.0	18.9	20.9
RWANDA	12.4	11.7	15.0	15.2	17.1	15.1	13.9
SAO T. & PRINC.	16.8	29.5	68.1	43.5	49.2	18.5	44.9
SENEGAL	10.9	13.8	16.7	18.4	18.7	11.7	16.8
SEYCHELLES	38.3	24.6	25.8	26.6	25.7	26.2	28.7
SIERRA LEONE	17.7	9.4	-1.7	8.0	10.0	11.7	5.2
SOMALIA	17.4	15.5	...	...	...	25.6	...
SOUTH AFRICA	29.9	17.2	18.0	15.5	14.6	23.1	16.0
SUDAN	14.7	7.0	...	...	...	7.1	...
SWAZILAND	40.7	19.6	32.9	37.1	37.0	27.1	32.0
TANZANIA	37.8	26.1	19.8	16.2	17.0	28.8	20.0
TOGO	28.7	33.1	18.2	20.5	21.2	23.0	18.1
TUNISIA	29.4	27.1	24.7	27.4	27.6	28.6	26.7
UGANDA	4.8	11.9	17.1	22.6	15.7	6.9	16.9
ZAMBIA	27.0	17.3	13.1	16.9	18.7	19.6	14.3
ZIMBABWE	18.8	17.4	19.6	4.4	2.5	18.2	15.9
AFRICA	**24.8**	**20.3**	**19.7**	**20.2**	**20.8**	**22.3**	**19.8**

TABLE 2.5
TERMS OF TRADE
(1995 = 100)

COUNTRY	1980	1990	1996	2000	2001	Average Annual Growth (%) 1980-1990	1991-2001
ALGERIA	153.1	123.4	111.4	166.8	166.6	-0.3	5.1
ANGOLA	307.4	155.1	141.9	174.5	157.2	-3.7	2.6
BENIN	56.4	100.1	91.2	75.6	88.1	9.7	-0.2
BOTSWANA	14.4	59.6	145.7	186.0	184.0	18.6	12.2
BURKINA FASO	63.4	91.0	93.3	84.2	94.5	4.0	0.6
BURUNDI	123.8	68.9	80.3	72.2	76.4	-3.2	2.3
CAMEROON	160.8	98.9	91.5	169.4	174.2	-3.3	9.2
CAPE VERDE	268.1	186.4	94.1	147.3	139.8	6.0	2.1
CENTRAL AFRICAN REP	117.4	114.4	95.8	84.4	85.1	1.1	-2.2
CHAD	60.8	73.5	104.3	90.5	107.3	3.1	4.1
COMOROS	267.8	209.6	87.0	168.9	151.0	-2.1	1.9
CONGO	249.8	122.5	140.7	180.0	157.5	-6.7	4.4
CONGO, DEM. REP.	64.4	80.8	118.8	140.3	124.6	2.9	4.7
COTE D'IVOIRE	93.8	74.0	82.5	68.5	63.7	-1.2	-0.6
DJIBOUTI	372.2	249.6	98.4	98.8	98.8	-3.4	-6.9
EGYPT	123.5	107.7	104.1	113.0	114.3	-0.3	0.8
EQUAT. GUINEA	137.3	123.8	89.0	90.5	111.4	-0.0	3.7
ERITREA							
ETHIOPIA	85.8	105.6	75.9	66.2	58.7	4.3	-3.3
GABON	63.0	82.4	117.9	254.6	161.4	3.2	15.5
GAMBIA	49.6	100.0	100.0	103.3	107.0	10.2	0.6
GHANA	131.3	86.8	98.3	86.0	90.2	-1.5	0.8
GUINEA	85.9	145.1	88.5	102.1	94.4	6.4	-2.3
GUINEA BISSAU	153.6	118.3	99.8	141.6	147.7	-1.4	2.6
KENYA	137.2	70.6	102.4	94.2	90.3	-5.7	2.4
LESOTHO	113.5	74.0	90.2	117.9	117.2	-3.9	4.5
LIBERIA	127.3	117.8	102.0	110.6	...	-0.5	...
LIBYA							
MADAGASCAR	72.5	83.5	83.0	67.4	69.0	3.7	-0.6
MALAWI	87.9	81.5	104.9	95.2	94.8	0.1	2.5
MALI	106.8	107.0	122.9	97.0	110.9	0.4	1.5
MAURITANIA	51.6	80.6	97.2	84.7	84.1	5.7	1.8
MAURITIUS	64.0	95.7	100.6	106.6	99.0	4.3	0.4
MOROCCO	128.6	87.7	101.4	98.8	98.2	-3.3	1.2
MOZAMBIQUE	87.0	99.4	99.6	99.4	81.7	2.5	-1.5
NAMIBIA	148.3	119.3	105.6	87.2	83.1	0.2	-2.9
NIGER	176.3	97.8	91.3	73.5	74.3	-4.4	-2.1
NIGERIA	137.4	121.4	121.6	175.1	163.5	2.4	5.2
RWANDA	112.8	42.5	76.5	58.5	61.6	-6.7	11.7
SAO T. & PRINC.	294.3	104.9	102.6	126.1	103.8	-7.5	0.5
SENEGAL	96.1	112.8	100.0	100.8	101.7	1.9	-0.8
SEYCHELLES	20.4	108.2	86.3	72.1	68.3	27.0	-3.4
SIERRA LEONE	76.9	76.9	95.1	91.3	92.1	-0.0	2.2
SOMALIA	112.8	100.8	99.9	99.5	...	-1.0	...
SOUDAN	67.1	87.7	...	...	...	3.2	...
SOUTH AFRICA	59.3	98.5	103.5	99.7	101.2	6.2	0.3
SWAZILAND	94.0	96.6	98.0	94.4	94.9	0.3	-0.2
TANZANIA	193.9	89.8	88.4	103.7	103.7	-7.2	2.0
TOGO	228.2	151.3	107.7	87.1	82.5	-3.6	-3.4
TUNISIA	126.0	102.7	103.3	96.8	97.0	-1.9	-0.5
UGANDA	131.4	119.3	91.7	46.6	41.2	4.3	-6.6
ZAMBIA	176.6	119.0	81.0	73.6	74.7	-1.6	-3.7
ZIMBABWE	61.9	93.8	109.5	142.6	145.1	4.7	4.3
AFRICA	**119.9**	**104.6**	**106.6**	**124.7**	**118.0**	**-1.0**	**1.4**

TABLE 2.6
CURRENT ACCOUNT
(AS PERCENTAGE OF GDP)

COUNTRY	1980	1990	1995	2000	2001	Annual Average 1980-1990	Annual Average 1991-2001
ALGERIA	0.6	3.0	-5.3	16.8	12.0	-0.5	3.3
ANGOLA	1.3	-2.9	-28.5	7.0	-2.8	-4.0	-12.4
BENIN	-6.8	-2.2	-6.6	-8.1	-7.5	-10.3	-5.6
BOTSWANA	-15.4	-0.5	6.3	22.0	19.3	0.6	10.4
BURKINA FASO	-1.1	-3.4	-5.2	-9.4	-9.7	-2.6	-7.3
BURUNDI	-9.1	-11.1	-0.4	-4.5	-11.0	-9.5	-4.3
CAMEROON	-5.0	-4.4	-0.9	7.4	-2.0	-1.6	-2.1
CAPE VERDE	-49.9	-5.9	-11.0	-12.0	-15.3	-9.5	-10.1
CENTRAL AFRICAN REP	-15.1	-6.0	-6.8	-3.1	-5.9	-7.6	-3.5
CHAD	-0.0	-11.1	-7.7	-13.7	-40.1	-7.6	-13.0
COMOROS	-1.8	-13.0	-14.3	-3.6	-8.3	-13.2	-12.0
CONGO	18.0	-9.0	-15.7	-11.0	-10.4	7.9	-21.0
CONGO, DEM. REP.	-1.6	-7.9	-7.7	-5.9	-8.2	-5.1	-8.4
COTE D'IVOIRE	-11.8	-12.2	-6.7	-5.4	-5.5	-6.5	-6.4
DJIBOUTI	10.0	-2.3	-3.4	-7.2	-4.5	-9.4	-5.1
EGYPT	-0.9	-2.8	0.6	-1.2	-0.2	-3.8	1.1
EQUAT. GUINEA	-65.2	-26.4	-61.0	-25.4	-18.0	-36.2	-48.0
ERITREA							
ETHIOPIA	-3.4	-4.6	1.2	-5.3	-5.5	-3.4	-3.7
GABON	29.1	2.5	3.2	12.2	0.5	5.2	1.6
GAMBIA	-46.5	-2.7	-4.3	-4.6	-2.4	-6.6	-4.0
GHANA	0.2	-3.5	-2.4	-9.1	-6.9	-1.6	-6.9
GUINEA	3.1	-9.2	-4.5	-2.9	-2.6	-4.9	-3.9
GUINEA BISSAU	-43.9	-13.6	-17.6	-8.2	-22.8	-27.0	-17.7
KENYA	-15.3	-5.6	-5.6	-2.1	-5.6	-5.4	-2.5
LESOTHO	-9.5	-10.1	-34.5	-18.1	-12.9	-13.3	-27.6
LIBERIA	5.0	-1.2	0.3	0.4	...	1.9	...
LIBYA	...	...	...	...	...	...	...
MADAGASCAR	-13.8	-10.7	-9.7	-5.6	-7.6	-7.8	-7.3
MALAWI	-16.7	-3.7	-10.4	-4.8	-4.4	-6.0	-9.2
MALI	-7.7	-5.8	-9.2	-9.5	-13.1	-7.4	-7.6
MAURITANIA	-21.9	-9.1	-5.4	0.8	-7.2	-16.3	-4.4
MAURITIUS	-9.9	-5.3	-5.3	0.5	-1.2	-3.9	-1.5
MOROCCO	-4.7	-2.8	-3.6	-1.7	-2.1	-5.9	-1.5
MOZAMBIQUE	-10.9	-15.9	-20.5	-17.0	-23.6	-13.1	-19.3
NAMIBIA	0.3	1.2	6.2	5.6	1.1	1.7	3.7
NIGER	-11.1	-4.4	-4.7	-4.9	-5.4	-5.0	-3.6
NIGERIA	8.5	7.4	-4.6	4.8	-0.8	-4.8	-2.5
RWANDA	-3.7	-8.1	4.2	-1.3	-10.3	-6.4	-5.4
SAO T. & PRINC.	-0.0	-0.1	-0.1	-0.0	-41.6	-0.0	-3.8
SENEGAL	-14.5	-7.8	-5.3	-6.5	-5.1	-10.6	-6.0
SEYCHELLES	-11.0	1.3	-7.4	-10.5	-5.6	-12.2	-8.3
SIERRA LEONE	-14.1	-10.9	-10.1	-9.8	-11.3	-8.5	-8.7
SOMALIA	-6.9	-8.7	-8.4	-4.2	...	-6.8	...
SUDAN	-8.8	-9.0	...	...	...	-13.1	...
SOUTH AFRICA	4.4	1.8	-1.5	-0.3	0.1	0.9	-0.2
SWAZILAND	-23.9	5.9	-2.3	-3.0	-4.1	-5.9	-2.1
TANZANIA	-8.6	-4.9	-17.7	-0.7	-2.6	-4.7	-7.7
TOGO	-10.4	-6.1	-4.0	-11.0	-13.2	-7.2	-8.6
TUNISIA	-4.1	-5.5	-4.3	-4.2	-3.1	-6.4	-4.4
UGANDA	-3.1	-5.9	-2.5	-8.8	-7.6	-1.8	-5.2
ZAMBIA	-15.2	-2.5	-4.2	-12.4	-14.3	-10.7	-7.1
ZIMBABWE	-5.6	0.2	-0.6	-0.7	-1.3	-2.6	-1.7
AFRICA	**2.1**	**-1.2**	**-2.9**	**1.2**	**-0.2**	**-2.8**	**-1.6**

TABLE 2.7
BROAD MONEY SUPPLY (M2)
(PERCENTAGE ANNUAL CHANGE)

COUNTRY	1980	1990	1995	2000	2001	Annual Average 1980-1990	Annual Average 1991-2001
ALGERIA	17.4	11.4	9.2	13.2	17.2	14.4	17.2
ANGOLA	...	...	...	...	...	...	...
BENIN	48.9	28.6	-1.8	26.0	9.6	12.7	14.3
BOTSWANA	19.0	-14.0	12.3	1.4	9.4	22.6	17.2
BURKINA FASO	15.1	-0.5	22.3	6.2	0.8	11.8	9.2
BURUNDI	1.4	9.6	-11.2	4.3	7.2	11.6	13.0
CAMEROON	21.4	-1.7	-6.2	19.1	2.8	11.1	3.9
CAPE VERDE	30.6	14.6	13.2	13.7	3.1	18.7	11.6
CENT. AFR. REP.	35.0	-3.7	4.3	2.4	7.9	8.4	8.2
CHAD	-15.3	-2.4	48.7	18.5	9.0	8.4	8.1
COMOROS	...	3.9	-6.1	14.5	10.5	12.7	4.3
CONGO	36.6	18.5	-0.1	58.5	-21.5	14.0	6.5
CONGO DEM. REP.	...	...	...	...	...	...	...
COTE D'IVOIRE	2.8	-2.6	18.1	-1.9	-2.2	4.0	6.8
DJIBOUTI	...	3.6	5.3	1.1	2.0	7.6	-0.7
EGYPT	51.4	28.7	9.9	11.6	2.2	25.7	11.4
EQUAT. GUINEA	...	-52.0	48.9	36.2	3.1	-9.0	32.5
ERITREA	...	...	...	...	...	...	...
ETHIOPIA	4.2	18.5	8.7	14.2	1.8	11.9	10.9
GABON	24.6	3.3	10.1	18.3	7.4	8.6	7.3
GAMBIA	10.4	8.4	14.2	34.8	0.3	18.8	13.5
GHANA	33.8	13.3	40.4	38.4	12.6	42.2	33.0
GUINEA	...	...	11.3	26.9	4.2	...	12.2
GUINEA BISSAU	...	574.6	43.0	60.8	0.2	...	37.7
KENYA	0.8	20.1	24.8	4.5	-0.9	12.7	18.1
LESOTHO	...	8.4	9.8	1.4	7.7	18.0	11.0
LIBERIA	-23.3	...	29.5	18.3	11.5	8.4	26.6
LIBYA	26.6	19.0	9.6	3.1	2.2	7.2	5.3
MADAGASCAR	20.6	4.5	16.2	17.2	5.3	16.9	21.0
MALAWI	12.6	11.1	56.2	41.4	9.5	17.6	32.1
MALI	4.5	-4.9	7.3	12.2	7.9	8.1	11.8
MAURITANIA	12.5	11.5	-5.1	16.1	4.3	13.0	3.7
MAURITIUS	23.2	21.2	18.7	9.2	2.2	21.0	13.4
MOROCCO	10.8	21.5	7.0	8.4	1.4	14.1	9.1
MOZAMBIQUE	...	37.2	47.5	38.4	12.3	39.5	38.5
NAMIBIA	...	...	24.2	13.0	0.7	...	19.0
NIGER	20.8	-4.1	3.8	12.4	-2.9	7.5	-1.9
NIGERIA	46.1	32.7	19.4	48.1	14.9	18.1	32.6
RWANDA	8.1	5.6	69.5	15.6	0.3	7.8	13.8
SAO T. & PRINC.	...	...	...	19.0	19.2	...	39.9
SENEGAL	10.3	-4.8	7.4	10.7	5.9	7.6	8.8
SEYCHELLES	33.2	14.5	10.5	9.1	3.3	11.7	15.2
SIERRA LEONE	21.6	74.0	19.6	12.1	12.6	51.8	28.2
SOMALIA	...	...	...	...	...	...	...
SOUTH AFRICA	22.8	11.4	16.0	7.2	3.9	17.2	12.1
SUDAN	29.4	48.8	73.3	36.9	12.0	38.0	58.3
SWAZILAND	13.7	0.6	3.9	-6.6	0.7	17.1	11.6
TANZANIA	26.9	41.9	33.0	14.8	3.4	25.7	22.5
TOGO	9.1	9.5	22.3	15.2	-0.4	9.0	5.3
TUNISIA	18.5	7.6	6.6	14.1	1.6	14.9	9.5
UGANDA	34.8	...	13.9	18.1	0.9	83.6	22.4
ZAMBIA	9.0	47.9	55.5	73.8	-10.1	38.6	43.2
ZIMBABWE	29.6	15.1	25.5	68.9	23.8	16.8	32.8
AFRICA	**23.2**	**18.2**	**20.7**	**17.2**	**15.0**	**11.2**	**22.3**

TABLE 2.8
REAL EXCHANGE RATES INDICES (PERIOD AVERAGE)
(NATIONAL CURRENCY PER US $, 1995 = 100)

COUNTRY		1980	1990	1995	2000	2001	Annual Average Growth (%) 1980-1990	1991-2001
ALGERIA	DINAR	36.7	53.9	113.0	131.6	133.5	4.4	10.2
ANGOLA	NEW KWANZA	...	22.8	113.4	99.2	107.3	...	24.2
BENIN	CFA FRANC	...	76.1	117.1	134.4	135.9	2.3	6.4
BOTSWANA	PULA	75.0	104.4	132.6	139.2	153.7	3.6	3.7
BURKINA FASO	CFA FRANC	44.3	63.5	119.4	143.2	145.3	4.2	9.2
BURUNDI	FRANC	67.3	98.0	127.9	136.0	144.5	4.6	4.2
CAMEROON	CFA FRANC	71.2	66.7	117.9	139.2	143.9	0.9	8.2
CAPE VERDE	ESCUDO	...	104.6	116.5	139.3	149.1	-0.8	3.6
CENT. AFR. REP.	CFA FRANC	42.9	65.0	131.0	151.9	156.2	5.5	9.8
CHAD	CFA FRANC	...	67.2	108.7	125.2	125.7	1.3	6.9
COMOROS	FRANC	...	87.4	119.8	136.9	140.8	-0.9	5.0
CONGO	CFA FRANC	74.1	72.2	103.1	124.3	131.0	1.2	6.4
CONGO DEM.REP.	FRANC	22.0	89.1	39.1	33.5	119.4	18.4	20.2
COTE D'IVOIRE	CFA FRANC	59.0	73.0	119.9	139.9	142.1	3.1	7.7
DJIBOUTI	FRANC	...	110.8	97.4	98.7	101.4	-0.8	-0.8
EGYPT	POUND	101.5	74.8	90.9	93.5	108.4	-1.6	5.4
EQUAT. GUINEA	CFA FRANC	...	67.5	101.4	114.4	114.9	-7.5	6.0
ERITREA	NAKFA	...	...	...	...	...	...	...
ETHIOPIA	BIRR	51.4	53.0	126.6	135.4	142.7	1.3	11.5
GABON	CFA FRANC	48.3	56.1	126.7	147.7	154.2	2.5	10.6
GAMBIA	DALASI	66.2	97.6	119.6	137.6	162.1	3.9	4.9
GHANA	CEDI	14.3	75.3	100.7	171.7	169.3	25.4	9.6
GUINEA	FRANC	...	93.6	132.3	161.7	169.3	108.6	5.7
GUINEA BISSAU	CFA FRANC	...	68.7	101.8	112.1	115.7	18.9	5.0
KENYA	SHILLING	70.3	112.4	112.9	119.4	123.9	4.5	1.7
LESOTHO	MALOTI	75.1	112.9	136.2	150.7	181.5	4.1	4.8
LIBERIA	DOLLAR	163.5	131.4	3,132.3	2,877.9	3,235.6	-1.9	358.6
LIBYA	DINAR	...	167.1	63.9	69.4	64.8	0.5	-7.8
MADAGASCAR	FRANC	38.5	85.1	110.2	109.5	101.5	8.0	2.3
MALAWI	KWACHA	53.9	64.7	111.7	120.4	113.7	2.1	7.2
MALI	CFA FRANC	...	62.2	123.3	148.4	151.1	1.8	9.9
MAURITANIA	OUGUIYA	...	75.2	143.3	163.6	...	-1.3	-1.4
MAURITIUS	RUPEE	74.0	103.2	121.8	126.0	137.8	3.2	2.8
MOROCCO	DIRHAM	67.4	110.9	116.6	128.2	139.9	5.7	2.3
MOZAMBIQUE	METICAL	...	61.2	96.5	105.7	138.6	10.0	8.4
NAMIBIA	DOLLAR	68.2	106.6	135.9	152.7	186.0	5.8	5.6
NIGER	CFA FRANC	36.9	61.2	121.8	141.5	144.5	5.6	9.1
NIGERIA	NAIRA	66.4	219.4	280.2	298.3	281.5	16.8	19.8
RWANDA	FRANC	85.7	79.1	111.6	129.6	144.1	-0.0	6.2
SAO T. & PRINC.	DOBRA	...	34.0	138.0	152.3	163.2	4.0	16.3
SENEGAL	CFA FRANC	56.2	65.1	126.7	150.3	157.0	2.7	9.4
SEYCHELLES	RUPEE	106.0	104.1	113.0	117.5	116.0	0.1	1.1
SIERRA LEONE	LEONE	85.9	110.3	101.5	122.7	120.9	5.5	1.4
SOMALIA	SHILLING	6.3	2,600.0	9,000.0	11,000.0	20,000.0	95.4	28.3
SOUTH AFRICA	RAND	77.7	104.3	140.5	156.6	189.9	3.1	5.9
SUDAN	POUND	44.9	23.6	102.5	98.0	96.2	-2.1	47.8
SWAZILAND	EMALANGENI	75.0	102.6	140.8	147.4	185.7	2.8	5.9
TANZANIA	SHILLING	37.3	97.7	82.9	86.9	93.2	9.9	-0.0
TOGO	CFA FRANC	53.7	76.4	117.9	138.3	146.6	4.3	7.1
TUNISIA	DINAR	67.0	105.5	120.4	139.8	148.9	4.8	3.5
UGANDA	SHILLING	...	93.7	134.6	153.0	161.1	19.8	6.1
ZAMBIA	KWACHA	69.1	92.8	107.5	114.8	127.0	6.0	3.2
ZIMBABWE	DOLLAR	49.4	81.3	160.4	123.5	109.7	5.1	4.3

* estimates

TABLE 2.9
INTERNATIONAL RESERVES
(MILLIONS OF US DOLLARS)

COUNTRY	1980	1990	1995	2000	2001	Average Annual Growth (%) 1980-1990	1991-2001
ALGERIA	4,021.8	980.7	2,295.6	12,278.5	18,666.3	-4.3	42.5
ANGOLA	...	...	212.8	1,198.2	1,080.4	...	...
BENIN	8.6	69.1	202.2	...	...	116.0	...
BOTSWANA	334.0	3,331.5	4,695.5	6,318.2	6,274.0	29.2	6.0
BURKINA FASO	68.7	304.7	351.7	...	...	17.8	...
BURUNDI	104.7	111.6	216.1	37.7	22.2	8.4	-10.1
CAMEROON	206.5	37.0	15.3	...	...	12.7	...
CAPE VERDE	42.4	77.0	36.9	28.2	31.8	6.8	20.6
CENT. AFR. REP.	61.5	122.6	237.9	...	...	10.3	...
CHAD	11.6	131.8	...	...	...	33.5	...
COMOROS	...	29.9	44.7	...	...	...	...
CONGO	92.5	9.9	63.6	224.1	...	-0.4	...
CONGO DEM. REP.	357.2	261.3	157.4	...	...	1.2	...
COTE D'IVOIRE	21.7	20.9	546.2	...	...	1.2	...
DJIBOUTI	...	93.6	72.2	67.8	66.7	...	-2.7
EGYPT	1,149.0	3,324.6	16,885.2	13,628.6	...	19.5	...
EQUAT. GUINEA	...	0.7	0.0	23.0	42.0	...	363.7
ERITREA	...	...	...	...	...	...	...
ETHIOPIA	104.6	29.6	782.9	306.7	425.2	6.6	45.1
GABON	115.1	278.4	153.0	...	...	107.4	...
GAMBIA	5.7	55.4	106.1	109.4	...	98.9	...
GHANA	199.4	282.1	774.9	311.3	286.7	6.0	...
GUINEA	...	...	86.8	147.9	...	...	...
GUINEA BISSAU	...	18.2	20.3	66.7	61.4	...	23.3
KENYA	501.1	218.9	368.8	897.7	1,028.1	-4.9	53.9
LESOTHO	50.3	72.4	456.7	417.9	415.8	...	20.2
LIBERIA	5.5	...	28.1	0.3	0.3	...	...
LIBYA	13,220.4	5,991.2	...	12,655.0	14,298.7	5.9	...
MADAGASCAR	9.1	92.1	109.0	285.2	351.2	49.4	...
MALAWI	69.0	137.7	110.5	247.4	267.4	33.8	23.0
MALI	15.4	197.7	330.2	...	...	47.4	...
MAURITANIA	146.8	58.5	89.9	3.1	...	-2.3	...
MAURITIUS	95.3	742.6	867.4	909.8	829.2	62.4	2.4
MOROCCO	427.4	2,082.0	3,831.4	5,007.3	8,280.0	39.5	15.6
MOZAMBIQUE	...	...	195.3	725.1	707.3	...	...
NAMIBIA	...	...	221.0	260.0	268.6	...	...
NIGER	126.4	226.4	99.0	...	...	13.8	...
NIGERIA	10,269.7	3,866.4	1,444.3	...	...	18.4	...
RWANDA	186.6	44.3	99.1	190.6	200.1	-7.5	23.7
SAO T. & PRINC.	...	...	5.1	...	16.0	...	...
SENEGAL	9.4	22.0	283.0	...	...	9.7	...
SEYCHELLES	18.4	16.6	27.1	43.8	38.0	10.7	11.1
SIERRA LEONE	30.6	5.4	34.6	50.9	27.2	-5.8	23.7
SOMALIA	...	...	...	...	...	...	...
SOUTH AFRICA	7,238.2	2,423.3	4,300.6	7,533.8	7,570.3	-1.2	19.6
SUDAN	48.7	11.4	163.4	...	...	17.2	...
SWAZILAND	158.7	216.5	298.2	351.8	312.9	8.9	6.2
TANZANIA	20.3	192.8	270.2	974.2	1,137.3	68.4	22.3
TOGO	78.1	357.9	135.2	...	...	20.4	...
TUNISIA	598.3	800.0	1,610.1	1,814.2	1,672.0	8.2	8.9
UGANDA	3.0	44.0	458.9	808.0	760.2	103.5	33.3
ZAMBIA	88.6	...	222.7	244.8	...	...	...
ZIMBABWE	326.4	218.8	735.2	238.5	146.9	-0.9	7.2
AFRICA	**40,646.7**	**27,609.5**	**44,752.3**	**68,405.9**	**77,982.8**	**4.3**	**8.6**

TABLE 2.10
CONSUMER PRICE INDICES (GENERAL)
(1995 = 100)

COUNTRY	1980	1990	1999	2000	2001*	Average Annual Change (%) 1980-1990	Average Annual Change (%) 1991-2001
ALGERIA	18.3	29.9	135.2	135.6	137.6	9.7	15.6
ANGOLA	...	0.0	97,807.1	378,806.9	978,458.2	(9.5)	1,007.3
BENIN	54.7	61.5	115.2	120.0	126.2	3.0	7.2
BOTSWANA	33.9	55.1	137.5	148.9	159.0	10.9	10.1
BURKINA FASO	75.5	73.6	112.9	112.5	118.6	4.5	4.7
BURUNDI	44.1	60.0	192.8	239.7	268.9	7.2	15.0
CAMEROON	56.9	70.1	114.4	115.8	119.8	8.4	5.4
CAPE VERDE	53.9	74.7	125.3	122.3	126.0	10.0	4.9
CENT. AFR. REP.	78.4	71.9	102.9	106.1	109.8	3.3	4.3
CHAD	76.9	69.6	124.1	128.8	150.5	3.9	8.0
COMOROS	61.2	71.4	112.5	117.7	121.8	6.1	5.0
CONGO	60.6	64.7	130.8	129.7	131.0	7.9	7.2
CONGO, DEM. REP.	...	0.0	16,012.7	104,674.8	417,652.6	59.2	3,147.6
COTE D'IVOIRE	51.0	64.1	112.5	115.2	120.3	6.1	6.1
DJIBOUTI	50.1	77.4	112.0	114.7	115.2	5.3	3.7
EGYPT	21.2	52.4	120.4	123.7	126.6	17.3	8.5
EQUAT. GUINEA	88.2	69.2	120.6	127.8	135.5	17.0	6.8
ERITREA	...		132.2	158.5	187.2	...	...
ETHIOPIA	50.9	54.4	106.6	104.9	105.1	4.6	6.7
GABON	75.5	83.4	106.4	109.1	110.2	6.6	3.2
GAMBIA	27.7	72.6	109.1	110.0	113.8	17.0	4.2
GHANA	7.9	30.9	241.5	302.3	421.7	47.3	27.6
GUINEA	16.0	61.0	115.6	123.5	132.0	31.2	7.4
GUINEA BISSAU	1.6	15.1	237.7	258.2	266.7	45.8	32.1
KENYA	20.8	34.0	132.4	140.1	143.8	12.1	14.8
LESOTHO	28.8	54.2	135.2	143.5	152.8	13.7	10.0
LIBERIA	38.8	65.2	146.2	160.8	176.9	7.9	9.5
LIBYA	...	42.0	246.9	282.5	320.9	4.5	20.5
MADAGASCAR	17.3	35.3	146.1	163.7	177.2	17.9	16.5
MALAWI	9.9	23.7	282.4	365.6	485.3	16.3	32.8
MALI	67.4	75.2	109.4	108.6	113.6	3.4	4.1
MAURITANIA	50.0	70.8	123.1	127.1	135.2	13.3	6.1
MAURITIUS	49.8	71.0	130.0	135.4	142.0	11.4	6.5
MOROCCO	59.2	74.6	107.7	109.7	110.8	7.5	3.7
MOZAMBIQUE	1.3	14.4	160.3	179.4	189.6	52.3	28.3
NAMIBIA	30.9	57.4	135.5	148.1	161.7	12.9	9.9
NIGER	89.0	76.4	110.7	113.9	118.7	3.2	4.6
NIGERIA	4.9	14.3	164.6	176.0	210.2	21.6	29.6
RWANDA	30.6	34.1	124.7	129.6	137.0	4.7	14.3
SAO TOME & PRINC	7.7	25.4	397.0	416.8	445.6	17.4	30.8
SENEGAL	71.3	71.8	106.5	107.2	109.3	6.3	4.2
SEYCHELLES	83.5	92.3	108.6	114.5	122.9	4.0	2.7
SIERRA LEONE	0.7	15.6	257.2	255.1	252.6	67.3	31.5
SOMALIA	1.7	27.5	173.3	193.2	215.4	62.5	21.2
SOUTH AFRICA	28.7	58.6	131.1	138.2	146.1	14.6	8.7
SUDAN	0.4	2.8	463.8	510.2	540.8	38.6	68.6
SWAZILAND	31.2	59.6	130.8	146.7	161.1	14.9	9.5
TANZANIA	7.7	29.8	170.9	181.1	190.5	30.6	18.7
TOGO	58.8	61.2	114.3	116.5	117.1	4.7	6.6
TUNISIA	53.4	75.5	113.9	117.2	119.0	8.3	4.2
UGANDA	0.8	40.5	121.9	125.4	131.4	102.8	12.1
ZAMBIA	0.2	3.2	280.9	354.0	429.8	46.9	64.0
ZIMBABWE	16.3	29.8	301.3	469.6	807.2	13.2	36.0
AFRICA	12.1	26.8	180.2	204.8	229.8	14.6	22.0

* : estimates

TABLE 2.11
OVERALL GOVERNMENT DEFICIT(-) / SURPLUS(+) AS A PERCENTAGE OF GDP AT CURRENT PRICES
(PERCENTAGE)

COUNTRY	1980	1990	1995	2000	2001	Annual Average 1980-1990	Annual Average 1991-2001
ALGERIA	9.9	3.6	-1.4	9.9	6.3	1.3	0.3
ANGOLA	-9.9	-23.7	-37.3	4.8	5.6	-10.2	-14.4
BENIN	-4.2	-4.1	-3.2	-1.8	-0.8	-4.7	-1.2
BOTSWANA	-1.5	10.3	1.9	4.4	-0.4	11.6	4.0
BURKINA FASO	-7.6	-4.6	-1.9	-5.7	-6.1	-4.9	-3.5
BURUNDI	-6.2	-2.7	-4.6	-2.1	-7.1	-7.6	-4.8
CAMEROON	0.3	-7.6	-3.1	1.4	2.4	-2.7	-3.2
CAPE VERDE	-8.0	-3.3	-12.9	-18.9	-4.0	-8.7	-10.3
CENT. AFR. REP.	-8.5	-6.8	-4.8	-1.8	-1.6	-3.0	-3.8
CHAD	6.4	-5.9	-4.5	-7.5	-10.2	-0.5	-6.1
COMOROS	-16.0	-1.7	-7.3	-1.9	-3.8	-8.4	-3.4
CONGO	-0.9	-6.6	-8.2	1.1	-1.9	1.3	-9.8
CONGO DEM. REP.	-0.4	-10.9	-9.3	-5.7	0.9	-6.3	-10.2
COTE D'IVOIRE	-12.8	-12.0	-4.1	-1.4	-1.2	-8.4	-5.4
DJIBOUTI	6.3	-7.3	-8.5	-1.8	-1.4	-4.4	-5.4
EGYPT	-9.6	-12.6	-1.2	-6.0	-5.8	-16.5	-4.6
EQUAT. GUINEA	-16.3	-5.3	-5.3	9.0	20.4	-10.5	-1.4
ERITREA	...	...	...	...	...	...	...
ETHIOPIA	-3.6	-9.7	-3.9	-11.5	-6.5	-6.0	-6.6
GABON	7.4	-4.1	2.8	11.8	10.6	-2.7	0.2
GAMBIA	-23.0	-1.7	-3.3	-1.4	-1.0	-7.4	-2.0
GHANA	-11.7	-2.2	-6.4	-7.9	-8.2	-4.2	-7.9
GUINEA	-0.5	-5.2	-2.7	-3.2	-3.2	-2.8	-3.1
GUINEA BISSAU	12.2	-5.9	-1.4	-7.6	-13.7	-5.3	-11.7
KENYA	-7.8	-6.8	-0.3	-0.7	-2.1	-5.8	-2.6
LESOTHO	-10.1	-0.9	4.9	-2.3	0.2	-9.7	-0.4
LIBERIA	-14.5	-18.5	...	...	...	-13.7	...
LIBYA	...	...	...	...	...	...	...
MADAGASCAR	-14.2	-0.6	-6.2	-3.0	-4.3	-6.1	-5.2
MALAWI	-11.6	-2.8	-4.7	-4.8	-0.5	-7.1	-6.1
MALI	-14.3	-19.9	-3.4	-3.8	-8.9	-18.6	-9.1
MAURITANIA	-13.7	-5.4	1.1	-3.2	1.5	-7.3	0.2
MAURITIUS	-10.6	-2.1	-3.7	-3.8	-5.9	-6.3	-4.0
MOROCCO	-11.2	-0.6	-5.5	-6.5	-7.1	-7.8	-3.8
MOZAMBIQUE	-2.0	-5.9	-3.1	-4.1	-9.0	-7.6	-3.6
NAMIBIA	...	0.5	-3.3	-2.9	-2.8	-0.1	-3.4
NIGER	-1.0	-7.0	-3.9	-3.4	-4.7	-3.7	-3.9
NIGERIA	-3.4	3.1	3.5	2.2	-1.0	-5.2	-1.7
RWANDA	-3.3	-7.2	-2.4	0.1	-5.3	-4.2	-5.3
SAO T. & PRINC.	-27.7	-42.2	-37.4	-16.5	-6.8	-26.7	-30.3
SENEGAL	-8.2	-0.5	-0.2	-0.2	-1.2	-4.2	-0.9
SEYCHELLES	-6.6	0.2	-9.7	-14.5	-13.8	-8.3	-10.9
SIERRA LEONE	-12.1	-8.8	-6.3	-9.3	-13.8	-9.1	-7.5
SOMALIA	-10.0	-1.1	...	...	...	-7.1	...
SOUTH AFRICA	-1.0	-3.1	-5.2	-1.9	-2.6	-4.0	-4.6
SUDAN	-8.9	-14.9	...	...	...	-11.1	...
SWAZILAND	...	6.7	-0.2	-1.5	-2.9	-0.7	-0.9
TANZANIA	-5.7	-3.2	-3.3	-0.9	-0.5	-5.8	-1.7
TOGO	-5.7	-3.1	-6.5	-5.5	-4.1	-4.3	-6.3
TUNISIA	-2.8	-5.4	-4.2	-3.1	-2.5	-4.9	-3.5
UGANDA	-4.7	-4.1	-2.6	-7.6	-0.8	-5.7	-2.9
ZAMBIA	-18.5	-8.3	-3.8	-5.8	-4.4	-13.2	-3.9
ZIMBABWE	-9.6	-6.2	-10.1	-21.7	-16.8	-7.8	-9.1
AFRICA	-3.6	-4.5	-3.3	-1.7	-2.5	-5.8	-3.8

TABLE 2.12
TOTAL EXTERNAL DEBT
(MILLIONS OF US DOLLARS)

COUNTRY	1980	1990	1995	2000	2001	Average Annual Growth (%) 1980-1990	1991-2001
ALGERIA	18,685.9	27,877.0	32,810.0	25,500.0	22,508.6	4.5	-1.6
ANGOLA	9,165.4	11,000.0	11,422.2	9,367.0	8,515.6	1.9	-2.0
BENIN	334.3	1,176.8	1,621.2	1,419.5	1,382.0	14.3	1.8
BOTSWANA	160.0	653.0	871.4	1,217.6	1,214.0	16.0	6.0
BURKINA FASO	220.5	611.1	1,204.0	1,578.7	1,512.5	14.0	8.8
BURUNDI	158.3	885.0	1,183.4	1,144.8	1,081.4	19.4	1.9
CAMEROON	1,288.4	5,102.2	8,475.0	7,472.6	7,025.2	17.0	4.1
CAPE VERDE	...	131.0	190.8	303.4	307.2	11.4	8.5
CENTRAL AFR. REP.	171.6	647.8	869.3	745.1	705.9	15.4	1.0
CHAD	976.2	483.2	818.1	1,052.8	964.4	2.8	6.8
COMOROS	30.1	197.0	218.3	224.6	182.9	23.0	-0.2
CONGO	1,156.7	3,888.7	5,561.0	5,255.6	9,863.4	23.6	11.0
CONGO, DEM. REP.	4,395.4	10,169.7	13,461.0	12,862.0	12,995.8	9.0	2.3
COTE D'IVOIRE	5,802.6	15,304.8	16,075.3	11,249.0	11,425.3	13.2	-2.2
DJIBOUTI	33.0	210.4	282.3	369.9	381.2	27.4	5.8
EGYPT	29,638.2	46,105.0	32,965.0	27,783.0	27,102.3	4.6	-4.4
EQUAT. GUINEA	44.0	212.3	234.2	217.3	101.3	17.9	-4.4
ERITREA	...	...	...	...	...	...	...
ETHIOPIA	754.1	8,404.9	9,787.5	5,451.9	5,062.7	30.4	-2.9
GABON	1,389.1	3,119.9	3,933.6	3,065.1	3,100.8	11.7	0.3
GAMBIA	212.8	259.1	402.3	511.3	538.1	3.9	7.0
GHANA	1,398.0	3,295.2	5,674.9	6,505.7	6,772.0	9.6	7.1
GUINEA	1,005.2	2,385.2	3,079.7	3,375.2	3,229.4	9.8	2.9
GUINEA BISSAU	445.4	738.4	944.6	796.7	700.0	5.2	-0.2
KENYA	4,236.3	6,388.6	6,082.1	5,224.5	5,530.8	4.2	-1.3
LESOTHO	75.0	357.3	546.7	547.3	624.7	17.2	33.0
LIBERIA	652.8	2,087.5	2,170.6	2,041.0	1,952.7	13.0	-0.6
LIBYA	...	...	...	...	...	...	...
MADAGASCAR	1,041.0	3,462.7	4,380.0	3,857.9	3,181.0	13.6	-0.4
MALAWI	799.4	1,674.6	2,080.8	2,674.3	2,847.8	8.1	5.1
MALI	708.0	1,977.6	2,731.2	2,653.4	2,730.6	10.9	3.1
MAURITANIA	838.6	1,889.6	2,351.5	2,056.4	1,708.8	9.2	-0.5
MAURITIUS	335.1	808.6	1,157.6	1,102.5	928.6	9.7	1.8
MOROCCO	9,552.8	20,759.0	22,903.0	17,977.1	15,676.8	8.2	-2.4
MOZAMBIQUE	891.1	4,395.6	5,523.7	2,905.3	3,258.7	17.8	-1.9
NAMIBIA	...	311.6	368.8	77.3	76.0	...	-5.5
NIGER	426.9	1,348.8	1,592.1	1,561.3	1,323.8	13.2	0.4
NIGERIA	6,478.0	33,764.0	31,929.6	31,937.4	29,650.5	19.6	-1.0
RWANDA	184.1	657.4	1,066.8	1,348.3	1,303.5	14.5	6.6
SAO T. & PRINC.	22.3	173.9	253.6	312.9	303.0	24.9	5.3
SENEGAL	1,224.1	2,977.3	3,443.1	3,064.0	3,216.4	10.4	1.1
SEYCHELLES	21.7	200.0	320.0	386.4	293.0	27.6	4.1
SIERRA LEONE	482.0	1,486.0	1,909.4	2,035.4	1,814.6	13.1	2.0
SOMALIA	791.0	2,048.3	2,712.8	3,291.8	3,006.3	10.1	3.6
SOUDAN	5,050.0	13,642.0	...	...	...	10.6	...
SOUTH AFRICA	15,500.0	19,627.1	35,335.0	36,858.0	35,854.9	2.8	6.1
SWAZILAND	280.3	225.2	250.7	365.6	381.9	1.0	5.4
TANZANIA	2,675.9	6,059.1	7,323.0	7,441.9	6,574.6	8.6	0.9
TOGO	976.2	1,181.6	1,449.3	1,042.6	962.0	2.8	-1.6
TUNISIA	3,586.0	8,046.1	11,151.7	11,505.9	9,697.4	8.7	2.0
UGANDA	657.4	1,570.0	3,387.0	3,444.0	3,824.7	9.5	9.7
ZAMBIA	3,352.6	7,406.2	7,264.1	6,019.6	4,148.0	9.3	-4.5
ZIMBABWE	1,269.8	3,239.8	5,322.7	5,352.2	4,676.0	9.9	3.9
AFRICA	138,626.5	295,306.8	341,699.5	310,329.6	305,152.7	7.9	0.4

TABLE 2.13
TOTAL DEBT SERVICE
(MILLIONS OF US DOLLARS)

COUNTRY	1980	1990	1995	1999	2000	Average Annual Growth (%) 1980-1990	Average Annual Growth (%) 1991-2000
ALGERIA	4,080.0	8,940.0	9,415.7	4,890.0	4,690.0	8.5	-5.8
ANGOLA	181.3	698.3	1,131.9	985.4	2,043.3	-10.1	29.7
BENIN	12.6	30.1	50.6	66.2	54.7	160.1	10.0
BOTSWANA	107.6	353.5	372.2	541.9	706.4	56.9	19.8
BURKINA FASO	16.0	69.0	63.5	68.0	73.1	48.6	13.2
BURUNDI	10.4	40.4	41.2	58.7	52.3	16.6	8.0
CAMEROON	...	151.4	307.3	401.5	339.7	-35.3	36.3
CAPE VERDE	...	12.6	19.2	34.2	35.4	47.5	26.0
CENTRAL AFRICAN REP.	5.2	10.7	7.8	9.2	7.9	6.8	43.3
CHAD	...	13.8	45.7	28.5	30.0	41.9	...
COMOROS	1.6	1.1	3.0	1.9	1.5	14.3	32.1
CONGO	108.8	379.5	328.7	138.8	150.2	17.9	402.9
CONGO, DEM. REP.	784.8	333.3	22.2	...	...	-4.3	...
COTE D'IVOIRE	1,094.1	1,029.3	1,933.4	995.6	1,057.8	3.8	5.5
DJIBOUTI	2.9	21.3	31.8	18.3	19.4	23.3	14.1
EGYPT	2,227.1	6,010.5	1,954.6	1,597.3	1,825.8	10.9	-8.1
EQUAT. GUINEA	5.3	8.6	25.2	17.6	16.4	14.4	-4.4
ERITREA							
ETHIOPIA	30.4	229.7	178.5	189.4	148.2	25.4	8.5
GABON	1,139.6	573.2	830.1	222.3	547.8	-1.1	9.4
GAMBIA	6.2	22.2	21.5	20.9	23.8	30.9	1.9
GHANA	...	374.4	637.4	459.5	533.5	12.9	6.6
GUINEA	116.2	174.2	188.9	131.5	172.1	6.6	2.1
GUINEA BISSAU	2.9	23.0	187.6	28.5	32.0	114.5	12.5
KENYA	248.3	794.5	729.1	744.9	471.9	19.0	2.4
LESOTHO	...	21.8	31.3	45.0	74.5	4.4	14.8
LIBERIA	41.6	116.6	113.8	126.9	130.6	38.1	1.4
LIBYA							
MADAGASCAR	157.0	81.7	96.6	92.2	98.4	5.3	18.7
MALAWI	134.3	124.0	135.6	106.3	...	1.4	...
MALI	16.4	164.7	100.0	85.4	82.8	29.8	-1.6
MAURITANIA	93.1	0.8	117.0	79.0	65.3	-15.3	1,223.8
MAURITIUS	11.2	174.5	187.8	200.2	204.7	71.0	8.0
MOROCCO	1,309.9	2,104.0	3,530.2	2,988.4	2,653.2	6.9	4.8
MOZAMBIQUE	145.0	70.0	97.3	143.4	150.1	...	31.3
NAMIBIA	51.6	51.5	30.0	20.9	21.8	9.2	-6.0
NIGER	84.0	...	104.8	68.8	77.6	...	-0.9
NIGERIA	835.6	2,768.1	2,094.6	1,900.0	1,942.0	27.4	1.3
RWANDA	...	...	20.3	11.7	13.5	...	-3.8
SAO T. & PRINC.	0.0	0.2	2.3	3.9	4.2	...	87.6
SENEGAL	166.1	462.4	273.8	200.6	188.2	11.6	-5.1
SEYCHELLES	0.2	35.0	42.0	63.7	60.3	171.1	5.8
SIERRA LEONE	39.3	55.7	294.7	53.6	52.7	2,416.1	36.8
SOMALIA	23.8	0.0	187.7	206.0	212.1	-21.8	...
SOUDAN	327.5	98.0	...	...	...	-1.9	...
SOUTH AFRICA	3,861.0	3,452.8	5,822.0	7,295.1	7,253.2	1.5	8.5
SWAZILAND	16.9	58.8	40.2	49.1	...	15.9	...
TANZANIA	...	...	...	...	164.9	...	...
TOGO	...	82.3	25.2	26.1	113.8	20.6	31.1
TUNISIA	470.1	1,333.2	1,642.9	1,562.8	1,889.9	18.3	3.9
UGANDA	88.3	363.7	143.8	110.6	90.3	16.8	-4.6
ZAMBIA	767.5	961.0	1,640.8	136.4	158.3	51.0	10.5
ZIMBABWE	202.7	440.0	537.0	478.4	125.5	8.4	-6.2
AFRICA	18,922.0	32,739.6	35,770.5	28,271.0	29,606.9	6.0	-0.7

TABLE 3.1
LABOUR FORCE BY SECTOR
(PERCENT IN)

COUNTRY	AGRICULTURE				INDUSTRY				SERVICES			
	1980	1985	1990	1996	1980	1985	1990	1996	1980	1985	1990	1996
ALGERIA	31	25	19	14	27	29	32	35	42	46	49	51
ANGOLA	74	72	70	68	10	10	11	11	17	18	19	21
BENIN	70	65	59	54	7	7	8	10	23	28	32	36
BOTSWANA	70	61	52	42	13	19	28	41	17	20	20	17
BURKINA FASO	87	86	85	84	4	5	5	5	9	10	10	11
BURUNDI	93	92	92	91	2	3	3	3	5	5	5	6
CAMEROON	70	63	56	49	8	10	13	15	22	27	32	36
CAPE VERDE	52	46	40	35	23	27	31	36	26	27	29	29
CENT. AFR. REP.	72	67	61	56	6	8	10	12	21	25	29	32
CHAD	83	80	76	72	5	5	6	7	12	15	18	21
COMOROS	83	81	79	77	6	6	7	8	11	12	14	15
CONGO	62	61	60	58	12	12	12	13	26	27	28	29
CONGO DEM. REP.	71	68	64	60	13	14	16	17	16	18	20	23
COTE D'IVOIRE	65	60	54	49	8	10	12	14	27	30	34	37
DJIBOUTI	...	...	...	...	...	...	...	...	...	...	...	...
EGYPT	46	42	39	36	20	22	24	27	34	35	36	37
EQUAT. GUINEA	66	61	57	52	11	13	15	18	23	26	28	30
ERITREA	...	...	...	...	...	...	...	...	...		...	...
ETHIOPIA	80	77	74	72	8	9	10	12	12	14	15	16
GABON	75	73	71	69	11	12	12	13	14	15	16	18
GAMBIA	84	83	82	80	7	7	8	9	9	10	11	11
GHANA	56	54	53	52	18	18	19	19	26	27	28	29
GUINEA	81	78	76	74	9	10	11	13	10	11	12	13
GUINEA BISSAU	82	81	80	79	4	4	4	5	14	15	15	16
KENYA	81	79	77	75	7	7	8	9	12	13	14	16
LESOTHO	86	84	82	81	4	5	5	6	10	11	12	13
LIBERIA	74	73	71	70	9	9	9	9	16	18	20	21
LIBYA	18	14	11	8	29	30	32	34	53	55	57	58
MADAGASCAR	81	79	78	76	6	7	7	8	13	14	15	16
MALAWI	83	78	75	70	7	10	13	17	9	11	12	13
MALI	86	84	82	80	2	2	3	3	12	14	16	17
MAURITANIA	69	61	53	45	9	12	16	21	22	27	31	34
MAURITIUS	28	25	23	20	24	24	23	23	48	51	54	57
MOROCCO	46	40	35	30	25	29	35	40	29	31	31	30
MOZAMBIQUE	84	83	82	81	7	8	9	10	8	8	9	9
NAMIBIA	43	44	43	40	22	20	27	37	36	6	31	23
NIGER	91	89	88	86	2	2	2	2	7	9	10	12
NIGERIA	68	67	65	64	12	12	13	13	20	21	22	23
RWANDA	93	92	92	92	3	3	3	3	4	5	5	5
SAO T. & PRINC.	...	...	...	...	...	...	...	...	...	...	...	...
SENEGAL	81	79	78	77	6	7	7	7	13	14	15	16
SEYCHELLES	...	...	...	...	...	...	...	...	...	...	...	...
SIERRA LEONE	70	67	64	61	14	15	16	17	16	18	20	22
SOMALIA	76	74	72	70	8	9	10	11	16	17	18	19
SOUTH AFRICA	17	...	14	...	35	...	32	...	48	...	54	...
SUDAN	71	68	65	62	7	8	9	11	21	23	25	27
SWAZILAND	74	71	67	64	9	10	12	13	17	19	21	23
TANZANIA	86	84	81	79	5	5	6	7	10	11	12	14
TOGO	73	71	69	67	10	10	11	12	17	18	20	21
TUNISIA	35	31	28	25	36	43	49	56	29	26	23	19
UGANDA	86	84	82	81	4	5	6	6	10	11	12	13
ZAMBIA	73	71	70	68	10	11	11	12	17	18	19	20
ZIMBABWE	73	70	68	66	10	12	13	14	17	18	19	20
AFRICA	70	67	65	62	11	12	13	15	19	21	22	23

TABLE 3.2
LABOUR FORCE PARTICIPATION RATE
(Percentage of population of all ages in labour force)

COUNTRY	TOTAL			FEMALE			MALE		
	1980	1995	2000	1980	1995	2000	1980	1995	2000
ALGERIA	26.0	31.1	34.5	11.0	15.2	19.3	41.1	46.5	49.4
ANGOLA	49.4	46.0	45.2	45.7	42.2	41.4	53.3	50.0	49.2
BENIN	47.9	45.2	45.2	44.5	42.9	42.9	51.5	47.5	47.5
BOTSWANA	43.6	43.0	43.7	41.8	39.0	39.1	45.5	47.3	48.5
BURKINA FASO	53.6	49.1	47.6	51.5	46.6	45.3	55.9	51.8	50.0
BURUNDI	54.9	53.4	52.6	53.2	51.1	50.4	56.9	55.7	54.9
CAMEROON	41.9	40.5	41.0	30.5	30.1	31.0	53.7	51.0	51.2
CAPE VERDE	32.5	38.8	40.7	20.4	28.8	30.3	46.7	50.6	52.3
CENT. AFR. REP.	52.5	47.9	47.1	48.7	43.4	42.8	56.6	52.6	51.8
CHAD	48.0	46.4	45.8	41.1	40.8	40.7	55.2	52.2	51.1
COMOROS	45.2	46.0	46.9	39.5	39.7	40.6	50.9	52.0	53.1
CONGO	42.1	41.4	40.8	34.8	35.1	34.7	49.8	48.0	47.2
CONGO DEM. REP.	44.5	41.6	40.6	38.8	35.8	34.9	50.4	47.4	46.4
COTE D'IVOIRE	40.7	39.8	40.8	26.6	26.2	27.4	54.0	52.7	53.5
DJIBOUTI	...	...	...	...	...	...	...	...	...
EGYPT	35.0	36.4	38.0	18.9	21.3	23.6	50.7	51.0	52.0
EQUAT. GUINEA	44.7	41.9	41.4	30.7	29.2	28.9	58.3	54.9	53.8
ERITREA	...	50.1	49.9	...	47.2	46.9	...	53.1	52.8
ETHIOPIA	49.5	44.6	44.2	41.6	37.1	36.7	57.5	52.3	51.7
GABON	52.5	46.8	45.1	46.3	41.1	39.8	58.8	52.7	50.6
GAMBIA	51.5	51.1	51.3	45.6	45.2	45.7	57.6	57.0	57.1
GHANA	46.6	47.9	49.2	47.2	48.3	49.4	46.1	47.6	49.1
GUINEA	51.8	49.8	49.6	48.8	47.3	47.1	54.8	52.2	52.1
GUINEA BISSAU	48.6	46.4	45.8	38.1	36.9	36.7	59.5	56.1	55.2
KENYA	47.2	49.5	51.6	43.5	45.7	47.8	50.9	53.3	55.4
LESOTHO	42.5	42.1	42.5	31.1	30.2	30.8	54.5	54.2	54.4
LIBERIA	42.1	38.3	40.2	32.6	30.5	32.0	51.5	46.0	48.3
LIBYA	31.0	31.7	33.9	12.2	13.7	16.4	47.7	48.1	50.2
MADAGASCAR	49.6	48.2	47.8	44.2	42.9	42.4	55.2	53.6	53.2
MALAWI	50.3	48.7	48.2	49.3	47.1	46.4	51.4	50.3	49.9
MALI	51.5	49.9	49.0	47.0	45.4	44.3	56.2	54.6	53.7
MAURITANIA	48.1	44.5	44.3	42.8	38.8	38.4	53.5	50.4	50.3
MAURITIUS	35.5	42.3	43.7	18.0	26.5	28.5	53.5	58.1	59.1
MOROCCO	35.9	38.2	39.4	24.1	26.5	27.4	47.7	49.9	51.4
MOZAMBIQUE	54.6	52.9	52.4	52.7	50.5	50.1	56.6	55.3	54.8
NAMIBIA	41.4	40.1	39.6	33.1	32.8	32.4	50.1	47.8	46.9
NIGER	48.1	46.6	46.2	42.2	40.6	40.3	54.0	52.6	52.0
NIGERIA	41.2	39.6	39.6	29.3	27.9	28.4	53.1	51.1	50.7
RWANDA	51.1	53.4	54.3	49.6	51.5	52.2	52.6	55.4	56.5
SAO T.& PRINC.	...	...	...	...	...	...	...	...	...
SENEGAL	45.9	44.5	44.2	38.7	37.9	37.7	53.1	51.1	50.7
SEYCHELLES	...	...	...	...	...	...	...	...	...
SIERRA LEONE	38.6	37.3	37.0	26.9	26.4	26.7	50.8	48.5	47.7
SOMALIA	45.2	43.2	42.8	38.8	37.1	36.8	51.8	49.4	48.8
SOUTH AFRICA	36.8	40.3	41.6	25.8	30.2	31.4	48.0	50.7	52.1
SUDAN	37.0	38.5	39.3	20.0	21.8	23.3	54.0	54.9	55.0
SWAZILAND	35.7	36.2	37.0	23.5	24.8	25.8	48.0	47.9	48.5
TANZANIA	51.2	51.4	51.5	50.2	50.3	50.2	52.2	52.6	52.8
TOGO	42.8	42.1	42.3	33.2	33.3	33.5	52.6	51.0	51.2
TUNISIA	34.3	37.6	40.4	20.1	23.2	26.1	48.0	51.8	54.5
UGANDA	51.7	49.9	48.9	48.9	47.2	46.1	54.5	52.7	51.7
ZAMBIA	43.1	42.7	42.2	37.7	37.0	36.4	48.6	48.4	47.9
ZIMBABWE	44.4	44.9	44.6	39.1	39.4	39.1	49.8	50.5	50.1
AFRICA	**42.7**	**42.7**	**43.1**	**34.1**	**34.1**	**33.8**	**51.7**	**50.9**	**49.7**

TABLE 3.3
COMPONENTS OF POPULATION CHANGE

COUNTRY	TOTAL FERTILITY RATE (PER WOMAN)			CRUDE BIRTH RATE (PER 1000 POPULATION			CRUDE DEATH RATE (PER 1000 POPULATION)			RATE OF NATURAL INCREASE (PERCENT)		
	1980	1990	2001	1980	1990	2001	1980	1990	2001	1980	1990	2001
ALGERIA	6.7	4.4	2.9	42.4	30.9	23.9	11.6	7.1	5.4	3.1	2.4	1.9
ANGOLA	6.9	7.2	7.2	50.7	51.2	51.2	23.5	20.6	19.2	2.7	3.1	3.2
BENIN	7.1	6.6	5.8	51.5	47.0	41.4	19.2	15.2	12.5	3.2	3.2	2.9
BOTSWANA	6.1	5.1	4.0	44.7	38.2	31.2	10.2	8.2	23.0	3.5	3.0	0.8
BURKINA FASO	7.8	7.3	6.8	49.8	47.5	46.8	19.4	17.9	16.3	3.0	3.0	3.0
BURUNDI	6.8	6.8	6.8	45.8	46.3	43.4	18.3	20.4	20.9	2.8	2.6	2.3
CAMEROON	6.4	5.9	4.8	45.1	41.7	36.6	16.6	14.2	14.6	2.9	2.7	2.2
CAPE VERDE	6.5	4.2	3.3	37.2	34.7	29.6	10.4	8.2	5.8	2.7	2.6	2.4
CENT. AFR. REP.	5.8	5.6	5.0	43.2	41.5	37.9	19.4	18.0	18.7	2.4	2.3	1.9
CHAD	6.7	6.7	6.7	48.1	48.5	48.5	22.9	20.5	18.8	2.5	2.8	3.0
COMOROS	7.0	6.1	5.0	48.6	40.6	37.9	14.4	10.9	8.7	3.4	3.0	2.9
CONGO	6.3	6.3	6.3	44.7	44.5	44.3	16.3	14.9	14.1	2.8	3.0	3.0
CONGO DEM. REP.	6.6	6.7	6.7	48.0	48.0	47.3	16.8	15.0	13.9	3.1	3.3	3.3
COTE D'IVOIRE	7.4	6.2	4.7	50.8	41.4	35.4	16.4	14.6	15.3	3.4	2.7	2.0
DJIBOUTI	6.6	6.3	5.8	52.8	45.5	38.5	20.8	17.6	20.2	3.2	2.8	1.8
EGYPT	5.1	4.1	3.0	38.8	31.3	23.9	13.3	8.6	6.2	2.6	2.3	1.8
EQUAT. GUINEA	5.7	5.9	5.9	43.1	43.6	43.2	21.7	18.6	15.4	2.1	2.5	2.8
ERITREA	6.4	6.2	5.4	45.2	43.9	39.0	19.6	16.0	13.4	2.6	2.8	2.6
ETHIOPIA	6.8	6.9	6.8	46.3	46.2	44.0	20.9	18.8	19.3	2.5	2.7	2.5
GABON	4.5	5.1	5.4	33.0	36.4	37.6	18.5	16.6	15.3	1.4	2.0	2.2
GAMBIA	6.5	5.8	4.9	48.3	44.5	37.8	23.9	20.5	17.3	2.4	2.4	2.1
GHANA	6.8	5.6	4.3	45.9	38.9	32.9	13.8	11.5	10.5	3.2	2.7	2.2
GUINEA	7.0	6.5	5.9	51.5	45.1	43.9	24.5	19.9	17.1	2.7	2.5	2.7
GUINEA BISSAU	6.0	6.0	6.0	45.0	45.1	44.6	25.4	22.2	19.5	2.0	2.3	2.5
KENYA	7.7	5.9	4.2	50.8	41.3	34.4	13.3	10.7	13.4	3.7	3.1	2.1
LESOTHO	5.6	5.1	4.5	40.9	37.4	33.0	14.7	11.9	20.4	2.6	2.5	1.3
LIBERIA	6.8	6.8	6.8	47.2	42.0	54.4	16.8	19.7	13.1	3.0	2.2	4.1
LIBYA	7.3	4.7	3.4	46.3	27.6	26.7	11.6	4.9	4.8	3.5	2.3	2.2
MADAGASCAR	6.4	6.2	5.8	45.6	44.7	42.0	17.6	16.4	13.5	2.8	2.8	2.9
MALAWI	7.6	7.3	6.4	55.0	50.9	45.4	22.5	20.9	22.5	3.2	3.0	2.3
MALI	7.0	7.0	7.0	50.4	50.1	49.7	21.9	19.3	17.5	2.8	3.1	3.2
MAURITANIA	6.4	6.1	6.0	43.3	44.1	43.7	19.1	16.5	14.4	2.4	2.8	2.9
MAURITIUS	2.7	2.2	1.9	23.9	20.2	16.0	6.4	6.5	6.7	1.7	1.4	0.9
MOROCCO	5.6	4.2	3.1	38.0	30.6	25.2	12.0	8.1	6.1	2.6	2.2	1.9
MOZAMBIQUE	6.6	6.4	5.9	46.0	45.2	42.3	20.9	20.4	23.6	2.5	2.5	1.9
NAMIBIA	6.5	6.0	5.0	42.2	41.6	35.1	13.9	12.7	17.8	2.8	2.9	1.7
NIGER	8.2	8.0	8.0	56.7	55.5	55.2	24.6	22.6	19.4	3.2	3.3	3.6
NIGERIA	6.9	6.5	5.5	47.6	44.8	39.9	18.0	15.4	13.5	3.0	2.9	2.6
RWANDA	8.3	6.8	5.9	51.4	43.5	42.2	19.5	34.4	20.8	3.2	0.9	2.1
SAO T. & PRINC.	...	...	...	...	...	...	...	...	...	...	...	...
SENEGAL	6.8	6.2	5.2	48.0	43.0	38.0	20.4	16.0	11.9	2.8	2.7	2.6
SEYCHELLES	...	...	...	...	...	...	...	...	...	...	...	...
SIERRA LEONE	6.5	6.5	6.5	48.9	49.3	49.2	28.8	28.8	23.9	2.0	2.1	2.5
SOMALIA	7.3	7.3	7.3	51.8	51.9	51.9	22.4	23.2	17.3	2.9	2.9	3.5
SOUTH AFRICA	4.7	3.5	2.9	34.3	28.3	25.0	11.2	9.1	15.8	2.3	1.9	0.9
SUDAN	6.1	5.4	4.6	42.4	38.3	34.1	16.7	13.9	11.3	2.6	2.4	2.3
SWAZILAND	6.2	5.5	4.5	43.1	39.4	33.8	14.7	11.6	21.2	2.8	2.8	1.3
TANZANIA	6.7	6.1	5.1	46.6	43.5	38.4	15.2	12.9	13.1	3.1	3.1	2.5
TOGO	6.9	6.3	5.4	46.1	42.9	39.1	16.5	14.2	13.3	3.0	2.9	2.6
TUNISIA	5.2	3.5	2.1	35.2	27.4	18.6	9.0	6.7	6.5	2.6	2.1	1.2
UGANDA	7.1	7.1	7.1	50.4	50.5	50.6	18.3	20.7	17.8	3.2	3.0	3.3
ZAMBIA	7.0	6.3	5.2	46.3	44.8	42.0	15.4	16.5	19.2	3.1	2.8	2.3
ZIMBABWE	6.7	5.7	4.6	44.5	41.4	35.6	10.5	13.0	17.8	3.4	2.8	1.8
AFRICA	**6.5**	**5.8**	**5.1**	**45.0**	**41.0**	**37.0**	**16.6**	**14.5**	**13.9**	**2.8**	**2.7**	**2.3**

TABLE 3.4
MORTALITY INDICATORS

COUNTRY	INFANT MORTALITY RATE (PER 1000)			LIFE EXPECTANCY AT BIRTH (YEARS)					
	1980	1990	2001	1980		1990		2001	
				M	F	M	F	M	F
ALGERIA	98	64	44	59	61	61	67	68	72
ANGOLA	153	131	120	40	43	43	46	44	47
BENIN	115	99	82	46	48	50	50	52	52
BOTSWANA	71	59	68	56	60	59	63	38	37
BURKINA FASO	125	110	89	45	51	46	54	46	56
BURUNDI	122	129	113	45	49	42	45	40	41
CAMEROON	108	90	81	48	51	51	54	49	51
CAPE VERDE	85	68	51	59	63	62	68	67	73
CENT. AFR. REP.	117	104	95	43	48	45	49	43	46
CHAD	148	131	117	40	44	43	46	45	47
COMOROS	110	88	69	50	54	54	58	59	62
CONGO	88	80	67	47	53	49	54	49	54
CONGO, DEM. REP.	112	96	80	47	51	50	53	51	53
COTE D'IVOIRE	112	97	83	48	51	49	52	48	48
DJIBOUTI	136	121	117	43	46	46	49	40	43
EGYPT	121	68	42	54	57	61	64	66	70
EQUAT. GUINEA	142	121	101	42	45	46	49	50	53
ERITREA	128	107	83	43	46	47	51	51	54
ETHIOPIA	142	125	108	42	45	44	47	43	44
GABON	114	97	82	47	50	50	53	52	54
GAMBIA	159	138	117	39	42	42	45	45	48
GHANA	94	79	63	52	55	54	57	56	58
GUINEA	161	139	116	39	40	43	44	48	49
GUINEA BISSAU	169	145	123	37	40	41	44	44	47
KENYA	87	71	60	53	57	55	59	49	51
LESOTHO	121	103	110	51	55	56	58	43	42
LIBERIA	138	143	85	49	52	43	45	53	55
LIBYA	53	33	26	59	62	67	70	69	73
MADAGASCAR	119	111	93	47	49	48	50	52	54
MALAWI	167	153	132	44	45	44	45	40	39
MALI	162	139	122	45	47	48	50	51	53
MAURITANIA	120	112	99	45	48	48	51	51	54
MAURITIUS	32	22	17	63	69	66	73	68	76
MOROCCO	102	68	44	56	59	62	65	66	70
MOZAMBIQUE	140	135	130	42	45	42	45	38	39
NAMIBIA	91	81	68	52	55	54	56	44	44
NIGER	158	148	128	40	41	42	42	46	46
NIGERIA	120	101	81	47	48	50	51	52	52
RWANDA	131	131	120	44	47	31	32	40	41
SAO T. & PRINC.	...	...	...	...	...	...	...	...	...
SENEGAL	91	71	58	43	48	48	52	52	56
SEYCHELLES	...	...	...	...	...	...	...	...	...
SIERRA LEONE	190	190	150	34	37	34	37	39	41
SOMALIA	145	152	115	41	44	40	43	47	50
SOUTH AFRICA	70	57	59	53	60	56	64	48	51
SUDAN	117	98	80	47	50	51	54	55	58
SWAZILAND	100	82	91	49	54	54	58	40	41
TANZANIA	105	89	75	49	52	51	54	50	52
TOGO	110	93	77	48	49	50	52	51	52
TUNISIA	78	41	27	61	62	66	68	69	72
UGANDA	121	121	96	45	49	42	44	45	46
ZAMBIA	104	99	83	49	52	47	48	42	41
ZIMBABWE	69	69	57	57	61	52	53	43	42
AFRICA	115	95	79	48	51	51	54	52	54

Note : M and F refer to Male and Female respectively

TABLE 3.5
POPULATION WITH ACCESS TO SOCIAL INFRASTRUCTURES
(PERCENT OF POPULATION)

COUNTRY	SANITATION			SAFE WATER			HEALTH SERVICES		
	1985	1990-93	2000	1985	1990-93	2000	1985	1991	1992-96
ALGERIA	59	90	73	69	90	94	...	...	98
ANGOLA	18	31	44	28	31	38	70	24	...
BENIN	10	70	23	14	70	63	...	42	18
BOTSWANA	36	70	...	77	70	...	...	86	...
BURKINA FASO	9	42	29	35	42	...	70	...	90
BURUNDI	52	58	...	23	58	...	45	80	80
CAMEROON	36	41	92	36	41	62	20	15	80
CAPE VERDE	10	67	71	31	67	74	...	...	...
CENT. AFR. REP.	19	18	31	24	18	60	..	13	52
CHAD	14	33	29	31	33	27	30	26	30
COMOROS	...	48	98	63	48	96	82	...	...
CONGO	40	27	...	20	27	51	...	...	83
CONGO DEM. REP.	23	60	20	33	60	45	33	59	26
COTE D'IVOIRE	50	82	...	17	82	77	...	60	...
DJIBOUTI	37	24	91	43	24	100	...	...	...
EGYPT	80	64	94	75	64	95	99	99	99
EQUAT. GUINEA	...	95	53	...	95	43	...	...	...
ERITREA	...	68	13	...	68	46	...	...	...
ETHIOPIA	19	27	15	16	27	24	44	55	46
GABON	50	67	21	50	67	70	80	87	...
GAMBIA	...	76	37	45	76	62	90	...	93
GHANA	26	57	63	56	57	64	64	76	...
GUINEA	21	55	58	20	55	48	13	45	80
GUINEA BISSAU	25	27	47	31	27	49	64	...	40
KENYA	44	49	86	27	49	49	...	...	77
LESOTHO	22	62	92	36	62	91	50	80	80
LIBERIA	21		...	37	...	...	35	..	39
LIBYA	91	97	97	90	97	72	100	100	95
MADAGASCAR	3	16	42	31	16	47	65	65	38
MALAWI	60	77	77	32	77	57	54	80	35
MALI	21	49	69	17	49	65	35	...	40
MAURITANIA	...	72	33	37	72	37	30	...	63
MAURITIUS	97	100	99	99	100	100	100	99	100
MOROCCO	46	58	75	57	58	82	70	62	70
MOZAMBIQUE	20	24	43	15	24	60	40	30	39
NAMIBIA	14	60	41	52	60	77	72	...	59
NIGER	9	52	20	37	52	59	48	30	99
NIGERIA	35	40	63	36	40	57	66	67	51
RWANDA	58	79	8	49	79	41	80	...	80
SAO T. & PRINC.	15	70	...	42	70	...	...	...	...
SENEGAL	55	50	70	44	50	78	40	40	90
SEYCHELLES	99	97	...	95	97	...	99	99	...
SIERRA LEONE	21	34	28	24	34	28	36	...	38
SOMALIA	15	37	...	31	37	...	20	...	...
SOUTH AFRICA	...	87	86	...	87	...	...	...	...
SUDAN	5	77	62	40	77	75	70	70	70
SWAZILAND	...	60	...	54	60	...	...	55	...
TANZANIA	64	49	90	52	49	54	73	93	42
TOGO	14	63	34	35	63	54	61	...	...
TUNISIA	52	99	...	89	99	...	91	100	...
UGANDA	13	42	75	16	42	50	42	71	49
ZAMBIA	47	59	78	48	59	64	70	75	...
ZIMBABWE	26	74	68	52	74	85	71	...	85
AFRICA	35	55	60	42	55	62	61	66	62

TABLE 3.6
SCHOOL ENROLMENT RATIO (GROSS)

	PRIMARY						SECONDARY					
	1975		1990		1996		1975		1990		1996	
		Ratio		Ratio		Ratio		Ratio		Ratio		Ratio
COUNTRY	Total	F/M	Total	F/M	Total	F/M	Total	F/M	Total	F/M	Total	F/M
ALGERIA	93	0.69	100	0.84	108	0.90	20	0.53	61	0.80	63	0.95
ALGERIA	93	0.69	100	0.84	108	0.90	20	0.53	61	0.80	63	0.95
ANGOLA	130	0.60	92	0.92	68	0.89	9	0.40	12	0.66	12	0.66
BENIN	50	0.45	58	0.50	78	0.59	9	0.34	12	0.41	18	0.44
BOTSWANA	71	1.23	113	1.07	108	1.01	15	1.06	43	1.12	65	1.10
BURKINA FASO	14	0.56	33	0.63	40	0.67	2	0.46	7	0.53	9	0.55
BURUNDI	21	0.63	73	0.83	43	0.83	2	0.43	6	0.57	8	0.61
CAMEROON	95	0.80	101	0.86	85	0.87	13	0.50	28	0.70	25	0.68
CAPE VERDE	127	0.90	121	0.96	144	0.95	7	0.86	21	0.95	...	0.94
CENT. AFR. REP.	73	0.53	65	0.64	60	0.65	8	0.23	12	0.41	10	0.42
CHAD	35	0.35	54	0.45	58	0.52	3	0.20	8	0.23	10	0.25
COMOROS	64	0.43	75	0.73	73	0.86	13	0.39	18	0.68	24	0.81
CONGO	136	0.75	133	0.88	111	0.91	48	0.54	53	0.69	52	0.72
CONGO, DEM. REP.	93	0.67	70	0.62	70	0.69	17	0.36	22	0.48	30	0.62
COTE D'IVOIRE	61	0.57	67	0.71	71	0.74	12	0.39	22	0.47	24	0.48
DJIBOUTI	30	0.54	38	0.71	39	0.74	7	0.36	12	0.65	14	0.70
EGYPT	70	0.67	94	0.85	101	0.88	40	0.56	76	0.81	75	0.88
EQUAT. GUINEA	140	...	...	...	...	...	14	0.25	...	...	...	...
ERITREA	...	...	23	0.96	53	0.82	...	...	15	0.93	20	0.71
ETHIOPIA	21	0.49	33	0.67	43	0.55	6	0.38	14	0.77	12	0.79
GABON	178	1.65	163	...	...	...	30	0.55	...	...	...	...
GAMBIA	33	0.49	64	0.68	75	0.75	9	0.36	19	0.43	26	0.56
GHANA	72	0.77	75	0.83	75	0.85	36	0.61	36	0.64	31	0.63
GUINEA	31	0.52	37	0.47	53	0.58	14	0.35	10	0.34	13	0.35
GUINEA BISSAU	65	0.45	56	0.58	70	0.58	4	0.40	9	0.45	11	0.48
KENYA	104	0.86	95	0.96	84	0.99	13	0.55	24	0.73	24	0.85
LESOTHO	106	1.42	112	1.23	108	1.12	13	1.17	25	1.48	31	1.46
LIBERIA	40	0.52	30	0.69	33	0.69	17	0.32	14	0.40	14	0.40
LIBYA	137	0.82	105	0.94	112	1.00	55	0.54	86	1.03	100	0.94
MADAGASCAR	92	0.72	103	1.00	93	0.99	13	0.71	18	0.97	16	0.99
MALAWI	56	0.62	68	0.84	133	0.91	4	0.34	8	0.29	...	0.55
MALI	25	0.56	27	0.57	45	0.64	7	0.35	7	0.48	12	0.51
MAURITANIA	20	0.56	49	0.74	79	0.89	4	0.12	14	0.48	16	0.51
MAURITIUS	105	0.98	109	1.00	107	0.99	38	0.83	53	1.00	65	1.04
MOROCCO	62	0.58	67	0.69	86	0.76	17	0.57	35	0.74	39	0.76
MOZAMBIQUE	83	0.55	67	0.75	62	0.72	3	0.50	8	0.62	7	0.63
NAMIBIA	...	...	129	1.10	131	1.01	...	...	44	1.27	61	1.18
NIGER	19	0.54	29	0.56	29	0.62	2	0.37	7	0.43	7	0.54
NIGERIA	50	0.64	91	0.76	82	0.83	8	0.53	25	0.73	34	0.84
RWANDA	55	0.84	70	0.98	...	0.97	4	1.23	8	0.78	13	0.77
SAO T. & PRINC.	...	...	...	...	...	...	...	...	...	...	...	...
SENEGAL	40	0.73	59	0.74	68	0.81	11	0.40	16	0.52	16	0.60
SEYCHELLES	...	...	96	...	...	...	...	...	...	...	...	...
SIERRA LEONE	39	0.64	50	0.69	52	0.69	12	0.46	17	0.57	17	0.58
SOMALIA	42	0.71	10	0.52	8	0.52	4	0.30	6	0.53	5	0.53
SOUTH AFRICA	104	1.02	122	0.98	129	0.98	27	1.00	74	1.16	84	1.19
SUDAN	47	0.57	53	0.75	51	0.84	14	0.44	24	0.80	21	0.90
SWAZILAND	97	0.94	111	0.96	118	0.94	32	0.83	44	0.99	54	0.99
TANZANIA	53	0.71	70	0.98	66	0.97	3	0.55	5	0.71	5	0.88
TOGO	98	0.53	109	0.65	120	0.71	19	0.31	24	0.34	27	0.36
TUNISIA	97	0.67	113	0.89	116	0.94	21	0.55	45	0.80	65	0.97
UGANDA	44	0.66	71	0.80	76	0.85	4	0.33	13	0.54	14	0.59
ZAMBIA	97	0.84	99	0.93	88	0.94	15	0.52	24	0.61	29	0.63
ZIMBABWE	70	0.84	116	0.98	113	0.97	8	0.70	50	0.87	49	0.85
AFRICA	71	0.68	78	0.85	79	0.85	14	0.54	25	0.77	29	0.81

Explanatory Notes

The main objective of the notes below is to facilitate interpretation of the statistical data presented in Part III of the Report. Data shown for all African countries are annual totals or five year averages. Period average growth rates are calculated as the arithmetic average of annual growth rates over the period. These statistics are not shown in the tables when they are not significant or not comparable over years.

Section 1: Basic Indicators

This section contains one table (Table 1.1) which presents some basic indicators as background to the tables in this part of the Report. The table provides cross-country comparisons for area, population, GNI per capita, Consumer Price Inflation, life expectancy, infant mortality and adult literacy rates. The main sources of data in this table are the United Nations Organizations, the World Bank, Country reports and ADB Statistics Division's estimates.

Area refers to the total surface area of a country, comprising land area and inland waters. The data is obtained from the Food and Agriculture Organization (FAO). The population figures are mid-year estimates obtained from the United Nations Population Division.

GNI per capita figures are obtained by dividing GNI in current US dollars by the corresponding mid-year population. GNI measures the total domestic and foreign value added claimed by residents. It comprises GDP plus net factor income from abroad, which is the income residents receive from abroad for factor services less similar payments made to nonresidents who contribute to the

domestic economy. The data are obtained from the World Bank Atlas.

Life expectancy at birth is the number of years a new born infant would live, if patterns of mortality prevailing at the time of birth in the countries were to remain unchanged throughout his/her life. The infant mortality rate is the annual number of deaths of infants under one year of age per thousand live births. Adult literacy rate is the percentage of people aged 15 and above who can, with understanding, both read and write a short simple statement on their everyday life. The data are obtained from UNESCO.

Section 2: Macroeconomic Indicators

Table 2.1. Gross Domestic Product, real

National accounts estimates are obtained from regional member countries' data, the World Bank, the IMF and the United Nations Statistical Division. In several instances, data are adjusted or supplemented with estimates made by the ADB Statistics Division. The concepts and definitions used for national accounts data are those of the United Nations System of National Accounts (SNA), Series F, no. 2, Revision 3.

Gross Domestic Product (GDP) measures the total final output of goods and services produced by a national economy, excluding provisions for depreciation. GDP figures are shown at constant 1995 market prices, and have been converted to US dollars using constant 1995 exchange rates provided by the IMF and the World Bank. For a few countries where the official exchange rate does not reflect effectively the rate applied to actual foreign exchange transactions, an alternative currency conversion factor has been used.

Aggregate growth rates for Africa are calculated as weighted averages of individual country growth rates using the share of the country's GDP in aggregate GDP based on the purchasing power parties (PPP) valuation of country GDPs.

Table 2.2. Gross Domestic Product, nominal

Data shown in this table are given at current market prices and are obtained by converting national currency series in current prices to US dollars at official exchange rates. Annual changes in GDP are presented in nominal terms.

Table 2.3. Gross National Savings

Gross National Savings (GNS) is calculated by deducting total consumption from GNP at current prices and adding net private transfers from abroad.

Table 2.4. Gross Capital Formation

Gross Capital Formation consists of gross domestic fixed capital formation plus net changes in the level of inventories.

Table 2.5. Terms of Trade

Terms of trade estimates are obtained from the IMF and supplemented by ADB Statistics Division estimates. These are obtained by dividing unit value indices of exports by unit value indices of imports. The terms of trade indices for the entire set of regional member countries are also ratios of the unit value of exports and the unit value of imports.

Table 2.6. Current Account

Data in this table are obtained from the IMF, and based on the methodology of the fifth edition of the Balance of Payments Manual. The current account includes the trade balance valued f.o.b., net services and net factor income, and current transfer payments. The data is given as percentage of GDP.

Table 2.7 Broad Money Supply

Broad Money supply (M2) comprises currency outside banks, private sector demand deposits, (and, where applicable, post office and treasury checking deposits) and quasi-money.

Tables 2.8 Real Exchange Rate Index

The real exchange rate index is defined broadly as the nominal exchange rate index adjusted for relative movements in national price or cost indicators of the home country and the United States of America.

Table 2.9. International Reserves

International Reserves consist of country's holdings of monetary gold, Special Drawing Rights (SDRs) and foreign exchange, as well as its reserve position in the International Monetary Fund (IMF).

Table 2.10. Consumer Price Index

Consumer price index shows changes in the cost of acquisition of a basket of goods and services purchased by the average consumer. Weights for the computation of the index numbers are obtained from household budget surveys.

Table 2.11. Overall Fiscal Deficit / surplus

The overall surplus/deficit is defined as current and capital revenue and official grants received, less total expenditure and lending minus repayments. The data is given as a percentage of GDP.

Tables 2.12-.2.13 Total External Debt; Debt Service.

The main source of external debt data is the IMF. Total external debt covers outstanding and disbursed long-term debt, use of IMF credit, and short-term debt. Debt service is the sum of actual repayments of principal and actual payments of interest made in foreign exchange, goods, or services, on external public and publicly guaranteed debt.

Section 3: Labor Force and Social Indicators

This section presents data on labor force by sector (agriculture, industry and services) and also labor force participation rates, total and by sex.

Other tables in the section give data on components of population change (i.e. fertility, births, deaths and rate of natural increase), infant mortality rates, and life expectancy at birth, access to social infrastructure (sanitation, safe water and health services) and school enrolment ratios for primary and secondary levels.

Table 3.1. Labor Force by Sector

The labor force includes economically active persons aged 10 years and over. It includes the unemployed and the armed forces, but excludes housewives, students and other economically inactive groups. The agricultural sector consists of agriculture, forestry, hunting and fishing. Industry comprises mining and quarrying, manufacturing, construction, electricity, gas and water. Services include all other branches of economic activity and any statistical discrepancy in the origin of resources.

Table 3.2. Labor Force Participation Rates

The table shows the percentage of the population within each sex and age group that participates in economic activities (either employed or unemployed) from ILO data. Figures shown are ratios of the total economically-active population to the total population of all ages. Activity rates for females may be difficult to compare among countries because of the difference in the criteria adopted for determining the extent to which female workers are to be counted among the "economically active".

Table 3.3. Components of Population Change

Total fertility rate indicates the number of children that would be born per woman, if she were to live to the end of the child-bearing years; and bears children during those years in accordance with prevailing age-specific fertility rates. The crude birth rate represents the annual live births per thousand population. The crude death rate is the annual number of deaths per thousand population. Rate of Natural increase of the population is the difference between Crude Birth and Crude Death rates expressed as a percentage. The data in the table are obtained mainly from the United Nations Population Division, UNICEF and the World Bank.

Table 3.4. Mortality Indicators

The variables presented in this table - namely infant mortality rate and life expectancy at births - are as defined in Table 1.1. The sources of data are also the same.

Table 3.5. Population with Access to Social Infrastructures

The percentage of people with access to sanitation is defined separately for urban and rural areas. For urban areas, access to sanitation facilities is defined as urban population served by connections to public sewers or household systems, such as pit privies, pour-flush latrines, septic tanks, communal toilets, and other such facilities. In the case of the rural population, the definition refers to those with adequate disposal, such as pit privies and pour-flush latrines. Applications of these definitions may vary from one country to another, and comparisons can therefore be inappropriate.

The population with access to safe water refers to the percentage of the population with reasonable access to safe water supply (which includes treated surface water, or untreated but uncontaminated water such as that from springs, sanitary wells, and protected boreholes). The threshold for the distance to safe water in urban areas is about 200 meters, while in rural areas it is reasonable walking distance to and from sources where water can be fetched.

The population with access to health services refers to the percentage of the population that can reach appropriate local health services by local means of transport in no more than one hour. Data in this table are obtained from the World Bank.

Table 3.6. School Enrolment

The primary school enrolment ratio is the total number of pupils enrolled at primary level of education, regardless of age, expressed as a percentage of the population corresponding to the official school age of primary education. School enrolment ratios may be more than 100 per cent in countries where some pupils' ages are different from the legal enrolment age. Data in this table are obtained from UNESCO.

The secondary school enrolment ratio is the total number of pupils enrolled at secondary level of education, regardless of age, expressed as a percentage of the population corresponding to the official school age of secondary education.

Data Sources

1.	**Basic Indicators**	Food and Agriculture Organization: FAOSTAT Database, 2000. United Nations Population Division: The 2000 revision. World Bank: African Development Indicators, 2001/2002. Regional Member Countries, ADB Statistics Division.
2.	**Macroeconomic Indicators**	
2.1 - 2.4	National Accounts	United Nations: National Accounts Yearbook, various years. World Bank: Africa Live Database, February 2002. IMF: World Economic Outlook data files, December 2001. ADB Statistics Division. Regional Member Countries.
2.5 - 2.6	External Sector	IMF: World Economic Outlook, Data files, December 2001.
2.7 - 2.10	Money Supply, Exchange Rates and Prices	IMF: International Financial Statistics, February 2002, and International Financial Statistics, Yearbook, 2001. ILO: Yearbook of Labor Statistics, various years. ADB Statistics Division, Regional Member Countries.
2.11	Government Finance	IMF: World Economic Outlook Data files, December 2001.
2.12 - 2.13	External Debt	IMF: World Economic Outlook, December 2001. ADB Statistics Division.
3.	**Labor Force and Social Indicators**	
3.1 - 3.2	Labor Force	ILO: Labor Force Statistics, various years. World Bank: African Development Indicators 2001/2002 ADB Statistics Division.
3.3 - 3.6	Social Indicators	UNICEF: The State of the World's Children, various years. World Bank: African Development Indicators, 2001/2002. UN: Human Development Report, 2001. UN: Population Division, The 2000 Revision. Regional Member Countries. ADB Statistics Division.

This publication was prepared by the Bank's Development Research Department (PDRE). Other publications of the Department are:

AFRICAN DEVELOPMENT REVIEW
A semi-annual professional journal devoted to the study and analysis of development issues in Africa.

ECONOMIC RESEARCH PAPERS
A working paper series presenting the research findings, mainly by the research staff, on topics related to African development policy issues.

COMPENDIUM OF STATISTICS
An annual publication providing statistical information on the operational activities of the Bank Group.

GENDER, POVERTY AND ENVIRONMENTAL INDICATORS ON AFRICAN COUNTRIES
A Biennial publication providing information on the broad development trends relating to gender, poverty and environmental issues in the 53 African countries.

SELECTED STATISTICS ON AFRICAN COUNTRIES
An annual publication, providing selected social and economic indicators for the 53 regional member countries of the Bank.

AFRICAN ECONOMIC OUTLOOK
An annual publication jointly produced by the African Development Bank and the OECD Development Centre, which analyses the comparative economic prospects for African countries.

Copies of these publications may be obtained from:

Development Research Department (PDRE)
African Development Bank

01 BP 1387 Abidjan 01, CÔTE D'IVOIRE
TELEFAX   (225) 20 20 49 48
TELEPHONE   (225) 20 20 44 44
TELEX   23717 / 23498 / 23263
WORLD WIDE WEB: http://www.afdb.org
EMAIL: afdb@afdb.org